Tim Keefe

ALSO BY CHARLIE BEVIS
AND FROM MCFARLAND

Jimmy Collins: A Baseball Biography (2012)

Doubleheaders: A Major League History (2011)

*The New England League:
A Baseball History, 1885–1949* (2008)

*Sunday Baseball: The Major Leagues' Struggle to
Play Baseball on the Lord's Day, 1876–1934* (2003)

*Mickey Cochrane: The Life of a Baseball
Hall of Fame Catcher* (1998)

TIM KEEFE

*A Biography of the
Hall of Fame Pitcher and
Player-Rights Advocate*

Charlie Bevis

McFarland & Company, Inc., Publishers
Jefferson, North Carolina

ISBN 978-0-7864-9665-5 (softcover : acid free paper) ∞
ISBN 978-1-4766-2231-6 (ebook)

LIBRARY OF CONGRESS CATALOGUING DATA ARE AVAILABLE

British Library cataloguing data are available

© 2015 Charlie Bevis. All rights reserved

No part of this book may be reproduced or transmitted in any form or by any means, electronic or mechanical, including photocopying or recording, or by any information storage and retrieval system, without permission in writing from the publisher.

Manufactured in the United States of America

*McFarland & Company, Inc., Publishers
Box 611, Jefferson, North Carolina 28640
www.mcfarlandpub.com*

Table of Contents

Preface   1

1. Sir Timothy   5
2. Irish Roots and Artisan Thinking   11
3. Carpenter's Son Growing Up Near Boston   16
4. Infielder on Amateur and Semipro Teams   24
5. Pitcher in the Minor Leagues   34
6. Pitching in the National League for Troy   49
7. College Baseball Coach   61
8. With the Metropolitans in New York City   66
9. Transfer to the New York Giants   83
10. Secretary of the Brotherhood   92
11. Strategic Pitcher with League-Leading 42 Wins   101
12. Land Owner in Cambridge   114
13. Adapting to Numerous Pitching Rule Changes   118
14. Clara Helm, the Future Mrs. Keefe   135
15. Record-Setting 19 Consecutive Wins   140
16. Sporting Goods Proprietor   159
17. Successful Salary Holdout   163
18. Establishing the Players' League   180
19. Capitalists Desert the Ballplayers   191
20. Aftermath of the Players' League   203
21. Ending His Pitching Career in Philadelphia   212
22. Harvard Baseball Coach   220

23. Umpire in the National League	223
24. Retirement from Baseball in Cambridge	235
25. Hall of Fame Selection	244
25. Unsung Pioneer of Ballplayer Rights	250

APPENDICES
A: Tim Keefe on Pitching — 255
B: Tim Keefe on Shorthand — 257
C: Tim Keefe on Strategic Pitching — 258
D: Pitching Changes Keefe Adapted to, 1880 to 1893 — 260

Chapter Notes — 263
Bibliography — 279
Index — 283

Preface

In 2012 my daughter Kelly lived in an apartment on Dickinson Street in Somerville, near Inman Square, an area that straddles the border between the cities of Cambridge and Somerville just outside Boston. When I first heard of her plans to move there, I grabbed a map to see how close she would be to the house at 1653 Cambridge Street in Cambridge. The answer: about half a mile.

Although it had been more than 20 years since my last visit to the neighborhood around Inman Square, I had a distinct recollection of a baseball memory. The former home of Hall of Fame pitcher Tim Keefe is located at 1653 Cambridge. Back in the early 1980s, my friend Bob Leach lived near Inman Square at 116 Concord Avenue in Somerville, about a block from Dickinson. Bob first introduced me to Tim Keefe's house; a sign indicated that the Hall of Fame pitcher had once lived there. Since discovering the Keefe home, I had periodically dug into Keefe's baseball life. He was a great pitcher in the late nineteenth century, accumulating 342 wins and pitching in three early incarnations of the World Series, so I began to consider writing a full-length biography of the Massachusetts native.

While there was lots of information about his baseball career, there were several immediate obstacles. What kind of person was Keefe? He left little indication. What was his motive for being the secretary of the Brotherhood of Professional Base Ball Players, baseball's first player collaborative? No clues there. Was he really that wealthy from baseball that he could live off the rents from his multi-family houses in Cambridge? No clues there either. I needed to go beyond his baseball life to have a truly viable biography.

From my experience as a writer of five books and numerous journal articles on baseball history, I knew I needed to verify the accepted "facts" by chasing down the primary sources, which often yielded details different from the "facts." Keefe was no exception. All secondary sources indicated that he was born in Cambridge in 1857 and grew up there. However, I could only find Keefe's immediate family in Cambridge in the 1860 federal census; they weren't there in the 1870 or 1880 censuses. It turned out that Keefe and his family lived in the neighboring city of Somerville in 1870, when the surname was spelled "Keef" in the census listing, without the "e" at the end. In the 1880 census the Keefe family was living at 54 Springfield Street in Somerville, very near to the building my daughter lived in some 130 years later. Using the city directories of Cambridge and Somerville and the Massachusetts census listings, I was able to fill in the other years. It turns out that young Keefe lived most of his early life in Somerville, with only a scant few years spent in Cambridge. That was just the beginning of new revelations about Keefe.

When I went to the Middlesex South Registry of Deeds in Cambridge to research the house that Keefe had lived in at 1653 Cambridge, I found little about Keefe himself owning the parcel after he had purchased the land in 1886 (the house wasn't built until 1896). Most of the deeds were in the name of his mother or his sisters. There were also mortgages galore after he retired from baseball, indicating that he wasn't wealthy. Discovered in the bowels of the Registry of Deeds was a carpenter's lien filed in 1877 when Keefe sought to enforce payment from a property owner for compensation for his carpentry work to help build a house on Springfield Street. This document was a window into understanding why Keefe was so active in the Brotherhood movement.

I've postulated that Keefe's initial motive to help form the Brotherhood stemmed from his carpentry background, where the apprentice–journeyman–master system still operated when Keefe was a youngster. His father was a journeyman carpenter and Keefe had apprenticed under him. The mobility of these craftsmen, their freedom to negotiate pay, and their advancement to the master/owner level were all hallmarks of the Brotherhood movement, which eventually led to the creation of the Players' League in 1890. The mobility and compensation threads provide a better understanding of Keefe's progress through baseball.

A static outline of his baseball life was not enough to explain why Keefe was such a great pitcher. One thread that I developed was how he adapted to the numerous changes to pitching rules during the 1880s. This enabled him to become a strategic pitcher with intimate knowledge of how to utilize the rules to his best advantage. This also connects back to the apprentice–journeyman–master system, where Keefe proceeded from apprentice as an amateur to journeyman in the major leagues. He became a master pitcher in several ways. He demonstrated his mastery of the pitching craft by writing two book chapters, one in the 1889 book *Scientific Ball* and the other in the earlier 1884 book *Batting and Pitching*. Keefe also developed young pitchers as a college baseball coach. In 1889 he opened his own sporting goods store, Keefe & Becannon, to leverage his pitching mastery into a business venture.

Good research sources also help form a good biography. Here, I happened upon the writing of William Ingraham Harris at the obscure *New York Press*. Harris, who knew Keefe from his days with the *Boston Globe*, wrote many insightful articles about Keefe that included comments from him that no other New York City newspapers published. Harris provided a different perspective on Keefe's salary holdouts in 1888 and 1889 as well as his role in the formation of the Players' League in 1890. If Harris had not died in 1891, we might have an even better understanding of Keefe as a man.

For web access to the *New York Press*, I thank the Old Fulton NY Post Cards website, which also provided access to the digitized archives of the *New York World*, the *New York Sun*, and other New York City newspapers to augment the more widely available *New York Times*. For web access to the digitalized archives of other periodicals, I especially thank the Boston Public Library for access to the *Boston Globe* and several other newspapers across the nation, the LA84 Foundation for access to *Sporting Life*, and the University of Illinois at Urbana-Champaign for access to the *New York Clipper*.

Several primary sources were used in my research effort. The aforementioned real estate records at the Middlesex South Registry of Deeds in Cambridge were a useful source for this biography. Other archival materials used were state and federal census records, cemetery records, church records, vital records at the Massachusetts Archives, naturalization records at the National Archives, and athletic committee meeting minutes at the Harvard University Archives.

Special thanks go to Holly Klump, the interlibrary loan coordinator at Rivier University, for her diligent efforts to locate numerous obscure books and periodicals. I am particularly appreciative of her effort to locate one of the very few extant copies of the 1884 book *Batting and Pitching*.

1
Sir Timothy

In May 1888, the *New York Press* newspaper first published the nickname "Sir Timothy" to describe New York Giants pitcher Tim Keefe. In its account of a Pittsburgh victory over the Giants, the *New York Press* reported that first baseman Al Maul "took revenge on Sir Timothy by smashing the ball in the nose for two bases" for one of Pittsburgh's nine hits off Keefe that afternoon.[1] Later that season when Keefe gained national fame by pitching the Giants to the National League pennant, other New York City daily newspapers adopted the nickname. By 1889, newspapers nationwide routinely referred to Keefe by this sobriquet.

William Ingraham Harris, the sports editor of the *New York Press*, was the individual who coined the Sir Timothy nickname. Because the *New York Press* was a brand new publication in 1888 and sought to capture readership in the highly competitive New York City newspaper market, Harris created a memorable nickname for one of the city's most popular ballplayers to attract readers away from the more popular *New York World* and *New York Sun*. Harris had cut his teeth in baseball reporting in Boston, where he had been the baseball writer at the *Boston Globe* for the two years prior to joining the *New York Press* in April 1888.[2] At the *Globe*, Harris knew Keefe not just from his exploits in the pitcher's box for the Giants but also on a personal level, since Keefe was a neighbor of the *Globe*'s sports editor, William D. Sullivan, as both men resided in the same Boston-area neighborhood.[3]

Harris wrote much about Keefe's thoughts and actions from interviews with him in 1888 and 1889, using access gained from his relationship with Keefe from his days at the *Boston Globe*. Through his reports in the *New York Press*, Harris provided historians with some of the best insights into Keefe's beliefs among the baseball writers of the day. Unfortunately, Harris became ill in 1890 and died in 1891. The reverence for his work contributed to the added integrity of the Sir Timothy nickname that he had dubbed Keefe. "His opinions were regarded in the height of authority," Sullivan wrote about Harris in an obituary. "His reports had a peculiar fascination in them, in fact so much so that he has been frequently classified as sui generis" (that is, a man with special characteristics that the world may never see again). "Being of a most observing nature, a ready thinker and a lightning calculator, he managed to foretell many of the leading base ball events of the year weeks ahead."[4]

Sullivan also wrote articles that provided valuable insight into Keefe's thought process during the 1888–1890 period, after Harris left the *Globe* to work for the *New York Press*. When former ballplayer Tim Murnane joined the *Globe* in 1888 to become its baseball writer, Sullivan was promoted to city editor but still retained the sports editor title for two more decades.[5]

Sir is an honorary title in the British Honours System, which is conveyed to men with hereditary peerage (e.g., duke or earl) and to those with knighthood, either through an order of merit (e.g., Garter or Thistle) or as a knight bachelor. Traditionally, the title is used in conjunction only with the man's formal first name, without including his surname; thus Keefe was Sir Timothy, not Sir Tim Keefe.

Knighthood had its genesis in the Middle Ages when successful soldiers were viewed as lower nobility by the British gentry, who valued the ideal of chivalry, a code of conduct for a warrior who fought not only skillfully but also bravely and honestly.[6] Knighthood served as the foundation for the modern concept of the English gentleman, who was respected for his virtue and honor. "Originally, the gentleman meant a man of gentle birth, i.e., 'good' or 'high' birth in the feudal hierarchy, as opposed to the common or villainous birth of the mere villager," British historian Harold Perkins wrote in his book *The Origins of Modern English Society*. "The aristocratic ideal of the gentleman was a moral ideal based on the chivalrous code of honour."[7]

By the nineteenth century, knighthood had transitioned from its heritage of bravery and honesty as a quasi-gentleman to mean simply a highly skilled person who performed admirable service to his country or profession. Thus, the term Sir Timothy referred to Keefe's mastery of the pitcher's craft on the baseball diamond as well as to his honesty and integrity that would befit a gentleman. Off the ball field, Keefe had the outward appearance of a gentleman, in contrast to his humble beginnings as an Irish-American carpenter's son in Somerville, Massachusetts. Like most successful businessmen of that era, Keefe sported a well-groomed mustache, dressed in suit and tie, and went by his initials "T.J." rather than by his full given name to sport the appearance of a gentleman. As one contemporary observer described Keefe:

> Keefe was a hard and faithful worker and everybody that knew anything about the National game liked him and his quiet and gentlemanly ways and he gained praise in every city in which he played, even though he was pitching against the home team. Personally Keefe is an admirable man. He is of commanding

appearance, dresses in a becoming manner and as he walks the street his handsome face, good figure and gentlemanly bearing command attention.[8]

His gentlemanly persona was ironic, from a linguistic perspective, since the surname "Keefe" is the Anglicized version of the Irish surname "Caomh," which in the Gaelic language of Ireland means "gentle."[9] Also ironic is that Keefe accepted a nickname associated with English gentry, given the distaste that Irish-Americans in the late nineteenth century had for all things English. But Keefe was not the typical Irish-American of the time.

Tim Keefe, shown here on an 1887 tobacco card, was dubbed "Sir Timothy" by William Harris of the *New York Press* in 1888 based on his mastery of pitching knowledge, exemplary performance as a strategic pitcher, and integrity on the baseball field (Library of Congress, Prints and Photographs Division, LC-DIG-bbc-0005f).

Keefe carefully nurtured his dignified image to be the antithesis of the stereotypical Irish Catholic, whom the Protestant majority in America considered to be "innately ignorant and violent" and consequently "idle, thriftless, poor, intemperate, and barbarian."[10] Keefe tried very hard to dissociate himself from the "Paddy, the illiterate ditch digger" image portrayed in many newspaper cartoons, such as those by Thomas Nast in *Harper's Weekly*, who, when drawing Irish-American characters, "invariably produced a cross between a professional boxer and an orangutan."[11] Contrary to the Irish-American stereotype, Keefe was a diligent worker, saved and invested his money wisely, was studious, and planned ahead for a career after baseball. He also lacked a clannish nature, being neither overtly religious as a Catholic nor a resolute Irish nationalist who despised the English.

Keefe was also the antithesis of the stereotypical baseball player of the 1880s. "The status of the professional baseball players was not high," historian Steven Riess wrote. "The main reason for this low prestige was the ballplayers' poor moral conduct and their ill-mannered behavior both on and off the field."[12] There was also an overlap of the stereotypes, since two-fifths of new ballplayers entering the major leagues between 1876 and 1884 possessed an Irish surname.[13]

Despite his impeccable public persona, Keefe was no choirboy in private, where he exhibited the manly traits of the times. He drank in moderation, gambled and swore on occasion, and didn't back off when challenged to a fight. He was also headstrong in attitude and often blatant in his choice of words, especially when he was defending issues that he was passionate about, such as the repressive activities pursued by the owners of National League ballclubs.

Keefe grew up in an environment where his father was guided by the elements of competence, independence, and morality that had been traditional measures of success in America for the 250 years after the Pilgrims landed at Plymouth Rock in 1620. As conveyed by Rex Burns in his book *Success in America: The Yeoman Dream and the Industrial Revolution*, the goal was modest: "wealth somewhat beyond one's basic needs, freedom from economic or statutory subservience, and the respect of the society for fruitful, honest industry."[14] The two building blocks of Piligrim-defined success were hard work and frugality. Adapting his father's version of success, Keefe embraced the character ethic that was the heart of the American definition of success in the 1880s. "Character—and all of the carefully cultivated, personal virtues it symbolized—was the foundation of the self-made man and the common denominator of all who were truly successful," explained historian Judy Hilkey in her book *Character Is Capital: Success Manuals and Manhood in Gilded Age America*.[15]

There was one aspect of his father's version of success that Keefe explicitly subscribed to. Keefe was not a child of poverty where his father was a wage-slave to industrial America and thus forestalled from prosperity. His father, Patrick Keefe, was a carpenter, a trade that for centuries had adhered to the apprentice–journeyman–master system of progression within the craft, which ultimately led to a man establishing his own business as a master carpenter. As explained by labor historian Bruce Laurie in his book *Artisans Into Workers*:

> Tradesmen thought of themselves and were considered to be part of a fluid hierarchy that consisted of master craftsmen, journeymen, and apprentices. Masters were proprietors who did everything from waiting on customers to ordering supplies and raw materials ... they also laid out work, supervised hirelings, and worked alongside their employees. Most were former journeymen, skilled workers paid by the day or the piece depending on the trade. Journeymen were onetime apprentices who usually began their indentures as teenagers and spent three to seven years learning the "art and mystery" of their callings under

the stewardship of a master.... Journeymen were masters in the making, busily accumulating resources in order to set up shop on their own.[16]

Keefe considered himself to be an artisan of the baseball profession. By 1888 when the *New York Press* dubbed him Sir Timothy, he was a journeyman pitcher well on his way to being a master craftsman. Keefe was not only competent at the day-to-day tangible skills of a pitcher, but he strove to understand the intangibles that made a pitcher more successful at his craft. "Keefe is considered a student; that is to say, there is a great amount of real brain-work connected with his play," one observer wrote in a nationally syndicated article in 1888. "His careful survey of every part of the field before delivering the ball, [and] his close study of the weak points of every batsman against whom he pits his strength and skill ... have given him a widespread reputation as the greatest 'head-work' pitcher on the ball field."[17] In 1884 Keefe wrote "Curve Pitching," a treatise that covered not only the technical aspects of throwing a ball in different ways but also the strategic aspects of winning the confrontation with the batter. He followed that up with another treatise in 1889, a chapter entitled "Pitching" in the book *Scientific Ball*. Keefe also shared his knowledge with young men seeking to be pitchers, through his college coaching activities during the baseball offseason. In 1889 he established Keefe & Becannon, a sporting goods business.

Keefe, though, had a broader perspective beyond the apprentice–journeyman–master system that promised independence. He was a proponent of what labor historians now call artisan republicanism, which had a long history dating back to the American Revolution. Carpenters and other artisans in the post–Revolutionary society "viewed themselves as the heart and soul of a republic of 'small producers,' essential to wise government and political stability," which they saw as an extension of Thomas Jefferson's vision of "a nation propelled by yeoman farmers and urban mechanics."[18]

The acceleration of industrialization by the 1880s pressured the future of artisan republicanism, as capitalists increasingly controlled businesses and favored the use of wage earners over artisans in order to maximize profit. When wage labor rapidly replaced artisans, the term "wage slavery" gained prominence, since wage workers were perceived to be economic captives of capitalists. This led to the concept of "free labor," where workers had an opportunity "to achieve ownership of capital" to participate in "equalization in the distribution of wealth."[19] Put more simply, the free labor ideology called for workers to have reasonable prospects to rise from wage-earner status to independent businessman.

In October 1889 Sir Timothy was at the top of the baseball player profession, having led the New York Giants to consecutive National League titles and postseason World Series championships in 1888 and 1889. At that point, though, the bottom fell out. Keefe helped lead a revolt of National League ballplayers to form the Players' League, which was founded on the artisan and free labor concepts. The Players' League was a dismal failure, though, at extending the independent master craftsman concept to professional baseball; the league dissolved after the 1890 season. Keefe put too much faith in the capitalists who backed the Players' League, who openly espoused sympathy for the plight of the ballplayer within the free labor ideology, but failed to adhere to that resolve through their actions. In the aftermath, Sir Timothy retained his admirable character, but he paid dearly for sticking to his beliefs in the independent artisan.

2

Irish Roots and Artisan Thinking

As a result of the Great Famine caused by the infestation of the potato blight, one million people died in Ireland between 1845 and 1852 and another one million left the island during that time period. Among the tens of thousands of those Irish emigrants who landed in Boston, Massachusetts, was Patrick Keefe, the father of Hall of Fame pitcher Tim Keefe. Born on May 27, 1826, Patrick Keefe left his home in the town of Bandon in County Cork and arrived in Boston in September 1847.[1]

Bandon is 20 miles southwest of the city of Cork, the second-largest city in Ireland next to Dublin. At the time of Patrick's birth, Bandon was a thriving market town for agricultural products from the farms in western County Cork, which provided opportunities for Irish Catholics like the Keefe men to become tradesmen in the Protestant-dominated society, and not have to be relegated to subsistence farming. Patrick's father, Timothy, worked as a blacksmith and Patrick acquired carpentry skills as a young man.[2] Patrick was likely an all-purpose carpenter in Bandon, who made anything involving wood, including buildings, windows and doors, furniture, and tools; the latter he could collaborate with his father the blacksmith.[3]

Throughout Patrick's childhood in the 1830s, though, Bandon was on an economic downturn, as the town was ravaged by the rise of industrialization and expansion of the railways, which fundamentally changed the town's economy. By 1845 Bandon already had a bleak future, as described in this report in the *Cork Examiner* newspaper: "Mr. Ray describes, accurately and minutely, the miserable condition to which the once-flourishing town of Bandon is now reduced. Mouldering factories—rotting machinery—idle looms—dismantled houses—ruined streets—a starving population—aye, and, surest sign of all of the progress of ruin and decay, a *diminished population*. In 1841 the population of Bandon was little over 9,000; while some 30 years before, it had a population of 4,000 more—13,000!"[4]

The Great Famine devastated the town of Bandon, as it did much of

County Cork, which was one of the areas hardest hit by the Great Famine. Many people in County Cork were subsistence farmers who relied on the potato as their main food source. Skibbereen, 30 miles southwest of Bandon, was one of the worst afflicted localities, where the dead were buried in their rag clothing in a mass grave. In 1847 the most available job for carpenters like Patrick Keefe was building coffins, especially the slide coffin, named "because the bottom slid out, allowing the body to drop into the grave, [which] became commonplace since it could be used again and again for those families who could not afford a coffin to bury their dead."[5]

Like many Irish families that had the means to escape Ireland, the Keefe family determined that they would be better off in America. "After 1845, craftsmen and entrepreneurs saw little reason to remain where 'there's neither trade nor business of any sorts going on,'" Kerby Miller wrote in his book *Emigrants and Exiles: Ireland and the Irish Exodus to North America*. "For many artisans and farmers, the Famine was simply the last straw, final proof after three decades of depression that Ireland was irredeemable."[6]

While by no means prosperous, the Keefe family with its artisan skills could afford to send Patrick Keefe alone to America to establish a foothold for his entire family to eventually live there. This was a common strategy for aspiring Irish emigrants, called chain migration, "where one of the older children goes first and, after acquiring some money, sends it home to finance the journey of another member of the family, eventually the entire family emigrates."[7] Even in the unlikely event that the Keefe family had enough money for everyone to secure a £5 ticket for the trip to America, Patrick's mother was pregnant with his brother Dennis, which would have made the six-week ocean voyage a particularly perilous journey.

The family invested in Patrick, who took an enormous risk going to America; at the same time, he was under significant pressure to succeed in America once he arrived. When he landed in Boston in September 1847, there was no time for visiting and relaxation. Patrick had a mission to accomplish: make enough money to bring the rest of his family to America. After spending a brief time in the Irish enclave in the North End of Boston, Patrick Keefe crossed the Charles River Bridge into the town of Charlestown, where he developed friendships with Thomas Dinneen, a grocer, and Patrick Twigg, a laborer, who both would later attest to knowing Patrick for five years when he filed his U.S. citizenship application.[8]

To save money to fund his family's passage to America, Patrick had to live cheaply, which he could as a boarder within another enclave of Irish immigrants, which he found in Somerville, a town five miles northwest of Boston. Somerville was a rural town in 1847, having just split off in 1842 from the mercantile town of Charlestown to its east, but was positioned for expansion as a railroad suburb of Boston. Houses were being built in East Somerville for residents who commuted by train to Boston, as "some lands in East Somerville were lotted and put on the market, but little if any elsewhere," among the farms, brickyards, and marshes of the town.[9] This housing development provided work opportunity for Patrick the carpenter.

Patrick Keefe likely resided most often in East Somerville during his first few years in America, but he would have moved around a lot to take advantage of house-building opportunities. "Most Famine emigrants were almost constantly on the move for at least several years after their arrival, searching for relatively secure, well-paid employment," Miller wrote in *Emigrants and Exiles*. Since carpenters and bricklayers were the most promising jobs available to Irish men, Patrick would have been one of the "many Famine emigrants [who] had sufficient skill, luck, and perseverance to find fairly secure employment."[10] While not held back by "No Irish Need Apply" signs, Patrick still no doubt encountered prejudice from his native Protestant employers and fellow carpenters, if only in attitude, due to his Irish nationality and Catholic religion. But Patrick earned enough money within five years to fund the transport of his family to America.

According to his citizenship papers filed in 1853, Patrick Keefe resided the previous five years in both Somerville and Cambridge.[11] Just to the south of Somerville, Cambridge was a city located across the West Boston Bridge over the Charles River that separated Boston from Cambridge. By 1852 Patrick was living in a dwelling on Columbia Street near Washington Street in the Cambridgeport section of Cambridge.[12] Here, he scouted potential locations where his family could live once they arrived from Ireland, since his father, a blacksmith, needed proximity to a built-up area like Cambridge since it would have been difficult to survive in a rural town like Somerville.

Of the three neighborhoods in Cambridge during the early 1850s, Cambridgeport was geographically and socially in the middle between Old Cambridge to the west, which was the haven of highbrow Harvard College, and East Cambridge to the east, which was the locus of low-brow Irish laborers who worked in the area's glassworks and furniture factories. There were distinct jealousies among the residents of the three sections. "Most of the new population and wealth were in the new villages" of Cambridgeport and East Cambridge, Samuel Eliot wrote in his book *A History of Cambridge*. "Both the new villages had a long-standing grievance against Old Cambridge because of the real or supposed unwillingness of the taxpayers who lived there to be taxed for the building of schools and streets in the newer parts of town."[13] In the early 1850s, Cambridgeport, particularly the Central Square area, had become the business and government center of the city, supplanting the former economic and political hub of Old Cambridge.

The one common thread among the three sections of the city was Cambridge Street, a two-mile stretch of road that traversed through all three sections, from the Harvard College campus through the open lands of Cambridgeport to First Street in East Cambridge. Young Tim Keefe would travel this thoroughfare often as he visited places in all three sections of the city. As an adult, he would eventually buy property on this street.

By 1853 Patrick's family had arrived from Ireland, where they had weathered the Great Famine crisis, escaped eviction from their rented land (and not be forced into the workhouse), and survived famine fever. His parents (Timothy and Catherine) and five siblings (Timothy, Ellen, John, Dennis, and three-year-old Thomas, all born in Ireland) settled in Cambridgeport, where they lived next door to Patrick in a two-family house on Columbia Street near Hampshire Street.[14] At the time, this area of Cambridge was open field, near a nursery on the outskirts of Central Square in northern Cambridgeport, near the city line with Somerville.

With his family now safely transported from Ireland and earning a decent living as a carpenter after eight years on American soil, 29-year-old Patrick could afford to take a wife and start a family of his own. On October 2, 1855, Patrick Keefe and Mary Leary, age 20, were married in a Catholic wedding ceremony performed by Father Lawrence Carroll at St. John's Church in East Cambridge.[15] One year later, on November 1, 1856, Patrick Keefe became an American citizen.[16]

At the time he became a U.S. citizen, Patrick Keefe was once again living in Somerville, where the rents were cheaper than in Cambridge and the carpentry work was more plentiful.[17] It is unclear exactly where he and his wife lived, since the extant editions of the *Somerville Directory* do not begin until 1869, but it was likely in the Union Square neighborhood of Somerville near Cambridgeport. This was relatively near his family, but, more importantly, close to the houses then being built in Somerville. As recounted by Charles Elliot in his book *Somerville's History*, "By 1855, land valued in 1842 at only fifty or one hundred dollars an acre had advanced to two or three thousand dollars per acre, and flourishing settlements began, not only in East Somerville, but near Union Square and on Prospect, Spring, and Winter Hills, each a little village of itself."[18]

Patrick Keefe supported himself as a journeyman carpenter. The carpentry trade in the United States was modeled on the European guild system, where the carpenter was considered to be an artisan and progressed within his profession through the apprentice–journeyman–master system. "Carpenters in Massachusetts were respected members of their communities in the mid–1800s," Mark Erlich wrote in his book *With Our Hands: The Story of Carpenters in Massachusetts*. "Their work was a 'calling,' not just a job, and their pay rates reflected this position," being 41 percent higher than factory workers and 49 percent higher than common laborers; only blacksmiths and machinists earned more than carpenters.[19] Journeyman carpenters earned their higher pay through intricate "finishing" work, wrote Robert Christie in his book *Empire in Wood: A History of the Carpenters' Union*, which required "fashioning by hand all of the complicated detail work—doors, windows, newel posts, mantels—outside on the site of the building."[20] Another skill was chiseling wooden joints that held together the widely spaced timbers in the post-and-beam framing then used to construct houses.[21]

It wasn't long before Patrick's carpentry work also supported a growing family. Mary soon gave birth to two boys, both of whom would adopt their father's artisan faith in the apprentice–journeyman–master system, and eventually six girls to form a family numbering eight children.

3

Carpenter's Son Growing Up Near Boston

Tim Keefe was born on January 1, 1857, the second child of Patrick and Mary Keefe. Although Tim steadfastly maintained over the course of his life that he was born in Cambridge, his birth was recorded in the neighboring town of Somerville, according to records in the Massachusetts Archives.[1] Tim contended that his birthplace was Cambridge likely because he was baptized at St. John's Church in East Cambridge.[2] This was the closest Catholic church at the time to the Keefe family's home in Somerville.

Another reason that Keefe identified with Cambridge was that the area of Somerville where his family lived was geographically cut off from the rest of the town by the Fitchburg Railroad tracks. He identified with the more proximate Cambridgeport area, which was within one-quarter mile of most of the Somerville houses where the Keefe family resided while Tim was growing up. In the late 1870s when Inman Square was developed in Cambridgeport, the neighborhood itself spilled over into Somerville, making it indistinguishable to residents like the Keefe family on Springfield Street who were only one hundred yards from the Cambridge city line. Later in the 1880s, Keefe actively sought the more prestigious provenance of Cambridge to enhance the perception of his character. While Somerville hadn't yet obtained its derisive mid-twentieth-century nickname "Slummerville," the town rapidly became a densely packed city populated by working-class residents in stark contrast to the more upscale nature of Cambridge.

Carpentry jobs for Patrick Keefe were limited by the national financial crisis in 1857, which slowed down house building in Massachusetts and caused out-of-work carpenters to bid down wages for those jobs that were available. Traveling on the nearby Fitchburg Railroad, Patrick became an itinerant carpenter—a journeyman in the truest sense of the word—who traveled to jobs outside of Boston, spending days or weeks at a particular job site. Since he was traveling so much for work, he moved the family back to Cambridge in 1860 where they lived on Columbia Street, near Patrick's parents.[3] By 1860 there were four children in the Keefe family: Tim, his older brother Daniel, and his sisters Katherine and Mary.[4] This was the only time that young Tim physically lived within the city limits of Cambridge.

In 1860, Patrick Keefe traveled to Washington, D.C., where the pay for carpenters was higher than the work he could obtain in Massachusetts. He worked as a civilian carpenter for the U.S. Army Corps of Engineers, which was building military defenses for the federal capital since war seemed imminent between the North and the South over the institution of slavery.[5] However, when the Civil War began in April 1861, Patrick was trapped in Washington.

The family lore, as told by Tim's nieces to *Boston Globe* sportswriter Harold Kaese in 1964 when Keefe was selected for the Hall of Fame, is that "Keefe's father was a builder working in the South when the Civil War began, was arrested, refused to fight for the South, and spent three years in prison."[6] Lee Allen, then the historian at the Hall of Fame, expanded on this family lore a few weeks later in his "Cooperstown Corner" column in *The Sporting News*: "Two of [Tim's] uncles, Frank and John, were killed in the Civil War. Tim's father was constructing a plant below the Mason-Dixon Line at the time the terrible war began. When he refused to fight against his brothers, he spent three years in a Confederate prison making bullets."[7]

Patrick Keefe could have been captured by the Confederate Army in its victory at the first Battle of Bull Run, which occurred in July 1861 in Manassas, Virginia, just 30 miles from Washington, D.C. Northern prisoners of war from that battle were sent to Richmond, and, indeed, some of the prisoners there did work there in munitions factories. Because there were both informal as well as formal programs to exchange prisoners between the two combatant sides, Patrick easily could have returned to the North soon after his capture. The formal program began in July 1862, and while promising "all prisoners of war would have been exchanged or paroled within 10 days of their capture," disputes over interpretations of the agreement disrupted that timeline. By mid-summer 1863, prison exchanges ended because the North could see the end of the war in sight due to weaknesses in the Confederate position.[8]

By mid–1863, Patrick was back in Massachusetts, and living in Somerville, when, despite his previous wartime experience, he registered for the military draft in June.[9] It appears his incarceration lasted less than two years, not three years, which is fairly precise for legend purposes (the three years could have originally meant three years away from home, not in prison). His fifth child, Margaret, was born in March 1864, so Patrick was definitely back in Massachusetts by June 1863.[10] In conjunction with the family lore that two of Patrick's brothers were killed in the Civil War, the headstone atop Tim Keefe's burial site contains this inscription relating to his deceased uncles: "In memory of John Keefe, age 19, Timothy Keefe, age 25, both killed in the Civil War in 1862."[11] Verification of that family lore cannot be confirmed, though.

After Tim's grandfather, Timothy the blacksmith, died in December 1863, Patrick and his family resided in Somerville during the rest of his lifetime, and never again lived in Cambridge.[12] Patrick and his family are recorded in the 1865 Massachusetts state census as living in Somerville, and thereafter he was consistently listed as a resident in the *Somerville Directory*.[13] So, Tim grew up in Somerville, not Cambridge. Interestingly, Tim never asserted in print that he *grew up* in Cambridge, only that he was *from* Cambridge. In fact, he never once discussed his childhood for publication, as no writer in Keefe's lifetime ever wrote about his days as a youth. It was as if Sir Timothy, without any prior background, began his existence at age 17 as a ballplayer on his first organized baseball team in 1874.

By 1865, the Keefe family was living on Oak Street in Somerville, in the area south of Union Square toward the Cambridge city line.[14] During the postwar building boom, Patrick probably worked in the area to build houses for the workers at the nearby Union Glass Company. "The building of horse-railroads and introduction of water, sewers, and gas gave a wonderful impetus to real estate transactions, which even the financial depression occurring a few years later failed to check," Elliot wrote in *Somerville's History*. One of the earliest real estate ventures in Somerville was "the lotting and building up of the property between Webster Avenue and Prospect Street, and west of that street, the Oak and Houghton Street district, the owners being Francis and Amory Houghton, the projectors of the Glass Works."[15]

Amory Houghton had founded the Union Glass Company in Somerville in 1854, but he sold it in 1864 to concentrate on his glass works in Brooklyn, New York, which eventually became the renowned Corning Glass Company.[16] Under new management, Union Glass flourished in the postwar boom and provided carpentry opportunities for Patrick Keefe.

The good economic times for the Keefe family, though, were offset by arguments between young Tim and his father. Allen, the historian at the Hall of Fame, explained: "Tim was only nine years old when his father returned to Cambridge, but even at that time he had demonstrated a love for baseball. His father, anxious that the boy learn mathematics and the science of precise measurement, considered baseball a waste of time and administered many a thrashing to Tim for his stolen moments of joy."[17]

Given all the sacrifices that Patrick faced in his life, it would not be surprising that tension developed between father and son about baseball. Patrick had come to America alone, worked feverishly to bring his parents and siblings here, worked hard to support his own family, and endured a prison camp while helping his adopted country fight a war. Patrick had given a lot of his life to others. So when Patrick believed that his son should not waste his time playing the game of baseball and instead get an education to prepare for a life of work using his head and not his hands, it was inevitable the two would clash.

Working for the Army Corps of Engineers in Washington, D.C., does explain Patrick's engineering obsession for his son Tim, as Patrick had likely been exposed to the design merits of the timber truss to carry heavy loads in the defense fortifications he helped build. A viable truss required precise design by an engineer, which would have convinced Patrick that engineering, not carpentry itself, was the better future. Becoming an engineer, though, required an advanced education. Patrick surely believed that using your brain to design buildings certainly beat using your hands to build them, thus making education important and baseball irrelevant to life as an adult. He likely imparted to young Tim that baseball had no tangible connection to making a living and thus was only for prosperous young adults who could afford to join a club (and pay dues) and take time off from work in the afternoon to play baseball.

Young Tim played baseball with his friends, both from Somerville and Cambridge, in the general Cambridgeport area, most likely on open land within Somerville, since he would have had to walk a good distance to play baseball within Cambridge. By the late 1860s, there were very few public spaces in Cambridgeport to play baseball, so Tim would have had to travel more than one mile to Old Cambridge to use the Cambridge Common just west of Harvard College or try to use a portion of Jarvis Field, land that Harvard had acquired in 1867 to stage its athletic events. However, by the time Tim was 12 years old, the Cambridge Board of Aldermen began to restrict the use of these two facilities. The Aldermen instructed the city police to prohibit the use of Jarvis Field for ballgames not authorized by the college, as well as enforce limited use of the Cambridge Common for ball playing activities.[18]

Tim likely had little desire to be the pitcher at this point of his baseball life. Playing in the field was where the action was in the 1860s, since the pitcher and batter were not yet adversaries. The role of the pitcher at the time was simply to toss the ball to the batter so that he could put the ball in play, to either reach a base or be put out by one of the nine barehanded fielders. By 1869 the pitcher's role hadn't changed appreciably since 1845 when the

Knickerbocker Club rules were codified, and included "the ball must be pitched, not thrown, for the bat." This original idea was the so-called "square pitch," where the pitcher had both feet on the ground and delivered the ball from 45 feet away with the "arm swinging perpendicular to the ground," to release the ball at the knee.[19] Keefe would have been much more interested in batting than being the lowly pitcher.

Besides playing the game, young Tim also watched the ballgames of the local organized teams, which in the late 1860s were all based in Cambridge rather than Somerville. The Cambridge-based Franklin and Putnam clubs fielded baseball teams and played wherever some green space could be procured. For example, the Putnam club played its games on the green in front of the Webster School in the southern portion of Cambridgeport.[20]

However, the most talented ballclub in the area was the Harvard College baseball team, which was one of the top three amateur teams in the Boston area and played many of the top ballclubs in the country. Tim may have attended the Harvard-Lowell championship match in 1867 at Jarvis Field, or even the game on June 12, 1869, at Jarvis Field between Harvard and the all-professional Cincinnati Red Stockings team, managed by Harry Wright. Although Harvard lost the game to Cincinnati by a large margin, 30–11, the game may well have whetted the appetite of Keefe for the play-for-pay aspect of professional baseball.

In 1870, Patrick Keefe made the leap from journeyman to master carpenter, when he established his own business, McCloskey & Keefe, in partnership with Hugh McCloskey, a carpenter in East Cambridge.[21] At the time, there were now eight children in the Keefe family, with the births of Ellen in 1866, Annie in 1868, and Elizabeth in 1870.[22] To keep expenses low during the start-up phase of the business, Patrick moved the family to a house in Somerville on Columbia Street "near the marsh," just one hundred yards north of the city border with Cambridge and half a mile south of Union Square.[23] It was one of the nastier sections of Somerville, located near slaughterhouses and the Boynton Meat Packing factory, both of which discharged waste matter into the nearby Miller's River and pungent stenches into the air.

The slaughterhouses were a particular problem. Given the numerous horses used in the local economy to haul goods and transport people in conveyances (omnibus and streetcar), facilities were needed to handle the rendering of dead horses. There were several rendering plants along the Cambridge Street axis in East Cambridge and Somerville below the Fitchburg Railroad tracks, where the animals were killed and then cut up to process hair, skin, hooves, bones, and meat to recycle them into productive uses, such as knife handles from bones and glue from hooves. Noxious fumes were one of

3. Carpenter's Son Growing Up Near Boston

[Census table image]

This listing from the 1870 federal census shows the Keefe household as tabulated by the census enumerator in Somerville, Massachusetts. Tim, then 13 years old, was the second oldest child of Patrick and Mary Keefe, sandwiched between his older brother and his six younger sisters. The youngest child was the not-yet-named Elizabeth, just two months old at the time of the census.

the outputs from the boiling of the body parts in outdoor vats, which often made nearby residents nauseous and caused them to vomit. By the late 1870s health regulations were established to curtail many of these unhealthy activities. However, the Keefe family lived in this environment where "the air reeked horribly" while Patrick established himself as a master carpenter, while many of their neighbors were "willing to trade good air for slaughterhouse jobs."[24] It was not a pleasant place for young Tim to live as a teenager.

It appears that Tim's formal education lasted only until the seventh or eighth grade. In the late 1860s this would have entailed completing two years at a primary school, two years at a sub-grammar school, and then four years at a grammar school. Keefe likely attended grammar school at the Prospect Hill School in Union Square, which was the nearest Somerville grammar school to the Keefe household "near the marsh."

While his parents did list Tim's occupation in the 1870 federal census as "student," when he was 13 years old, Keefe likely went to work soon thereafter, since state law then mandated compulsory school attendance only until age 14.[25] He did not graduate from Somerville High School, as there were no Keefe names listed among the graduates published in the *City of Somerville Annual Report* for the years before 1880.[26] In any event, Keefe would have had to pass a test to attend Somerville High School. The entrance requirements in the 1870s mandated not just passing a test but also a certification from the grammar school that the student had attained certain educational requirements to be able to handle a high-school-level curriculum. Tim was not listed among the exam-passers in the *City of Somerville Annual Report* during the period 1868 to 1871. Not many students attended Somerville High School in that era; for instance, in 1875, there were only 32 graduates, with just nine students in the college preparatory course.

Since Tim wasn't interested in pursuing an education to become an engineer, his father would have insisted that he use his time to become an apprentice carpenter to begin his journey through the apprentice–journeyman–master system that Patrick had taken to support his family. As Patrick found out in America, being an independent artisan like a journeyman carpenter was the track to rise into the middle class.

As a master carpenter with his own business, Patrick Keefe could tutor apprentices and likely did have Tim as an apprentice to teach him the skills needed by a carpenter. His older brother Daniel was an apprentice plumber at the time.[27] Tim became no stranger to working dawn-to-dusk hours as an apprentice carpenter, who, as W.J. Rorabaugh explained in *The Craft Apprentice*, "sought to learn his trade well so that he might be hired as a journeyman, save some money, and then set up as a master."[28] His pay was learning the craft from the master, not cash wages, over the traditional three-year period of apprenticeship. By 1870, the apprentice system was unraveling in many trades, since "the transformation from craft to factory that had begun fifty years earlier with the first textile mills was now spreading throughout the artisan world."[29] Crafts such as tailoring, shoemaking, printing, weaving, and iron molding had become largely mechanized, which eliminated the artisan and destroyed his middle-class stature. Carpenters were some of the few remaining artisans, although now they needed to be specialists rather than generalists.

The timing to start a carpentry business seemed auspicious, since "the period from 1869 to 1875 saw many old estates [in Somerville] laid out and built over. Among these were ... the Concord Avenue and Springfield Street district owned by John O'Brien."[30] However, in reality, the timing was bad. In the early 1870s, the nature of carpentry work changed dramatically when non-tradesman contractors acting as independent capitalists revolutionized how houses were built. Also, a host of woodworking machines were invented to save time and money, such as sanders and compound carvers, and ready-to-install windows and doors were manufactured by unskilled men in a factory and delivered to the job site.

Contractors segmented work to maximize profits and minimize the time needed to employ expensive carpenters, by hiring women and children as "green hands" to do the simpler tasks. As Christie wrote in *Empire in Wood: A History of the Carpenters' Union*, "Carpentry was gradually divided into door hanging, floor laying, stair building, and a score of other special tasks by competing contractors who paid one-half the wage of a fully trained, all-around carpenter."[31] Design innovation in the trade also hurt, as the use of balloon framing, rather than traditional post-and-beam, was increasingly utilized, since the use of 2" by 4" studs nailed close together made more efficient use of wood and labor, since the technique required a lower level of carpentry skills.[32] The long economic depression that began in 1873 exacerbated the situation, according to carpenter historian Erlich, since "contractors imposed whatever wage levels they wanted ... [and] desperate carpenters worked for subsistence pay—if they worked at all."[33]

It appears that Patrick Keefe left his own business and returned to journeyman status by 1873. Being undercapitalized in a rapidly changing trade no doubt contributed to the failure as a master carpenter. The unexpected burial expenses resulting from the 1872 death of his eighth child, two-year-old Elizabeth, were also a factor.[34]

Since most carpenters at the time had no protection of a union, the changes in how carpenters were employed devastated the economics of the Keefe household. The impact was so drastic that in 1875 Patrick Keefe took a wage-earning job in an East Cambridge lumber yard rather than continue to try to work as an independent carpenter.[35] This drastic change in the nature of the employer-artisan relationship surely impacted Tim's perspective on the working world.

If there is any truth to the Keefe family lore about father-son disagreements about the value of baseball, it was disagreements related to money. The tough economic times that hit the Keefe household during the economic depression of the 1870s would have sparked this tension if Tim, now a journeyman carpenter after completing his apprenticeship, was sneaking away to watch or play baseball games rather than toil from dawn to dusk for a meager day's pay. However, Tim had a solution to the family financial problem that involved baseball.

4

Infielder on Amateur and Semipro Teams

Tim Keefe came of age during the formative years of professional baseball in the 1870s. Harry Wright, formerly of the all-professional Cincinnati Red Stockings, came to Boston in 1871 to organize the Boston ballclub in the newly formed National Association of Professional Base Ball Players. Wright's team dominated the competition, winning four of the five championships during the association's five-year existence, before its better teams left in 1876 to form the National League.

Before 1876, Wright's team was the only recognized professional team in the Boston area; all other organized teams competed for amateur championships. However, there was a sizeable gray area between the seemingly polar philosophies of professional and amateur teams. The amateur system in Boston was classified into two levels: amateur and junior. As the name implies, the junior teams were less skilled than those in the amateur rank. Junior teams were generally stocked with purely amateur players, who played the game just for the fun of it, perhaps with aspirations to move up to a team at the amateur level. However, teams at the amateur level gradually morphed from purely non-paid players in 1871 to a sizeable portion of players being openly compensated by 1875, either through a division of gate receipts or direct payments by the team sponsor. The term "semiprofessional" was not used much before 1876, but essentially the majority of teams in the amateur bracket were semipro teams that paid ballplayers to some degree.

The need for additional income for his family led Keefe into the murky world of amateur baseball in the Boston area, where he could be paid to participate in a game he loved. Much like the apprentice–journeyman–master system in carpentry that he was steeped in after being an apprentice carpenter, Keefe needed to develop sufficient skills to advance within a similar hierarchy in baseball. By 1874, "first-class competitive baseball was transformed from an avocation primarily of clerks and skilled craftsmen into a form of skilled work in its own right," historian Warren Goldstein related in his book *Playing for Keeps*. "The relative scarcity of baseball craftsmen earned them high wages and substantial freedom of movement."[1]

To tap into the ranks of amateur baseball to begin his journey to becoming a paid ballplayer, Keefe had to cross the city line from his home in Somerville into Cambridge to join a club that sponsored a baseball team. In this era, "club" was a literal term, i.e., a fraternal organization comprised of members who paid dues. Having a baseball team generally was secondary to the club's main function as a social organization.

As an amateur ballplayer, Keefe was an infielder. His callused hands from carpentry work helped him easily field balls in an era when players did not wear a glove on their non-throwing hand. Keefe first played on an organized baseball team in 1874 when he played first base for the junior team of the Franklin club in Cambridge, according to a detailed record of his early playing days in the earliest published biography of Keefe in the *New York Clipper* in 1880.[2] His earliest exploits on the diamond with the Franklins have gone unrecorded, though, since the local Cambridge newspapers at the time only sporadically published the results of any baseball games and rarely any box scores. Later in 1874 Keefe moved to the Tremont club of Cambridge, which competed for the upper-echelon amateur title. However, the Tremonts weren't very good; by July 1874 the Tremonts had a 0–11 record against other teams at the amateur level.[3]

The oldest extant box score of Keefe's amateur baseball career was published in the *Boston Daily Advertiser* in August 1874, which summarized the 21–6 defeat of the Tremonts by the Beacons.[4] Keefe played second base and batted fourth in the order that day, but he did not produce any of the team's three base hits or score any of their six runs. He did make four putouts and had two assists in the field. The game was played at Boston's South End Grounds, home to the city's professional team and, courtesy of Harry Wright, also home to the Beacon club. Wright helped to foster the amateur game within the city by making the field available to the purely amateur Beacons. Keefe must have relished the chance to play baseball on the same second-base turf that Ross Barnes patrolled for the Boston team of the National League.

In 1874 Keefe faced pitching that was increasingly adversarial and deceptive to the batter, rather than be an innocent feeding of the ball to the batter. Two years earlier the baseball rules had been liberalized to allow the pitcher to use a wrist-snap with a release point at or below the hip.[5] This rule change allowed the pitcher to throw a curveball rather than be restricted to a straight pitch. When umpires began to allow a bent-arm delivery with the wrist-snap, the ball could also be delivered with increased speed.

Keefe learned to pitch by observing the professional pitchers at the South

End Grounds. He likely took the horse-drawn trolley from Somerville to downtown Boston and transferred to the Tremont Street trolley line to get to the South End. While he certainly could not afford the 50-cent admission price, he may have negotiated it down to a nickel or dime for a late-inning entry. Or he may have simply watched the ballgames from a perch overlooking the fence.

Three men were Keefe's early pitching idols, based on remarks he wrote in his treatise "Curve Pitching," which was published in 1884 as a chapter of the book *Batting and Pitching*. "From the straight arm and strategic work of Al Spalding, of the Bostons, and Dick McBride, of the Athletics, the delivery became a square, underhanded throw, beautifully exemplified by Thomas H. Bond, of the Bostons," Keefe wrote. "From about the year 1874, the delivery became more and more of a throw, the arm rising higher and higher, and the curve came into effect."[6]

While Arthur Cummings is generally credited with "discovering" the curveball, Bond in particular became a model curveball pitcher for Keefe. Bond, a first-generation Irish-American who in 1874 played for the Atlantic club of Brooklyn, elevated the wrist-snap rule of 1872 into a side-arm delivery by 1874. As Spalding recalled in his 1911 book *America's National Game*, "In 1874 Tom Bond inaugurated the present style of pitching, or, rather, underhand throwing, with its in-curves and out-shoots," which, while technically in violation of the straight-arm pitching rule, was permitted by the umpires.[7] Bond defeated Spalding several times during the 1874 season, as the Atlantics challenged the dominance of the Boston team in National Association competition.

The *Boston Daily Advertiser* continued to maintain the fictional bifurcation between professional and amateur teams in an early 1875 article entitled "The Diamond Field," in which the newspaper printed sub-headlines "Professional Clubs," to describe the 13 teams with membership in the National Association, and "The Amateurs," to list the other local teams.[8] Although the *Boston Daily Advertiser* left no middle ground, there were many teams in the Boston area that considered themselves something between professional and amateur. At a meeting in May 1875 of the Massachusetts Association of Amateur Base Ball Players, the Taunton club moved to pass an amendment to the constitution to allow "a player [to] be recompensed for the [work] time lost in playing the game." The initiative lost by a vote of 11 to 11, since a two-thirds majority was required to modify the constitution. The *New York Clipper* called the motion "a very singular amendment for an 'amateur' association" and went on to propitiously speculate "an evident split must occur next year, to be 'truly amateur' or 'professional-amateur' as the semi-professionals are called."⁹ The vote indicated that one-half of the amateur teams in Massachusetts considered themselves to be semipro.

Keefe began the 1875 season with the more-than-amateur Mutual club of Boston, which likely dispensed a share of gate receipts to its players. While Keefe had been uninterested in being a pitcher as a younger lad, the advent of the curveball and the heightened dynamics of the pitcher-batter interaction changed his mind. By 1875 the game of baseball had evolved to the point where the recipe for success became "preventing the other team from scoring, instead of just trying to pile up more runs."¹⁰ The pitcher was now a pivotal player on a baseball team. With the Mutuals in 1875, for the first time, Keefe had the opportunity to be a pitcher, a fact that he later confirmed in an 1895 interview.¹¹

In his first year of pitching, Keefe likely used the traditional underhanded delivery, taking one step forward within the six-foot-by-six-foot pitcher's box, whose front line was 45 feet from the batter, to toss the ball with medium speed toward the batter. He may have mixed in a soft curveball, which he learned through observing the more proficient experimenters with the curveball. He had to be somewhat precise in his delivery, since the batter could call for a high or low pitch to define his strike zone (waist to shoulders or waist to knees). Nine unfair pitches to the batter created a base on balls (a "ball" was called for every three unfair pitches) and four fair pitches taken or missed by the batter created a strikeout (after two "strike" calls, a warning was issued to the batter when the third strike occurred, so the fourth fair pitch taken was technically the third strike). But the pitcher was only as good as his catcher was capable of receiving his throws with his bare hands. In this era of no gloves, no mask, and no protective equipment whatsoever, the catcher normally played 20 feet behind the batter until runners were on base. Then he would move closer to the batter, but in amateur games not likely directly behind the batter. Therefore, speed was not a big consideration in pitching; accuracy and a bit of deception were more important.

Keefe pitched at least two games for the Mutual club in 1875. On May 22, Keefe pitched in the 15–3 loss to the Beacons; he gave up only nine hits, but 25 errors by the Mutuals (including seven by the catcher) were his downfall.¹² On June 12, Keefe pitched more effectively against the Boston Amateurs, as the Mutuals lost, 5–4, in 11 innings.¹³

On August 7, the *Boston Daily Advertiser* published a brief item about a "semi-professional" baseball team in Lewiston, Maine, called the Androscoggins, which was being organized "on a basis similar to that of the Graftons, Live Oaks, Lowells, and others in the State," namely one that paid its players.¹⁴ Several players from the local Chelsea amateur team had already been engaged to play for the Androscoggins, including the team's shortstop, Jim Mutrie. Keefe either read the newspaper that day and acted upon the report, or had been previously recruited by Mutrie, because he soon packed his grip and boarded a train on the Boston & Maine Railroad for the 150-mile journey north to Lewiston to cast his lot with a team that was willing to pay him more than a share of gate receipts.

Mutrie, who at the time was considered one of the better players in the Boston area, was recruited by several people from Lewiston who had visited him in Boston. "They proposed that Mutrie should take charge of the Lewiston team and try and defeat the Portlands. After some haggling Mutrie agreed to go if he was guaranteed the sum of $18 a week," a writer later captured Mutrie's recollections of Lewiston. "Jim went to Lewiston full of energy and determination to carry out his contract. But fate was against him. In the first game he was done for. He undertook to catch a swift pitcher ... [but] intercepted a foul tip, and he was sorry afterward, as the ball smashed his collarbone and he was laid off for the season."[15]

Keefe stayed with Lewiston for the 1875 season, probably receiving about half of what Mutrie had negotiated, perhaps $10 a week. That was roughly what Keefe could earn as a journeyman carpenter, but with much less physical exertion and greater certainty of having an income. He no doubt quarreled with his father about his decision to leave Somerville to play baseball in Lewiston. Playing ball in Boston was one thing, but to go to Maine for baseball was quite another. Money was likely the linchpin to winning over his father, who was experiencing such hard times as a carpenter during the nation's long economic depression that he had recently swallowed his pride to be a wage-worker in a Cambridge lumber yard. Keefe may have also used the several examples of Irish-born men who were successful as professional ballplayers, such as Tommy Bond, who was born in County Langford.

After playing for two months with the Androscoggins against the competition in Maine, Keefe played several games in Massachusetts in October when the Androscoggins barnstormed through the home state of many of the team's players. Although the Androscoggins often lost, they exhibited batting skills. In the 15–9 loss at Taunton, the boys from Lewiston banged out 16 hits, as the *Taunton Gazette* reported that "they bat heavily and pounded Waterman's pitching in a style frightful to contemplate."[16] When the Androscoggins rapped out another 16 hits in a 14–10 loss at Lowell, the *Lowell Courier* reported, "The Maine boys scored one each in the fourth and sixth and in the seventh by very heavy batting—five base hits, seven total bases—made five runs, tieing [*sic*] the game."[17] Keefe had two of the team's 16 hits against Lowell and fielded flawlessly at first base with 15 putouts and no errors.

The veil shielding the fiction of the non-existence of semipro ballclubs was lifted at a meeting in November 1875 of the Massachusetts Association of Amateur Base Ball Players, when "various charges of 'paying' players were brought against the Lowells, Live Oaks, Tauntons, and Graftons, and it was finally voted not to award any championship prizes this year."[18] By February 1876 the veil was completely removed.

The baseball landscape changed in 1876 when Boston, Chicago, and other top clubs bolted from the National Association to form the National League. This effectively gutted the two-tier professional/amateur system in place the previous five years, since it fostered the creation of a new layer of "minor" professional clubs. In 1876 clubs with fully professional teams sprouted up within 50 miles of Boston in the cities of Lynn, Lowell, and Fall River in Massachusetts, as well as in Manchester, New Hampshire, and Providence, Rhode Island.[19] All these clubs were part of the loosely organized New England Association, which competed for the glory of the New England Championship. All other clubs with paid players were considered to be semipro. Purely amateur clubs comprised of adults became virtually extinct in the Boston area. As the *New York Clipper* reported, "The Beacon Club of Boston—about the only legitimate Knickerbocker amateur club in the Hub—has retired from the field, having no opponents of their own class to play with, semi-professionalism having gobbled up all the other so-called amateur clubs of Boston in its vicinity."[20]

Having switched ballclubs in mid-season during both 1874 and 1875, Keefe had formed his own player mobility philosophy at the time, since there were no formal rules. In the strictly amateur period prior to 1869, the National Association of Base Ball Players had a policy to forestall "revolving," or changing, clubs, by requiring a 60-day probationary period before playing for a new club.[21] Thereafter, the norm for professional ballplayers was a one-season agreement, which was formalized with the establishment of the National Association of Professional Base Ball Players in 1871. However, this standard was often ignored by both players and ballclubs. As for non-professional players between 1871 and 1875, there were no guidelines to abide by, since there was no national governing body for amateur ballclubs after 1871 and a general lack of formal recognition of semipro ballclubs within state amateur associations. However, there was a need for a guiding principle, since the fraternal social club concept was rapidly converting into a business structure with paid employees (such as the Androscoggins) and there were fewer clubs (such as the Harvard College and Beacon clubs) where the players "give their time to the national game from pure love of the sport, and not for any pecuniary benefit."[22] With little formal guidance about switching ballclubs in 1874 and 1875, Keefe simply switched when it benefited him.

With the formal recognition of minor professional and semipro teams in 1876, Keefe adopted the one-season commitment philosophy of professional players in the National League, to emulate Al Spalding and several other well-compensated ballplayers who left the Boston ballclub after their one-season contracts ended in 1875 to accept better deals with the Chicago ballclub for 1876. Keefe saw this combination of limited ballclub commitment with negotiation freedom thereafter as consistent with the world of the journeymen carpenter, who had no long-term ties to anyone he had worked for in the construction of a house. Naturally, he believed that the commitment to a ballclub ended sooner if it disbanded before the end of the season.

Since he was not ready to advance up to either the National League or the New England Association, Keefe returned to play with the semipro Androscoggins for the 1876 season, where he played "at times the respective positions of first base, short-stop and pitcher."[23] Few box scores have survived from Keefe's tenure with the Androscoggins, since the *Lewiston Evening Journal* rarely printed much about the team. However, the newspaper did print an extensive account of a Fourth of July holiday game between the Androscoggins and the team from Bates College. Keefe played shortstop in his team's 9–1 drubbing by the college students.[24] It is unclear how much longer Keefe remained with the Androscoggins after that holiday ballgame. According to an article in the *Somerville Journal* a decade later, he may have been asked to leave due to his poor habits. "He used to lie around in the sun, and sleep and dream and be indolent," a Lewiston baseball fan recalled. "We didn't think he would ever be a great ballplayer or anything else in those days."[25]

Keefe did not return to Lewiston for the 1877 season. Instead, he worked full-time with his father, who was able to leave his job at the lumberyard and return to being a journeyman carpenter who built houses. The opportunity was right in Somerville, in the burgeoning Inman Square neighborhood that straddled the Cambridge/Somerville border. It was one of the rare times that Keefe put down enough roots to find his way into a public record of his employment, as he was listed as a "carpenter" in the 1877 *Somerville Directory*. The house-building opportunity also allowed the Keefe family to live near the construction activity, at 68 Concord Avenue, to leave behind the putrid conditions of their home on Columbia Street near the slaughterhouses and meat packing plants.[26]

Together, Keefe and his father teamed up to built two-family houses on land developed by John O'Brien, a relatively prosperous Irish-American who operated a grocery and butcher store in Union Square in Somerville, about one-half mile north of Inman Square. O'Brien owned several acres of land in the area of Somerville that was south of the Fitchburg Railroad tracks but north of the Cambridge city line, having purchased a number of the old farms there. He carved the land into house lots and sold them off to individual buyers to build their own houses on them.

There was a need for worker housing in the Inman Square area, since it was close to the Union Glass Company factory in Somerville as well as other manufacturers in Cambridge. In an effort to make the land more valuable, O'Brien petitioned the Cambridge Board of Aldermen to formally name the intersection at Cambridge Street and Hampshire Street to be Inman Square, to replace the current informal name of Atwood's Corner. Ralph Inman had owned 180 acres of pasture and woodland in Cambridgeport when he died in 1788; his family began selling off the land in 1862 as individual house lots. The petition was approved on December 29, 1875.[27] Since "square" implied urban and "corner" implied rural, O'Brien's land was now more valuable. Soon the lots sold more briskly, houses sprung up, and a neighborhood evolved. St. Joseph's Catholic Church was soon erected nearby, so that the Irish-American residents of the new houses no longer needed to travel to East Cambridge to worship. The Keefe family would soon be numbered among those Irish-American residents.

During the summer of 1877 Keefe occasionally played baseball for the Our Boys semipro team in Boston, which played a schedule that ranged from college and amateur teams to professional teams in the New England Association; there was even one game with the Boston team of the National League. The Our Boys played their home games at the South End Grounds in Boston, where the Boston club of the National League staged its games, thanks to the largesse of manager Harry Wright who still tried to foster the growth of amateur baseball in the city (as well as give himself an advantage to scout the local amateur talent for future major leaguers). This association with the National League ballclub helped Keefe form relationships with Wright as well as with some of the ballplayers on the Boston team, particularly Tommy Bond who was in his first year pitching for the Boston team.

When he did play for the Our Boys, Keefe substituted for Dan Cronin, the second baseman and team captain, when Cronin was needed to man the outfield. In this limited action, Keefe began to ascend into competence as a ballplayer. His best effort came in the game against the Lowell professional team, when he was 1-for-5 at the plate in a 9–7 loss.[28] Keefe didn't play in the August 15 game when the Our Boys lost, 5–1, to the Boston National League team.[29] Instead, he watched the game from the stands to observe Tommy Bond shut down the Our Boys, giving up just three hits, and see George Wright flawlessly play second base.

Several of Keefe's teammates on the Our Boys went on to play in the major leagues. Pitcher John Driscoll compiled a 38–39 record during the 1880–1884 period, predominantly in the American Association. Jerry Sweeney played 31 games in the Union Association in 1884, while Cronin got into two games in the same league.

A major turning point in Keefe's baseball career came on October 18 when the Our Boys played Harvard College at the South End Grounds. Keefe was in the lineup at second base that day, and collected two of his team's six hits in an 8–3 loss to Harvard. He was rewarded for his effort that day with his first press mention in a Boston newspaper: "Keefe, Donovan and Driscoll did the fine playing for the Our Boys."[30]

The game against Harvard shows that working full-time as a carpenter during the spring and summer of 1877 had sparked Keefe's ambition to take the game of baseball more seriously than he had when he played for the Androscoggin club in Lewiston, Maine. More importantly, after watching the Harvard battery of pitcher Harold Ernst and catcher James Tyng, Keefe now wanted to become a pitcher rather than remain an infielder. Tyng, by wearing a mask during the game, enabled Ernst to throw curveballs more effectively, since Tyng could play closer to the batter more often. Tyng popularized the catcher's mask in 1877 while playing for Harvard, even though "it was a subject of ridicule to the 'bleaching board' element" and he "was subjected to good natured though somewhat derisive pity" by the opposing players.[31] Ernst was so good a pitcher that he could have easily played professionally, but the amateur philosophy of sports at Harvard precluded that possibility. Ernst, instead, became a medical doctor.

Further inspiration to become a professional baseball player came from a house construction job that he started just one week after playing in the Harvard game. Keefe accepted a carpentry job to help build a house outside of Inman Square on Lot 72 on Springfield Street in Somerville, for which he had a verbal agreement to be paid $2 a day for labor and materials. Keefe worked on the house for 11 days between October 26 and November 8 and was owed $22. When the property owner, Martin L. Cate, a recent graduate of Harvard College who lived in Cambridge, refused to pay Keefe and three other carpenters on the job, Keefe sued Cate and recorded a lien on the property. The problem was that there was no written agreement, just a handshake deal. According to the lien filed by Keefe at the Middlesex County Registry of Deeds, "The erection of a wooden dwelling house ... was performed by virtue of an oral agreement made by me with one George Moyers who had authority from and was rightfully acting for said owner, in procuring and furnishing such labor and materials and by and with the consent of said owner."[32]

This incident helped to shape Keefe's attitude about professional baseball in relation to making a living as a carpenter. He decided that he would be just as well off as a professional baseball player, if it took these lengths to collect payment as a carpenter (Keefe must have settled with Cate, since Cate sold the property in January 1878 and needed the lien to be discharged to sell the property).[33]

Keefe and the other three carpenters who sued Cate for payment did not belong to a carpenters' union, but rather simply joined forces for their mutual good as individuals who worked in a common craft. There had been carpenter unions in the Boston area, but they typically imploded when economic depressions occurred. The earliest carpenter union in Boston was established in 1834, but disappeared by the 1857 depression; a state federation of carpenters was created in 1864, with eight local affiliates, but it perished by the 1873 depression.[34]

By 1877, after swinging a hammer as a carpenter for six years, Keefe was more interested in pursuing the independence promised by the apprentice–journeyman–master system than in improvements in daily wage or limits on hours worked that were the focus of craft unions. Probably meaningless to Keefe was the fact that Massachusetts was a leader in laws benefiting workers and organized labor, such as the 1842 court decision in *Commonwealth v. Hunt* that permitted unions to organize or the 1874 first-in-the-nation 10-hour workday law for women and children. Also meaningless would have been the February 1877 strike by the Boston & Maine Railroad engineers, a precursor to that summer's nationwide railroad strikes. Keefe was driven by the principle of free labor, not negotiated labor. Since becoming an independent master carpenter seemed an unlikely future occurrence for Keefe, given the dramatic changes in how houses were constructed, he decided to pursue independence through baseball.

Keefe took his first step toward independence as a professional ballplayer two days after finishing his work building Cate's house in Somerville. On November 10, he played third base for an aggregation of semipro players cobbled together under the banner of the Westboro team in a game against the Boston National League team during its extended postseason exhibition tour. In this game Keefe batted against Tommy Bond for the first time in competition; like most of his teammates, he went hitless as Bond yielded just three hits in the 9–2 victory over the Westboros.[35] Also playing for the Westboros that day were pitcher Gid Gardner and catcher Barney Gilligan, who both hailed from Cambridge. Together with Keefe, the trio would navigate the turbulent landscape of professional baseball over the next two years in their ultimate quest to play in the National League.

5
Pitcher in the Minor Leagues

Since the ballplayers on the Our Boys team in 1877 were an ambitious bunch, the team broke up when many of them, including Tim Keefe, sought full-time employment in 1878 as a professional ballplayer. In March 1878 the *Boston Daily Advertiser* reported that Hudson, Massachusetts, a town 30 miles west of Boston, would field "a paid nine," having agreed to terms with Keefe and Gid Gardner of the Our Boys as well as with Barney Gilligan of the Alerts of Charlestown. The town of Westboro, Massachusetts, located 10 miles southwest of Hudson, also planned to field a team, having engaged Dan Cronin of the Our Boys to be its second baseman and field captain.[1]

It appears that Keefe, as well as the other two players, used a verbal agreement with Hudson as leverage to negotiate better terms with the Westboro team. By May 1878, Keefe, Gardner, and Gilligan had all abandoned the Hudson team to join the Westboro team captained by Cronin. Jerry Sweeney, first baseman for the Our Boys, also joined them, as a fourth former member of the Our Boys on the Westboro team.

Professional baseball in the Boston area settled into a four-tier structure for the 1878 season. The Boston team in the National League was, of course, at the top of the professional pyramid. At the next rung down on the ladder were the pro teams in Lowell and Lynn, which competed in both the International Association and the New England Association. Teams could compete in multiple leagues, since they only needed to play each other league team a certain number of times during the season, in this era before fixed schedules.

The International Association was the second tier, with its other teams located in nearby Manchester, New Hampshire, but also in Buffalo, Rochester, Syracuse, and Utica in New York as well as in London, Ontario, Canada. The New England Association, more geographically compact, was the third tier of pro ball in the Boston area, encompassing teams from the Massachusetts cities of Holyoke, New Bedford, Springfield, Westboro, and Worcester in addition to Lowell and Lynn; Manchester, New Hampshire, was also in this league. Providence, Rhode Island, which had competed in the New England Association in 1877, moved up to the National League for the 1878 season.

At the bottom fourth rung were the many independent teams throughout the region, in small cities such as Hudson and Clinton in Massachusetts.

Westboro was the smallest locale to compete for the New England Association championship in 1878.[2] George Fayerweather, the manager of the Westboro team, later recollected about Keefe: "What an excellent fellow he was! He then evinced those head qualities and that keen judgment as a player and man that have advanced him to where he is today."[3] Keefe, who wasn't yet sporting a mustache on his face, earned between $12 and $18 a week with the Westboro team.

Keefe began the 1878 season playing third base for the Westboros, who, other than a few victories against the Worcester team, didn't fare well against the New England Association competition. For example, Westboro was soundly defeated, 13–6, in the May 22 game at Lynn against the Live Oak team. Keefe received his first press mention in a national publication for his 2-for-4 performance in that game, when the *New York Clipper* reported that "the batting of Gardner and Keefe of the Westboros was heavy."[4] By June Keefe had moved from third base to center field, since Fayerweather had secured Bill Crook, a veteran professional ballplayer, to play third base.

During this era of the one-man pitching staff, Gardner was the starting pitcher in every game for Westboro. "At this time [1878] Tim Keefe was regarded as possessing few qualities as a twirler, but he thought he could pitch some," Fayerweather recalled ten years after the team disbanded. "But Gardner didn't take too kindly to another man in the [pitcher's] box, and many a time have I seen Tim walk into his patch of ground with a heart heavy as a boarding-house biscuit and the tears almost on his cheeks, because his ambition to pitch was not gratified. Yet he occasionally put the ball over the plate for us."[5]

Keefe received his one chance to start a game in the pitcher's box for Westboro when Fayerweather tapped him to pitch the afternoon game of the Fourth of July holiday twin bill with Worcester, after Gardner had pitched the morning game. Keefe had little success in the pitcher's box, though, as he gave up four runs early in the game. As reported by the *Westboro Chronotype*, "They seemed to have but little trouble in striking Keefe's balls, but when Keefe was changed for Gardner, it was fatal to the Worcesters."[6] With Gardner in the box, the Westboros rallied for an 8–4 victory.

In his role as "change pitcher," Keefe pitched in at least three more games for Westboro in 1878. His best effort was on July 13 against New Bedford when Keefe was the hero of Westboro's 2–1 victory. He relieved Gardner in the seventh inning of a 1–1 tie and gave up only one hit in three innings, as Westboro scored the game-winning run in the eighth inning.[7]

In this first time as a pitcher against strong competition, Keefe likely used a mix of fastballs and soft curves. He would have had some zip on his fastball, since a rule change for 1878 permitted his arm motion to be at waist level, up from hip height. If a pitcher hitched up his pants so that the belt line was near chest level, he could really generate some speed on the ball. Since most catchers now wore a mask and stooped behind the batter frequently, his curveball would fool some batters. However, at this stage of their baseball careers, Gardner was a much more talented pitcher than Keefe.

A pitcher with a good curveball was one thing, but without a catcher who could catch the curveball and prevent it from rolling to the backstop, that pitcher was far less effective in retiring batters and stopping the opposition from scoring. Catchers in this era needed to be tough and courageous, given the risk to bodily injury by standing close to the batter to receive the pitch and stop baserunners from stealing bases. "While toughness was the most conspicuous attribute of catchers of the early 1870s, it was becoming clear that they also needed tremendous skill," Peter Morris wrote in his book *The Catcher*. "The difficulty of finding someone who could satisfy both requirements meant that a good catcher was indispensable." Disfigured fingers were common in these days before the catcher's mitt, since the catcher caught the ball with his fingers, not the palm of his hands, by using "a trap or spring box made of the fingers" to avoid a stone bruise or split hand.[8] These qualities made Gilligan a valuable component of any team he played for.

After the Westboros played a series of games in early August with the team from the nearby town of Clinton, the Westboro team disbanded and its players joined the Clinton team. As the *Clinton Conant* reported, the Clintons "were entirely reorganized from the Westboros (only Thomas Burke remaining of the original nine)."[9] One of the benefits of playing in Clinton was the brand new ball field that had been constructed that season. Keefe patrolled center field at the site of today's Fuller Field in Clinton, which Guinness World Records has recognized as the oldest baseball diamond in continuous use.[10] On the downside, Clinton did not compete for the New England Association championship, and thus played most of its games against small-city teams such as Brockton, Natick, and Fitchburg with just a few games against the likes of New Bedford and Springfield.

Keefe's perspective on the workplace was impacted in early September when third baseman Crook died in an accident at a hotel in Springfield, after the Clintons had defeated Springfield, 3–2, that afternoon. The writer for the *Clinton Conant*, who may have witnessed the tragedy, described the accident in a stream-of-conscientious manner:

5. Pitcher in the Minor Leagues

Crook was on his way upstairs about ten o'clock, for the night, and stopped on the second floor for a little sport, when in the dim light he backed against what he supposed was the side of the house, but in reality was merely a low railing which surrounded an aperture, covered by glass, beneath which the chandelier hung; he fell backwards upon the glass, which of course gave way; Sweeney caught him by one leg, but his clothing gave way, and he fell, striking the chandelier and falling from thence, twenty-eight feet in all, to the floor striking his head; he was taken up unconscious, and remained so till about six the next morning when he died.[11]

Crook's family received no financial compensation from the owners of the Clinton ballclub. Instead, the Clinton ballplayers chipped in a week's salary for Crook's family, while his former employer, the Athletic club of Philadelphia, donated the proceeds from one of its games.[12] Keefe was back playing third base after Crook's death, as Clinton continued to play ballgames through mid–October before disbanding for the season.

An October 26 game played by many of the Clinton ballplayers as the revived Our Boys team against the General Worth team from Stoneham encouraged Keefe to become a full-time pitcher, rather than continue as an infielder. Keefe started the game that day in the pitcher's box, as Gardner didn't participate in the game. Keefe pitched well through eight innings, when his team led, 2–1, but he then yielded five runs in the ninth inning, as the Our Boys reunion team lost, 7–3.[13] Keefe gave up just seven hits and struck out nine batters. Since he had been repeatedly hitless in Clinton's games against New England Association teams, as box scores in the *Clinton Conant* show, Keefe concluded that being a pitcher would give him the best chance to play professionally for the longest period of time, since he was, at best, just an average infielder.

Keefe was encouraged at the prospect for a good income as a professional ballplayer by the postseason negotiations of Boston players Jim O'Rourke and George Wright. Like all ballplayers at the time, they were only contractually obligated to play one season with their current team, and thus could negotiate with others teams in the National League for their services for the next season. O'Rourke and Wright decided to play for the Providence team in 1879, to the dismay of the president of the Boston club, Arthur Soden, who would engineer the infamous reserve rule at the end of the 1879 season to prevent such high-profile departures in the future.

Over the winter of 1879, Keefe and Boston's star pitcher Tommy Bond likely "bonded" during the conversations they had during the informal gatherings of professional baseball players in the club room of the Boston National League team, which was located above the Wright, Howland & Mahn sporting goods store in Boston. During these "hot stove" talks, so named for the heating arrangement in the club room, Bond and Keefe would have discussed pitching techniques.

Chroniclers of Keefe's life have long noted that Bond tutored two future Hall of Fame pitchers, Keefe and John Clarkson, associating the timeframe with Bond's Harvard coaching stints, but never quite pinning down the exact years, which ranged from 1881 to 1883 or so.[14] Since Keefe was an established pitcher by 1882, the Harvard-related timing seems off for him, but on target for Clarkson, who made his major-league debut in 1882 with the Worcester team when Bond also pitched there. Spring of 1879 would have been a more logical time for Bond to have coached Keefe, since the 22-year-old Keefe was then a novice pitcher. Bond was also at the top of his pitching game in 1879, having won 40 games for Boston in each of the 1877 and 1878 seasons before fading in 1880. Keefe's rapid advancement as a pitcher in 1879 makes this timing all the more appropriate.

Keefe, the self-educated man, likely asked good questions of Bond, a master craftsman in the art of pitching, to secure as many tips to being a successful pitcher as he could. Bond wouldn't have been reticent about sharing information, since he worked with the pitchers on the Harvard College baseball team.[15] From these conversations, Keefe likely developed an effective curveball to replace his rudimentary one developed through observation.

In the preface to his treatise "Curve Pitching" published in 1884, Keefe indicated that he considered Bond to be a pitching mentor to him. Regarding the understanding of the faults of the batter, Keefe wrote, "Bond was also very successful in this art, and contrived to place his field with remarkable success." After Bond retired prematurely due to arm problems, Keefe regretted that Bond was "compelled to withdraw [from the game] when the high throwing came into vogue" due to the increased stress on the arm. Keefe mentions Bond three times in the preface, more than any other pitcher.[16]

In 1879 the Keefe family now lived in one unit of a two-family house at 54 Springfield Street in Somerville, in the Inman Square neighborhood that straddled Cambridge and Somerville. The Keefes would call this place home for the next 15 years.[17] The work building houses in the Inman Square area had been good to Patrick Keefe, the patriarch of the family, and his second-oldest son, Tim, the budding ballplayer, who was still listed as a carpenter in the *Somerville Directory*. Their incomes were supplemented by those of Tim's older brother, Daniel, who was a plumber, and his sister Katherine, who worked as a dressmaker.[18] The Keefe family was now living the lifestyle of a typical carpenter in Massachusetts, where the family earned about $700 a year, lived in a six-room tenement in a pleasant neighborhood, with rooms that were well furnished and carpeted, with a well-dressed family and a wife having a sewing machine.[19] It wasn't a lavish life, but it was demonstrably a step up from subsistence living in a shanty.

For the 1879 season, professional baseball in the Boston area, below the level of the National League team, provided greatly diminished opportunities for ballplayers. The National League had taken steps to eviscerate the competition posed by teams at the higher level of what are now called "minor leagues," but at the time were simply other professional leagues. The International Association was in shambles, since the National League had poached the Buffalo and Syracuse teams (as well as the Troy team from the New York State Association) and the team in London, Ontario, Canada, no longer existed. In Massachusetts, the Lowell and Lynn teams also disbanded, further eroding the International Association field but also causing the demise of the New England Association. The remnants of both leagues congealed into one league for the 1879 season, called the National Association (having to drop the "inter" since there were no longer any Canadian teams), with teams in Holyoke, New Bedford, Springfield, and Worcester in Massachusetts; Manchester, New Hampshire; Albany, Rochester, and Utica in New York; and the Nationals of Washington, D.C.

Because there was no room in the National Association for a team from a town as small as Clinton, Massachusetts, the Clintons competed in the Eastern Massachusetts Association for the 1879 season.[20] However, this was really a semipro circuit mostly comprised of cooperative teams that paid their players by a percentage of gate receipts rather than weekly salaries. Other teams in this league were the Aetnas of Boston, King Philip of Rockland, and a team from the city of Brockton.

Due to the drastic reduction in the number of professional teams in the Boston area, there was a glutted market for professional ballplayers seeking employment for the 1879 season. Keefe had little bargaining power to negotiate with other teams and thus had no choice but to return to the Clinton team. This was especially the case since he wanted to become a pitcher and forsake his infielder role in professional baseball.

In April 1879 the *Clinton Conant* published short biographical sketches of the Clinton ballplayers, which described Keefe thus: "Center Field—Timothy J. Keefe of Cambridgeport. Formerly with Our Boys, Androscoggins of Lewiston, Me., and Westboros."[21] The newspaper also listed pitcher Gardner and catcher Gilligan as being from Cambridgeport. Although described initially as the team's center fielder, Keefe played third base once the 1879 season began.

Keefe also pitched a few games for Clinton, as new manager George Brackett rested Gardner more often than Fayerweather had during the prior season. The narrower pitcher's box in 1879, now six-feet-by-four-feet, seemed to agree with Keefe. In the May 7 game against the Aetnas, Keefe pitched the Clintons to an 8–2 victory.[22] In left field for Clinton that day was John Gaffney, a capable ballplayer who would soon turn pro as an umpire, to begin a long career as a major-league umpire. Keefe also pitched on May 30 in the afternoon game of the Decoration Day holiday twin bill, an 8–5 loss to New Bedford.[23]

Since few spectators attended the ballgames, especially the two holiday ones, the Clinton team disbanded on the evening of June 10 when, as the *Clinton Conant* reported, the ballclub directors were "convinced that the receipts did not and would not pay expenses, [and] voted to discharge the nine and stay further costs." The next day the ballplayers "bade their Clinton friends good bye and took the 9:28 train for Boston."[24]

Many of the Clinton ballplayers weren't unemployed for long, as several struck deals with ballclubs at a higher level of competition. Barney Gilligan, the catcher, caught on with the Cleveland team in the National League; he made his major-league debut on June 12 in Cleveland's game at Boston. Gid Gardner, the pitcher, joined the Worcester team in the National Association; he was soon pitching for the Troy team in the National League, making his major-league debut on August 23.

Keefe got a tryout with the Utica team in the National Association, which was traveling through the area to play the Massachusetts teams in the league. In Utica's exhibition game on June 13 in South Boston against the Harvard College team, the *Boston Herald* reported that "Keefe, late of the Clintons, pitched effectively for the Uticas."[25] After another good outing against Yale College on June 14, Keefe became the regular pitcher for Utica. This was a spectacular jump for Keefe, from infielder and change pitcher on a semipro team in a state league to the primary pitcher for a professional team in a regional league. The catch was that the Utica team was not very good, lingering near the bottom of the league standings.

On June 23 Keefe received his baptism by fire in the pitcher's box for Utica against the Nationals of Washington, one of the best teams in the league. After the *Utica Morning Herald* had commented that "the ability of Keefe, who has not yet been called upon to do his best, will be taxed to the utmost," Utica lost, 4–3, when Keefe was victimized by a passed ball that allowed the winning run to score.[26] However, the next day, Keefe rebounded to defeat the Nationals, 3–1.

While Keefe pitched well in his first few outings for Utica, he was soon fatigued by the pace of being in the pitcher's box every day. On the Fourth of July holiday, Keefe was battered by Manchester, 10–4, when he allowed

13 hits and Utica made 16 errors, although "the majority of their errors was due to Keefe's wild pitching," according to the *Utica Morning Herald*.[27] Then on July 8 Albany blasted Keefe, 8–0, when "Keefe's pitching was badly punished the first three innings by the Albanys, and then he gave way to Alcott."[28] Keefe was soon playing right field for Utica, while Alcott, the man he had replaced in June as the team's primary pitcher, returned to be the starting pitcher.

The Utica team disbanded on July 13. Despite Keefe's evident failure as a pitcher, the *Utica Morning Herald*, in its analysis of the curtailed season, called Keefe "a moderately effective pitcher" and went on to say, presciently, that "Keefe has the elements of a good pitcher, and in time can gain proper command over the ball, and be a strong man in the center for the best of clubs."[29]

After resting his right arm for a week and a half, Keefe joined the New Bedford team of the National Association, which was looking to replace Ed Kent as its pitcher. With little tangible evidence from his Utica trial that he was a viable pitcher, Keefe had to rely on relationships to secure this next baseball job. George Fayerweather, the manager of the New Bedford club, who had been manager of the Clinton team the prior season, was willing to give Keefe a chance. After a tryout in two exhibition games against Eastern Massachusetts Association competition, Keefe became the new pitcher for the last-place New Bedford team.

Keefe lost his first two league outings with New Bedford on August 1 and 2 against Albany. He rebounded with a victory on August 4 against Holyoke, when he gave up only five hits as the *New Bedford Evening Standard* reported "the visitors were unable yesterday to make anything effective off Keefe."[30] Keefe was able to pace himself better with New Bedford than he had with Utica, although his pitching style was classified by one writer as "that class of wild, swift pitchers who depend mainly upon speed and the curve for effect."[31] After Fayerweather was ousted as manager in mid–August, the new skipper, Jim Mutrie, kept Keefe in the pitcher's box. Keefe seemed to mature under Mutrie's tenure as manager, capping his season with a three-hit shutout against the Nationals of Washington on September 23, another shutout against Jersey City on September 27, and a very respectable showing in a 6–5 loss to the Boston team of the National League on October 1.

Having been told that New Bedford was not going to field a team for 1880, Keefe began to scout for pitching opportunities for the next season while still throwing for New Bedford. He landed a job with the team in Albany, New York, one of the few clubs expected to return for the 1880 season, to be the change pitcher to spell Morrie Critchley when needed. However,

Keefe was immediately pressed into service by Albany for its postseason exhibition series with the Troy team of the National League, when Critchley couldn't pitch due to a sore arm.

The two-week postseason stint with Albany that October was a good test of Keefe's pitching progress, as he faced National League competition in four games and the Nationals of Washington in two makeup games. Granted the games were mere exhibitions, but the batters were still the best hitters in baseball. Keefe seemed to modify his approach to pitching in these games by using less speed and more finesse. "Keefe put on an extra lot of curves and twists and was hard to hit," the *Albany Evening Times* reported on his effort against Troy on October 6.[32] These games put Keefe on the road to becoming a strategic pitcher.

His power of observation started Keefe down that road, as he had watched several pitchers on the other teams in the National Association who would soon rise to prominence in the National League: Larry Corcoran and Fred Goldsmith with Springfield, Lee Richmond with Worcester, and Mickey Welch with Holyoke. While at the barbershop, where he began to shape his mustache that was the trend among up-and-coming young men, Keefe no doubt read the *New York Clipper* and the *National Police Gazette*. Before the specialty baseball publications *Sporting Life* and *The Sporting News* came into existence in the mid–1880s, the *Clipper* and the *Police Gazette* were the premier national publications of the day for baseball coverage.

A November 1879 article in the *New York Clipper* was further impetus for Keefe to change his pitching style. In a review of the 1879 National Association season, the Jersey City correspondent to the *Clipper* labeled Keefe as "overrated" as a pitcher and slotted him in the category of "wild-curve pitcher," defined as a pitcher who "can curve the ball and send it in with speed, but who has but little command of the ball and no strategic skill."[33] The Jersey City correspondent spelled out what he believed was the successful nature of the "strategic pitcher":

> Strategy is the great thing in the art of pitching. Without this no battery can be worked to advantage. Of what avail is the finest rifle cannon to an artillery corps without the judgment to use it with strategic effect? The pitcher who watches his batsman's style of play, and who pitches accordingly; who can change his pace quickly and disguise the change well; who, when he finds hard hitters before him, can pitch for catches; who can return the ball quickly to the catcher when he sees the batsman temporarily out of form; who, when he sees men on the bases, will pitch for his catcher to throw, and who will readily send men to bases on balls in order to afford his catcher a chance to play his best point; such a pitcher is a strategist, and when he combines this with the other strong points of telling curves and swift pace, he necessarily must excel in the position.[34]

Also important to the strategic pitcher was to have a catcher who was familiar with the pitcher's style, so that the pitcher and catcher would be considered "as a partnership that should not be broken up if at all possible ... to yield a whole that was greater than its individual parts."[35] While pitching for the lowly Utica and New Bedford teams, though, Keefe did not have that opportunity to form a lasting relationship with a catcher behind the plate, nor during his two weeks in Albany in October. Over the winter, however, he would have more opportunity to work with top-flight catchers to advance towards becoming a strategic pitcher.

After pitching for Albany in October, Keefe drew the attention of Frank Bancroft, manager of the Worcester team in the National Association. Bancroft took his team to Cuba in December 1879 as the barnstorming Hop Bitters, named for the popular patent medicine produced by the trip's financier, Asa Soule, owner of the Rochester, New York, company of the same name. With civil unrest in Cuba, Bancroft moved the team in January 1880 to New Orleans, Louisiana, where the Hop Bitters enjoyed a more comfortable setting playing the local amateur teams. Bancroft left New Orleans in mid–January for two reasons.[36] First, he needed to finalize negotiations for Worcester to join the National League for the 1880 season, to replace the expelled Syracuse club. Second, because the New Orleans tour was so lucrative, he planned to return with a second squad so that multiple games could be staged in New Orleans during the Mardi Gras festival week in February.

Bancroft's second team was comprised of a variety of ballplayers from the New England area, including pitchers Keefe of the Albany team and John Ward of the Providence team in the National League. On February 4, Bancroft's second team left New York City by train for New Orleans and arrived on February 8, just a few hours before the team's first scheduled game that afternoon.[37] Keefe pitched that initial game, yielding just three hits and ringing up 13 strikeouts in the 0–0 tie with the J.S. Wright team, which was strengthened by the addition of the Worcester battery of pitcher Tricky Nichols and catcher Doc Bushong.[38]

The allocation of players in the games in New Orleans was often loosely arranged, to avoid having an unentertaining game where the professional Northerners ran up the score against the amateur Southerners. The Worcester players and the new arrivals in the second squad were often sprinkled into the opposing team to improve the competitiveness of the games, particularly when it came to pitchers and catchers.

Keefe enjoyed pitching in the warm weather at New Orleans. In the February 11 game with the Eckfords, Keefe pitched a no-hitter; the next day he pitched for the local Lone Stars against the Hop Bitters, in the first Ward–

Keefe pitching duel of his career, yielding five hits in the 1–1 tie.[39] Reports to the *New York Clipper*, likely penned by Bancroft, noted that Keefe "pitched with remarkable effectiveness" and that his pitches "proved puzzling."[40]

Helping Keefe improve his pitching while in New Orleans were the catchers on the Worcester team, Doc Bushong and Charlie Bennett. They were thinking-man catchers, who sought to avoid injury but also improve the effectiveness of the pitcher. Bennett popularized the chest protector in 1883, while Bushong popularized the use of one-handed catching around 1884, by using a padded kid glove on the catching hand.[41] By 1886, both catchers were considered the best at their trade, since the pitchers who worked with them were so effective.

With a substantial black population, New Orleans was vastly different in racial composition from the Boston area, a little more than a dozen years after the end of hostilities in the Civil War. Keefe pitched at least two games against black teams on the New Orleans trip. On March 4 he threw a second no-hitter, this time against the Orleans "colored club."[42] Keefe and Bennett teamed up for another victory on April 4 against the unidentified "colored champions of that city," using just five players in the field to defeat the black team, 17–3.[43]

While Keefe stayed in New Orleans until mid–April, Ward left in March and stopped over in New York City, where he dropped into the *Clipper* office to discuss the trip. Among his many comments was praise for Keefe, saying that "Keefe has greatly improved in his delivery and become very effective."[44]

Keefe had plenty of time to talk with Ward during their six weeks together in New

The *New York Clipper* published this picture of Tim Keefe in 1880. Keefe had just returned from playing winter ball in New Orleans, where he alternated in the pitcher's box with John Ward, star pitcher of the champion Providence team of the National League. Keefe was still a novice pitcher at this time, since he had spent only one year as a minor-league pitcher in 1879.

Orleans. They surely exchanged thoughts about pitching delivery and the role of a competent catcher. No doubt Ward also shared his frustration over the institution of the five-man rule, soon to be known as the reserve rule. The National League ballclub owners, at their September 1879 meeting in Buffalo, had instituted a league-wide rule proposed by Boston president Soden to stem the widespread financial losses being suffered by clubs in the league. Soden believed the root cause was the high salaries being paid to ballplayers, who were free to negotiate with all ballclubs after the end of each season. Soden wanted to restrict competition among the ballclubs for ballplayers. As reported by the *Buffalo Commercial Advertiser*: "It was proposed that each delegate be allowed to name five desirable players from his own club as a nucleus for a team in 1880, and that these chosen men should not be allowed to sign with any other club without permission. This would prevent unhealthy competition and at the same time give each club a majority of its players for next season."[45]

Because Ward had been one of the five men allowed to be reserved by the Providence team, the 19-year-old pitcher was forestalled from negotiating with the other clubs in the league.[46] Rather than improve his financial position after posting 47 wins for Providence during the 1879 season, Ward could only return to play for Providence in 1880 at a salary level dictated by the ballclub, with little recourse. This concerned Ward since it was a serious erosion of the free labor principle that had permeated the American economy for more than a century since the American Revolution.

The conversations between Keefe and Ward in New Orleans began a decade-long partnership to fight for the employment rights of major-league ballplayers. While Keefe had likely read about the five-man rule in the October 25 issue of the *New York Clipper*, hearing Ward's experience with it would have made a deep impression on him. Keefe viewed a ballplayer akin to his former trade as a carpenter, where a man was an independent artisan who progressed through the apprentice–journeyman–master system within the craft. To Keefe, an amateur ballplayer was the apprentice stage and a professional ballplayer was a journeyman, who could negotiate his own employment deals and, once they were completed, move on to the next job without being encumbered by the previous job. While carpentry jobs might last only two weeks, such as his 1877 disagreement with Cate over the building of a house in Somerville, and ballplayers worked for their clubs for seven months of the year, the difference in time period was immaterial. If thrifty, the ballplayer could advance to the master stage by starting his own baseball club or other business that took advantage of his inherent artisan skills.

In late April 1880, Keefe joined the Albany team for its preseason games in New England against Providence on April 22 and Boston on April 23, where he faced his pitching mentors Ward and Bond, respectively. During the preseason, Albany manager Jack Chapman used both Keefe and Critchley, the team's pitcher the previous season. With his two-month, warm-weather training session in New Orleans, Keefe was in mid-season form while Critchley was still loosening up the winter kinks. Keefe easily outdueled Critchley to secure the Albany pitcher job, as Chapman released Critchley. On May 1, 1880, Keefe was in the pitcher's box for Albany in its season opener with the Nationals of Washington.

Albany was one of only three teams in the National Association for the 1880 season, as the league was ravaged by the National League's efforts to minimize competition and thus establish a monopoly. Besides the Nationals of Washington, the other league team was in Baltimore. With so few league games, Albany played an extensive slate of exhibition games with major-league teams, which numbered a dozen in the first two months of the 1880 season. This level of competition provided Keefe with another great opportunity to showcase his improved pitching talent against the game's best hitters.

Keefe was a far different pitcher in the National Association in 1880 then he was in 1879, based on his increased command of the ball that he developed in New Orleans under the tutelage of catcher Bushong.[47] This aspect of becoming a strategic pitcher was conveyed in a biographical sketch of Keefe, likely written by Bancroft, which was published in the *New York Clipper* that spring:

> Manager F.C. Bancroft of the Worcesters some time ago singled out Keefe as one of the most effective pitchers in the fraternity.... He combines in a remarkable degree all the needed qualifications to excel in his chosen profession, having wonderful speed, a troublesome curve, and great command of the ball. He fields finely, both in his position and at third base, and, moreover, evidences much headwork in delivering the sphere.... The faithful discharge of his duties, combined with his quiet, gentlemanly deportment, has deservedly made him a great favorite.[48]

A portrait of Keefe accompanied the biographical sketch, which showed Keefe now sporting a bushy mustache.

Despite the high praise of the *Clipper* sketch, though, beneath the surface Keefe seemed reluctant to fully embrace professional baseball as his future and jettison his carpentry roots. The federal census enumerator, who arrived at the Vandewerkin boarding house at 719 Broadway, where Keefe lived while in Albany, recorded that Keefe's occupation was cabinetmaker, not ballplayer.[49]

Those doubts were dispelled in June when two exhibition games with major-league teams within a span of six days soon led to Keefe joining the

Troy team in the National League. On June 10, Keefe pitched a no-hitter against Troy, when, as the *Troy Daily Times* reported, "the heavy hitters of the Troy club could do nothing with Keefe's curves, and did not secure a single base hit during the game."[50] On June 15, Keefe dueled with old friend Gid Gardner, now the change pitcher for Cleveland, who was part of an all-Cambridge battery with Barney Gilligan at catcher. While Gardner defeated Keefe that day, 3–2, he had a very mediocre year with Cleveland, posting a 1–8 pitching record. Gardner may have been the hare in the race with Keefe to get to the National League the quickest, but the tortoise Keefe eventually won the larger contest by pitching in the League until 1893 while Gardner's last League game was in September 1880.

At this juncture of the season, the *Albany Evening Times* called Keefe "one of the best, most puzzling, and most scientific pitchers in the country." After the no-hitter on June 10, the *Times* questioned the pitching practices of the Albany team: "It is good policy, to our thinking, to substitute the change pitcher to relieve Keefe, but it does seem an extremely foolish policy to allow Keefe to pitch in an exhibition game and substitute McCormack for an entire game in a championship contest." The newspaper went on to comment that "no one could blame Keefe very much if he should ask for his release unless he gets better support from the home nine."[51]

By mid–June, Keefe knew he wanted to leave Albany, as he believed he was ready to pitch in the National League. He probably did ask management for his release, but since there would be no competitive Albany team without Keefe, he would have been turned down. Troy manager Bob Ferguson knew he wanted Keefe to be his change pitcher rather than Terry Larkin, who had been unimpressive in his six games to spell Mickey Welch. Ferguson didn't want to wait until the 1881 season to get Keefe. The *Troy Daily Times* reprinted a report from an Albany newspaper that the Troy directors met with Keefe in an Albany cemetery "and there in the night time made him the advances which in the city and during the day time they were ashamed to offer," adding that Keefe refused the "flattering offer" and will remain with Albany "to keep his contract obligations."[52] While the story is no doubt apocryphal, the clandestine aspect of it has a ring of truth to it, as Ferguson would have used whatever methods needed to obtain Keefe's services for Troy. Ferguson might have even suggested some skullduggery.

There are indications that Keefe faked a lame arm to force Albany to release him. In a June 18 exhibition game with Cleveland, Keefe pitched only five innings before retiring. After that, he pitched only sporadically for Albany. He last pitched for Albany in the afternoon game of the Fourth of July holiday twin bill with the Nationals of Washington, but left the pitcher's box early. "Keefe, after pitching the first inning, owing to his sprained back, had to give up and was put into centre field," the *Albany Evening Times* reported.⁵³ Albany disbanded immediately following the holiday twin bill. The *Troy Daily Times* then reported the next day "Troy has engaged Keefe, the pitcher of the disbanded Albanys. He will report about August 1."⁵⁴ If Keefe really did have a lame arm, Troy would not have been so eager to sign him at that juncture.

During his month-long hiatus between Albany and Troy, Keefe was back in Massachusetts at his family's home in Somerville. While ostensibly resting his tired right arm, he found the time to attend at least one National League game at Boston's South End Grounds. On Wednesday, July 21, Harry Wright called Keefe from the stands to be the substitute umpire for the game between the Boston and Cincinnati teams.⁵⁵ Wright obviously respected Keefe's knowledge of the game to entrust him with the umpire duties in the absence of a league-approved official. With two excellent pitchers in the box that day, Boston defeated Cincinnati, 4–2, as Tommy Bond prevailed over Will White.

Two weeks after his inaugural stint as an umpire in the National League, Keefe was in a Troy baseball uniform pitching curveballs to the Cincinnati batters.

6

Pitching in the National League for Troy

Donning the uniform of the Troy, New York, team in the National League, Tim Keefe made his major-league pitching debut on August 6, 1880, against Cincinnati in Troy. "Cincinnati could not hit Keefe, who made his first appearance here to-day, and pitched excellently," a wire-service account told newspaper readers across the country.[1] Keefe yielded just four hits in the 4–2 victory, as he struck out seven batters and walked three. He also contributed to Troy's offense by collecting two hits in four at-bats.

Three factors helped Keefe make an auspicious debut in the National League. First, Cincinnati, the last-place team in the league that year, was not very good. Second, the Cincinnati players were tired, as Troy was the tail end of a month-long road trip through the league's eastern cities, with previous stops in Buffalo, Boston, Providence, and Worcester. Third, and perhaps most importantly, Keefe had umpired the July 21 game that Cincinnati had played in Boston, where he was able to obtain an up-close observation of the few strengths and multiple weaknesses of the Cincinnati batters as they battled the serves of Boston pitcher Tommy Bond.

In this era of reliance on one man to pitch virtually every game for his team, Mickey Welch had pitched 41 of Troy's previous 48 league games. Troy manager Bob Ferguson hired Keefe to be the change pitcher, to give Welch a break from his grueling work schedule as Troy began its own four-week road trip through the league's western cities. Keefe proved to be "fully equaling expectations," as the writer for the *Troy Daily Times* judged him, as he won both of his next two starts against next-to-last-place Buffalo and yielded just 11 hits in his first three games in the pitcher's box for Troy.[2]

After compiling a 5–2 record in the first seven games he pitched for Troy, Keefe's pitching results began to attract notice around the National League. "His delivery is very deceptive, hard to hit, and full of curves," the *Cleveland Herald* reported, "and the good support he receives from [catcher] Holbert helps him largely."[3] In Chicago, which had a huge 13-game lead over second-place Providence, Keefe faced a clearly superior team to any of the competition that he had faced to date. Led by Cap Anson, Chicago was steamrolling to a first-place finish. However, Keefe was able to secure one victory over the formidable White Stockings in his three starts against them. On September 2, Keefe lost the morning game of a separate-admission twin bill in a close contest, 1–0, before he tamed the Chicago batters to win the afternoon contest, 5–1. This Chicago defeat was one of just 17 losses the team suffered in its 86 games played during the 1880 season.

Back in Troy, Keefe faced the Boston team on September 4, but lost another tight game, 4–3, as Boston had to rally in the seventh to tie the game and then score the go-ahead run in the ninth inning to overcome a 3–1 Troy lead. Keefe then lost another 1–0 game on September 9, this time to Providence, as he was outmatched by John Ward, his friend from Bancroft's New Orleans tour earlier in the year. The catcher for Keefe in that September 9 game was newcomer Buck Ewing, rather than Bill Holbert who had been Keefe's catcher for all his previous games with Troy.

This was the beginning of a long friendship between Keefe and Ewing on the baseball diamond. "I have known Ewing since the latter seventies," Keefe told a baseball writer shortly before Ewing died in 1906. "I first met him while I was playing with Albany. He played with Rochester and afterwards he and I joined the Troy team."[4]

Following the Providence game, though, Keefe, then with a 6–6 pitching record, left the Troy team for the remainder of the 1880 season, forcing Welch to once again carry the entire burden of pitching for Troy. His reason for leaving is still unclear. Was his arm ailing? This seems unlikely, given his excellent pitching performances in September. Since the Troy-Providence game the next day was rained out, did Keefe and Ward meet to further their conversations in New Orleans to concoct a strategy for Keefe to leverage his negotiation position for the 1881 season? This explanation is more probable.

The *Troy Daily Times* was relatively quiet about the reason for Keefe's departure, generally inferring that Keefe had another tired arm, similar to the avowed reason that he had left the Albany team earlier in the year. However, the newspaper did drop a hint in mid-September when it reported that Boston manager Harry Wright was tampering with Troy players, accusing Wright of talking to them about "the manner they should be treated by Manager Ferguson and the board of directors" and allegedly having "sent word to Keefe that he wanted to see him in Boston as soon as he could get away from Troy."[5] Wright was seemingly circumventing the rules by not directly discussing playing for Boston. But to a savvy man like Keefe, Wright's motivations were quite transparent.

6. Pitching in the National League for Troy

In Troy's September 4 game with Boston, Keefe had left a favorable impression of his pitching skills in the mind of Wright, whom Keefe had at least a casual business relationship dating back to his days with the Our Boys club that played its games at the South End Grounds in Boston, the home field for Wright's team. As secretary of the Boston ballclub and not just its manager, Wright was well aware of the league's secret five-man reserve policy, and he apparently believed that Troy wouldn't waste one of its five picks on Keefe, making him available to be signed for the 1881 season. While Keefe was haggling with Wright, and perhaps other ballclubs, Troy finished the season in fourth place in the National League standings.

In early October, though, Troy did place Keefe's name on its five-man reserve list for the 1881 season, along with Welch, Holbert, Evans, and Caskin.[6] Because he was reserved, other ballclubs wouldn't negotiate with Keefe. Although basically he was forced to accept Troy's salary offer, Keefe did try to negotiate with the Troy management. "I was considered a robber because I held out for $2,100," Keefe recalled later in life.[7] Keefe eventually agreed to a $1,500 salary for the 1881 season, which was 50 percent more than Troy was willing to pay its two other promising rookies from the 1880 team, Buck Ewing and Roger Conner.[8] The $1,500 sum was still good pay, from Keefe's perspective, since he would be paid twice what a good journeyman carpenter might, at best, earn in a year. And he only had to work half a year to receive that amount, as he took another step forward in his quest to be a master craftsman of the pitching profession. Keefe could put away his carpentry tools, as he no longer had to support himself during the winter months by performing manual labor.

Much has been made of Keefe's stingy 0.86 earned-run average that he compiled during the 1880 season. While he was a good pitcher in his dozen games for Troy, the low ERA was not an indicator of his innate pitching skill but rather that he was a fresh arm that opposing batters were unfamiliar with that season. His 1880 pitching success was misleading because it was just a small sample. If he had pitched a full six-month season, his ERA most assuredly would have risen sharply, as it did in the 1881 season.

When the 1881 season began, the Troy ownership may have regretted its decision to put Keefe on the team's reserve list. Keefe pitched the first seven games for Troy and lost all seven decisions. Following that 0–7 start, Keefe had a long season, compiling an 18–27 record with an 3.24 ERA for Troy in league contests. Troy also played numerous exhibition games in addition to its 84-game schedule against National League teams. The team made frequent 150-mile train trips to New York City to play the Metropolitan team. These games were played at the Polo Grounds, the first baseball grounds created within the New York City limits (basically Manhattan at the time). The Polo Grounds were located just north of Central Park within the rectangle bounded by Fifth Avenue, 110th Street, Sixth Avenue, and 112th Street.

Although seen at the time as just a bunch of exhibition games, the half dozen games played between the two intrastate teams each year in 1881 and 1882 provided a platform for Metropolitans manager Jim Mutrie (Keefe's former manager at New Bedford) and his financial partner, John Day, to observe the skills of the Troy players, as they pondered the elevation of the Metropolitans to major-league status. Keefe pitched his first game at the Polo Grounds on April 19, when Troy defeated the Metropolitans in a preseason game. Keefe may have preferred those games on the outskirts of bustling New York City than those on his home grounds in less cosmopolitan Troy. At the very least, those frequent excursions to Manhattan whetted his appetite to live and work in New York City.

This drawing from Tim Keefe's treatise "Curve Pitching" published in 1884 shows Keefe pitching with a sidearm delivery, which he used while pitching for the Troy team in the National League from 1880 to 1882. Even after the overhand delivery was legalized, Keefe continued to throw sidearm to lessen the strain on his right arm and lengthen his pitching career.

For the 1881 season, the National League increased the pitching distance by five feet by moving the pitcher's box farther from home plate. The new rule required the pitcher to throw the ball from behind the front line of the pitcher's box that was now located 50 feet from home plate, rather than 45 feet as it had been during the 1880 season.[9] Another rule change for 1881 was the reduction in the number of balls needed for the batter to walk, from eight to seven, as a disincentive for pitchers to waste as many pitches as they had been doing to test a batter's patience.

Certainly, Keefe held back to some degree during

the 1881 season, to ease the strain on his arm from the longer pitching distance as well as to conserve stamina as he attempted to pitch continuously over a full season for the first time in his pitching career. Perhaps he overestimated the impact of arm strain and let up too much. Or perhaps he sulked a bit too much over his failed salary negotiations due to his inclusion on the team's reserve list, reducing his motivation level since he knew he couldn't parlay good pitching into a higher salary, with either Troy or another ballclub. There were accusations of the latter by mid-season, when the *Troy Daily Times* reported that Troy management was "under the impression that Keefe is pitching poorly purposely in order to obtain his release," so that he could negotiate freely with other ballclubs.[10] Or perhaps Keefe didn't like Ferguson's strategy to alternate his two pitchers, believing he should have been the primary pitcher, not sharing the duty with Mickey Welch.

Ferguson used Keefe and Welch roughly equally in 1881, with Keefe in the pitcher's box for 45 games and Welch for 40 games. With the longer pitching distance in 1881 putting more pressure on the pitcher's arm, Ferguson and a few other managers adopted a two-man pitching staff to replace the one-man workhorse strategy (with change pitcher in reserve) that had previously been exclusively used. In Chicago, Cap Anson took the two-man strategy a bit further by actually rotating his two pitchers, Larry Corcoran and Fred Goldsmith, each game. Although he didn't invent the strategy (Ferguson had used it with the same two pitchers in 1879 when he managed the Springfield team in the National Association), Anson did popularize the two-man pitching rotation in the major leagues based on Chicago's successful defense of the National League title in 1881.[11]

The two-man pitching staff strategy had long-term benefits for both Keefe and Welch, since neither man blew out his pitching arm over the next dozen years, even if Keefe was resistant to the idea in the beginning. The lifespan of the workhorse pitcher was quite short, just a few years, as exemplified by Boston's release of the once-stellar Tommy Bond early in the 1881 season, following the rapid decline in his effectiveness during the 1880 season. By carefully observing the motion of other pitchers and correlating it to their eventual decline, Keefe began to make a science of comprehending the impact of pitching motion on the strength of the arm.

Another beneficial aspect of the two-man pitching staff to Keefe and Welch was their pairing with specific catchers, Keefe with Holbert and Welch with Ewing. Holbert was a great defensive catcher, who knew Keefe's moves and helped to steady him in the pitcher's box. Holbert, though, didn't add much to the Troy offense. "Even by the standard of the catchers of the era, he was an inept hitter, becoming the only player in baseball history to bat two thousand times without hitting a home run," Peter Morris described Holbert in his book *The Catcher: How the Man Behind the Plate Became an American Folk Hero*. "His defensive prowess alone enabled him to become one of only twenty-five nineteenth-century catchers to catch more than five hundred major league games."[12]

Not many people watched Keefe pitch in Troy, though, since the team had one of the worst attendance records in the National League. "Attendances were slim there, 300 persons was an average crowd, and the owners had a hard time making both ends meet," Keefe later recalled. "Twelve-hundred was a large crowd in Troy in those days."[13] The miserable attendance for Troy home games reached its low point at the September 27, 1881, game with first-place Chicago, when only 12 spectators watched the game in a driving rainstorm. The umpire didn't even show up, so Welch had to umpire the game. Later in life, Keefe vividly recalled this game:

> Whenever Cap Anson's Chicago team played in Troy, Larry Corcoran used to slip away when he wasn't pitching and go over to Springfield [Massachusetts]. One day this truancy cost him $100, and it also gave Ed Williamson a chance to display his versatility. Ed was playing third base for the Chicago team and Fred Goldsmith was pitching. I was pitching for Troy. It was pouring rain and there was nobody in the stand except the baseball writers. But management decided to play. The ball was naturally wet and slippery and Goldsmith couldn't curve it. This infuriated Anson, who was playing first base. Finally he ordered Goldsmith out of the game and plastered a fine on him. Then he turned to the stand and called for Larry Corcoran. Of course, there was no answer. Larry was in Springfield. So Larry received a $100 fine for his absence. Ed Williamson then stepped into the [pitcher's] box and beat us.[14]

Troy was ahead, 6–3, when Williamson went into pitch. "Williamson took Goldsmith's place in the third inning, the latter having sustained a strain," the *Chicago Inter Ocean* described the pitching change, but not explaining what kind of "strain" that Goldsmith suffered, i.e., Anson's yelling at him.[15] Anson was happier by the end of the game, after Chicago rallied for six runs in the seventh inning to win the rain-drenched game, 10–8.

Even though Troy finished in fifth place in the 1881 National League standings, there was little hope that Keefe would avoid being placed on the team's reserve list for the 1882 season (given the paucity of quality pitching available to replace him) or that he would be able to negotiate an increase in his salary. The team's financial situation was precarious, since so few people attended the ballgames.

Troy was a major producer of iron and steel products, such as cast-iron stoves, bells, wire and nails, as well as being renowned for its shirt collar and cuff industry, which was invented in the city in the 1830s. However, despite the numerous foundries and factories, Troy had the smallest population of the eight cities with ballclubs in the National League, ranking as the 29th largest city in America in the 1880 federal census. Worcester was only marginally better as the 28th largest city. The National League had counted on Troy's baseball heritage to draw spectators to the ballpark. From 1866 to 1870, the Union ballclub of Lansingburgh, just north of Troy, competed with other top amateur teams around the country, and then played two seasons in the professional National Association; the club disbanded in 1872 when it couldn't compete economically with other better-financed ballclubs.[16] When the National League brought Troy back in 1879, the baseball fans didn't return in droves.

Keefe was in the lower end of the pack of National League pitchers, with the third-most losses (27) during 1881. He was probably pleased with his technical progress as a pitcher. By 1881 his delivery would have been more advanced than it was two years earlier when he converted from infielder to full-time pitcher, as he perfected his sidearm motion. "Pitchers, little by little, began to cultivate a side-arm motion," John Foster wrote in his article "The Evolution of Pitching" in 1931. "They would try to deliver the ball as nearly as they could to conform with the hip line of their bodies. To do so they had to abandon strictly underhand pitching and become side-arm throwers." Many pitchers of that era, though, flaunted the rules. "More of them were mild transgressors and pitched the ball from a line that was above the hip.... It seemed to them that the higher they started their delivery, the more effective they were against rival teams."[17]

Keefe was no exception. He pushed the limits of the pitching rules, but didn't abuse them, which later became his hallmark during the decade of the 1880s. A Cleveland baseball writer once analyzed Keefe's attentiveness to the rules: "His delivery was better than was expected, as it was naturally supposed that he managed to get his arm up higher than he did. Several times yesterday did he do this, and if he hasn't a corn on his right ear it is no fault of his. [Cleveland pitcher Jim] McCormick was watching him pretty closely, and was on the alert to catch any overhanded work."[18]

Newspapers provided few details about Keefe's delivery, since the 1880–1882 period was a nascent time for baseball reporting in daily newspapers. Coverage of Troy's games in the *Troy Daily Times*, a Republican-leaning publication, provided little flavor to the newspaper's businessman audience beyond the basic details of the games. Keefe often received more intimate coverage in the National League's two most prominent cities, Boston and Chicago, as well as, curiously, in Cleveland, where the coverage in the *Herald* and *Leader* provided some details about Keefe's pitching style.

There is, of course, no video showing Keefe's pitching delivery or any action photographs, only a few staged photographs and drawings. The best modern replica of his standard delivery is likely to be that of Dan Quisenberry, the relief pitcher for the Kansas City Royals in the 1980s, who also had a bushy mustache to visually resemble Keefe. Roger Angell described the unusual delivery of Quis in his 1988 book *Season Ticket*:

> He is a true submariner—a man "from down under," in baseball parlance—and every pitch of his is performed with a lurching downward thrust of his arm and body, which he must follow with a little bobbing hop off toward third base in order to recover his balance. At perigee, ball and hand descend to within five or six inches of the mound dirt, but then rise abruptly; the hand—its fingers now spread apart—finishes up by his shoulder, while the ball, plate-bound at a sensible, safe-driving-award clip, reverses its earlier pattern, rising for about three-quarters of its brief trip and then drooping downward and (much of the time) sidewise as it passes the batter at knee level or below. One way or another, the pitch almost always finds part of the strike zone.[19]

His knowledge of the strike zone, and his patience at the plate, enabled him to be an effective batter by collecting many walks even though his batting average wasn't impressive. Keefe had the second-most walks as a batter on the Troy team in 1881, with 21, despite playing in half as many games as Ferguson who drew 29 walks.

Keefe was no doubt content with his salary level (despite wanting more), which allowed him to both save some money and contribute to the family finances back home in Somerville, Massachusetts. It is unknown how accepting his father, Patrick Keefe, was of his second-oldest son's chosen profession or whether he ever journeyed to the South End Grounds in Boston to watch him pitch when Troy played there. Did Patrick favor the route taken by his oldest son, Daniel? He was active in the state militia and had followed in his father's footsteps to learn a trade and became a journeyman plumber. Did Patrick think more highly of his educated daughter, Margaret? She was nearing graduation from Somerville High School, a level of education neither of her older brothers had attained. Since Tim never talked about his father for publication, we'll never know how Patrick felt about his baseball-playing son. A good supposition, though, is that Patrick cracked a wry smile when thinking about how Tim could earn so much money playing a game.

For the 1882 season, the American Association began to compete with the National League. The new league was a six-city circuit with ballclubs in Baltimore, Cincinnati, Louisville, Philadelphia, Pittsburgh, and St. Louis. In theory this added competition provided Keefe with negotiation leverage to barter for a better deal with Troy, or join one of the teams in the new league at a higher salary (and without mobility restriction, since the Association didn't utilize the reverse-list principle in its agreements with ballplayers in 1882).[20] He may have contacted some of the Association ballclubs to determine their interest in having him be one of their pitchers. If he did put out some feelers, it didn't help out, since he was back with Troy in 1882 and at the same salary level as the previous year.[21] His unimpressive pitching statistics from the 1881 season apparently didn't imbue confidence that he'd pitch any better in the American Association.

At the beginning of the 1882 season, the 25-year-old Keefe had one of his best pitching efforts for Troy, when he hurled a four-hit shutout on May 11 against Worcester. His pitching opponent that day was 21-year-old Cambridge native John Clarkson. After that shutout, Keefe statistically didn't improve much from the 1881 season, compiling a 17–26 record for Troy by the end of the 1882 season. Ferguson did use Keefe more often than Welch in 1882, 43 games to 33, with left-hander Jim Egan as a third pitcher in 12 games. Ewing caught very few games that Keefe pitched that year, as Ferguson placed Ewing at third base and other field positions to keep his bat in the lineup and to keep him healthy. When Ewing did catch, it was with Welch, as Holbert caught for Keefe.

Keefe also umpired in three games during the 1882 season. For the three-game Troy-Buffalo series from June 9 to June 12, when the designated umpire was a no-show, the Troy pitchers substituted as umpire. Keefe umpired the game on June 9, Welch on June 10, and Keefe again on June 12. However, in the last game, Keefe had to relieve Welch in the pitcher's box in the fourth inning when Welch sprained his ankle, forcing Cassidy to relieve Keefe as the umpire. In his third appearance as an umpire in 1882, on August 23, Keefe's impartiality as an arbiter was recognized by the *Troy Daily Times* when the paper commented, "Keefe umpired the game in a satisfactory manner. His decisions were not once questioned," even though Troy lost to Cleveland.[22]

In August 1882 there were already rampant rumors that the Troy and Worcester franchises would be eliminated by the National League, to make room for ballclubs in the far more populous cities of New York and Philadelphia, which both had thriving independent professional teams in 1882. Enthusiasm quickly dampened among the small coterie of Troy businessmen who crossed the Congress Street Bridge over the Hudson River to attend the afternoon ballgames played in West Troy.

By far the most impressive game that Keefe pitched in 1882 was a one-hitter on August 9 against Detroit, although it was witnessed by only 500 spectators. After a rocky first inning when Detroit scored two runs on a triple by Ned Hanlon, an error, and a base on balls, Keefe then retired 25 consecutive Detroit batters until he issued a second base on balls in the ninth inning.

The last home game played by a major-league team in Troy, New York, occurred on August 26, 1882, before the Troy team went on the road for the remainder of the season. One hundred and ten years later in 1992, a granite monument was erected in Troy's Knickerbocker Park to commemorate the city's major-league baseball history. Keefe, Ewing, Connor, and Welch—all future Hall of Fame selections—are depicted on that monument, as is Hall of Famer Dan Brouthers who played briefly with Troy in 1880.[23]

To eliminate the need for a spare ballplayer in case there was an injury, and to keep expenses low on the team's final road trip, Keefe and Welch played in the field when they were not pitching (or umpiring). Keefe played third base and some outfield for Troy down the stretch, which also enhanced his negotiation position for 1883 by positioning himself as more than just a pitcher.

During September, Keefe and many of the other Troy ballplayers sought or fielded offers from other ballclubs, from both the National League as well as the rival American Association, for their services during the 1883 season, in anticipation of the demise of the Troy ballclub. When it became public that the National League owners, at their meeting on September 22, had voted to expel Troy and Worcester and admit teams from New York and Philadelphia, the imminent death of the Troy franchise set off an accelerated flurry of rumors regarding the team and its ballplayers. Claims that Boston, Cleveland, and Detroit had made offers already were reported by the *Troy Daily Times*.

Keefe pitched his last game for Troy on September 28 in Worcester, when he hurled a three-hitter for a 4–1 victory. Troy ended its season the next day, finishing in seventh place in the National League standings.

The Troy players, except Ewing, continued on to Philadelphia and New York to play a few postseason games with the two future National League ballclubs. The ballplayers also entertained verbal offers to play the next season in Philadelphia, as well as accepted telegrams from other ballclubs interested in their services. "Troy players are waiting for bids and refuse as yet to bind themselves," the *Cleveland Herald* reported. "It is certainly a fact that all the players not bound by the five-man rule are in a position to demand big prices, and are putting their services up at auction to the highest bidder."[24] While this newspaper account recognized the reality of the reserve rule restricting five Troy players, the ballplayers themselves acted as if all the Troy players were free to negotiate their own deals and that the five-man rule didn't apply.

6. Pitching in the National League for Troy

As the Troy ballplayers measured their worth on the open market, they played a ballgame in New York City on October 5 with the Metropolitans at the Polo Grounds. The game was, in effect, a tryout for an offer to join the Metropolitans for the 1883 National League season. Welch pitched Troy to an 8–2 victory over the Metropolitans, with Holbert as his catcher rather than the still-absent Ewing. Keefe played third base, and impressed with two hits and flawless fielding of six chances.

Ewing was the prize that all the ballclubs sought from the Troy team, since he was considered to be the best catcher in the league. After receiving a $2,800 salary offer from the Detroit ballclub, Ewing eventually agreed to a $3,100 offer to play for the Metropolitans in New York.[25] Ewing, though, was part of a cooperative effort by six of the Troy players to negotiate a group deal that would also serve each individual well. The other five players were Keefe, Welch, Connor, Gillespie, and Roseman.

The Troy Six deftly played the Metropolitans against both the Troy management and the other ballclub owners to overpay for their services. As the *New York Herald* reported in mid–October, "The [Troy] players have been coquetting, however, to a considerable extent, holding off from signing with the various managers, and thereby increasing the bidding by saying that they intended remaining in Troy, while at the same time they declined signing with that club."[26]

On the evening of October 10, the Troy Six met with the Troy ownership. Because they were trying to hold the team together to apply for a franchise in the American Association, the owners were motivated to offer the six players a substantial salary increase and asked the ballplayers to sign contracts at those amounts.[27] The ballplayers essentially laughed in ownership's face and walked out of the meeting. Ewing was the first to refuse to sign, then "the remainder of the players followed Ewing's lead and refused to sign, making no secret of the fact that they were engaged to play next year."[28] The Troy stockholders were indignant. "See how these men have treated us. It is shameful," one stockholder told the *Troy Daily Times*. "We have been played for a lot of suckers."[29] Three days later the *Troy Daily Times* reported that several Troy players had signed with the New York City team.

Keefe no doubt relished this final interaction with the Troy ballclub club, as he exercised what he thought was his right to negotiate his own deal with any ballclub he wished, since the Troy club was going of out business. Keefe was able to obtain a sizeable salary increase, as he signed with Day for a $2,000 salary.[30] Unbeknownst to Keefe, besides outbidding the other ballclub owners for the services of all six Troy ballplayers (plus a seventh, Holbert, who was Keefe's battery mate), Metropolitans owner John Day also had to pay an additional fee to contract with the players. Day must have paid some tribute to the Troy management for the five players who were on that ballclub's reserve list. Otherwise, the other ballclub owners would have cried foul.

In his three seasons with the Troy ballclub, Keefe compiled a decidedly uninspiring 31–59 pitching record. He hardly looked to be Hall of Fame material at this stage of his baseball career. That perspective changed in 1883 when he developed a new pitch to add to his repertoire.

7

College Baseball Coach

In mid–October 1882, having settled on New York City as the home location of his pitching exploits for the 1883 baseball season, Tim Keefe focused on his college coaching duties, as the *Troy Daily Times* reported that "Keefe, late of the Troy nine, will train the Amherst College nine for a week or ten days, beginning his work to-day."[1] He also returned to train the Amherst nine during the winter of 1883, as the college tried to improve its competitiveness in the American College Baseball Association, in which it competed along with teams from Harvard, Yale, Princeton, Brown, and Williams.[2]

The coaching stint at Amherst College in 1883 was the third winter of Keefe's annual ritual of giving back to the game by providing instruction to college baseball teams. During the winter of 1881, Keefe was "giving instruction to the students at Harvard College and will shortly go to Dartmouth to teach the students how to bat curved pitching."[3] His connection to pitchers Tommy Bond and John Ward helped him secure these coaching jobs, since Bond had worked with the Harvard students for several years and Ward had coached at Dartmouth during the winter of 1879.[4]

College coaching in the early 1880s was unofficial, since college baseball teams were not sponsored by their colleges at this time, but rather were merely independent social clubs comprised of the college's students.[5] The club controlled its own finances, collecting member dues and admission fees from games to pay its expenses, such as travel to games and the services of a coach. The team captain was in charge of the team, but during the preseason he often hired professional ballplayers to "coach" the players in specific skills, such as pitching. Therefore, the coaching job was more trainer than leader.

Keefe found many benefits in college coaching, even though it only paid roughly $100 for the season. The job expanded his resume as a craftsman in his profession, as one who knew the art of pitching, not just the brute execution of pitching. To Keefe, coaching advanced him within the apprentice–journeyman–master system, where as a journeyman major-league pitcher and budding master he could help mold young pitchers (apprentices). Enjoying the "imparting knowledge" aspect of the master–apprentice relationship with young pitchers, Keefe extended his college instructor role to other young pitchers on an informal basis. One beneficiary was John F. O'Brien, who grew up near Troy, New York. The *New York Clipper* reported years later that "in 1882 Tim Keefe was pitching for the Troy team, and took enough interest in young O'Brien to give him several points on how to curve the ball."⁶ O'Brien went on to be a major-league pitcher in Cleveland from 1888 to 1890.

Coaching also gave Keefe the ability to slowly limber up his right arm over the winter months in indoor conditions. This better prepared him for the start of the playing season in May, compared to the rushed process in April in colder outdoor weather that most players had to endure. Keefe had observed how pitching in New Orleans during February and March had better prepared him for the 1880 season with Albany. Formal spring training in warm-weather states was still years away, as it was considered too expensive at the time. Keefe, therefore, conducted his own cold-weather version of spring training each winter as a college baseball coach.

A third benefit to the coaching job was to slowly adapt to changes in the pitching rules for the upcoming season by experimenting with different approaches. This was an incredible benefit to Keefe, since rule changes occurred almost on an annual basis during this era when ballclub owners struggled to find the right balance between pitching and hitting in the game. For the 1881 season, his coaching duties allowed Keefe to experiment with the new five-foot longer pitching distance. For 1883 he had the opportunity to experiment with different delivery motions when the rules were changed to elevate the release point from the waist to the shoulder.

Keefe and Ward were two of the early adopters of this approach to baseball training in 1881, with Keefe at Harvard and Ward at Princeton, along with a third pitcher, Fred Goldsmith at Yale.⁷ While the major-league pitchers and college baseball players all saw the benefits to this instruction, the colleges themselves frowned on the practice of hiring professional coaches. They considered such actions a breach of the amateur model of sport, which was patterned after the principle espoused at the Oxford and Cambridge universities in England, where, in essence, amateur was good and professional was bad. However, the English model was steeped in social elitism, where "the line between amateur and professional sport is mainly a line between the unpaid members of a privileged class and the paid members of an underprivileged class."⁸ As the *Princetonian* commented during the winter of 1881, "The element of professionalism is gradually working its way into our college athletics. This year Harvard, Princeton, Brown, and Dartmouth have professional trainers for their nines and Yale must perforce follow suit."⁹

Keefe coached again at Harvard College during the winter of 1882. The

7. College Baseball Coach

Harvard Crimson reported in March that "Keefe of the Troys was practicing with the nine yesterday" on Holmes Field during the first day of outdoor practice by the varsity team.[10] However, Keefe had also worked out with the Harvard players a month earlier, as the *Yale News* reported that "Keefe of the Troys is pitching for and 'coaching' the Harvard nine in their gymnasium practice."[11] These twin actions caused a firestorm at Harvard, a bastion of the amateur model of sports, which considered a professional athlete tutoring its students on the college grounds to be heresy.

In June 1882, to forestall any further incursions into professionalism, Harvard established the Harvard Athletic Committee, comprised of three faculty members, to take an active oversight role with all the athletic teams formed by its students. The committee sought to prevent abuses that conflicted with education, such as the number of games played (especially those away from campus that caused students to miss classes), as well as to eliminate threats to the college's amateur philosophy. One of the first actions of the Harvard Athletic Committee was to effectively prohibit the hiring of professional coaches, by decreeing that no instructor or trainer be permitted on the college grounds without written authority of the committee.[12]

When the committee requested information from the captain of the baseball team about the trainer hired during the winter of 1882, the Harvard ballplayer didn't give Keefe's name to the committee. Instead, he reported that the team had paid $100 to a Mr. Richardson, whom the committee promptly notified that his services would no longer be needed.[13] In February 1883 the Harvard Athletic Committee explicitly voted to not permit the baseball team to hire a trainer.[14] Without a professional instructor during the winter, the Harvard baseball team had a mediocre record against other college teams in 1883, which spawned this criticism by the *Harvard Crimson*:

> We were handicapped at the start by not having the use of a professional pitcher to bat against in the winter. The result has been lamentably weak batting on the part of almost every man on the nine. Our pitchers were dependent entirely on their own ingenuity while the pitchers of Yale, Princeton and Amherst had the benefit of the best professional advice in the country.... The pitching, consequently, devolved on Nichols and Allen, who have each done remarkably well, in spite of the disadvantageous circumstances under which they undertook the task. Still it could not be expected that without previous practice or training in the position they could do as well as men who have enjoyed the advantages of training under Ward, Goldsmith and Keefe.... If, as is very probable, the antiprofessional rule shall be made less stringent next year, there is no reason why we should not put into the field a strong and victorious nine.[15]

During the fall of 1883, the Harvard Athletic Committee tried to convince the other elite institutions in its universe to prohibit the hiring of professional athletic coaches. While philosophically on board with the idea, no college was willing to actually take action on the idea. As the committee pondered what to do on its own, the *Boston Globe* reported in early January 1884, "There isn't much doubt that a [baseball] coach will be allowed, and Keefe will doubtless be engaged to fill the position. He has one of the best heads in the business, and he was universally liked when he was at Harvard two years ago."[16] The *Globe* was wrong. At its January 21, 1884, meeting, the Harvard Athletic Committee voted to adopt the following policy: "The appointment of oarsmen, ball players or other professional athletes by students either for contest or practice shall be absolutely prohibited."[17]

With the crack down on professional coaches at Harvard, Keefe coached at rival Williams College in western Massachusetts in 1884 and returned there in 1887.[18]

Keefe reflected on his experience coaching college pitchers in the section he wrote about pitching in the 1889 book *Scientific Ball*. "During my experience as a pitcher and also as an instructor I find that young pitchers, and especially the college pitcher, use far more curves than any experienced League pitcher," Keefe commented. "The college pitcher has the up, down, in and out and numerous other curves—in fact, too many altogether. The effective pitcher to-day has no time to use so many curves. He must have good command of his delivery, and by so doing can dispense with many curves that are used by beginners and still be effective."[19]

In 1888 the Harvard Athletic Committee was expanded to nine men, to include three students and three graduates in addition to the three faculty members. With a broader spectrum of opinion, the committee finally allowed the baseball team to hire a professional trainer after conducting a review of the situation. This editorial by the *Harvard Crimson* summed up the situation: "Hire some professional base-ball trainer for the nine, or at least allow the nine to play with professionals. We have a professional trainer for track athletics—the only sport in which Harvard has been almost uniformly successful—why not have one for base-ball? The secrecy which has surrounded the actions of our base-ball teams of late has insidiously brought about many abuses which only openness and frankness in the matter can eradicate."[20]

In November 1888 the Harvard Athletic Committee discovered that the baseball team had niftily, and quite properly, evaded the committee's edict, since "the nine has not been allowed to employ a professional player as a coach in the gymnasium or on the field, but no notice has been taken of their employing a man who coaches them outside, that practice not being covered by the rule."[21] The following month the committee voted to authorize the baseball team to hire John Clarkson of the Boston National League team as a coach.²² The committee vote was the height of hypocrisy. As Ronald Smith pointed out in his book *Sports and Freedom: The Rise of Big-Time College Athletics*, Harvard's solution to compete at a high level in intercollegiate sports was to "claim amateurism to the world while in fact accepting professionalism."²³

Clarkson was in; Keefe was out. Keefe would not return to coach at Harvard College until the winter of 1892.

8

With the Metropolitans in New York City

When Tim Keefe and the other six Troy ballplayers negotiated deals with John Day in October 1882 to play in New York City during the 1883 season, they believed they would continue to perform in the National League. Little did they know that Day was hatching a plan to field two major-league teams, one for the National League and the other in the rival American Association.

Day needed two teams, since he had an abundance of quality ballplayers, 18 in all among the existing Metropolitan squad, the seven Troy players, and newly signed John Ward from Providence, who had been left off his team's reserve list. By late October, Day had separated the group into National League and American Association rosters. Since both teams were owned by Day under the umbrella of the Metropolitan Exhibition Company, there was no problem shifting around the Troy players. The Metropolitans played in the Association, with Jim Mutrie staying on as manager; and a new team was assembled to represent New York in the League. Although the Metropolitans were the established team in the city, they needed to play in the Association, because the League required teams to be named after the city they played in. The Association had no qualms about its teams using club names, so the Metropolitans joined three other similarly themed ballclubs, the Athletic of Philadelphia, Eclipse of Louisville, and Allegheny of Pittsburgh.

Keefe was assigned to the Association team, along with his Troy teammates Bill Holbert and Jim Roseman. The other four Troy players (Mickey Welch, Buck Ewing, Roger Connor, and Pete Gillespie) were assigned to the League team. Welch recalled that the decision to allocate pitchers was not a matter of whether Day thought Welch was better than Keefe, but rather about where to assign the pitcher-catcher battery combinations. "We had two batteries in Troy; me and Buck Ewing was one and Tim Keefe and Billy Holbert was the other," Welch remembered. "He put Keefe and Holbert with the Mets and me and Ewing with the Giants."[1] Since Ward was considered to be the best pitcher among the 18 combined ballplayers and Jack Lynch was returning to pitch for the Metropolitans, there was room for only one change pitcher on each team between Keefe and Welch. Since Ewing was considered to be the best player of the bunch, he and Welch were allocated to the League team. Therefore, in the fall of 1882, Keefe was considered to be the fourth-best pitcher in New York City and was more highly regarded for his ability to play third base when not pitching.

Keefe no doubt was not all that disappointed that he was assigned to the Association team rather than to the League team. First, there was his familiarity with Mutrie, from his days with the Lewiston and New Bedford teams that Mutrie had managed. Second, he would be pitching to batters that hadn't seen his delivery before, which would give him an advantage. This was particularly the case with the rule change instituted for the 1883 season that allowed the pitcher to release the ball up to shoulder height.[2] Third, the Association didn't yet subscribe to the concept of the reserve list, which would give him greater mobility (that changed in February 1883, though, when the two rival leagues made peace and established a working relationship, which included a mutual recognition of reserve lists).

The big downside to being with the Metropolitans was the ballpark, since the team no longer could be the sole tenant at the Polo Grounds. Mutrie initially considered leasing property at the corner of 135th Street and Eighth Avenue, which was even further uptown than the Polo Grounds, for the team to have its own grounds. Ultimately, Day's two teams shared the Polo Grounds, with the League team considered to be the primary tenant to use the southeast diamond, which had been used the previous two years by the Metropolitans, at the corner of 110th Street and Fifth Avenue. When the League team was on the road, the Association team used the southeast diamond. However, when both teams were scheduled to play at home, both teams played at the same time, with the Metropolitans relegated to a newly built southwest diamond, at the corner of Sixth Avenue and 110th Street, while the League team used the southeast diamond. A flimsy canvas fence separated the two fields.[3]

The difference between the two fields at the Polo Grounds was like night and day, with the Metropolitans on the southwest diamond getting the decided second-class status. The southeast diamond had plenty of seating, with a double-decked grandstand and bleachers down the foul lines, while the southwest diamond had a much smaller seating capacity with only hastily arranged bleachers. The southeast diamond was proximate to an evolving fashionable neighborhood of brownstones on the east side of Central Park and the evolving neighborhood of Harlem to the north, while the southwest diamond bordered a desolate area on the northwest side of Central Park dominated by dilapidated shanties where there were any people living there at all.

Another downside to playing for the Metropolitans was being associated with the "beer and whisky league," the disdainful name that the owners of League teams called the Association, since it appealed to working-class spectators rather than more respectable patrons by charging a 25-cent admission (not the 50-cent fare of the League), sold beer at the ballpark, and played ballgames on Sunday. Keefe, though, was inspired by the huge Sunday crowds at the ballparks in the Association cities that he had only rarely experienced in his three years with Troy in the League.

Keefe had to devise a strategy over the winter of 1883 to adapt to the new pitching rule that allowed the ball to be delivered up to shoulder height. He likely worked on alternatives while coaching college players, although it is uncertain at which college he practiced, since there were no newspaper reports of his whereabouts that winter. He decided to primarily rely on his existing at-the-hip motion and not take full advantage of the close-to-overhand delivery, since he had concerns with arm strain.

After observing many a professional pitcher throw his arm out during his five years in the major and minor leagues, Keefe was determined to avoid such a problem with his right arm. "Men who follow pitching usually last only four or five years. Then they have what is called the 'pitcher's arm,' which is not much better than no arm at all," a syndicated article about Keefe later commented on his perception of injured pitching arms. "Through the constant and violet use of certain ligaments, their power not only becomes impaired but is sometimes lost altogether."[4] Since he had no medical training and only a rudimentary formal education, Keefe must have relied on advice from a physician to form this philosophy. Quite possibly his source was former Harvard College pitcher Harold Ernst, who had graduated from Harvard Medical School following his illustrious years as an amateur pitcher on the baseball diamond.

During the 1883 season, Keefe began to perfect his graceful pitching motion that put minimal stress on his right arm. "The beauty of Keefe's work was the ease with which it was accomplished. It was once said of him that he could pitch a game of ball on the hottest day in summer, wearing a paper collar, and not wilt it in the least," Will Rankin, an astute observer of New York City baseball, later wrote about his observation of Keefe's delivery. "His every motion was grace and ease personified, and he could send a ball over the plate with great speed, with apparently as little exertion as he required in delivering one of his 'slow ones' to a batsman."[5]

Rather than radically modify his arm motion, Keefe changed his assortment of pitches by adding a "slow ball," or change of pace, to his basic repertoire of fastball and curveball. "Change of pace for pitchers was important in those days," Keefe said decades later about his renowned pitch. "It was then, as now, largely a case of outguessing the batter."[6] The key to an effective change of pace was to disguise its delivery by throwing the ball with the exact same motion as he did with his other pitches. "His real effectiveness lay in his change of pace," the *New York Tribune* explained. "He could pitch a speedy ball with the same preliminary movements as he used with a slow cut-curve; consequently the batsman never knew just what kind of a ball to expect when he was pitching."[7]

Keefe revealed the change of pace in an April 13 preseason game against the Cleveland team of the National League, when he gave up just one hit in nine innings. The *New York Clipper* report, likely written by Rankin, was very specific about Keefe's success that day: "The visitors could do nothing with Keefe's pitching. It was not his speed or his curve so much as it was his well-disguised change of pace, which bothered the Cleveland batsmen."[8]

Keefe seemingly picked the Cleveland game to unveil his change of pace because the next day the Metropolitans began to play the New York League team in the first of several not just intercity but also intercompany games. Keefe wanted to make a good impression against the League team, but errors in the field undid Keefe's strategy as the Metropolitans lost, 8–1. The Mets lost most of the games in this series. Keefe even umpired the April 30 game, where one writer noted that he "was decidedly off on calling strikes, but he was impartial."[9]

To intimidate batters, Keefe also decided to pitch inside more often. While this resulted in more hit batsmen, there was no significant penalty to the pitcher, just another called ball, which he had several to waste since the batter needed seven balls to take first base for a base on balls. The combination of the change of pace and closer-to-the-batter pitching resulted in many more strikeouts than Keefe had registered in the past.

Keefe got off to a rocky start in his first few regular-season games in the Association, as the Metropolitans began the season on the road. He lost his first two starts against lowly Baltimore, a rag-tag outfit that had finished in last place in 1882 and was destined to repeat that dismal performance in 1883. On May 1, Keefe lost the opening game of the season, 4–3; two days later he lost again, but was more impressive. He registered 13 strikeouts, but yielded four runs in the ninth inning to lose, 5–1. As the *Baltimore Sun* noted in its game account, "Their battery yesterday afternoon was Keefe, pitcher, Holbert, catcher, and a good one it was. The pitching of Keefe was so effective that he managed at different times during the game to retire every Baltimore player on strikes."[10] He won his first Association game on May 7 against the Allegheny team from Pittsburgh, in a pitching duel with former Our Boys teammate John Driscoll. Back in New York for the first home game of the season on May 12, Keefe took the pitcher's box on the big stage of the southeast diamond at the Polo Grounds, but lost again, this time to the Athletic team of Philadelphia.

After several games on the southeast diamond, the Metropolitans switched over to the less-desirable southwest diamond for the Decoration Day holiday games on May 30, when both the Association and League teams were first slated to play in New York. There were five games played at the Polo Grounds complex on the holiday, as both teams played separate-admission twin bills, with one game in the morning and a second in the afternoon. In between the games of the League twin bill on the southeast diamond, Princeton and Yale played a college game. The Metropolitans played most of their games for the next two weeks on the southwest diamond, before finishing up against the St. Louis Browns on June 14, when both teams took the long train trip to St. Louis to begin a series there on Sunday, June 17. In St. Louis, Keefe experienced a completely different viewpoint of Sunday compared to staid version in New York City and Boston.

Sunday was the designated day of rest for most people in the 1880s, as the workweek extended six days from Monday through Saturday. The way "rest" was best utilized, however, differed between states in the eastern and western portions of the country. States in the East still clung to the strict Sunday observance of their Puritan forefathers, with laws that prohibited most work activities, including baseball. Residents in many cities west of the Allegheny Mountains, especially immigrants from Germany, observed a Continental Sabbath where people participated in festivities and sporting events. In cities such as St. Louis and Louisville, Sunday was a day of leisure, not simply a day of rest for greater intellectual and physical well being as it was considered to be in the East. Consequently, Sunday baseball was permitted in St. Louis and Louisville, but prohibited in New York City and Boston.

Playing a major-league baseball game on Sunday was a new experience for Keefe, who reveled in the opportunity to pitch before a huge crowd of working people, whose only opportunity to watch a ballgame was on Sunday after six straight days of labor. There was nothing in his Catholic upbringing that prevented him from forsaking his day of rest to work on the Sabbath. During the winter baseball tour in New Orleans in 1880, Keefe had shown no reluctance to pitch on Sunday. However, there was one player on the Metropolitans, outfielder John O'Rourke, who chose to strictly observe the Sabbath and refused to play on Sunday.[11] Without any extra players on the 11-man squad, the only option to replace the center fielder was to use one of the alternate battery, so catcher Charlie Reipschlager (rather than pitcher Jack Lynch) played in the outfield that Sunday. Keefe lost a close battle, 7–5, in front of a crowd of 11,000 spectators, which was "the biggest crowd that ever attended a ball game in St. Louis," according to the *St. Louis Globe-Democrat*, and the biggest crowd that Keefe had ever seen.[12]

In addition to playing on Sunday in St. Louis and Louisville, Keefe also experienced tremendous crowds to watch baseball on the Independence Day holiday. Keefe pitched and won both games of a Fourth of July twin bill before an overflow crowd in Columbus, Ohio. He surrendered just three combined hits to the Columbus batters, which established a still-standing major-league record for fewest hits allowed by a single pitcher in two nine-inning games on the same day.[13] In the inexact yet hyperbolic writing of the times, the Columbus correspondent to *Sporting Life* reported that "Keefe pitched both games for the visitors and gave the greatest exhibition of strategic twirling ever seen there."[14]

Upon the team's return to New York City, the Metropolitans needed to play just three more games on the southwest diamond at the Polo Grounds, as they played most of their remaining home games on the better southeast diamond. The simultaneous-games strategy was jettisoned since "the canvas separating the two diamonds enabled the spectators to view the game in progress on either side of it, and destroyed the interest of both games."[15]

Keefe was the workhorse of the Metropolitans pitching staff in 1883, manning the pitcher's box for 68 of the team's 97 games in the Association's 98-game schedule. He could not have pitched that many games without his relaxed sidearm motion that created less arm strain. Keefe finished the season with a 41–27 record, the first of six consecutive 30-win seasons for Keefe. He led the Association in complete games (68), innings pitched (619), and strikeouts (359) and was second in wins (41). Most impressive was the strikeout figure, which greatly exceeded the next highest total, by Bobby Mathews of the Athletic club of Philadelphia with 203. Keefe had found his footing as a strategic pitcher, who could continually fool batters with an assortment of pitches and deliveries.

The 1883 season was a financial success for the majority of the Association ballclubs, as reportedly seven of the eight made money; only the Metropolitans failed to turn a profit. Despite some decent success on the playing field, the Metropolitans became the "redheaded stepchild to their owners, the Metropolitan Exhibition Company," headed by John Day, at the expense of the other New York City team playing in the National League.[16] The culprit was admission price, which at 25 cents was half that of the 50-cent tariff for the League team. Day and Mutrie couldn't generate a big enough volume of spectators to watch the Metropolitans for half the price of a League game. On the other hand, Day's team in the League, which finished in sixth place, had no trouble turning a profit at double the fare charged to see the Association team.

In the fall of 1883, the Association adopted a number of changes, including expanding the schedule to 112 games and adding four more teams to become a 12-team league. The Association also instituted a new rule for batters hit by a pitch, who now were entitled to take first base. This rule allegedly was passed "because Tony Mullane and Tim Keefe made a practice of hitting batters."[17]

There were nearly twice as many major-league ballclubs in 1884 than in 1883, after the Association expanded by four teams and a third league was established, the Union Association, which added eight more teams. This rapid expansion of major-league jobs created another opportunity for Keefe to improve his salary, which was manifested in an aggressive offer from the St. Louis ballclub in the Union Association to sign Keefe and his battery mate Holbert.[18] Keefe used this interest from the Union Association to renegotiate his deal with the Metropolitans, which resulted in increasing his salary from $2,000 up to $2,800 for the 1884 season as well as retroactively for the 1883 season.[19] Keefe leaked his new salary information to *Sporting Life*, which printed that "Keefe of the Mets gets $2,800 and Holbert his catcher $2,500."[20] Effectively, Keefe wanted to acknowledge publicly that he wasn't interested in playing in the Union Association by making the price for his services (and the entire battery) too costly for the new league.

Unintentionally, Keefe also signaled that he wanted to stay in New York City, to take advantage of the better opportunity for Irish-Americans there than back in the Boston area. Many Irish-Americans had become business owners and moved into the middle class in New York City as a result of the Democratic political organization known as Tammany Hall. Keefe had read about the infamous Boss Tweed, head of Tammany Hall in the 1870s, who had been sent to jail for graft and corruption of city funds, but whom many working-class Irish-Americans viewed "as a modern Robin Hood who provided them with food, fuel, and jobs."[21] By 1883 the new leader of Tammany Hall was John Kelly, the son of Irish immigrants who had learned the mason trade, established his own business, and then entered politics. "Kelly became the first in Tammany's long line of Irish-Catholic bosses," historian Terry Golway wrote in his book *Machine Made: Tammany Hall and the Creation of Modern American Politics*.[22] Kelly established a cross-class coalition between the downtrodden Irish and the city's business elite, to be able to achieve the goals of both sides of the social spectrum. In 1880 Kelly successfully engineered the election of William Grace as mayor, the first Irish-born man to be mayor of New York City. Things looked auspicious in New York City for ambitious Irish-Americans, like Keefe, for the remainder of the 1880s.

While the National League revised its pitching rules for the 1884 season to permit an unrestricted overhand delivery, the American Association stayed with the shoulder-height restriction. Keefe thought the overhand delivery was a bad idea:

> The higher the ball is thrown the harder it is upon the arm. No pitcher can stand the strain, and the result will be that the arm must be kept down. Whitney, Radbourn and Galvin kept their arms up as high as they cared to last season, which is the best reason in the world for the fact that they won't throw any harder this season. Then a high-thrown ball is not so deceptive nor so hard to hit as a ball delivered from below the shoulder. The pitcher delivering the ball above the shoulder will probably deliver it straight, as the curve entails too much a strain on the arm.[23]

Some National League pitchers, such as Hoss Radbourn, weren't full converts to overhand pitching. "Radbourn, who had risen to the top [in 1883] as a sidearm man, would have little use for the rule change," Edward Achorn wrote in his biography of Radbourn. "He might pull out the occasional overhand throw from his bag of tricks, along with throwing sidearm and underarm, dancing around the pitcher's box, and mixing up fastballs and junk curves."[24]

By 1884, Keefe was skilled at throwing six types of pitches, as conveyed in his treatise "Curve Pitching," written for the book *Batting and Pitching*, published that year by Wright & Ditson. In "Curve Pitching," partially reproduced in Appendix A of this book, Keefe describes in detail how to throw a straight ball, out-curve slow ball, swift drop ball, swift out-curve, in-shoot, and rising ball.[25] Keefe is thought by some to also have thrown a spitball, since he reportedly "wet his thumb before delivering the ball," which he likely learned from his mentor, since Tommy Bond "used to wet his fingers and produce a peculiar shoot on his ball," reportedly by doctoring the ball with glycerin, which he kept in a bottle in his hip pocket.[26]

The Metropolitans had new home grounds for the 1884 season. Metropolitan Park, located on First Avenue between 107th Street and 109th Street, was "on a site formerly occupied by the city dump" and across the East River from factories that emitted foul odors.[27] Keefe pitched the opening home game there on May 13, an 18–4 demolition of the Alleghenys. While the *New York Times* described the visual aspects of the new ballpark ("the diamond was well sodded and presented a neat appearance"), the *New York World* commented on its smell, by writing that the ballpark was "decidedly unpleasant to the olfactory organs."[28]

The Metropolitans began the season on the road on May 1, where Keefe demonstrated his newly developed drop ball to the consternation of the Baltimore batters, which included his old friend Gid Gardner, now an outfielder after he had thrown out his arm as a pitcher. "In Keefe's pitching lay the strengths of the visitors," the *Baltimore Sun* reported. "His delivery has lost none of its eccentric curves since last year, and he has added a drop ball to it which is particularly puzzling. He struck out no less than 15 of the 27 hands, and the seven hits made off him were all singles except one by Sommer, which was a doubtful two-bagger."[29] Keefe also hit one batter, Clinton, who was given first base under the new rule for the 1884 season. Keefe, though, hit only 15 batters during the season, which didn't even place him within the top ten among the Association pitchers in that category despite his reputation for throwing inside to batters. After losing the opener, though, Keefe didn't lose another game for nearly four weeks, winning nine straight games before losing to St. Louis on May 27.

Although nearly universally despised by the ballplayers, Metropolitan Park did provide a significant home advantage for the Metropolitans, as the team won 26 of its 32 home games played there. Spectators also hated the new ballpark, as they stayed away in droves. Before the team headed west on its first long road trip, there were rumors that the Metropolitans would disband before the Fourth of July holiday, and transfer their best players (including Keefe) to the New York team in the National League. "The Mets will disband after playing their first series of home games," one out-of-town newspaper reported. "The club has been losing money

This drawing from Tim Keefe's treatise "Curve Pitching" published in 1884 shows Keefe demonstrating how to throw a drop ball, by putting the hand directly under the ball so that in the delivery the ball would slide off the ends of the fingers.

rapidly in their new grounds and the attendance at home games has been very meager."[30]

The Metropolitans did go on the road trip, but when they returned to New York City Mutrie scrambled to mitigate the financial losses by scheduling the team to play once again at the Polo Grounds (on the southeast diamond) when the League team didn't have a home game. Mutrie also publicly refuted the notion that Keefe would be transferred to another team. "Tim Keefe will not be released from the Mets," *Sporting Life* reported in June. "Mutrie says $5,000 would not purchase his release."[31] Keefe showed his multiple talents, and the trust in him, on the road trip by umpiring the June 21 game at Louisville, when the scheduled umpire didn't arrive in time. American Association secretary Wheeler Wickoff authorized the substitution of Keefe as umpire via telegraph.[32]

With three major-league teams in the New York City area in 1884, with the addition of the Brooklyn ballclub in the expanded American Association, the daily newspapers ramped up their coverage of baseball as they quickly discovered that they could attract more readers with enhanced reporting of the games. At the time, baseball writers were part of the news department, often covering both sports and general news. There were few specialist writers in baseball when Keefe arrived in the city in 1883, notably June Rankin at the *New York Herald* and Jim Kennedy at the *New York Times*.[33] Will Rankin, June's brother, who wrote for the *Brooklyn Eagle*, was a contributor to the weekly *New York Clipper*, and was the New York correspondent for the *Boston Globe* and the *Boston Herald*, where Keefe already had relationships with William Sullivan and Edward Stevens, respectively.[34]

By 1884 the *New York World* was on its way to becoming the dominant newspaper in the city by the end of the decade, after establishing the first sports department within a newspaper staff, i.e., with its own editor, which covered baseball as well as horse racing, boxing, and marathon walking.[35] Best remembered today for its sensationalism and lurid accounts of crime and violence, the *New York World* was a moribund newspaper with low circulation in 1883 when it was purchased by Joseph Pulitzer. The new owner instituted changes to increase circulation among working people and immigrants, by using human-interest stories, illustrations, an expanded Sunday edition, and sports articles. "The *World*'s coverage of sports provides one of the clearest indications of its determination to treat authoritatively, and in detail, the subjects that interested the masses of men," George Juergens wrote in his history of the newspaper.[36]

Peter J. Donohue became the baseball specialist at the *New York World* in 1884, which accelerated the newspaper's influence in the baseball world.[37]

Keefe, himself originally one of the working masses, had a symbiotic relationship with Donohue, as each helped the other to attain acclaim in their field. Keefe was included in a *World* pictorial as one of the 14 "bold knights of the ash," along with other well-known baseball men such as Harry Wright, Albert Spalding, Buck Ewing, and Cap Anson.[38] Keefe had seen the benefit to baseball through the working-class crowds attending ballgames in the American Association, so he was more than happy to tap into that popularity in New York City to advance his own agenda.

Weekly baseball-specific publications were just in their nascent stage of life in 1883, with the inception that year of *Sporting Life*, published by Francis Richter in Philadelphia. George Stackhouse of the *New York Tribune* doubled as the New York correspondent to *Sporting Life*.[39] While the *New York Clipper* had been around for a while, it catered primarily to the theater and had a waning influence on baseball in the 1880s, even with Will Rankin as its baseball editor beginning in 1885.[40] *The Sporting News* didn't begin publishing until 1886, but it had a minimal influence on Keefe's career given the paper's St. Louis perspective during his active pitching years.

The *National Police Gazette*, based in New York City, was another source of publicity. Renowned for its mix of sex, sin, scandal, and sports, the weekly *Police Gazette* was "read gratis in almost every barbershop, hotel, pool hall, fire company, and street-corner saloon" by an estimated half a million men each week.[41] The *Police Gazette* was blunter and more detailed than most reporting at the time, as exemplified by this dispatch about the challenges Keefe faced with his catcher in a July 1884 game:

> Keefe virtually pitched five men out on strikes, although three runs were scored without a single base-hit being made. Bobby Mathews was the first man to go to the bat and he was easily disposed of on three strikes; Knight, the next man, should also have retired on three strikes, but Holbert let the third strike slip through his butter fingers; Storey then hit a ball to Keefe, and the latter, in his anxiety to do something grand, tried for a double play, but throwing the ball wild to Troy he lost the play. Houck then came to the bat and made three vigorous plunges at the ball without removing the cover, and Holbert, as might be expected, let the third strike go past him, which placed three men on bases with no one out. Corey then came to the bat, struck at the first good ball pitched, missed it, and Holbert, as in the case of previous two third strikes, allowed it to go past him, which brought Knight home and advanced each of the other men a base. Corey's second attempt to hit the ball had the same effect. Holbert, greatly to the surprise of all present, allowed the ball to pass him, while the man on third scored, and the man on second went to third. Corey again made a desperate effort to hit the ball and once more missed it. Holbert followed suit, and, without making any attempt to hold the man on third base, threw the ball to first and put Corey out, while Houck ran in from third base and scored the third run of the inning.[42]

Keefe lost that game, 5–2, to Mathews, whom he admired as a strategic pitcher, having written in his treatise "Curve Pitching" that "Mathews probably understands the player who faces him as well as any one who occupies the points to-day."[43] But readers of the daily newspapers in New York City didn't get that level of detail as to how Keefe lost the game. The *New York Times* reported simply that "Keefe pitched with telling effect for the home team, but met with poor support ... [when] the local players lost the contest through the errors of Holbert and Keefe."[44] The *New York World* had even scantier detail, writing that Keefe "out-generalled and out-pitched 'little Bobby' but he was not supported in the field or behind the bat ... [as] the runs were scored off two errors of Holbert."[45]

After that defeat on July 17, which dropped the team into third place in the Association standings, the Metropolitans proceeded to rattle off 11 consecutive victories to take first place, before Keefe lost to Brooklyn in the team's first trip across the recently constructed Brooklyn Bridge to play the Brooklyn expansion team. The Metropolitans remained in first place for the rest of the season, clinching the pennant in early October to finish with a 75–32 record, a .701 winning percentage, six games ahead of second-place Columbus. Truth be told, Lynch was the team's premier pitcher in the drive to retain first place, not Keefe. Lynch won 14 straight games between July 12 and August 19, while Keefe won seven and lost four.

Despite the summer lull, Keefe had a very successful year pitching for the Metropolitans in 1884, compiling a 37–17 record in the pitcher's box, as Mutrie deployed an alternating strategy that year to use Keefe and Lynch each half the time as pitcher. Keefe's strikeout total of 334 was lower in 1884 than in 1883, but, on an adjusted basis for the fewer games pitched, he was more proficient at striking out batters, with 6.2 strikeouts per nine innings in 1884 compared to 5.2 strikeouts per nine innings the previous year. He also walked fewer batters in 1884 than in 1883, on both an absolute basis (71 vs. 108) as well as a relative basis (1.3 per nine innings vs. 1.6).

These statistical conclusions indicate that Keefe became a more strategic pitcher in 1884. In an article entitled "The Pitching of 1884" published in *Sporting Life*, Keefe was named one of the Association's top pitchers based on his "combination of strategy and change of pace."[46] An anecdotal story also advances this conclusion. "While with the Mets he time and again has six bad balls called on him and then would strike out the batsman on the next three balls pitched," Will Rankin recalled about Keefe's ability to waste pitches to accomplish his ultimate goal. "Only a man with perfect control over the ball is able to perform such feats."[47] Keefe was also helped by the diluted competition in 1884 with 12 teams in the Association and an entire third league

As a leader in the newspaper industry to publish artwork to accompany text, the *New York World* selected Tim Keefe (shown as number 7, top figure on the far right) as one of 14 luminaries of the baseball world in an October 1884 issue of the *World*. Keefe, who had led the Metropolitans to the American Association pennant, ranked with more well known figures such as Albert Spalding, Harry Wright, Henry Chadwick and Cap Anson.

in Union Association, which had recruited some talented hitters from the Association.

On the other hand, the Metropolitans were stronger on offense in 1884, with the addition of hard-hitting first baseman Dave Orr (.354 batting average and nine home runs) and significant improvement in third baseman Dude Esterbrook (50 point increase from 1883 to a .314 batting average). The Mets had the second-highest team batting average (.262) in the Association. Keefe also contributed at bat, with a .238 batting average and three home runs. It was the last year that Keefe still concentrated on hitting in addition to his pitching duties, as he never again hit above .200 during his career (excluding the 1887 season when walks counted as hits).

The now-recognized first World Series was played in 1884, between the Metropolitan team of the American Association and the Providence team that was champion of the National League. The series was a less than stellar affair. While described by the *New York Clipper* as a "set of games to decide as to which of the two champion teams of the League and the American Association would be entitled to be champions of the United States," the series was one-sided in favor of the Providence team, which completely dominated the Metropolitans.[48]

Mutrie and Frank Bancroft, the Providence manager, haggled for several weeks via telegrams over the conditions to apply to the privately arranged series of postseason games. With no institutional infrastructure to dictate the details, Mutrie and Bancroft determined the number of games to play, where the games would be played, what rules would apply (when they differed between the two leagues), and, most importantly, how to divide the profits. The two men agreed to a three-game series to be played entirely in New York City, on October 23, 24 and 25, where the audience for the games was likely to be the largest. Bancroft conceded to play under Association rules, with two big exceptions: National League admission prices would apply as would the National League pitching rules, so that Providence's star pitcher, Hoss Radbourn, could throw overhand.[49]

Radbourn, who had won 60 games for Providence in 1884, was so effective because he was one of the first "to combine the two styles of slow and swift delivery, or 'change of pace,' without varying the motion of the arm and body," according to historian Peter Morris in his book *Game of Inches*. Radbourn kept batters guessing, mixing up an explosive fastball with curveballs that broke in different directions, along with "a perplexing slow ball" that would "come toward you and then change its route all of a sudden," akin to a spitball.[50] In many ways, Radbourn was a model for Keefe's eventual bag of pitching tricks.

The festivities surrounding the Championship of the United States began with a bad omen for the Metropolitans, when a rainstorm canceled the scheduled parade on October 22 to celebrate their Association championship. The storm also ushered in a cold front that brought windy conditions and brisk temperatures that dissuaded many potential patrons from attending the first game of the series on October 23. Whereas Mutrie and Bancroft expected a crowd approaching 10,000 spectators, only about 2,500 people went through the turnstiles.

The bad omens continued in the first inning of the opening game, when Tim Keefe resembled the raw pitcher he was back in 1878 with the Westboro team rather than the sharp hurler he was in 1884 with the Metropolitans. It didn't help that his regular catcher, Holbert, was injured and couldn't play, forcing Reipschlager to try to catch his serves. Keefe hit the first Providence batter, Paul Hines, which under Association rules put him on first base. He then threw a wild pitch to advance Hines to second base. Keefe also hit the second batter, Cliff Carroll, to put another runner on base. Two passed balls later, Hines was at third base and Carroll on second base. After Radbourn popped out, Joe Start grounded out to the second baseman, to score Hines and advance Carroll to third base. Then Keefe uncorked another wild pitch to allow Carroll to score and give Providence a 2–0 lead. For all intents and purposes, though, the series was over.

The Metropolitans lost the first game, 6–0, as they could only reach Radbourn for two hits (one by Keefe) in a miserable display of incompetence on the ball field. Kennedy, the baseball writer for the *New York Times*, took the team to task: "The curves of Radbourn struck terror to their hearts, and they fell easy victims to his skill. Some of the local players who have good batting records were like so many children in the hands of the pitcher of the Providence team. They made ineffectual plunges at balls that would reflect discredit on some of our third rate amateurs."[51] Things didn't get much better in the second game on October 24.

Although featuring a rematch of Keefe against Radbourn, the second game attracted only 1,000 spectators. While Keefe was more effective in the second game, his teammates could garner only three hits off Radbourn. Keefe shut down Providence for four innings, but in the fifth a Cambridge buddy, Barney Gilligan, doubled home the first run of the game and Jerry Denny hit a two-run home run to give Providence a 3–0 lead, which held up for a 6–1 victory when darkness halted the game in the eighth inning. Keefe yielded just five hits, but the Gilligan and Denny blasts came at inopportune times for the Metropolitans, as Providence clinched the series by winning the first two games.

Both teams went through the motions in the third game played on Saturday, October 25. Only a few hundred people showed up at the Polo Grounds to watch a meaningless game, which had originally been conceived as the big-attendance game of the series, hoping that the two teams would split the first two games to set up a deciding third game. With nothing on the line for the Metropolitans, Keefe umpired the third game as Mutrie put Jim Becannon into to the pitcher's box. Providence belted the serves of Becannon to cruise to an 11–2 victory, as umpire Keefe mercifully stopped the game after six innings to keep the score from becoming even more embarrassing.

The Metropolitans finally got their celebratory parade in the evening of October 27, which left from the corner of Eighth Avenue and 59th Street and wound its way down to Canal Street, then up Bowery to finish at Union Square. The players rode in a four-horse tally-ho coach, with Keefe sitting prominently near the front along with his catcher, Holbert. Players from dozens of amateur baseball teams followed the featured tally-ho coach over the parade route.

Keefe may have been disappointed in his two losses to Providence mostly because he ostensibly had failed in his tryout to join the New York League team and escape the second-class conditions that he worked under with the Metropolitans. However, his performance against Providence did not hurt his chances at moving to the more prominent, and profitable, of the two major-league teams owned by the Metropolitan Exhibition Company. Keefe wanted to stay in New York City, as he had grown accustomed to its majesty and opportunity, compared to the limitations that faced him back home in Boston. Although he lived during the baseball season at the Harlem House hotel, which was a few blocks further uptown from the Polo Grounds, at 115th Street and Third Avenue, he regularly traveled downtown in the evenings to sample the entertainment and education options readily available to him.[52]

Despite winning the Association championship, the Metropolitan ballclub lost money for a second year in a row. As Day began shopping the ballclub to sell it to a new owner, the exit for Keefe from the Metropolitans began to take shape. The plan was leaked in a November piece in *Sporting Life*: "The Metropolitan Club has not been a source of profit to the Metropolitan Exhibition Company, while the New York League Club has made money despite its ill success. Now why should not the company devote all its energies and resources to strengthen the team in which the money is, and the let the non-paying barnacle slide ... it is by no means improbable that one battery will be transferred therefrom and the rest of the team turned over to Brooklyn."[53]

At the National League meeting in November 1884, the owners had a long discussion about their objections to "swift pitching, which the over-hand throw yielded, creat[ing] the class of games known as 'pitchers' battles' in which the competing batteries had the brunt of the fight thrown on them," with fielders or hitters having little impact on the game results. To provide for a better balance between pitching and hitting, the owners instituted a new rule for the 1885 season requiring the pitcher to have "both feet touching the ground" in his delivery.[54] Presuming that the Association would adopt a similar rule, Keefe got right to work experimenting with how to modify his delivery to respond effectively to this rule change.

While back at his parents' house in Somerville, Massachusetts, for the winter, Keefe experimented with indoor baseball, in a game staged at a Boston roller polo rink on December 22. In the game, local pitching favorites Keefe and John Clarkson, now a pitcher for Chicago in the National League, illustrated "the style of pitching which will be in vogue next season, namely the pitcher to keep both feet on the ground while delivering the ball."[55] The Red team, with Keefe as its pitcher, defeated the Blue team, which had Clarkson, 10–4, in a game played under difficult conditions, as the soft ball used was tough to see under artificial light and the ball bounced high off the asphalt surface of the rink the few times it didn't directly contact the netting hung around the rink to protect spectators.[56] Astutely, the *New York Clipper* didn't think there was a future for indoor baseball, because "an equivalent substitute for natural light is what is lacking."[57]

Three months following the indoor baseball game, Keefe's status within the world of New York City baseball dramatically changed.

9

Transfer to the New York Giants

The two baseball teams owned by John Day under the umbrella of the Metropolitan Exhibition Company were complete opposites in 1884. The Metropolitans, largely due to the pitching of Tim Keefe and Jack Lynch, were champions of the American Association but lost money, while the National League team finished in fourth place but made money. If Day could only blend the best of both teams, and jettison the rest, he would have a blockbuster in a championship-caliber team that could turn a big profit.

The League team needed pitching to augment Mickey Welch, the team's stalwart hurler who had a 39–21 record in 1884. John Ward had thrown out his arm pitching and was now a shortstop, as outfielder Mike Dorgan alternated with Welch in the pitcher's box by the end of the season. Moving either Keefe or Lynch from the Metropolitans to the League team would be a perfect solution. If only Day could have easily accomplished that maneuver, though.

There were no trades at the time, only releases, which came with a 10-day period recognized by both major leagues where the released player could offer his services to other teams but could not sign with another team during those 10 days. This provision was intended "to prevent clubs from exchanging players without giving other clubs a chance to bid for their services," which is precisely what Day wanted to do.[1] Keefe or Lynch, who both had 37 wins in 1884, would be highly sought by other teams. Day, though, was only interested in Keefe for the League team, given his temperate habits vis-à-vis alcoholic beverages, as opposed to Lynch who operated a saloon near the Polo Grounds.[2]

Given Keefe's history of contentious salary negotiations, it would have been a huge risk for Day to release the 28-year-old pitcher without a lot of assurance that he could re-sign him at a reasonable price. How to mitigate that risk was a big stumbling block for Day. Fortunately, Lynch provided help with that conundrum. Right after the 1884 World Series with Providence, Lynch had taken a four-week trip to Europe.[3] This extended absence gave Day the idea that if he could ensure that Keefe was physically unavailable to communicate with other teams for the 10-day period following the release, he could re-sign Keefe without much risk. A trip to Europe was not in Day's budget, but an excursion by boat to the island of Bermuda in the Atlantic Ocean was more reasonable.

By January 1885 Day had decided to move Jim Mutrie from the Metropolitans to be the manager of the League team and also transfer Keefe and Dude Esterbrook from the Association team to the League team. The ruse to transfer Keefe and Esterbrook to the League team was an open secret in New York City. "Tim Keefe, of the Metropolitans, was in this city recently," the *New York Herald* reported in February 1885. "As he has not yet been signed it is the general impression that he is to be released by the Mets and signed by the New Yorks."[4]

One reason Keefe was in New York City was to play in several roller polo games at Madison Square Garden with his team from Boston. In one game, Keefe, who played offense as the cover-point, scored two goals in his team's 5–0 victory.[5] Keefe was also spotted in the corridors of the Fifth Avenue Hotel during the National League meeting in early March. Keefe, "the pitcher of the Metropolitans, who has been playing polo on roller skates," was interested in whether or not the League owners would agree to reinstate the "deserters" whom they had blacklisted for jumping to the Union Association during the 1884 season.[6]

Before his departure to Bermuda, Keefe likely received a salary advance from his future 1885 earnings, because he made his first real estate investment in March 1885. Keefe cautiously dipped his toe into the real-estate market by investing $2,000 into a mortgage loan on a piece of land in his hometown of Somerville, Massachusetts, opposite the Fitchburg Railroad Station. The landowner, Richard Blackwell, who owned a livery stable, was obligated to repay the $2,000 principal at the end of ten years and to pay six percent interest to Keefe each year in two semiannual payments.[7]

On March 26, following his formal release from the Metropolitans, Keefe sailed for Bermuda on the *Trinidad* along with Mutrie, Esterbrook, and Fred Davis (Day's brother-in-law). When they encountered choppy seas on their two-and-a-half-day ocean voyage, all four men got seasick. Mutrie reportedly had the worst of the heaves, with Keefe a close second. After landing in Bermuda on March 29, they stayed at the Hamilton Hotel. On April 6, the end of the 10-day release period, Keefe and Esterbrook signed contracts to play for the New York League team and soon departed from Bermuda on the *Oronoco*. They arrived back in New York City on April 12.[8] Keefe and Esterbrook got in one game of baseball while in Bermuda, on a cricket field at the military camp there. Keefe was the catcher and Mutrie the pitcher for one team, while Esterbrook caught and a Harvard College student pitched for the other team. Keefe's team won, 16–2, as soldiers filled in at the other positions while hotel guests observed the action.⁹

The American Association ballclub owners howled about the deal, but they had no recourse to reverse the transaction, only to issue penalties. "It was through the vexation and mortification of the American Association Club managers and officials in being outwitted by Manager Mutrie in their efforts to get Keefe," the *National Police Gazette* reported, "that the Metropolitan Club was fined $500 and Manager Mutrie unjustly expelled from an association with which he had no connection. Keefe's Bermuda trip will long be remembered."¹⁰ Day actually paid the fine, since he wanted to sell the Metropolitan ballclub to recoup his losses from the previous two seasons.

In his negotiations in Bermuda, Keefe chose long-term security over a high salary in the short term, by having a three-year agreement. Keefe negotiated a three-year deal, because he received the same $3,000 salary for each of the 1885, 1886, and 1887 seasons.¹¹ Given his pitching performances during the 1885 and 1886 seasons, Keefe would have wanted to dicker with Day for a salary increase, but there were no newspaper reports of such activity following those two seasons as there would be for his highly public salary negotiations in 1888 and 1889.

Keefe's arrival back on U.S. soil coincided with the birth of the nickname for Day's League team. Peter Donohue, the baseball writer for the *New York World*, popularized the name "Giants" after he began to use the term to often describe the team in his game reports in May 1885. According to the *Dickson Baseball Dictionary*, "Baseball folklore has long held that New York manager Jim Mutrie ... bounded from the dugout and exclaimed 'My big fellows! My giants!'" to inspire Donohue to pen the name; however, there is little evidence to indicate that Mutrie ever uttered this phrase.¹² Donohue seems to have crafted the nickname on his own, perhaps at the urging of his publisher, Joseph Pulitzer, to enliven the reporting of the ballgames in order to attract more readers.

There were some taller than average players on the New York Giants in 1885, which may also have inspired Donohue. First baseman Roger Connor was 6-foot-3, outfielder Pete Gillespie was 6-foot-1, and second baseman Joe Gerhardt was 6-foot-0. Most of the rest of the lineup ranged from 5-foot-11 to 5-foot-9. Keefe, at 5-foot-10 and 180 pounds, was at the upper end of that range along with third baseman Esterbrook and catcher Ewing. At the lower end were shortstop Ward, outfielders Jim O'Rourke and Mike Dorgan, and catcher Tom Deasley. Welch and utilityman Danny Richardson were the smallest men on the team at 5-foot-8. Six of these dozen men would eventually land in the Hall of Fame: Keefe, Welch, Ewing, Connor, Ward, and O'Rourke.

After his two-year hiatus from the National League, Keefe began the 1885 season auspiciously on May 9 when he pitched a shutout to defeat Radbourn and Providence in a rematch of the 1884 World Series. However, after losing his next outing on May 12, Keefe pitched only two more innings during the next four weeks. The combination of the traveling to Bermuda in April and playing rough-and-tumble roller polo during March didn't serve Keefe's right arm well.

The new pitching rule mandating that pitchers keep both feet on the ground while delivering the ball to the batter didn't last long. In late April League president Nick Young, to appease some concerned owners, announced that the new pitching rule would be just an experiment for the first month of the 1885 season, after which the new rule could be repealed if the owners desired.

The both-feet-on-the-ground rule was a boon to the Giants at the beginning of the 1885 season. By Decoration Day the Giants had rocketed into first place behind the pitching of Welch and Richardson, who filled in for a tired Keefe. With New York atop the League standings, though, it didn't take long before some teams began to grumble about the new rule and call for its jettisoning. A week later, Boston, in concert with Providence, officially called for the rule's repeal just before the start of the Giants' series in Boston. Young had no choice but to mandate that the 1884 pitching rules would apply beginning on June 9 for the remainder of the 1885 season.[13] When Keefe recalled the situation three years later in an article for the *Boston Globe*, there was an unmistakable disdain in his tone concerning one owner's disregard for the integrity of the game:

> During the season of 1885 the New York club was playing in Boston when everything looked favorable for the Giants winning the championship. But here they struck a snag. The Boston club had already struck a toboggan, and where they would stop [in the standings] was a very uncertain question. But Mr. Billings, one of the Boston club directors, came to the rescue. He held a consultation with the Providence club and, after considerable pleading, they joined hands with him and objected to the new rule. It was immediately changed, previous to the New York club going on the grounds that day. The words of Mr. Billings must still be very fresh in the memory of Mr. Mutrie. As he shook his finger at the genial manager, he [Billings] said in a voice never to be forgotten, "I changed that rule, and you can tell your president so." Does any one think that Mr. Billings had the interest of the national game, or self-interest, at heart?[14]

That day, though, the return of the hop-step-and-jump delivery served to help the Giants and hinder the Boston team. "Welch seemed to be at home while jumping around in the box, but the privilege did not make Buffinton's delivery any more effective," the *New York Times* reported on the victory by the Giants. "Welch was very effective. The 'jumping jack' tactics seemed to impart new life to his pitching, and it was with the greatest difficulty that the ball was hit out of the reach of the fielders."[15] However, a week later, New York dropped into second place, where the team was destined to reside for the remainder of the season. Over the course of the season, this pitching rule change benefited the pennant-winning Chicago team.

Chicago and New York completely dominated the National League in 1885. Both teams won more than three-fourths of their games, while only one other team won more than half of its games. For the next three months following the pitching rule change, the Giants nipped at the heels of the Chicago team, but could not catch them.

With his arm healthy again by mid–June, Keefe reunited with former Troy teammate Mickey Welch to form a formidable two-man pitching rotation for the Giants to make a run at Chicago for first place. Welch experienced his best season in the major leagues in 1885 when he produced a 44–11 pitching mark. The renewed legalization of the hop-step-and-jump delivery was a boon to Welch, who was known for "continually dancing while in the act of delivering the ball."[16] Welch compiled a 17-game winning streak between July 18 and September 4. The Giants won 29 games and lost only four during that stretch, but could gain only one game in the standings on Chicago.

Keefe posted a 32–13 pitching record for the Giants in 1885, with a contrasting style to that of Welch, since Keefe did not use the hop-step-and-jump delivery. Newspaper accounts are sparse about Keefe's delivery at the time, calling it "puzzling" and "deceptive," but never reporting that he jumped or danced in the pitcher's box as Welch was often described as doing. The techniques that Keefe wrote about in his 1884 treatise on pitching never mentioned the hop-step-and-jump, or any motion for that matter. He described what to do before the delivery, then the throwing of the ball, but nothing about any intermediary motion. Keefe's focus on command of the ball likely would have been disturbed by using the hop-step-and-jump motion. Three years later, he derisively termed the hop-step-and-jump to be "contortionist's movements in the box."[17]

During the summer of 1885, the Giants became the darlings of New York City. Attendance for games at the Polo Grounds surged, with several thousand at each weekday game and more than 10,000 on Saturday. "The team had generated enormous fan interest, drawn huge crowds, become fashionable, and made a pot of money for John B. Day," James Hardy wrote in his history of the nineteenth-century New York Giants. "It was hard to complain after all that," when the Giants didn't cop the pennant that year.[18]

Several actors who performed in *Black Hussar*, a comic opera then being staged at Wallack's Theater, were at the July 22 game, including rabid baseball fans DeWolf Hopper and Digby Bell. They all sat with Giants president Day in the directors' box in the upper deck of the Polo Grounds grandstand. "Digby Bell had converted me to baseball," Hopper reminisced in his memoir *Once a Clown, Always a Clown*. "We were at the Polo Grounds every free afternoon." Hopper wrote that a gold-headed cane from the team and "the friendship of Buck Ewing, Tim Keefe and John M. Ward were my proudest chattels."[19]

Keefe and his Giants teammates were soon accustomed to performing in front of the theater crowd that Day courted. In the victory over Detroit that Bell and Hopper witnessed on July 22, "Keefe was the king pin of the nine. To say that he pitched splendidly would be putting it mildly," one baseball writer described his performance. "He was an absolute conundrum to the hitters of the visiting club. The fact that only three of the thirty-three men who went to the bat made base hits is sufficient proof of his effectiveness."[20]

The actors had traveled a great distance from their place of employment, as Wallack's was located on Broadway at 30th Street, in the center of the theater district that was located on Broadway between 23rd Street and 42nd Street. Other big theaters of that day were the Lyceum, Bijou, and Casino. By 1885, "this once sparsely settled stretch of Broadway was ablaze with electric lights and thronged with crowds of middle- and upper-class theater, restaurant, and café patrons."[21] Horse-drawn coaches took the image-conscious actors to the Giants games, while the Third Avenue Elevated Railroad was the transportation mode favored by the more pedestrian spectators at the games of the Metropolitans.

While the Giants were having their best year so far in their three years in the National League, Keefe's former team, the Metropolitans, began to sink to new lows in the American Association. Although the team was no longer consigned to the crummy southwest diamond of the Polo Grounds that they had to endure in 1883, the Metropolitans were forced to play as a low-budget opening act on the southeast diamond prior to Giants games. In late August, Day borrowed the newfangled doubleheader idea, to offer two ballgames for the price of one. When he noticed an attendance spike, Day scheduled four more doubleheaders in September. Keefe pitched in the premier game of the September 10 twin bill, after watching the Association game that was the opening act. Day finally found a buyer for the Metropolitans later in the fall, when Erastus Wiman bought the team and relocated it to Staten Island to play next to the amusement park he operated there.

Although the New York Giants could not advance from their second-place position to overtake Chicago during the summer, the Giants still had a chance for first place when the team arrived in Chicago for a four-game series from September 29 to October 3. If the Giants could win at least three of the four games, but preferably all four, they would vault into first place. Instead, the Giants lost three of the four games, which expunged their championship hopes. After losing the first three games, the Giants won the last game, as Keefe defeated Chicago in a seven-inning game that was curtailed by darkness on a cold, rainy day. The Giants finished the 1885 season in second place with a 85–27 record, a .759 winning percentage, two games behind pennant-winning Chicago.

Keefe honed his reputation as a strategic pitcher during the 1885 season: "Keefe is said to be one of the most scientific pitchers in the country—that is, he uses his head as well as his hands while in the box."[22] Will Rankin provided a more detailed perspective on Keefe the strategic pitcher:

> The care with which Keefe surveyed every part of the field before delivering the ball, his study of the weak points of his opponents, and his work in changing pace, and in placing the ball over the corners of the plate, marked him as a great "head work" pitcher.... No one could stand behind the plate and watch the ball come in, now swift as a cannon shot, now so slowly as hardly to reach the plate, now over the inner corner of the plate, so close to the batsman as to make him wince, and now over the outer corner so that he reached for it in vain, and every ball delivered with practically the same motion of the arm, without becoming quickly convinced that there was a big brain controlling the motions of the stalwart right arm."[23]

With Ewing and Deasley as his catchers, Keefe had no problem advancing within the pitching profession without the aid of Bill Holbert, who had been his catcher for his previous five seasons in the major leagues. Keefe led the National League in earned-run average at 1.58 as well as in fewest hits allowed per nine innings at 6.8, the latter a category that he'd dominate between 1885 and 1889. His seven shutouts were the second most in the league.

Ewing's advancement within the catching profession immensely helped Keefe. He was the first catcher to play from a crouch position behind the batter, not stoop over from a standing position, and use a snap throw to stop baserunners from stealing bases.[24] Ewing was one of the first catchers to use a padded glove on his left hand and a thin glove on his right hand to enable him to throw the ball better. With more runners prevented from advancing on the bases, opponents scored fewer runs. Teaming with Ewing made Keefe a more productive pitcher and soon escalated him into the corps of elite pitchers in the National League.

Transferring from the Metropolitans to the Giants changed Keefe's life in many ways. With his $3,000 annual salary with the Giants, Keefe earned far more than he'd ever make as a carpenter. He began to distance himself from his blue-collar background. He took advantage of the opportunity to attend the theater and participate in other social activities that he could never experience in ethnically stratified Boston, which provided few such opportunities for those of Irish ancestry. Most importantly, he was now a teammate, not just a friend, of John Ward, who had recently graduated with a law degree from Columbia College. This tighter relationship facilitated their partnership in the establishment of the Brotherhood of Professional Base Ball Players following the end of the 1885 baseball season.

The proximate cause of the Brotherhood formation were the salary provisions adopted by the ballclub owners at a special joint meeting of the League and Association on October 17, which prohibited salary advances and capped a ballplayer's annual salary at $2,000. "This will produce ill-feeling among the players," the *New York World* astutely reported. "It is also likely to cause trickery by both managers and players."[25] The *New York Herald* took a more eloquent approach to describe the players' viewpoint: "While the laws formulated may be perfectly satisfactory to the club officials it is not at all likely that they will meet with the approbation of the players whom they are to govern. A reduction of salaries may be deemed necessary among the club officials in order to make their baseball enterprise a paying investment, but the players will no doubt have a voice in the matter. It is hardly likely that the heretofore large salaried men will quietly submit to the wholesale reduction of their salaries."[26]

When the Giants ballplayers arrived back in New York City on October 18 after their postseason exhibition games in Cincinnati and Washington, D.C., an unidentified ballplayer told the press: "The time has arrived when the players must take some action in the matter.... The players have been ignored at every meeting, and restrictions one after another have been placed upon them until now they can stand it no longer.... Players have been treated unfairly long enough, and I assure you that stockholders of clubs will find before long that they have placed the last straw on the camel's back. We make the money, and it is only just that we ought to get a fair share of the profits."[27] The unidentified player was undoubtedly Ward, given the loquacious nature of the explanation; Keefe would have been much more succinct.

On October 22, 1885, on the eve of the Giants' final postseason game before the team dispersed for the offseason, the Brotherhood of Professional Base Ball Players was formally organized, a gathering whose purpose was captured in the handwritten minutes that Keefe wrote in a ledger book:

9. Transfer to the New York Giants

We, the undersigned, professional base-ball players, recognizing the importance of united effort and impressed with its necessity in our own behalf, do form ourselves this day into an organization to be known as the "Brotherhood of Professional Base-Ball Players." The objects we seek to accomplish are: To protect and benefit ourselves collectively and individually; To promote a high standard of professional conduct; To foster and encourage the interests of the game of Base Ball.[28]

John M. Ward	139 E. 48th St. New York
T.J. Keefe	54 Springfield St. Somerville Mass.
J.J Gerhardt	[illegible] Cincinnati Ohio
Wm. Ewing	" " "
Roger Connor	60 E. 109 St. New York
Daniel Richardson	368 Fulton St. Elmira N.Y.
Michael Welch	87 Beech Street Holyoke Mass.
Michael C. Dorgan	Syracuse N.Y.
Jas. H. O'Rourke	57 Hamilton St. Bridgeport Conn.[29]

Only nine of the twelve New York Giants players were founding members of the Brotherhood; the other three players (Esterbrook, Deasley, and Gillespie) either didn't want to join or were excluded from consideration.

Ward was elected president of the Brotherhood and Keefe was elected as secretary.[30] History would forever link the two men as the renegade ringleaders of what would be called the first baseball players union, but which the two men saw merely to be a fraternal organization of ballplayers. While the Brotherhood didn't go public until nine months later in August 1886, the October 1885 meeting was the beginning of a contentious, soon to be vicious, confrontation between the ballplayers and ballclub owners.

10

Secretary of the Brotherhood

Keefe was well qualified to serve as secretary of the Brotherhood of Professional Base Ball Players, given his self-education in shorthand, which allowed him to take accurate notes of the organization's meetings. "Being secretary of the National Brotherhood of Base Ball Players, the minutes of the meetings are taken down in shorthand," Keefe wrote in an 1888 letter to a stenography magazine to which he subscribed. "It not only offers an opportunity for good practice, but it saves considerable valuable time."[1] A portion of this letter to *Browne's Phonographic Monthly* is reproduced as Appendix B.

There were only a few public hints that Keefe was training to be a stenographer. The earliest indication that Keefe was proficient in shorthand occurred in 1884, when *Sporting Life* ran this short item: "Keefe of the Mets has been learning stenography and is said to be quite an expert, being able to take down eighty words a minute."[2] Two years later, after the existence of the Brotherhood was publicly disclosed, *Sporting Life* reported that "Tim Keefe is studying stenography and becoming quite expert at it."[3] Not until 1888 did a New York City publication disclose his shorthand expertise, when the *New York Herald* noted that Keefe was "an expert shorthand reporter" who "would wrestle for hours with the mysterious twists, loops, arches and dots of stenography until he has acquired a very proficient knowledge of the art."[4]

Keefe studied shorthand to have a skill to provide an income once his pitching career was over. In the 1880s most stenographers were male, not the female stereotype that developed in the twentieth century. As Carol Srole wrote in her history of stenography, at the time Keefe studied shorthand, stenography was perceived "as a means to advance beyond the ordinary clerk" to be independent and create an identity as "middle-class men."[5] However, that image soon changed in the 1890s when typing and stenography became intertwined skills performed by women in the mechanization of the office, which relegated shorthand to a service performed by female clerks in the working class.

While his shorthand skills have always been the avowed reason why he held the secretary position in the Brotherhood, Keefe was not just a mere scribe. Keefe was the unsung officer of the Brotherhood, who operated, by choice, in the shadow of John Ward, who has received the lion's share of the credit for developing the organization as its president and highly vocal spokesman. However, Keefe was instrumental in membership recruitment and retention, as the oft-described "genial Keefe" bonded with the ballplayers better than did the gruff Ward. Keefe likely made a valuable contribution to its strategy by advocating the profit-sharing element of the eventual Brotherhood-spawned Players' League in 1890. And Keefe had a significant role in the formation of the Brotherhood.

The genesis of the Brotherhood prior to its first meeting on October 22, 1885, is undocumented and likely will remain murky and never completely understood. It was as if nine ballplayers on the New York Giants got together to rant about the National League's attempt to establish a salary cap and then four days later decided to form the Brotherhood, without any prior forethought. This is exactly the explanation that *Sporting Life* provided in August 1886, when the Brotherhood made its first public statement to acknowledge its existence: "Last fall the players of the New York Club met together for the purpose of formulating some scheme of organization."[6] Later, Ward more specifically wrote: "In 1885 the passage of the arbitrary $2000 salary limit rule forced the organization of the Brotherhood for mutual protection of the players."[7]

It appears, though, that the Brotherhood at least dated from August 1885, when a group of ballclub owners from both the League and the Association met in Saratoga, New York, in late August to discuss various changes to the national agreement between the two leagues. These changes included not only the prohibition of salary advances but also the "grading of salaries."[8] A November 1885 item published in *Sporting Life*, from the newspaper's Washington correspondent, provided an overt hint of the existence of the Brotherhood: "There is in existence an agreement among the players of the New York Club refusing to sign for the maximum salary as agreed upon by the late joint convention [on August 23–24]. This agreement was drawn up and signed by seven members of that club soon after the Saratoga meeting."[9]

The Brotherhood had an even earlier conception, though, as revealed by a note in a different section of the same edition of *Sporting Life*, in which one man denied responsibility for the recent agreement made by the New York Giants players: "The report that Billy Voltz is at the head of a scheme to organize ball players against managers is denied by that gentleman. The scheme attempted last spring was not for that purpose."[10]

William Voltz was the reason that neither Ward nor Keefe ever talked extensively for publication about the actual creation of the Brotherhood,

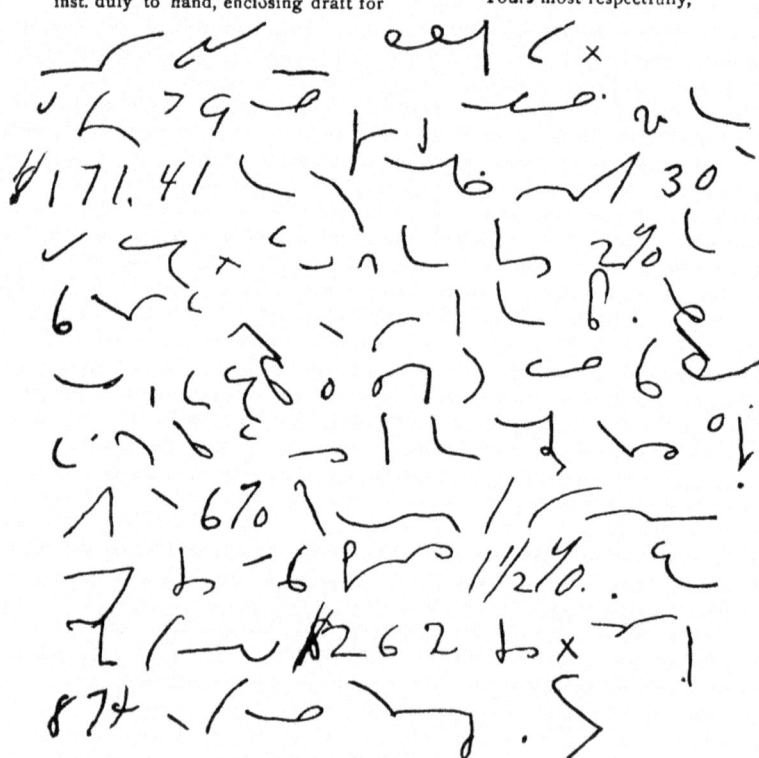

During his off hours during the baseball season, Tim Keefe taught himself the art of shorthand (illustrated above) to quickly and efficiently write down spoken words in meetings. This skill, which Keefe had hoped would lead to a lucrative post-baseball career, was the more overt reason why he was selected to be the secretary of the Brotherhood of Professional Base Ball Players. Keefe also had more intellectual contributions to the Brotherhood effort.

because the idea had been expropriated from Voltz. The Brotherhood's coming-out article in *Sporting Life* in August 1886 gave just a brief back story, without ever naming Voltz: "Last season [in 1885] a well known Philadelphia reporter, doubtless with the best intentions, made such an attempt [to organize players] and had secured the consent of a number of players, but it failed partly because, in his plan, the beneficial feature was too prominent and the protective [feature] not enough."[11]

In April or May 1885, Voltz, a former baseball writer in Cleveland, originally conceived the idea of a ballplayers' fraternity. "A movement is on foot among the professional ball-players to form a protective union. It is understood that the scheme emanated from the fertile brain of the versatile Billy Voltz, formerly of Cleveland," the *St. Louis Globe-Democrat* reported in July 1885. "Over 200 ball-players have signified their willingness to join such an association, and the plan is to assess them $5 per month, making a reserve fund of $1,000 a month, or $6,000 a season, to be used during the winter for sick and indigent subscribers to the fund."[12]

At some point before June 1885, Keefe and Ward must have met with Voltz, perhaps when Voltz tried to enlist them to be members of his fledging organization. Both players knew Voltz as a baseball writer for the *Cleveland Leader* between 1880 and 1882 when both were pitching in the National League and visited Cleveland to play its League team.[13] Voltz was at the *Cleveland Herald* in 1884, where Frank Brunell, the newspaper's chief baseball writer, seemed to have a more than casual relationship with Keefe, who was then pitching in the American Association.[14] Brunell, who later was secretary of the Players' League, printed numerous snippets in the *Cleveland Herald* about the trials and tribulations of the Metropolitan ballclub in 1884 and associated rumors about Keefe, which even the New York City newspapers didn't publish.[15] The linchpin to the Cleveland connection, whose information, which was of little interest to Cleveland readers, could only have come from Keefe, was this item in the *Cleveland Herald* in April 1884: "Tim Keefe of the Metropolitans is said to be a practical stenographer."[16] Because Cleveland did not have a team in either major league in 1885, Voltz had an overwhelming challenge to sign up ballplayers as members, so he shifted gears in June 1885 to become manager of a minor-league team. Keefe, no doubt, liked the concept and probably prodded Ward to help keep alive the nascent organization that Voltz had created.

The Brotherhood was a fraternal organization, not a labor union, which in the latter part of the nineteenth century, as Mary Ann Clawson points out in her book *Constructing Brotherhood*, was the model for "movements of every conceivable ideological stripe, as well as for literally hundreds of social organizations."[17] Masonic fraternalism, a concept imported from England to facilitate mutual aid, "exerted a special appeal to anyone seeking to establish or reaffirm a symbolic relationship to the figure of the producer-proprietor, especially as it was exemplified by the contradictory figure of the artisan ... [who] stands in a singularly problematic relationship to an emergent capitalistic order."[18] Much of the ritual of the Masonic fraternal movement related to stone masons, who were artisans that subscribed to the apprentice–journeyman–master system, to honor the way of life of a "paternalistic early capitalism ... [in which] a master craftsman as the hero of a morality play clearly affirms the dignity of labor and craft knowledge."[19]

Keefe had much clearer motivations than Ward did in making such a fraternal organization work. Keefe grew up in Somerville, Massachusetts, where his father was a carpenter. This was a trade that for centuries past had subscribed to the apprentice–journeyman–master system of progression within the craft, which ultimately led the budding apprentice to become a skilled journeyman and eventually to independence as the owner of his own shop as a master carpenter. This was roughly akin to company ownership in the industrialization era of the 1880s, but without the overbearing focus on financial gain. Keefe, himself a journeyman carpenter before becoming a professional baseball player, held onto these artisan beliefs as ruthless capitalism in the 1880s modified the basic tenet of ownership from independence to monetary gain. The former was a goal achievable by many, while the latter goal was obtainable only by a few. The carpenter's activities had two dimensions, craft and trade. The craft was the actual skills, tools, and logic of the work, while the trade was the control over the processes and products created by the craft. It was the trade aspect that led to the carpenter's independence.[20]

The motivations for Ward are far from obvious. He grew up in Bellefonte, Pennsylvania, where his father owned and operated a machine shop to make farm machinery; he was well educated, having attended a local college.[21] Because Ward grew up in a middle-class household, baseball historians have struggled to identify Ward's motivation in establishing the Brotherhood. Most have been stumped at any explanation beyond his legal training in contracts. Ward biographer Bryan Di Salvatore was blunt in his explanation: "Because his political philosophy comes to us more or less fully mature—with his newspaper and magazine articles—and because his upbringing was one, more or less, of middle-class comfort, the origins of his populist leanings—as we will call them for now—must remain a matter of speculation."[22] Geographer Robert Ross offered this explanation: "Ward's near universal reputation as one of the best, most intelligent, most honorable, and, indeed, manliest players—particularly compared to the outsider personas of journalists—must have been a strong factor in attracting such a high percentage of players to follow him. Just what influenced Ward is more difficult to discern."[23]

Whatever elements of their background moved the two men to embrace the fraternal benefits of the Brotherhood, Keefe and Ward believed in the "free labor" ideology of the time This was the glue that bound Keefe and Ward together in their efforts during the first two years of the Brotherhood. The free labor concept, advocated by the Republican Party since the days of Abraham Lincoln, called for "an open and dynamic economy that fostered economic independence for diligent and industrious farmers and workingmen."[24] By the mid–1880s, though, the Republican value of free labor had morphed into concern more for small-businessmen as the middle class became dominated by white-collar workers rather than blue-collar artisans and craftsmen as had been the case before the Civil War. By 1887 the ideology that tied together Keefe and Ward was a companion to free labor, what economists now call the "labor theory of value," which, simply put, advocates that labor creates all wealth or, alternatively, that workers are entitled to the fruits of their labor.[25]

In the Brotherhood, Keefe and Ward wanted to perpetuate the ballplayer as an artisan who was part of the middle class. However, artisans were rapidly disappearing from the middle class by 1887. During the 1880s there was an increased demarcation in urban society regarding social class into the three tiers of genteel, middle, and working beyond the previous distinction simply between manual and non-manual workers. The middle class of the 1880s was still in its formative stages, comprised mostly of businessmen, professionals, governmental workers, and a few clerical office workers, all of whom were non-manual workers. It was unclear where the remaining artisans stood, since most manual workers were shunted into the lowest social tier of the working class because their once skillful jobs were rapidly being converted into tasks performed either by machines or by unskilled workers. According to Stuart Blumin, author of *The Emergence of the Middle Class: Social Experience in the American City, 1760–1900*, the world of work had shifted from proprietors performing manual tasks to work that did not include making things but rather "buying, selling, shipping, and the managing of other people's production."[26]

While Keefe and Ward were ostensibly manual workers, though well paid, they considered themselves to be in the middle class and they wanted other major-league ballplayers to have the same prospects. The conflict facing Keefe and Ward was whether the remaining artisans in America could still aspire to middle-class status, and if so, would they be independent businessmen (under the free labor doctrine) or would they be highly paid wage-earners (partial impact of labor theory of value); otherwise the industrialization of work would doom artisans, like so many other previous craftsmen, to be lowly paid wage-earners.

The major intellectual problem that Keefe and Ward faced was the lack of an effective structural model to achieve their goals for ballplayers. The craftsman and artisan had been virtually left out of the predominant business structures in use in the late nineteenth century, which had reduced most production skills to menial wage labor. The philosophies of the two largest labor organizations of the era, the American Federation of Labor and the Knights of Labor, were of little assistance. The American Federation of Labor disavowed the artisan approach and instead focused on wages, hours, and working conditions for the wage-earner worker. This clearly was a direction that Keefe and Ward did not want to go. The Knights of Labor, while embracing the free labor ideal, focused its efforts on the cooperative approach, in which workers owned the business.

A cooperative capitalized itself by selling shares in the enterprise to cooperative workers, who earned both a fixed dividend and a share of the profits; members also had a voice in management decisions. According to labor historian Steve Leikin in his book *The Practical Utopians: American Workers and the Cooperative Movement in the Gilded Age*, "Cooperators believed that under the rubric of legitimate republican rights fell the privilege to set the price of their own labor and to receive the full value of its product ... [to be] competent citizens capable of managing their own affairs and controlling their own fate in an industrialized republic."[27] According to labor historian Gerald Grob, "Such optimism, following closely on the heels of paralyzing depression, appealed to working men, and for a brief time the vision of a new society captured the imagination of thousands of laborers."[28]

However, while the goals of the Knights of Labor were admirable, there were two big problems with the concept of the cooperative enterprise. First, the concept never advanced beyond local grocery stores and small workshops. Second, more importantly, the vast majority of cooperatives were business failures.[29] The cooperative concept experienced very few successes.

While the Players' League is often characterized as a cooperative enterprise, the Players' League was not an experiment in the ill-fated cooperative movement. If organized as a regional cooperative with non-players providing most of the capital, the league would have been doomed to failure from the start. The one substantive cooperative element to the league was that one-half of the board of directors was reserved for ballplayers; however, most of the ballplayers who served as directors were also stockholders, and thus owners, not simply workers.

It was obvious to Keefe and Ward that neither labor organization could be a template for the Brotherhood to achieve success for ballplayers. To handle the worker side of the league structure, the Brotherhood instead latched onto an alternative concept gaining traction during the mid–1880s—profit sharing—to incorporate into the structure of the Players' League.

Between Keefe and Ward, Keefe was the likely proponent for the profit-sharing concept. Given his ties to the Boston area and his thirst for knowledge, Keefe surely was familiar with the rise of the profit-sharing idea in Boston as well as the many high-profile failures of cooperative enterprises in the Boston area. "Co-operation, whether in production or distribution, needs but to be better understood and its advantages appreciated, to be more generally adopted," the *Boston Globe* wrote in an 1888 editorial. "Profit sharing, now not infrequent, is a step in the right direction. It is likely to become far more common as a safeguard against strikes and other labor disturbances."[30]

Profit sharing was a nascent movement in the mid–1880s, in which business owners shared profits with workers without requiring them to be owners, as in a cooperative. The profit-sharing movement began in America in 1884 following the publication of the book *Profit Sharing* written by Sedley Taylor. The movement gained momentum during the next few years, especially in Keefe's home state of Massachusetts, when in 1889 Nicholas Gilman wrote his treatise *Profit Sharing Between Employer and Employee*.

"Of the schemes that filled the vacuum left by the cooperative movement, profit sharing came the closest to a lineal relationship, both in its formula and in the enthusiasm it generated among the middle-class moralists," historian Daniel Rodgers wrote. "It was, in fact, cooperation split in half in a Solomon-like judgment; dismissing cooperative management as unworkable, the plan proposed to transform wage employment by the more limited device of adding to the wage earner's pay a share in the joint profits."[31] Terming this structure to be an "industrial partnership," Gilman wrote in the spring of 1889 that he believed profit sharing "to be the most satisfying and equitable adjustment of the relations of capital and labor, to remove the discontent that is now agitating the industrial world."[32]

Although it wasn't a perfect structure to meet the needs of the Brotherhood, profit sharing was the best available concept in 1889, when planning for the Players' League began in earnest. "Between 1886 and 1889, when profit-sharing articles could be found everywhere in the middle-class press, some thirty firms installed profit-sharing plans," Rodgers wrote about the concept's acceptance, with "the Proctor and Gamble soap-works outside Cincinnati the most prominent among them."[33] Much like the Players' League, though, profit sharing soon collapsed as a viable tool, as "profit sharing staggered under its heavy burden of hopes."[34]

While the free labor and labor theory of value ideals were enough to keep Keefe and Ward on the same page during the first few years of the Brotherhood, these concepts eventually drove a wedge between the two men. By 1888 they had divergent opinions on the top priority for the Brotherhood. That was two years into the future in 1886, when the two men were focused on expanding membership in the Brotherhood beyond just the players on the New York Giants.

11

Strategic Pitcher with League-Leading 42 Wins

New Orleans had served Tim Keefe well during the winter of 1880 and did so once again during his two-month stay there in the late autumn of 1885, when Giants manager Jim Mutrie organized a team to play a series at the North Central & South American Exposition against the St. Louis Browns of the American Association.[1]

Mutrie's team was a last-minute replacement, after League champion Chicago had backed out of its commitment following the disputed ending to the 1885 World Series between Chicago and American Association champion St. Louis. The unanticipated excursion to New Orleans was a huge balm for Keefe, who pitched for the Giants on November 17 in the opening game of what would be a five-game series. He pitched again in the third game on Sunday, November 22.

Before an overflow crowd of 8,000 people, Keefe lost the Sunday game, 3–2, in a close match with St. Louis. While Keefe was familiar with the crowds that assembled to watch Sunday baseball from his Association days, this was a new experience for many of his Giants teammates. In its account of the game, the *New Orleans Times-Picayune* captured not only the excitement but also the social implications of Sunday baseball, by reporting that baseball's "popularity with all classes was demonstrated by the crowd ... wealth and position fraternized with the humblest of workers for the time being."[2] The final game with St. Louis was played on the following Sunday, November 29, when Keefe finally pitched the Giants to victory.

When Mutrie and Buck Ewing returned to New York City at the end of the St. Louis series, Keefe and the remainder of the Giants stayed in New Orleans to operate the team, joining up with Doc Bushong and other members of the Browns who also stayed. The reconstituted Giants played another series at the Exposition against a Louisville team comprised mostly of players from the Eclipse ballclub of the Association, but augmented by Louisville native Fred Pfeffer who was the second baseman of the League's Chicago team. This

New Orleans series provided the setting for Keefe, Bushong, and Pfeffer to exchange thoughts that would three years later result in their collaboration on a book about strategic baseball, published under the title *Scientific Ball*.

The series with Louisville also gave Keefe the opportunity to work individually with Bushong, which had been so useful to Keefe when they first met in New Orleans during the winter of 1880 as part of Frank Bancroft's touring team. In 1880 those sessions had helped Keefe to convert from being a mediocre pitcher into a first-class pitcher. Bushong may have also helped Keefe during the late fall of 1885 as well. Bushong wrote the catching section of *Scientific Ball*, where he devoted a lot of space to signs with the pitcher. "All pitchers and catchers have a system of signs by which they have a perfect understanding with each other about what kind of ball is to be delivered," Bushong wrote, with the pitcher "allowing the catcher to make the signs, but reserving the right to give the sign of refusal, using his own judgment as to whether the ball delivered should be high or low, in or out."[3] The work with Bushong may have resulted in Keefe devising a better sign system with his New York catchers, which cut down on the number of his pitches that eluded the catcher, thus serving to improve his overall pitching performance.

Keefe returned to Boston in January 1886. "His arm troubled him somewhat down South, but he anticipates no trouble next season," one writer reported. "He will favor his arm for the rest of the loafing season, and will go into the gymnasium early in the spring."[4] Keefe had no publicly reported problem with Giants president John Day to sign for the 1886 season, in the second year of his $3,000-per-year salary deal, so they must have concocted a way to evade the League's stipulated $2,000 salary cap. One of the directors of the Giants, Walter Appleton, was reported visiting Keefe in Boston during January, where the writer noted that Appleton "will do a little business with the twirler on the quiet."[5] One alleged ruse to get around the League's salary cap, as described by Buck Ewing's biographer, was to have Mutrie pay an inflated value for Ewing's shirt after the catcher had signed to play for the $2,000 limit.[6] There was no report of what Appleton offered Keefe to stay within the bounds of the League rule.

At the League meeting in March, the ballclub owners actually encouraged the hop-step-and-jump delivery for the 1886 season by inexplicably lengthening the pitcher's box, from six feet to seven feet, to give the pitcher more room to move around. However, as the *New York Clipper* fumed in its report of the meeting, "The League did nothing to punish the pitcher for hitting batsmen with pitched balls, and so this will be a point for League pitchers to play this season."⁷

The hop-step-and-jump delivery assisted Keefe to his enormous success during the 1886 season, when he won a career-high 42 victories to lead the National League. "The batters had a tough time in those days, especially in the era of the hop, step and jump," Keefe recalled in his later years. "We were pitching from a 50-foot distance then, and honestly, I sometimes used to wonder how they ever hit us, with those advantages which we had."⁸ As a mature strategic pitcher, Keefe used the availability of the hop-step-and-jump delivery to give him psychological ammunition to baffle batters.

However, Keefe never said that he used the hop-step-and-jump delivery, only that it was overpowering. In April 1886 the *New York Sun* gave a detailed comparison of the deliveries of the two pitchers for the Giants. The writer described Keefe as doing "very little moving in the [pitcher's] box, and when delivering the ball he does it without an effort." In contrast, Welch used "movements [that] are always watched with care, as he keeps continually dancing about, so that it is never known when he intends to pitch."⁹ With Mickey Welch the only Giants pitcher who used the hop-step-and-jump delivery, batters were off balance the next game when Keefe pitched with his easy motion.

In addition to his distinct difference in forward motion compared to Welch, Keefe had an enormous number of other advantages in the pitcher's box. With his multiplicity of pitching combinations, batters were constantly mystified at how Keefe would deliver the ball once as he approached the front line of the box 50 feet from the plate. He threw half a dozen types of pitches, used several different arm motions (sidearm to overhand), positioned himself from a number of different angles toward home plate within the four-foot-wide box, and threw consistently at waist height which could be a called strike in either of the two strike zones chosen by the batter (high or low). He could also waste a number of outside pitches to entice the batter to swing at a bad pitch, since six called balls were required before a batter was awarded a base on balls. He could pitch inside with impunity, since a ball hitting the batter was just another called ball. When he combined these alternatives with his observed knowledge of each batter's strengths and weaknesses, Keefe had a substantial advantage over batters.

References to his "clever pitching" abounded to describe Keefe in 1886. He was now clearly a master at his craft. One writer even wrote about "Keefe's splendid strategic delivery, his pitching being masterly."¹⁰ However, at the beginning of the 1886 season, Mickey Welch, not Keefe, was the number one pitcher for the Giants; by the end of the season, though, Keefe was unquestionably the ace of the Giants' pitching staff.

The National League played a 126-game schedule in 1886, up from 112 games in 1885. While the owners added 14 games, they didn't lengthen the time frame of the season, but instead squeezed the extra games into the same 24-week period as in 1885. The result was fewer open days, for travel and rest, and more days where the players were required to play a doubleheader to make up postponed games.

Mutrie fielded the same lineup in 1886 as he had the prior year, and once again used Keefe and Welch as a two-man pitching rotation. The only difference was the addition of another utility player, Larry Corcoran. However, most teams now used a three-man strategy to staff the pitcher's box in order to more efficiently utilize pitching arms. New York did not adopt that strategy, though, as Keefe and Welch started all but one game for the Giants that season. Chicago used a three-man staff of John Clarkson, Jim McCormick, and John Flynn to capture its second consecutive pennant in 1886.

Also hurting New York's chances were injuries to Ewing, who missed more than 50 games. When he did play, he was the catcher in only 50 of his 73 games, playing in the other games as an outfielder. Tom Deasley caught 30 games, but Jim O'Rourke had to be pressed into service behind the plate for 47 games. Mutrie also used several other recruits to fill in at catcher as needed. The merry-go-round at catcher didn't faze Keefe, but it seemed to affect Welch, who had a sub-par season with a 33–22 record.

The season started auspiciously for the Giants on Opening Day, April 29, when a crowd of 11,946 filed through the turnstiles at the Polo Grounds to watch the Giants play Boston. "The grand stand was packed, every seat, chair, step, and railing was occupied," one newspaper described the scene, as "late comers were forced to go out on the field, where they formed a horseshoe and stood in the sun." As a band escorted the Giants from their clubhouse in the southwest corner of the grounds, John Ward led the team onto the field, followed by "the gigantic Connor, tall and lanky Gillespie, pretty Keefe, and modest looking Gerhardt" and the rest of the team.[11]

Both teams posed for a photograph before the game in front of the grandstand at the Polo Grounds. This appears to be the first team photo ever taken of the New York Giants. The nature of the spectator crowd is clear, all men wearing dark suits and bowler hats. The uniform worn by the Giants was plain, white shirt with lacing down the front, white pants, and dark stockings. The photographer, from the F.L. Howe Studio, "was compelled to take several plates, and the delay was annoying to the spectators," the *New York Times*

11. Strategic Pitcher with League-Leading 42 Wins

Following the 1886 season-opening win by the New York Giants, Jim O'Rourke (foreground) and John Ward (background) were carried off the field on the shoulders of spectators in a celebratory scene captured on the front page of the May 8, 1886, issue of *Frank Leslie's Illustrated Newspaper*. Publicity such as this elevated the Giants to celebrity status in New York City, just at the time that Tim Keefe began to hit his stride as a strategic pitcher.

reported, adding that one impatient fan yelled, "Three strikes, photographer's out."[12]

The overflow crowd saw a great game, as Welch pitched the Giants to victory over Boston in an 11-inning thriller. The Giants won the game in the bottom of the 11th inning when Ward singled, went to third base on Gerhardt's double, and scored on O'Rourke's fly ball to center field. "The spectators shouted themselves hoarse, staid business men seemed to forget their years and yelled as loudly as the small boys," the *Times* reported. "Young men whose voices had given out made up the deficiency by rapping on the floor of the grand stand with their canes, and for a few moments it looked as though the people would go frantic with joy."[13] Spectators carried O'Rourke and Ward off the field on their shoulders in a celebration captured in a woodcut that ran on the front page of *Frank Leslie's Illustrated Newspaper*.[14]

Before a less raucous crowd at the Polo Grounds the next day, Keefe secured his first victory of the 1886 season, when he limited Boston to six hits in a 10–2 win. Keefe had three hits (single, double, and triple) to help power the offense.

On May 10 the team left on a two-week road to four cities. By May 18, the Giants had settled into third place, where they would remain for the rest of the season and never seriously challenge for the pennant. More importantly on the road trip, Keefe and Ward signed up new members of the Brotherhood in all four cities. Keefe recorded in his ledger that seven players signed up in Detroit, six in Kansas City, nine in St. Louis, but only three in Chicago.[15] Given that the Haymarket riot by striking union workers had occurred in Chicago just two weeks before the Giants arrived, it was not surprising that Chicago players were skittish about joining the Brotherhood. Fred Pfeffer and Ned Williamson joined the Brotherhood; Keefe noted that Mike Kelly joined later in the season.

Back home at the Polo Grounds for a Decoration Day twin bill on May 31 (since May 30 was a Sunday), 7,000 people watched Keefe defeat first-place Detroit in the morning game and a record crowd of 20,000 attended the afternoon game. By noon time, several thousand people had amassed outside the three normal entrances to the Polo Grounds, causing Day to open the carriage and employee entrances to accommodate paying customers for the afternoon game. "When the time finally arrived for the players to don their uniforms and begin the conflict," the *New York Times* reported, "they found the diamond occupied by the surging mass ... [and] could not find standing room, let alone take their positions on the field."[16] A platoon of policemen on foot and another three dozen on horses had to be summoned to move back the enormous crowd to make room on the field for the ballplayers. In a game marred by the ground rule that a ball hit into the outfield crowd was just a single, New York, behind the pitching of Welch, lost, 4–1.

As the crowds for Opening Day and the Decoration Day holiday demonstrated, "the Giants were not only popular, they now had become fashionable," historian James Hardy wrote in his book *The New York Giants Base Ball Club*.[17] Keefe and his teammates were celebrities in New York City. The Opening Day woodcut on the front page of *Frank Leslie's Illustrated Newspaper*, a weekly publication for an upper-income readership, was just the beginning of the public adulation for the New York Giants in 1886.

Photographer John Wood shot individual photos of Mutrie and the 13 players on the Giants. Wood converted these photos into cabinet cards and packaged them for sale. This set contains the oldest known photograph of Keefe. The Wood photographs also served as the basis for many line-drawing illustrations of the Giants, which were published in newspapers across the country, such as the syndicated article "Nine Nimble Twirlers" that featured Keefe and Welch.[18] A July edition of *Frank Leslie's Illustrated Newspaper* contained an entire page of sketches of the Giants players.[19]

The Wood photos also found their way onto pieces of cardboard that were used as the backing for packages of Old Judge cigarettes, produced by Goodwin & Company, a New York City tobacco firm.[20] These 1886 Old Judge cards are typically recognized as the first true set of baseball trading cards, which cigarette makers used to increase demand for their product in the ruthless marketing battle for smokers during the 1880s.[21] The Old Judge cards seemingly came about through a business connection in the tobacco industry between Goodwin and Giants owner John Day, who was a wholesale dealer in tobacco leaves used for cigar wrappers.

The New York Giants were also a focus of two new baseball publications based in New York City. The *Official Record* was a daily paper devoted to baseball, published by June Rankin, the official scorer of the Giants' games at the Polo Grounds and baseball writer for the *New York Herald*.[22] The *Sporting Times* was a weekly paper, owned by Day and Mutrie, which employed former newspaper writers Peter Donohue of the *New York World* and Jim Kennedy of the *New York Times*, who had provided extensive coverage of the New York League team in its first three years in the city.[23]

Since most of the ballplayers lived downtown and had to travel uptown to the Polo Grounds, a former Giants batboy remembered that they would travel there "in an open, horse-drawn carriage to the resounding cheers of the fans who lined the streets."[24]

At some point during his tenure with the New York Giants, perhaps as early as 1886, Keefe began to live at the Grand Central Hotel, located at 673

The New York Giants pose in front of the grandstand at the Polo Grounds for this photograph taken at the season-opening game in 1886. Tim Keefe is in the middle row, seated third from the right. Also in the middle row are manager Jim Mutrie, in street clothes, and John Ward to the immediate right of Mutrie. Sitting in front of Mutrie and Ward is Mickey Welch, who teamed with Keefe as the team's pitching staff for the 1886 season (Library of Congress, Prints and Photographs Division, LC-USZ62-11348).

Broadway near Third Street, which was more urbane than the mundane Harlem House located far uptown on 115th Street where Keefe had first lived. The 10-story Grand Central Hotel was one of the first apartment hotels, offering "its permanent boarders suites of a parlor, bedroom, and closet," with a shared bathroom on each floor, which Elizabeth Cromley, author of *Alone Together: A History of New York's Early Apartments*, termed "lavish surroundings on a moderate budget."[25] These early bachelor flats provided affluent single men with a "multiple-room setting that combined the features of an apartment with those of a boarding house," such as maid and laundry services as well as common meals in a downstairs restaurant plus common rooms to entertain guests.[26] The Grand Central Hotel was much farther from the Polo Grounds than the Harlem House was, but it was closer to the theater district and more convenient for the evening and Sunday activities that Keefe was interested in.

Because New York state law and the National League constitution prohibited the playing of professional baseball games on Sunday, Keefe had the day off every Sunday while a member of the Giants. While he left no indications of how he observed this day of rest, his Sir Timothy demeanor provides a few clues as to what he likely did on Sundays.

Keefe could have attended mass on Sunday morning at St. Patrick's Cathedral, which had opened in 1879. Since the Catholic cathedral was located on Fifth Avenue at 50th Street, Keefe might have walked the four dozen blocks for exercise rather than spend the fare for a horse-drawn cab ride.

After mass, a carriage ride in nearby Central Park would have been a popular choice, since the roads within the expansive green space were designed for horse-drawn carriages of the city's elite, or "the great rendezvous of the polite world," as Roy Rosenzweig and Elizabeth Blackmar termed it in their book *The Park and the People: A History of Central Park*.[27] Only the rich could afford to stable their own horses and garage their own carriages, but Keefe could have easily rented a horse-drawn carriage for the late morning at the rate of $1 per hour at one of the many livery stables located near the park. Keefe later did own his own coach and team of horses.[28]

After lunch, he likely read the Sunday edition of the *New York World*, either purchasing his own copy or reading it at the New York Mercantile Library, which was open on Sundays. Entertainment options for the afternoon included a band concert in Central Park or a boat ride to view the recently erected Statue of Liberty on an island in New York Harbor.

In the evening, after dinner, Keefe likely attended a lecture at one of the many halls near the Grand Central Hotel, such as at the Cooper Union, or read a magazine in his hotel room. Keefe was a voracious reader. "Keefe has by no means allowed his mind to run to seed through the over-cultivation of his body," one writer described him. "He has always been a good deal of a reader of solid books of information and he has added to his early school education a wide command of general and valuable information."[29] Some of the more popular magazines of the day that published articles about issues impacting the country were *Literary Digest*, "a forerunner to *Time* and *Newsweek* in general news analysis," *Lippincott's*, and *Scribner's*; *Harper's Weekly* was also popular among educated and upper-middle-class readers for its combination of writing and illustrations.[30]

If the weather was warm, he might take the train to Coney Island in Brooklyn for an overnight stay at one of the upscale hotels there. The Manhattan Beach Hotel, at the more fashionable east end of the island, "was a bastion of the very rich," and the adjacent Brighton Beach Hotel "was patronized by the middle classes," both sufficiently segregated from the island's middle zone that "attracted working-class daily excursionists" and Norton's Point on the west end that had an "unsavory reputation as a resort of the underclasses."[31]

He could also have taken a day trip to watch some illicit Sunday baseball played by the Brooklyn team in the American Association, which staged its games on Sunday at Ridgewood Park in Queens. While the mores of influential Brooklyn residents forestalled the evasion of state law within the Brooklyn city limits, the population of the small towns in Queens County (and its police force) was more accommodating.[32] Brooklyn's Sunday games at Ridgewood Park attracted some of the largest crowds to watch a ballgame in the New York City area.

Keefe was least likely to be found at more lowbrow events, such as Buffalo Bill Cody's Wild West Show, or at all-male retreats like Nick Engel's saloon, on West 27th Street near Broadway, a tavern that was frequented by many ballplayers.[33]

In July Keefe and Ward finished their initial canvassing of the ballplayers on the other seven League teams, signing up 16 players in Boston, eight players in Philadelphia, and three in Washington.[34] They then decided to go public to announce the existence of the Brotherhood, using the pages of *Sporting Life*, courtesy of editor Francis Richter, to publish an article written by a friend of Ward.

In the article, Ward focused on the protective elements of the Brotherhood, but stopped short of espousing rebellion. Concerning the reserve list, Ward said, "I believe a majority of ball players regard the reserve rule as a necessary institution, though they may consider that some abuses have arisen under it." As for the salary limit, Ward thought it "already a practical nullity," but used the issue to launch into the problems of the basic contract between ballclub owner and ballplayer: "A great majority of the cases in which players are unfairly treated arise, not from the reserve rule or salary limit, but from a contract which legally is injustice—a contract in which the parties of the one part sign away all rights, and the party of the other 'reserves' all." Ward simply wanted a fair contract "in which the equities of each might be reasonably protected."[35]

Keefe also did some interviews following the publication of Ward's comments in August 1886. Keefe focused on the human aspects and building a foundation that the Brotherhood was organized to help, not hurt, the game:

> The brotherhood was formed with the intention of fostering and elevating the game of base ball. This we can do by conferences with the League officials and by disciplining players who behave themselves improperly. For instance, a player who becomes intoxicated will be liable to a fine from the brotherhood, as well as from his club.... We do not propose to work antagonistic to the League, and expect to do all we can toward bringing about improvements in the playing rules. Our influence will also extend to players unjustly treated by clubs of the League.... In these cases we shall ask for satisfactory treatment, and that being refused, we shall be obliged to resort to extreme measures.[36]

This photograph of 29-year-old Tim Keefe was shot in 1886 by photographer John Wood, who took individual photographs of all the ballplayers on the New York Giants. These Wood photographs served as the basis for one of the first sets of baseball tobacco cards, which were distributed in packages of Old Judge cigarettes produced by Goodwin & Company (Library of Congress, Prints and Photographs Division, LC-USZ62-138723).

While Keefe did not define "extreme measures," he had set in motion the actions the Brotherhood would take three years later.

One victory by Keefe in 1886 came at an emotional cost, when he hit Jack Burdock in the head with a pitch in Boston on August 12. "The third ball Keefe sent in with awful speed. Burdock couldn't get away from it and it caromed off the left side of his face with frightful force," the *Boston Globe* described the scene. "As a result he was knocked clean out and was led from the field with the blood streaming from his face."[37] Keefe no doubt had a genuine human concern for Burdock, as did his catcher that day, O'Rourke, who during the winter was pursuing a law degree at Yale College.[38]

Despite later claims by chroniclers of Keefe's life, he did not suffer a nervous breakdown following the Burdock incident.[39] Keefe remained in the game after Burdock was taken off the field. He threw out the next batter on a grounder hit to him, and pitched the Giants to an 8–1 victory. He didn't miss his turn in the pitcher's box, pitching two days later in another game against Boston. The *New York Clipper* reported "Keefe felt very badly over the matter, and offered to pay for all needed medical attention."[40]

The Giants suffered through a nine-game losing streak from August 30 to September 8, which included three to Detroit and four to Chicago, who were battling neck-and-neck for first place. After losing two games, one in the morning and the other in the afternoon, to Chicago on September 8, all hope for the pennant evaporated for the Giants.

On October 9, the last day of the regular season, Keefe won his 42nd game against sixth-place St. Louis at the Polo Grounds, in a five-inning contest shortened to allow St. Louis to catch a train back to St. Louis. It was Dude Esterbrook's last game with the Giants. Keefe's partner in the Bermuda ruse to transfer from the Metropolitans to the Giants was not included on the team's reserve list released by the League on October 13.

The Giants finished with a 75–44 record, in third place, behind pennant-winning Chicago. Keefe compiled a 42–20 mark in the pitcher's box. Since Mutrie used just a two-man pitching rotation in 1886, Keefe pitched more often than pitchers on other teams, so he led the National League in several pitching categories, including wins (42), innings pitched (535), and complete games (62). He was third in strikeouts with 297.

Keefe surpassed Welch during the 1886 season to become the ace of the Giants pitching staff. One reason was Ewing's part-time status in 1886. When he was healthy enough to catch, Ewing typically caught Welch while Keefe worked with O'Rourke and Deasley. Ewing had been Welch's battery mate for the previous five seasons, dating back to their days in Troy. Unlike Keefe, though, Welch seemed rattled without Ewing as his backstop. After Welch lost one game when Ewing couldn't play, the *New York Times* reported: "The everlasting smile for which he is famous has been missing during the past few games, and his work has lacked the vim and determination that made him a favorite on the Polo Grounds."[41]

Another reason why Welch was surpassed by Keefe was the financial concern that burdened Welch, which didn't allow him mentally to focus on pitching. Not only was Welch supporting a wife and children back home in Holyoke, Massachusetts, but he had also invested in a saloon there.[42] Money concerns had led Welch to hold out in April for a salary advance, which Day was prohibited from granting him, so Welch did not join the Giants until April 23, less than one week before the start of the season.[43] Welch had not prepared himself properly to weather the long playing season.

Keefe made sure not to replicate those mistakes in the future. He took great pains to keep his right arm in shape, enjoyed being a bachelor, and was frugal with his money. The latter was one reason why Keefe was now the treasurer of the Brotherhood in addition to his position as secretary.[44] During the 1886 season, rather than make a risky investment as Welch had in a saloon, Keefe made a more modest investment in real estate.

12

Land Owner in Cambridge

On July 26, 1886, Tim Keefe purchased three-quarters of an acre of land in Cambridge, Massachusetts, on the northern side of Cambridge Street, between Irving Street and Trowbridge Street. Keefe bought the 29,950 square feet of land from Mary Brown, of Baltimore, Maryland, who had inherited several acres of undeveloped land following the death of her first husband, Horatio Preston, in 1878. She subdivided the inherited land into small lots, hoping to sell it to people looking to erect individual houses. There were four house lots on the land that Keefe purchased.[1]

Keefe had consummated the deal on July 3, when the New York Giants were playing in Chicago, but didn't sign the paperwork until he was back in New York City on July 23. Signaling a change in his attitude about living in the Boston area, the land deed was made out to "Timothy J. Keefe of New York." After he signed in the presence of a justice of the peace, the papers were filed on July 26 at the Middlesex South Registry of Deeds in Cambridge.[2]

Keefe paid $5,614.50 for the land, $2,000 in cash with the remainder in a mortgage taken back by the seller for a one-year period, with five percent interest payable semi-annually.[3] Less than five months later, Keefe paid not only the first interest payment but also the entire principal value of the mortgage to own the land free and clear.[4]

At the time she sold the land to Keefe, Mary Brown was the wife of Frank Brown, whom she had married in 1879, a little more than one year after the death of her first husband.[5] Frank Brown was then campaign treasurer of the Democratic State Central Committee in Maryland, in addition to overseeing his family's country estate outside of Baltimore. A few years later, in 1892, Frank Brown would be elected governor of Maryland.[6]

To Keefe, the land purchase was a sign that he had reached middle-class status. To his parents, who were born in Ireland, it was a real cause for celebration. As Jay Dolan explained in *The Irish Americans: A History*, "In Ireland, owning one's own home was but a dream for most Irish ... [who were] driven from the land by famine and hard-hearted [English] landlords."[7] Such a purchase was not all that easy to accomplish in America in the late nineteenth century either. Keefe had to be thrifty in order to save enough money for the down payment on the house, since banks at that time generally required at least one-half of the sale price to be in cash in order to issue a mortgage loan for the remainder of the purchase price. Keefe also had to be wise with his money to maintain an exemplary credit status, because banks would only issue mortgage loans for short periods of time, from one to three years. A borrower needed to be creditworthy so that the mortgage could be refinanced at the end of its term if the entire principal couldn't be repaid.

In February 1888, Keefe transferred ownership of the land on Cambridge Street to his 19-year-old sister Annie.[8] Such a transfer was a common transaction in the late nineteenth century, which served to protect the man's property from the liens of his creditors by having it technically owned by a trusted woman. Often, this would be a transaction between husband and wife. Since Keefe wasn't yet married, he chose his youngest sister. Putting his real estate property in the name of his sister indicates that Keefe was planning to open a business, where the threat of owing money to creditors was a real risk.

Keefe's property on Cambridge Street was one-quarter mile east from Harvard College, one and a quarter miles west from his family home outside Inman Square, and across the street from the Rindge estate, which was owned by Frederick Rindge, following the death of his father, Samuel, in 1883. The undeveloped area bordering both sides of Cambridge Street seemed to be prime territory for development. It seemed to be a good investment for Keefe, as the land appeared ripe for a substantial increase in value within the next few years.

Less than a year after Keefe purchased the land on Cambridge Street, Frederick Rindge donated some of his land opposite Keefe's property to the city of Cambridge so that the city could build a public library. In a letter to Mayor William Russell in June 1887, Frederick Rindge wrote: "Dear Sir: It would make me happy to give to the city of Cambridge the tract of land bounded by Cambridge, Trowbridge, Broadway, and Irving Streets in the city of Cambridge and to build thereon and give to said city a Public Library building."[9] Four months later Rindge donated more land to the city, this time for a high school building and a manual training school, if the city could acquire adjoining land to allow sufficient space for the two buildings.[10] Construction on all three buildings began in 1888, but, unfortunately for Keefe, the city planners decided not to expand north of Cambridge Street to acquire land for either Cambridge English High School or the Cambridge Manual Training School for Boys.

There was no quick sale of Keefe's Cambridge Street property to reap a profit due to the proposed public construction projects across the street. When the public library was completed in 1889, the building was surrounded by a grass park, providing a soothing view from Keefe's land. He would have to settle for future development of the land, along the lines of a December 1887 newspaper report that "he owns some profitable real estate in Cambridge, Mass., and intends to build a home there for the future Mrs. Keefe."[11] Keefe did build a home on the property a few years later and Mrs. Keefe did live there, but it was his mother, not his wife.

Now that Keefe owned land in Cambridge, the phrase "from Cambridge" that the newspapers often attributed to Keefe had a larger element of truth to it, since he continued to live in the family home in neighboring Somerville when he visited Boston. In March 1888 the *Cambridge Tribune* published a short article about professional ballplayers from the city, naming Keefe along with John Clarkson, Barney Gilligan, Gid Gardner, and Walter Hackett.[12]

Keefe encouraged the New York City newspapers to write that he was "from Cambridge" to give him a more prestigious provenance, since most people outside of Boston equated Cambridge with Harvard College. For example, the *New York World* wrote in April 1888 that "Tim Keefe left for his home in Cambridge, Mass."[13] Occasionally, when *Boston Globe* sports editor Sullivan was involved, there would be some inconsistencies, since Sullivan and Keefe both lived in Somerville. "On his arrival [in Boston] Keefe at once visited his home, No. 54 Springfield Street, Somerville, where a representative of the *Evening World* [Sullivan] sought in vain to interview him," the *World* reported the next day.[14] Sometimes the reporting reached hyperbolic proportions: "Keefe came into life near the classic shades of Harvard College, in the

T. J. KEEFE, PITCHER.

This picture of Tim Keefe appeared in the July 10, 1886, issue of *Frank Leslie's Illustrated Newspaper*, along with pictures of the other New York Giants. This was part of the ballclub's publicity campaign to enhance the popularity of the team with upper-income residents of New York City, which Giants president John Day courted to attend ballgames at the Polo Grounds.

old town of Cambridge, Mass., in the year 1858 [sic]. He received a liberal education in the schools of that city."[15]

The Cambridge connection also helped to fuel a friendly rivalry with Cambridge native Clarkson, who grew up on Rockwell Street in the southern part of Cambridgeport.[16] The Clarkson home was two miles from the Keefe home in Somerville, which was just north of the Cambridge city line that separated Somerville from northern Cambridgeport. Clarkson was the oldest of five baseball-playing sons of jeweler Thomas Clarkson and his wife Ellen. His brothers Arthur and Walter would go on to play major-league baseball (Walter was the first Harvard College baseball player to disavow the amateur nature of sport at Harvard and turn professional before graduation). Henry and Frederick played high-school baseball at Cambridge High and Latin and later in the semipro ranks.

When Clarkson began to pitch for the Boston team in the National League in 1888, local fans would crowd into the South End Grounds when Keefe was matched up against Clarkson. The first such pitching duel occurred on June 21, 1888, when Clarkson propelled Boston to a 4–2 victory over Keefe and his New York Giants. As the *Boston Globe* reported, "Timothy Keefe, the twirler from the varsity city, bowed down to the delivery of his varsity friend on the Boston side, and hit the air," when Clarkson struck out Keefe at bat.[17]

Owning property in Cambridge was definitely good for Keefe as he prepared for the 1887 baseball season, which would propel him to national fame as a strategic pitcher.

13

Adapting to Numerous Pitching Rule Changes

The significant overbalance of pitching to batting during the 1886 season led the National League ballclub owners to consider substantial changes in the playing rules for the 1887 season. To discuss potential rule changes, the owners invited several ballplayers to their joint League-Association conference committee meeting in Chicago in November 1886, including John Ward of the Giants (as a ballplayer, not as president of the Brotherhood), Cap Anson of Chicago, and John Morrill of Boston.

One rule change that Ward proposed was to have the pitcher stand in the box facing the batter, with his left foot in front of his right foot, and to the left of an imaginary straight line to home plate, with the right foot to remain on the ground during the pitcher's delivery. "Today the successful pitcher is the man who takes a hop, skip, and a jump and makes the ball whiz past your face with the speed of the wind. If this thing continues it will be necessary to have a surgeon and coroner on every diamond," Ward said before leaving for Chicago. "These changes will bring back the old style of delivery, increase the batting and base running, and, in a word, increase the popularity of the game."[1]

This proposed change the pitching rules seemed to be crafted by Tim Keefe, secretary of the Brotherhood, since he believed that brains, not brawn, should be the foundation of pitching. "The retrogression of the hop, skip and jump pitching again placed a premium on brute strength. All it demanded to be an effective pitcher was plenty of speed and strength and a series of gymnastics to terrify the batter; no science whatever was required," Keefe wrote two years later. "The natural result, before the [1886] season was finished, was that very few batters could pick out a good ball to hit, and the pitcher had the batter completely at his mercy."[2]

While the owners adopted the Brotherhood's pitching suggestion, they also added the requirement that the pitcher keep one foot on the back line of the pitcher's box when delivering the ball to the batter. They shortened the length of the pitcher's box by a foot and a half, reducing its length from seven feet to five and a half feet. Most importantly, the owners mandated that "only one step" could be taken by the pitcher, thus outlawing the hop-skip-and-jump delivery.[3] Before the 1887 season began, one umpire attempted to condense the new pitching rules into one concise paragraph:

> In the first place the pitcher will have to face the batter. That means that the body and face must practically front the batsman. For instance, in the case of a right-handed pitcher, he will stand with his right foot on the rear line of his position. This, you will observe, will enable him to stand in a three-quarter position and yet show the umpire and batsman his whole front. This is what the umpire will exact. The ball, too must be in plain sight all the time. It cannot be hidden behind the back or upon the hip. Of course the pitcher will swing his arm back before the last motion is made to deliver the ball. This will be allowable, but when the ball is delivered both feet must be upon the ground. The pitcher can step forward one step in delivering the ball. And he can even be out of his box after the ball has finally left his hand and his delivery is completed without incurring a penalty.[4]

In effect, the new rule changes moved the pitcher farther from the batter when he delivered the ball. During the 1886 season, the pitcher released the ball at the front line of the box, which was 50 feet from the plate. In 1887 the pitcher released the ball about 53 feet from the plate, give or take a few inches depending on the pitcher's stride, since his back foot had to remain on the back line of the box, which was 55 and a half feet from the plate.

Other new rules for the 1887 season included increasing the number of called strikes for a strikeout from three to four, reducing the number of called balls for a walk from six to five, having one common strike zone for all batters between the knees and the shoulder (eliminating the option for the batter to call for a high or low strike zone), and putting the batter on first base when hit by a pitch. Additionally, batters were credited with a base hit if they received a walk and a balk was called on pitchers who, while in position to pitch, attempted to pick off a baserunner or otherwise attempted to deceive the runner (eliminating feints by pitchers).[5]

Keefe told the baseball writers that December that he didn't believe the new pitching rules would bother him that much. There was one rule, though, that Keefe disliked especially. "I don't think well of the new rule where a pitcher is allowed but five balls and a batter four strikes," Keefe said, "but I suppose I can get used to it." As for the new hit batsman rule being intended for him, he laughed and replied, "I have no fear of that rule; it won't bother me in the least."[6]

As he had done several times in his major-league career, Keefe started adapting to the newly promulgated rules over the winter. For 1887 he experimented with modifying his delivery to conform to the new pitching rules by resuming his college coaching duties. During the winter of 1887, Keefe coached the baseball team at Williams College in western Massachusetts.[7] Keefe sensed that the extra two or three feet of pitching distance would make a substantial difference in pitching results during the 1887 season, just as he had experienced six years earlier when an extra five feet was added to the pitching distance for the 1881 season.

Because Keefe was in the third year of his three-year salary deal with the Giants, the integrity-minded pitcher didn't haggle with owner John Day to increase in his salary for 1887 above the previously agreed-upon $3,000 level. However, seeking to obtain some reward for his fabulous 1886 season when he won 42 games for the Giants, Keefe did procrastinate a bit in signing his contract for the upcoming season. He sought the same deal that Day had given Mickey Welch the previous three seasons, to have a personal contract with Day, rather than the standard contract with the ballclub; the personal contract guaranteed payment of his salary whether or not the pitcher was healthy or injured. Day refused Keefe's request. "We care for our men when sick and pay good salaries," Day told the baseball writers. "I don't see why we should be compelled to make a personal contract."[8] Keefe thought the request was reasonable, since it wouldn't cost Day anything to

This Old Judge tobacco card distributed in 1887 shows one of the few photographs of Tim Keefe throwing the ball. Keefe had to adapt to numerous changes in the pitching rules instituted for the 1887 season, which included having to deliver the ball with one foot on the back line of the pitcher's box (Library of Congress, Prints and Photographs Division, LC-DIG-bbc-0267f).

grant; however, Day thought that it was unnecessary and wouldn't budge. Day even discontinued the use of a personal contract with Welch.

Manager Mutrie tapped Keefe to pitch the season opener, bypassing Welch who had the honor the previous two years. Keefe pitched a six-hitter, yielding four base hits and two walks, to lead the Giants to a 4–3 victory, with O'Rourke as his catcher. Ewing, whose hands were battered and would catch fewer than a dozen games in 1887, was the second baseman. Bill Brown and Tom Deasley spelled O'Rourke at catcher during the 1887 season.

Mutrie made other changes to the lineup. He put Danny Richardson, formerly a utility player, at third base and installed newcomers George Gore and Mike Tiernan in the outfield, relegating Mike Dorgan and Pete Gillespie to sharing left field. Mutrie also went to a three-man pitching rotation, to give Keefe and Welch more rest between starts during the long 126-game season. But Mutrie's obsession with having a left-hander for the third pitcher to complement right-handers Keefe and Welch hurt the Giants, since Mutrie couldn't locate a reliable southpaw to be the third pitcher. Bill George won his first three starts for the Giants, but then didn't win another ballgame all season, racking up nine losses. Ledell Titcomb barely won more games than he lost while Mike Mattimore turned out to be just a .500 pitcher.

By May 14, two weeks into the season, the Giants had settled into third place and the newspapers started to criticize the talented team that couldn't win consistently. The *New York Tribune*, whose readers were businessmen not laborers, wrote that the Giants' poor record was the result of "indifference and laziness," because the ballplayers were "flattered and petted until the high salaried and fortunate individuals have begun to imagine they owned all Manhattan Island."[9] While the Giants did remain within hailing distance of first place for the next four months, they never closed the gap to fewer than four games.

The Giants displayed new uniforms for the 1887 season, jettisoning the bland togs of 1886 in favor of more colorful attire. They wore striped shirts, with alternating maroon and black vertical stripes, white pants, and stockings with the same stripe pattern.[10] Although not considered to be part of the genealogy of the orange-and-black color scheme of the twentieth-century New York Giants, the 1887 uniforms were the first forerunner of that color palate.

Another new wrinkle in the National League for 1887, besides the numerous pitching rule changes, was a reward for the pennant-winning team, the Dauvray Cup. Actress Helen Dauvray, a frequent spectator at the Polo Grounds, donated the trophy, fashioned by the Gorham Silver Company in Providence, Rhode Island, which was to be presented to the winner of the world championship series between the pennant winners of the League and the Association. As baseball historian John Thorn wrote in "Baseball's Lost Chalice," his history of the Dauvray Cup, "Hers was not baseball's first self-promotional trophy."[11] Dauvray's acting career was flagging at the point, so she hoped the Cup would boost her theater prospects. At some point during the season, Ward was smitten by the affections of Dauvray.

It was a challenging season for pitchers, since batters now had a decided advantage over them. Keefe did not have fond remembrances of the 1887 season, as he recalled sarcastically one year later in an article in the *Boston Globe*:

> How pleasant [?] it was to pitch in Chicago or Detroit under those rules. Captain Anson and his men would step up to the plate and with perspiration covering my face I would foolishly attempt to try and outwit them. To see the way that they were driving in the bricks in the wall surrounding the grounds or carrying a leg off of some infielder was decidedly exhilarating and a sight I shall never forget—nor will the infielders either. In Detroit there was no brick wall around the grounds, but plenty of trees in the adjoining town and how Messrs. Brouthers, Thompson, Rowe, Richardson and White entertained themselves by knocking the branches from the trees and scattering the leaves is still fresh in my recollection. How sound my repose at night was under the four-strike rule![12]

Welch got off to a poor start in 1887, when the master of the hop-step-and-jump delivery couldn't successfully adapt to the new pitching rule that required one foot to be firmly affixed to the back line of the pitcher's box. Compounding the situation was that Ewing's hands were so badly injured that he only sporadically played catcher, forcing Welch to pitch to unfamiliar catchers. No longer having a guaranteed contract with the Giants no doubt increased his financial worries as well. After Welch was injured for much of June, he injured his foot covering first base in an early July game in Chicago, putting him out of action for two weeks.

After Keefe's July 1 victory over Indianapolis, the *New York World* headline read: "Tim Keefe and Victory: The Giants' Great Twirler Bowls Over the Hoosiers." However, the Giants' pennant hopes were dashed a few days later when both Keefe and Welch were unavailable to pitch. In an article entitled "The Giants Are Crippled," the *New York World* wrote: "At present the Giants are in a bad way for pitchers. Keefe is at home owing to the death of his father; Welch is laid up with a sore leg; Tiernan's arm is bad; and Roach and Mattimore are under the weather."[13]

Keefe was back home in Somerville, Massachusetts, for the funeral of his father, Patrick Keefe, who had died there on July 8.[14] His father was buried in the Keefe family plot in St. Paul's Cemetery, which is located near the Somerville city line in the town of Arlington.[15]

While Keefe didn't live up to his father's expectations for him to become an engineer, the rest of his siblings either met or exceeded their father's hopes

13. Adapting to Numerous Pitching Rule Changes 123

and dreams for them. Daniel followed the military route by joining the Cambridge militia, where he rose to the rank of captain; he also progressed within the plumbing trade to become a master plumber owning his own business.[16] Katherine and Mary contributed to the family income through the sewing trade as a seamstress. Margaret, Ellen, and Annie all graduated from the eighth grade at the Luther V. Bell School; Margaret also graduated from Somerville High School.[17] Margaret also appears to have taken some college courses before her early death in 1888, as her occupation listed on her death record was "college student."[18] Annie worked as a bookkeeper before her early death in 1889, working for Mrs. Ellen Cain, the proprietor of the grocery E. Cain & Son in East Cambridge.[19] Ellen worked in the composing room of the *Cambridge Tribune* newspaper, before taking on the traditional female role to raise a family; however, she did emphasize education with her nine children, who all graduated from college.[20]

To fill-in for Keefe while he attended his father's funeral, Mutrie recruited Bill Swarbush to take the pitcher's box. Swarbush lost both games he pitched for the Giants, on July 9 and 12, at the Polo Grounds. Swarbush never appeared in another major-league game. Mutrie called on Bill George to replace Welch, but George was just as ineffective as Swarbush.

Keefe returned to the Giants for the July 13 game, and Welch returned to pitch a week later. However, Keefe was now unquestionably the Giants' number one pitcher, as acknowledged by the *New York World* following Welch's return: "Mickey Welch is popular ... [and] he will grow in popularity until he again fairly divides the honors with his handsome associate, Tim Keefe."[21] Keefe never relinquished that popularity mantle while he and Welch both pitched for the Giants.

Although the Giants were not overly successful on the baseball diamond in 1887, the Giants were still popular in the city. The team topped the National League in attendance in 1887 for the third year in a row, attracting for the first time in league history more than a quarter of a million spectators to its games.[22] A number of people took the opportunity to exploit this popularity for commercial gain, which enabled Keefe and his Giants teammates to bask in greater glory.

Cigarette manufacturers stepped up their advertising efforts in 1887 by distributing a greater number of baseball card sets, in their attempt to compete with the dominant W. Duke, Sons and Company. Duke had established a cigarette factory in New York City, which utilized the recently invented Bonsack cigarette-making machine to eliminate the need for laborers to hand roll cigarettes. Duke was thus able to reduce the price of a package of cigarettes and increase the company's share of the burgeoning cigarette market.[23]

The 1887 Old Judge set of baseball cards, which were sepia-toned photographs not drawings, "stands as one of the greatest visual records of late-nineteenth-century baseball and the men who played it," according to Dave Jamieson, author of *Mint Condition: How Baseball Cards Became an American Obsession*.[24] Photographer Joseph Hall shot photos of the ballplayers in full-body poses, not simple facial portraits that Wood had done for the 1886 Old Judge cards. As Jamieson wrote, these photos "convincingly evoke the showmanship of the sport, often with genuine artistry ... as if Hall was trying to capture not the face but the personality."[25] Keefe, shown in his striped shirt worn by the Giants in 1887, was captured in several photos that show him throwing a ball as well as one wielding a bat.[26]

Allen & Ginter began distributing baseball cards with its cigarette products in 1887. Their cards were full-color drawings of the ballplayers, which differentiated them from the sepia-toned Old Judge cards. Keefe was captured on his Allen & Ginter card emulating the 1887 pitching rules by holding the ball in front of his body, to give the batter a complete view of it before its delivery to the plate.[27]

Evening newspapers began to proliferate in New York City in 1887. The *New York Sun* and *New York World* both began publishing evening editions to supplement their morning coverage, to join a growing number of afternoon newspapers like the *New York Evening Telegram*. The *World* often labeled editions of its evening paper as the "Baseball Extra." Because the morning newspapers focused on the "hard" news of reporting the details of the ballgames played the previous day, the evening newspapers introduced "soft" coverage of the New York Giants, which enlivened the ballplayers to readers.

For example, the *New York Evening Telegram* wrote in August 1887: "Keefe doesn't take to stealing very much. He is so honest that he refuses even to capture a base.... Ewing is contemplating getting a string to pull him down to second every time an opportunity is given to the former to get there."[28] Readers in September got further insight on Keefe's delivery when the *Telegram* reported: "Keefe has the greatest slow ball pitched. 'It comes up to the plate as though the twirler had a string on it drawing it back,' once remarked a player. Welch brings a ball from over his head, which is very effective."[29] From this description, we learn that Keefe continued to throw sidearm.

While the evening papers added some zest to the ballplayers, the morning papers began to provide more game analysis, not just play-by-play coverage. For example, after a victory over Pittsburgh, which had transferred to the League from the Association for 1887, the *New York Herald* reported: "Keefe pitched for New York and a great game he pitched. Some people thought he never pitched better. There was room for improvement in Brown's catching, but that will probably come in time. New York's fielding was generally sharp and brilliant."[30]

Another way to make money off the fame of the Giants was to organize a postseason tour of the team. Walter Appleton, a stockholder in the Giants, arranged for a series of baseball games to be played in San Francisco, California, from November 1887 through February 1888. Keefe, Ward, and several other members of the Giants signed up to play on Appleton's team.[31] Not to be shortchanged on the exploitation of their fame, Keefe arranged for a tour to New Orleans, Texas, and southern California prior to the commitment to be in San Francisco in mid–November; on Keefe's tour, the ballplayers retained all of the profits, not splitting them with Appleton.[32]

Before Keefe returned from his father's funeral, Ward stepped down as team captain, replaced by Ewing. That gave Ward more time to devote to his Brotherhood activities, which would consume much of his time in the coming months. Ward, outraged at the $10,000 sale of Mike Kelly from Chicago to Boston earlier in the year, was extremely motivated to have the National League recognize the Brotherhood, so that these perceived flagrant violations of ballplayer rights could be addressed and changes instituted. The Kelly transaction led Ward to write his treatise on the flawed employment relationship between ballplayer and ballclub under the title "Is the Base Ball Player a Chattel?"

Based on the beliefs of Keefe and Ward that were steeped in the labor theory of value, the Brotherhood position was that ballplayers' skills produced the game's profits, not the skills of management. Therefore, ballplayers should share equitably in the net proceeds and have greater control over their destiny. The Kelly transaction blatantly violated that principle. Chicago ballclub owner Spalding justified the sale of Kelly to Boston because it was mutual and benefited both sides, since Kelly got a higher salary from Boston and Spalding received value for what he considered a disruptive influence.[33] Ward believed that Kelly was entitled to a significant portion of the $10,000 sale price, if not all of it. Besides the philosophical issue, Ward was one of the few people that actually understood the complicated legal logistics involved in the sale of a player, which infuriated him even more. The payment for a player's release was contingent on the player first signing a contract with the purchasing ballclub. Thus the transaction happened in reverse, the player signed with a new club and then his old club released him (after receiving the negotiated payment).[34]

Given his artisan faith in the apprentice–journeyman–master system, Keefe was in complete accord with Ward that a released player should be free to negotiate his own deal, not be constrained by the existing cart-before-the-horse practice. However, the selling of players soon became the issue that divided the two men with regard to the policy direction of the Brotherhood to accomplish change.

Keefe and Ward had been a great team at organizing the Brotherhood during its first two years to represent a broad swath of the ballplayers in the National League. However, 1887 was a turning point in their relationship. Ward, as president, focused on the big picture and legal issues. He also worked with the council of delegates. The ballplayers on each of the eight teams voted one player to be the delegate for their team to vote on Brotherhood matters. Keefe, as secretary-treasurer, was more connected to the individual ballplayers in the membership, initially in recruiting them and then retaining them as dues-paying members. However, there were never any general memberships meetings, which diminished Keefe's influence drawn from the entire membership. Thus, Ward had more power within the Brotherhood structure. Ward's obsession with the selling of players was at odds with Keefe's top priority to remove impediments that reduced individual ballplayer salaries. This became a breaking point with the two men.

Ward's article "Is the Base Ball Player a Chattel?" was published in the August 1887 edition of *Lippincott's Magazine*, where he railed at the unfairness of the reserve rule. "The rule itself was an inherent wrong, for by it one set of men seized absolute control over the labor of another," Ward insisted in the article. "Clubs have seemed to think that players had no rights, and the blacklist was waiting for any man who dared to assert the contrary." Ward likened the sale of Kelly to be slavery, which at the time was an intensely powerful metaphor since the Civil War had ended only two decades earlier. "In the eye of the baseball magnate the player has become a mere chattel. He goes where he is sent, takes what is given him, and thanks the Lord for life." Ward concluded the article with a veiled threat that a new league could be created to cure these ills: "Shall [change] come from the clubs, or from the players, or from both conjointly?" Ward asked. "If the clubs cannot find a way out of these difficulties, the players will try to do it for them."[35]

Despite Ward's hatred of the reserve rule, though, he concluded that it was necessary for baseball to continue as a moneymaking proposition for ballplayers, not just for the ballclub owners. In his *Lippincott's* article, Ward summarized the three reasons for the reserve rule: "they wished to make the business of base-ball more permanent, they meant to reduce salaries, and they sought to secure a monopoly of the game."[36] Keefe would have vehemently disagreed with Ward's prioritization, believing the second reason "to reduce salaries" was the greater driver.

At the very least, Ward believed that to accomplish any change with the

National League, especially his desire to terminate "the present odious system of buying and selling players," he needed to overtly recognize his audience, the ballclub owners, who were firmly committed to the principle of the reserve rule. Despite the recent profits being earned by ballclubs, Ward was cognizant of the high mortality rate of ballclubs in the past (only Boston and Chicago had been in the league since 1882), so he believed that a healthy survival environment was needed to ensure that ballplayer jobs would still exist. Ward also wanted to differentiate the negotiation position of the Brotherhood to focus on tangible issues, rather than the ethical arguments like shortening the workweek then being articulated by many labor organizations across the country.

Ward used the article to successfully lobby the National League to recognize the Brotherhood later in the year. That was a tall order in 1887, since few employers then would even talk with a labor organization. Ward and National League president Nick Young were soon "engaged in epistolary sparring" about the possibility of the League recognizing the Brotherhood.[37]

On August 20, 1887, Keefe pitched for the Giants in a 5–5 tie with the Phillies. The game was not memorable from a pitching perspective nor did it impact where the Giants finished in the standings. What was memorable from this game, and provided everlasting fame to Keefe, was the future recollection of the opposing pitcher, Dan Casey, of his last appearance as a batter in that game. He contended that he was the model for the batter in the poem "Casey at the Bat," and Keefe was the inspiration for the pitcher in that poem.

In the top of the ninth inning with the Giants ahead, 5–3, the Phillies loaded the bases with Casey next to bat. "Casey then raised the crowd to its feet by hitting a fly to right, bringing in McGuire and Irwin," to tie the game.[38] This allegedly was the original inspiration for baseball's most famous poem, according to Jim Moore and Natalie Vermilyea, authors of the book *Ernest Thayer's "Casey at the Bat": Background and Characters of Baseball's Most Famous Poem*. Moore and Vermilyea postulate that Thayer, then living in San Francisco, read about Casey's exploits in *The Sporting News*, which included the phrase "Casey was at the bat," and modeled the pitcher in his poem after Keefe.[39]

Unfortunately, Casey's accurate memory of that August 1887 game in Philadelphia (i.e., Mudville in the poem) faded over the years, so he contended that he struck out, just as Mighty Casey did in the poem, rather than swat a base hit to tie the game. However, Casey always gave Keefe a top billing in his recreation of that game, such as this excerpt from a 1938 article in *Collier's* magazine:

> "The fans were cheering for me to knock the ball over the fence, but the only thing that was knocking was my knees! A week before, up in Boston, I'd busted

up a game with a lucky homer and the folks thought I could repeat. But I knew different. I looked at the pitcher and he looked at me. I got that sinking feeling. When the first ball came over it was fast and a little low. I just stood looking at it as it hit the catcher's glove. I couldn't have hit it with a shovel." *"Strike one," the umpire said.* "Well, that umpire was plenty right for one time. Then came the next pitch." *But Casey still ignored it, and the umpire said, "Strike two!"* "Ignore it? I hadn't even seen it! I was too busy getting my head out of the way! I didn't even wave my bat at it, either. Those were two swell called strikes. By then I wished I was somewhere else. Tim Keefe could throw that ball as fast as a fellow shooting at you with a gun." *And now the air is shattered by the force of Casey's blow.* "Well, that was that. For fifty years I've been trying to make people believe that I was a pretty good ballplayer, but no home-run king."[40]

Keefe umpired the Giants' game on Saturday, September 3, at the Polo Grounds when the scheduled umpire was ill. His integrity, unfortunately, was obvious when he tried to be impartial and not favor the Giants, who lost the game, 12–10. "The only trouble was that he was too afraid that he would not give the visitors all they were due them," the *New York Sun* reported, "and he made the home club suffer in more cases than one."[41] The *National Police Gazette* commented that "Tim Keefe is a model young man, but he is not the man that should ever again be selected to umpire a game for the New Yorks."[42]

On Monday, September 5, workers in New York celebrated the first state-sanctioned Labor Day holiday. Keefe pitched for the Giants to victory that day at the Polo Grounds before a crowd of 9,000 fans, as "Keefe was at his best and he proved a complete enigma to the heavy batters of the visiting team."[43] Because Labor Day was the creation of labor unions, who sponsored a large parade in New York City, Keefe probably felt sympathy for his former carpenter associates, but no special attachment to the celebration as far as the Brotherhood went.

Shortly after Labor Day the Giants fell into fourth place, where they finished the season with a 68–55 record, ten games behind first-place Detroit. Keefe compiled a 35–19 record as a pitcher, with his 35 victories being the second-best in the National League behind the 38 of Chicago's John Clarkson. Keefe advanced as a strategic pitcher during the 1887 season, producing one of the league's lowest earned-run averages (3.12) as well as the lowest ratio of walks and hits per inning pitched (1.12). Keefe wasn't bashful about yielding walks by wasting pitches to entice the batter into swinging at marginal pitches, finishing ninth in walks per nine innings (2.0), since he had confidence that batters would swing at his marginal pitches to make outs, as evidenced by his league-leading 8.1 hits per nine innings ratio. Keefe was also second to Clarkson in the ironman pitching categories of games (56), innings pitched (476), and strikeouts (189).

13. Adapting to Numerous Pitching Rule Changes

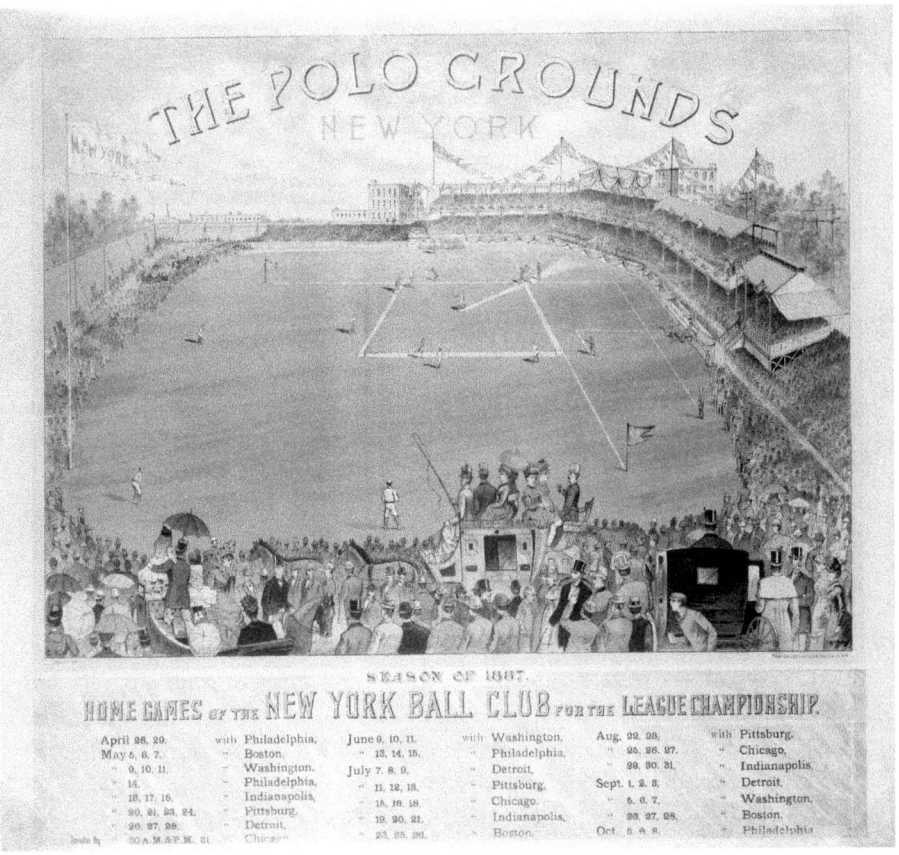

Most of Tim Keefe's pitching exploits in New York City occurred at the original Polo Grounds, shown in this 1887 painting, at the corner of Fifth Avenue and 110th Street. Strong attendance at the Giants' games at this first vintage of the Polo Grounds helped to establish Keefe's reputation as one of baseball's best pitchers (Library of Congress, Prints and Photographs Division, LC-DIG-pga-02288).

Ward had been very active in Brotherhood activities in August and September, following the publication of his article in *Lippincott's Magazine*. On August 28, the Brotherhood members met in New York City to devise a strategy regarding the signing of contracts for the 1888 season and gaining recognition by the National League ballclub owners.[44] Looking to obtain recognition at the League meeting in mid–November, Ward was the evangelist for the Brotherhood. He courted baseball writers to get the word out about the intentions of the Brotherhood. While he tried to keep a temperate voice, his frustration with the intransigent League sometimes flustered him. In mid–September he threatened to start another league if the owners didn't recognize the Brotherhood. "There is plenty of money at our disposal to organize any association or league. We know of any amount of capitalists who want to invest their money in baseball," Ward said. "We will all play next year whether the League people like it or not."[45] Although Ward had conceded to the ballclub owners the idea of the reserve rule, as being necessary to attract capital to the sport, he was adamant about minimizing the impact of the rule through an equitable contract that represented the rights of both player and ballclub.

The Giants' postseason tour helped to solidify the Brotherhood position that the ballplayer was the primary producer of earnings. Even the *New York Times* conceded that the California tour was successful because "Tim Keefe, Mike Kelly, and Buck Ewing were the attractions, and the people turned out in masses to see them play."[46] The ballplayers were on the cooperative plan on the tour, only being paid if spectators showed up to watch the ballgames. Their deal with Appleton gave them 40 percent of the receipts of the games in San Francisco; they divided 100 percent of the proceeds in the games played before arriving in San Francisco.[47]

Seven Giants ballplayers participated in the postseason baseball tour that left Jersey City, New Jersey, on October 25 headed for New Orleans en route to San Francisco: Keefe, Brown, Connor, Richardson, Ward, Tiernan, and Ewing. They were supplemented by Jerry Denny of Indianapolis and Kelly of Boston.[48] Basically, it was a Brotherhood team, not so much the Giants, since the vast majority (if not all) of its ballplayers were members of the Brotherhood, including its president and secretary. Following the surprise wedding announcement on October 12, Ward's wife, Helen Dauvray, was also on that train, which arrived in New Orleans on October 29.

The barnstorming Giants played their first game on Saturday, October 30, against the New Orleans Pelicans, with Keefe pitching the team to a 7–3 victory. "Keefe's pitching is as good as it ever was," the *New Orleans Times-Picayune* reported. "His command of the ball, coupled with the facility with which he changes speed, made it difficult for the locals to find the solution of his delivery."[49] Kelly and some of the ballplayers apparently partied hard into the night in the French Quarter, since they arrived hungover for the Sunday game the next day. Keefe had to relieve Richardson to secure a 4–4 tie.[50] The game on Monday was canceled, as the drinking episode made national headlines and nearly canceled the entire tour. After Kelly made amends with the locals, Keefe pitched the team to victory the following Sunday before the team departed for Galveston, Texas. In Texas Keefe tried to take a break from pitching, but to not disappoint the crowds he would pitch the last inning or two of each game.[51]

The seriousness of Keefe was implicitly revealed by Kelly in a book

13. Adapting to Numerous Pitching Rule Changes   131

ghostwritten for him in 1888, *"Play Ball": Stories of the Diamond Field*. In the book Kelly related a number of stories about this postseason excursion, such as quail hunting in Mississippi and riding bronco horses in Texas. While Kelly mentions Ewing, Connor, Tiernan, and Richardson as enjoying these aspects of the trip, he never once mentioned Keefe as a participant in the fun activities.[52] Not that Keefe didn't appreciate Kelly's sense of fun, which he revealed in this Texas story that Keefe later told author George Tuohey for his history of the Boston ballclub:

> More good stories are told about poor Mike Kelly than about any other ball player. I shall never forget one day in Austin, Texas, when we had a combination team on the way to Frisco. About the eighth inning Mike came to the plate and sent a corking hit to deep left. The ball went into a clump of bushes and the left fielder began to hunt for it. Kelly ran to first and instead of turning about for second he kept straight on for right field. "Hey Kel. Where are you going?" we all yelled. But Mike kept on until he reached the right fielder. The latter didn't know what was up until Mike ran around him and then trotted toward second base. When he touched the bag he ran out again toward left field. The centre fielder, who had run over there to take the throw from the left fielder when the latter found the ball, was simply dumbfounded. Kel ran around him and then galloped to third base. By this time the left fielder had found the ball and he quickly threw it in to the shortstop. The latter shot the ball to the catcher and Kel was headed off. Mike ran up and down several times with the whole Austin team chasing him until he saw he was cornered. Then he broke into a sprint and dashed across the diamond in the direction of right field. The third baseman who had the ball went after him full tilt. "Yer'll never catch me," yelled Mike, "if yer chase me ter Frisco." Kel ran out of the gate and never stopped until he reached the hotel.[53]

Ward left the team in Texas to return to New York City to attend the National League meeting, where he pushed to have the League recognize the Brotherhood as the representative of the ballplayers. Ward eventually embarrassed the League into inviting a Brotherhood committee (consisting of Ward, Ned Hanlon, and Dan Brouthers) to meet with a committee of the owners. Two notable aspects of this meeting were that Keefe was not a member of the Brotherhood committee and Chicago owner Spalding initiated a motion to recognize the Brotherhood. The next day, Ward was able to gain some concessions in contract terms, such as written notice of the grounds for a fine imposed on a ballplayer.[54] Action on the salary cap was tabled until the spring.

In other action at the League meeting, the owners reverted back to three strikes for a strikeout, rather than the four needed in 1887, and eliminated the batter being credited with a base hit for a walk. Keefe thought that going back to three strikes would be bad for the game. "Although the new three-strikes rule will make it easier for me I am very sorry they adopted it. It is a bad move for the good of the game. We will simply have a pitcher's game again," Keefe said. "As I look at it the batsman is going to be at the pitcher's mercy and that is exactly the opposite to what we want. Instead of more batting the new rule means less."[55]

Although Ward had seemingly won a huge victory over the ballclub owners and firmly established the Brotherhood as an effective protective organization, in reality he had awoken the proverbial sleeping dog. "The owners had been forced to give up their absolute authority over the management of the game. It seemed they had accepted the situation gracefully," historian Glenn Moore wrote in the *Journal of Sport History*. "But privately they seethed, and plotted all year to win back the control they had lost ... [and] arrived at a Machiavellian scheme" that they executed twelve months later.[56]

While Ward was back in New York City, the Giants had reached Los Angeles, California. Keefe maintained his abbreviated pitching duties there, as Ewing pitched and Keefe came in from center field to switch with Ewing near the end of the game. In the November 20 game, the *Los Angeles Times* reported that Keefe went 2-for-4 at bat and "was applauded to the echo for some brilliant running catches, one of which seemed almost impossible."[57]

On November 22, the Giants caravan arrived in San Francisco, where three other major-league teams were already playing ballgames: Chicago and Philadelphia from the National League and the St. Louis Browns from the American Association. Those three teams played among themselves at Central Park in San Francisco, while the Giants played the three local California League teams (Haverly, Greenhood & Moran, and Pioneer) at the Haight Street Grounds. With the protracted two-month stay in San Francisco, you could say that these barnstorming Giants were the first incarnation of the San Francisco Giants, who 70 years later were transplanted from New York to the City by the Bay following the end of the 1957 season.

The barnstorming Giants played their first games in San Francisco on Thanksgiving Day, November 24. In the morning Tiernan pitched the team to victory over the Haverlys; in the afternoon game the Greenhoods defeated the Giants, 10–4, before 20,000 people who jammed into the Haight Street Grounds.[58] Keefe continued his limited pitching duty, pitching just the first inning before taking over center field in favor of Kelly in the pitcher's box. Ward arrived back in San Francisco in time for the Sunday game against the Pioneers on November 27, when Keefe again pitched just a solitary inning.

Besides the games in San Francisco against California League teams, the Giants also played teams from other cities in the region. On November 26, the Giants handily defeated Stockton, 26–0, in San Francisco.[59] While unremarkable as a competitive event, this ballgame seemed to provide inspiration

13. Adapting to Numerous Pitching Rule Changes

for a *San Francisco Examiner* writer named Ernest Thayer, a native of Worcester, Massachusetts, to write his poem "Casey at the Bat" that was published in June 1888. Thayer did interview many of the Giants and covered several of their ballgames. Playing for Stockton that day were two men named Cooney and Flynn, the exact surnames of two characters in Thayer's poem.[60] The appearance of Kelly and Keefe, often cited as models for the batter and pitcher in the poem, lends some credence to this genesis of the famous baseball verse.

On December 6, the Giants journeyed 75 miles south of San Francisco to play a ballgame in Santa Cruz, where the weather was a bit warmer. They enjoyed the scenery as they traveled on a narrow-gauge railroad along the shore of San Francisco Bay south from San Francisco into San Jose before traversing the mountains into the coastal city of Santa Cruz. Keefe shut out the California all-star team picked for the occasion, 9–0, as the *San Francisco Evening Bulletin* reported "the Californians were unable to bat Keefe."[61] George Van Haltren, the opposing pitcher, told a Santa Cruz newspaper after the game, "The victory of the Giants was due to their batting and our inability to hit Keefe. I never saw Keefe play so well."[62] Van Haltren signed with the Chicago ballclub to play in the National League for the 1888 season.

While the details of exhibition baseball games played 3,000 miles from New York City may seem totally irrelevant, the trip to San Francisco had an extraordinary impact on Keefe's life. In San Francisco he met his future wife, participated in conversations that initiated the planning for the eventual Players' League, and began planning to start his own sporting goods business.

During the two months in San Francisco, Keefe had plenty of time to tour the city and revel in the Pacific Coast life with members of the touring party. San Francisco had an extremely lively theater district, so Keefe likely spent many evenings at the theater, where years earlier Ward's wife, Helen, had started her career as an actress. On those excursions as part of Helen's entourage, Keefe first met his future wife, Helen's sister Clara. Keefe also had time to socialize with the ballplayers from the other three major-league teams that were visiting San Francisco. Keefe was reunited with Doc Bushong, catcher for St. Louis, and Fred Pfeffer, infielder for Chicago. Keefe and Pfeffer, in conjunction with Ward, began to think about establishing a new league as an alternative if the Brotherhood negotiations with the ballclub owners failed. While these initial discussions were no doubt more of a dream scenario, they did begin the concept for the Players' League. Keefe no doubt also continued discussions with Bushong and Pfeffer that soon culminated in a writing collaboration in the 1889 book *Scientific Ball*, another step forward in Keefe being recognized as a master pitcher. A bigger step that Keefe considered in this regard was establishing a sporting goods business in New York City, which a year later came to fruition as Keefe & Becannon.

Besides San Francisco having no qualms about staging baseball games on the Christian Sabbath of Sunday, unlike the environment in New York City, San Francisco also tolerated ballgames on the Christian Holy Day of Christmas. The Giants were defeated by the Pioneers on Christmas Day, before losing to the Greenhoods the next day in the finale of their games with California League teams.[63] When Kelly and Connor left to return to the East Coast, Keefe and the remaining Giants lobbied Appleton for more money to stay in San Francisco, since the attendance had begun to dwindle at the games with the California League.

One issue leading to the meager crowds was Keefe's tired arm, exacerbated by the lack of a reputable substitute pitcher. Keefe found the weather in San Francisco, though temperate by New York City standards, to be chillier than in New Orleans, which didn't help to limber up his arm. Keefe reportedly told a San Francisco writer, after repeatedly being asked to pitch with his sore arm, "he would not pitch in such cold weather if he was paid $5 for every ball he threw over the plate."[64]

Appleton arranged for the Giants to play a three-game series with the St. Louis Browns, at a more leisurely pace by only playing on three Sundays in January. He enlisted local favorite Van Haltren to pitch for the Giants in the second game of the St. Louis series, which led to a larger crowd as well as a victory. However, by that point, Appleton had already milked about as much as he could from San Francisco baseball fans, so the barnstorming Giants disbanded.

Keefe left San Francisco in early February 1888. He was anxious to return east for a couple of reasons. First, he had family matters to attend to, since he received a telegram notifying him that his sister Margaret had died in January.[65] Second, he wanted to commence working to establish his sporting goods business. Third, he wanted to pursue a social engagement with Ward's sister-in-law Clara.

14
Clara Helm, the Future Mrs. Keefe

On Tuesday morning, April 24, 1888, before boarding a train in Providence, Tim Keefe purchased the morning newspapers to read on his trip back to Boston. He was shocked to see this story on the front page of the *Boston Globe*: "New York, April 23.—Somewhat of a sensation was caused in local base ball circles today by the report that Tim Keefe is about to marry the widowed Mrs. Helm, a sister of Mrs. John Ward, née Helen Dauvray."[1] The rumor was also published nationwide in newspapers such as the *Chicago Inter Ocean*, *Philadelphia Inquirer*, and *San Francisco Evening Bulletin*.

Soon after his arrival in Boston, Keefe stopped by the offices of the *Boston Globe* to speak with former baseball writer, now city editor, William Sullivan to correct the erroneous report. In the evening edition of the *Globe* that day, Sullivan reported that Keefe blushed when he talked about the marriage rumor:

> I am very sorry to spoil this little story for the sake of the newspapers, but I must contradict it for the lady's sake, at least. I'm very sorry that the story is being circulated. It is not a pleasant yarn to start about a lady. It will put Mrs. Helm in an uncomfortable position, and I don't know how the story started. Why, I never saw Mrs. Helm but once. When I came on from San Francisco in the spring she was on the train, traveling with her sister, Mrs. Ward. There were others in the party, and we had a very pleasant trip across the country to New York. I have not seen Mrs. Helm from that day to this.[2]

Keefe was no doubt fibbing just a bit to protect Clara's public reputation in this Victorian era of staunchly conservative morals when it came to courting women. Indeed, they likely attended the theater together while in San Francisco, either in a group outing or accompanied by a chaperone. Away from public view, they perhaps even shared some time alone at their hotel, where they met to just talk, of course.

Clara Helm, née Gibson, was a mysterious woman from an odd family. In his 2011 article about Clara's sister Helen Dauvray, baseball historian John Thorn tried his best to interpret what he termed "swirling data discrepancies" to paint a biographical sketch of the Gibson family and its two famous sisters. Clara was the fourth of six children of Charles H. Gibson and Louisa De Young, who were married sometime around 1847. The children, in birth order, were Adolph, Amelia, Laura, Clara, Ida, and Charles. Clara was born in Cincinnati, Ohio, around 1855. The Gibsons were an itinerant family, living in Missouri, Louisiana, and Ohio before landing in California around 1857 and then in Oregon by 1860. After the father disappeared in 1862 ("whether Charles died or deserted his family is not known"), the mother married San Francisco printer John L. Williams around 1864. They lived in San Francisco two blocks from Maguire's Opera House, where Clara's younger sister Ida made her theatrical debut in 1866 as Little Eva in the show "Uncle Tom's Cabin." A few years later Ida Gibson changed her name to Helen Dauvrey once she was an established actress. Clara was a teenaged bride when she married James Helm, but was a widow by 1875 at the age of 20, when she inherited his money. By 1880 the entire Gibson family was back in New York City.[3]

The extended Gibson family lived in a mansion at 49 Park Avenue, on the corner of East 37th Street, five blocks south of the Grand Central Depot.[4] The family employed four servants to work in the mansion, whose deed was in Clara's name.[5] A number of unfortunate incidents during 1887 forced Clara to sell the Park Avenue mansion. In March a stalker was arrested lurking outside the mansion; in May the first husband of Helen was cited in a lawsuit that dragged their marriage back into the newspapers; in October her brother Adolph was accused of sexually assaulting one of their servants; and also in October marriage rumors about Helen and Ward surfaced.[6] The address was just too public, so Clara sold the Park Avenue mansion in April 1888; she and her sister then resided in a hotel in the city.[7]

Clara attended the ballgames at the Polo Grounds with her sister Helen. The *New York World* ran a sketch in May 1888 of women spectators at the Giants' games, which included Clara, who wore a Gainsborough hat:

> Mrs. Helm, who invariably accompanies Mrs. Ward to the games, is larger than her sister and she, too, is quite an expert scorer. She is, however, more given to applauding good plays by individuals and her blue eyes twinkle merrily when the Giants win. It was some time ago rumored that Mrs. Helm would wed Tim Keefe, the handsome and popular pitcher of New York's club, but the report was promptly denied. Mrs. Helm apparently loves base-ball more than any being or thing, and her admiration for the game is apparent at all times. Her cheeks are reddened and her eyes are bright when New York's boys secure a run or make a brilliant play, but she is prone to pouting when they make errors or lose a game.[8]

In November 1888 the *New York Daily Graphic* described Clara as a beautiful woman: "Mrs. Helm is a very handsome woman—she has youth, beauty, brains and wealth—what could the heart of mortal ask more? There is a striking suggestion of Helen Dauvray in the face, though the coloring is so utterly different. Mrs. Helm has a fair, vividly tinted complexion, brilliant dark eyes and a profusion of exquisite hair of burnished bronze hue which she arranges with marked and most becoming individuality. One who looks at her picture in to-day's *Graphic* will scarcely need to be told that she is a very winsome woman."[9]

Clara was a budding sculptor. The *New York Daily Graphic* described her as "a young, handsome and rich widow who has gifts of unusual power as a sculptor ... [who] has worked at her chosen tasks in the studio of Launt Thompson, and beneath his critical eye, her work, which never lacks the master touch of genius, has acquired the polish and finish which practice alone can give."[10] She proposed to sculpt a statue of a newsboy atop a water fountain to be situated in City Hall Park near the major newspaper buildings. "The figure is to be in bronze and the base in rough granite," the *New York World* reported. "The spout of the fountain represents a printer's composing stick."[11] The publicity, with the added tidbit that she was traveling to Europe for some rest before undertaking the sculpture, undoubtedly was a cover, arranged by Keefe, to provide a public reason for Clara to sail alone to Europe.

This picture of Clara Helm appeared in the *New York Daily Graphic* on November 21, 1888, when it accompanied an article about her proposed newsboy sculpture. In August 1889, Tim Keefe married the wealthy widow in a quiet ceremony in Worcester, Massachusetts.

Keefe was smitten with Clara because she was unlike any woman he had ever met before, refined yet independent. Both were strong-minded persons, who cherished their independence as unmarried individuals. Neither person seemed to be in a rush to marry. Regarding Keefe, as Howard Chudacoff wrote in *The Age of the Bachelor: Creating an American Subculture*, "The availability of alternatives to marriage, such as opportunities for economic, social and sexual independence" led men "to forego or delay marriage as a means of attaining personal satisfaction."[12] As for Clara, she seemed to revel in being an independent woman, 75 years before the women's liberation movement began in the 1960s. Their relationship was consistent with Keefe's moving beyond his Somerville roots, especially since Clara was not Catholic. Their different religious beliefs didn't seem to be a problem for Keefe, although it very likely was a huge issue for his family, with one exception. The couple eventually did marry in August 1889.

In November 1888 Keefe pushed the limits of that independence as he apparently planned to accompany Clara to Europe. Four days after the *New York World* article about Clara and her plans to travel to Europe, Keefe arrived in New York City with his sister Annie, presumably to be his chaperone. "But very few of Tim's friends knew he was in town, for he has been quietly engaged in showing his sister the sights of the city, it being her first visit to Gotham," the *World* reported. "He had fully intended to take a trip abroad this winter, but the friend with whom he was to take the trip is unable to go, and that, together with several other matters, has led Tim to postpone his journey for another year" and "return to his home in Cambridge."[13] That unnamed "friend" was likely Clara. The trip to Europe by the couple was aborted since Clara's sister Helen had left her husband John Ward, Keefe's teammate on the Giants, in San Francisco rather than accompany him to Australia with the Spalding baseball tour. Instead, Helen was Clara's travel companion to Europe, not Keefe.[14]

Ward disapproved of Keefe's relationship with Clara from the beginning, as the two ballplayers reportedly did not speak to each other during the entire 1888 baseball season. After the Giants won the World Series in October 1888, newspaper reports surfaced that the two men were not on speaking terms. "They have not spoken to each other since last spring," *Sporting Life* reported in November. "Keefe says that Ward does not support him, while Ward has nothing to say. It is rather surprising that two men at the head of the Base Ball Brotherhood should become such bad friends."[15]

There were a variety of reasons why Ward didn't want Keefe courting Clara. Ward suspected that Tim would encourage Clara to continue to use her inheritance from her deceased first husband to finance his wife's acting dreams, while Ward adamantly wanted Helen to abandon acting. Ward may have also disapproved of the relationship because of its overt scandalous nature, since Clara and Tim both lived in hotels rather than in more respectable accommodations. But the real scandal that Ward wanted to be kept quiet was his extra-marital affair with Jessie McDermott, which he feared that Keefe would tell Clara who would then tell Helen.[16]

Ward also knew some, but surely not all, of Clara's secrets, some of which painted her as being less pristine than perhaps Keefe was aware. Clara was the legal guardian of Edward Gibson, a "nephew" within the Gibson family who has unknown parentage.[17] Perhaps Clara was his biological mother, or Helen was from her brief first marriage, or he was the result of a dalliance by one of her brothers. Edward Gibson was born in April 1880 in New York City and was educated at private boarding schools in France and England before attending Lawrenceville Preparatory School in New Jersey and then Cornell University.[18] One reason that Clara made frequent trips to Europe was to see her "nephew." The only known public reference to Clara and Edward appeared in 1891 in the *New York World*: "Mrs. Timothy Keefe sails to Europe tomorrow with her little nephew Eddie Gibson."[19] Otherwise, few people outside of relatives knew about Edward's existence. It is uncertain when Keefe first learned about Clara's nephew and, more importantly, how he felt about the situation.

Keefe tried to put at rest the rumors about his feud with Ward, but he came across as lukewarm: "The great pitcher laughed at the idea. He said that he and Ward were on the best terms, and that their friendship had not been in the least strained."[20] The frosty relationship between Keefe and Ward certainly did not detract from the Giants' chance to finally capture the National League pennant in 1888. Perhaps it even helped.

15

Record-Setting 19 Consecutive Wins

Following his return to New York City in February 1888 from San Francisco, where the extended postseason baseball tour of the New York Giants had concluded, Tim Keefe spent some time back home in Massachusetts before he coached the Amherst College baseball team in western Massachusetts that March.[1]

"Tim Keefe looks a little heavier than when he left us for the Pacific coast," Sullivan wrote in the *Boston Globe* about his interview with Keefe before heading out to Amherst. "I think Boston will get Clarkson," Keefe told Sullivan about the possibility of Boston buying his release from Chicago ballclub owner Albert Spalding. "John is not dependent on base ball. We are both Cambridge boys, you know, and I understand John pretty well. If he don't wear a Boston uniform you won't see him on the diamond this year.... When the time comes [Spalding] will release Clarkson to Boston, but John's release will come high. I shouldn't be surprised if Spalding wanted $15,000 for it, and Boston will pay whatever the price is."[2]

Keefe denied that he had talked to the Boston ballclub about the possibility of purchasing his release from New York, but he carefully chose his words, saying that he hadn't spoken to the Boston directors or anyone connected with the ballclub. That didn't preclude middlemen from doing the talking for him. "I should like to come to Boston, and I don't see as they need me in New York," Keefe told Sullivan. "The same reason that Clarkson has been wanting to come here holds equally for me. This is my home, too, and for that reason Boston is preferable to New York for me. Then, too, I believe it is well to change about. I have been in New York a long time, and it would be better all around for me to make a change and come to Boston."[3]

Despite his protestations to the contrary, Keefe had been, at least indirectly, in communication with the Boston ballclub regarding the salary it would pay him if his release could be purchased from New York. Before he left for Amherst College, Keefe communicated his position to the New York correspondent of *Sporting Life*:

> It is true that Keefe has been made uneasy by the unbusinesslike and you may say dishonest policy of other club officials. He has said to Mutrie: "Jim, I think it is not right to compel me to stay in New York and play ball for the money I get from the New York Club, when I have been offered one and one-half times more salary to pitch in another League city as soon as I get my release." That is all Tim will say, but it is enough.... It is not at all strange, therefore, that Keefe grows restless and talks about the slavery of pitching seven mouths for $3,000.[4]

Boston was the likely source of this salary number because that ballclub was seeking a first-class drawing card with local roots for the pitcher's box in order to fill the stands at the newly renovated South End Grounds. In early April, for a $10,000 price tag, Boston acquired the services of Clarkson from the Chicago ballclub to be that drawing card.

Sensing that Clarkson, rather than himself, was destined for Boston, Keefe decided to demand a $4,500 salary to play for the New York Giants during 1888. This was one and a half times his $3,000 salary for the 1887 season, equal to the higher salary that Keefe implied had been offered to him by Boston. Keefe determined that a 50 percent increase to $4,500 was appropriate based on his 109–52 pitching record (.677 winning percentage) over the previous three seasons, in which he had labored for a $3,000 annual salary as part of a three-year agreement he had negotiated in 1885 with the ballclub. That agreement expired at the end of the 1887 season. The $4,500 amount was the value that Keefe believed his services would be worth if there were an open market in the National League for baseball talent. He took the approach that any highly experienced journeyman within the apprentice-journeyman-master system would take, or, in modern parlance, anyone who subscribed to the free labor principle. Keefe and Brotherhood president John Ward both held out for a higher salary to play with the Giants in 1888, but for different reasons.

Keefe was miffed that the League had reneged on its agreement to eliminate the official $2,000 salary cap. Ward ostensibly had been successful in lobbying the League to eliminate the salary cap at a meeting in March, where the ballclub owners agreed to contract for the excess salary over $2,000 with a personal contract, so that "the surplus money will not be given in the shape of a present as heretofore."[5] However, the League failed to implement that agreement when it couldn't convince the American Association to also agree to its merits, as part of the pact between the two leagues to have consistent contract provisions.

Ward was motivated by the Clarkson transaction, the $10,000 deal that sent Clarkson from Chicago to Boston. This was yet another arrangement, similar to the $10,000 deal for Mike Kelly in 1887, where the ballplayer reaped none of the proceeds even though, as Ward would contend under the labor theory of value doctrine, it was the ballplayer's skill that created the price value.

Keefe and Ward soon leaked their negotiation positions to several baseball writers to try to put public pressure on the Giants' management to accept their salary demands. In mid–April headlines such as "Keefe and Ward, of New York, Refuse to Sign Unless They Get Increased Salaries" and "They Will Stick It Out: Ward and Keefe Have Named Their Figures and Will Not Sign for Less" appeared in newspapers across the country.[6] William Harris of the *New York Press* insightfully captured both sides of the negotiation:

> Keefe and Ward have named their figures and Mr. Day will not agree to them on the ground that they are exorbitant and beyond reason. The two men insist on their terms and President Day says he will not pay what they want. Ward refuses to talk about the matter except to refer questioners to Mr. Day. He admits that he has named his price and proposes to stick to it. Tim Keefe is just as obstinate. He will not sign, so he says, until Mr. Day accedes to his demand. It is not likely that the deadlock will continue many days longer. The New York Club must have Keefe and Keefe knows it as well as anybody. With Ward it is a little different, but Mr. Day cannot afford to let him go. There will be mutual concessions on both sides, and the matter settled before the 20th [Opening Day].[7]

Harris exploited his personal relationship with Keefe from his days at the *Boston Globe* to publish insights about Keefe in the *New York Press* that no other newspaper captured. The *Press* was a brand new newspaper in 1888 and needed an edge to take readers away from the more established *Sun* and *World* that also appealed to the common man. Keefe also exploited Harris in his new position as sports editor of the *Press* as a pulpit for his salary negotiations in 1888 and 1889. Decades later, these articles in the *New York Press* provide historians with some of the best available insights into Keefe's personality.

Initially, Keefe and Ward prudently didn't publicize their actual salary demands, but Harris soon revealed the numbers: Ward wanted $5,000 and Keefe $4,500. Harris, in a bylined dispatch in the *Boston Globe*, thought Ward asked for "more money that he is worth to the New York team," while, regarding Keefe, "Mr. Day will not pay him $4,500, but he will sign Keefe and Keefe will come pretty near being satisfied."[8] Day had offered $4,000 to each player.

Ward, who had the least favorable negotiation position, was the first to cave in. On April 19 he signed for $4,000 and played for the Giants in their season-opener on April 20, when Ledell Titcomb manned the pitcher's box. "Ward has accepted my offer and will join the club at once. I don't think he is worth the money that I am paying him, but public opinion and nothing else forces me to do it," Day told sportswriters. "He took a very sensible view of the case tonight and determined to sign at my figures. If he had not done so he never would have worn a New York uniform."[9] However, Keefe, who took the position that, as one writer put it, "there is but one Keefe and New York needs and must have him," continued to battle with Day, but did it 200 miles away from New York City in Boston.[10] Day played hardball with Keefe by reiterating that he would not pay the pitcher more than $4,000 under any circumstance.

As Day steadfastly refused to negotiate with his star pitcher, Keefe chatted several times in Boston with William Sullivan, the sports editor at the *Boston Globe*, who was also a neighbor of Keefe's family in Somerville. "On my arrival in New York I had an interview with Mr. Day, who made me an offer to sign with his club. I refused to agree, as there was a difference of $500 between us," Keefe told Sullivan on April 20. "I took it for granted that matters would be adjusted as soon as the time would come around for the League season to open up, but when Mutrie broached the subject he made me the same offer that Day did. Of course I refused to sign, and as I did not care to do any playing until the middle of May, I returned to my home in this city. Just at present I don't know what Mr. Day and Mr. Mutrie propose to do."[11] Keefe provided more detail to Sullivan a few days later:

> If Mr. Day had offered me the salary I wanted before I left New York, I don't doubt that I should have signed. He didn't do that and I am not at all sorry. You see this is the way it stands. I have business here in Boston to settle up that may take me a week, and it may take a month. I know that after the season opened and I had got to work I could not get away to come on and attend to my business. So I was not at all anxious to sign. I wanted to fix up my business, and I am here now to attend to it. ... I am not trying to play any bluff. When I get my business affairs fixed up and the weather is warmer we will fix it up if they want me, and I will jump in. They have got Welch, and Crane and Titcomb are both good ones. So they will get along well enough without me for a while.[12]

Keefe didn't specify what his "business" dealings were all about, but it likely involved initial footwork on behalf of the future Keefe & Becannon sporting goods enterprise that he would establish in January 1889.

When rookie pitcher Ed Crane was less than impressive for the Giants in his debut in the April 21 game, Keefe's subtle strategy to allege that Crane and Titcomb would be an adequate substitute for him appeared to give him the upper hand with Day. However, Day seemed to stoop to dirty tricks, by releasing a rumor to the newspapers that Keefe planned to marry Clara Helm, the sister of Ward's wife. The timing of these April 23 newspaper reports, in the midst of Keefe's salary negotiation with the Giants, led to the obvious conclusion that Day, or someone else affiliated with the Giants, had leaked the story as a nasty joke to inspire Keefe to sign at Day's salary offer. Keefe, taking the high road, told Sullivan at the *Boston Globe* on April 24 that Day "wouldn't joke about such a matter, and, by the way, when he says a thing he means it generally."[13]

Keefe went on to explain that he had just returned from a business trip to Worcester and Providence. "I found a telegram from Mr. Day, which had been received at my home in Somerville. That has made me think that it wouldn't be the best thing in the world for me to wait here any longer," Keefe told Sullivan. "I have just telegraphed Mr. Day that I will leave here tomorrow [April 25] and will see him at New York tomorrow night. Perhaps he doesn't want me now. He may not. If he does, and we can come to terms, I shall undoubtedly sign tomorrow."[14] Keefe never explained exactly what was communicated in that telegram, but on April 27 he suddenly agreed to Day's offer of $4,000 to pitch for the 1888 season.[15]

Day and Keefe may have settled their dispute by the results of the April 26 game that Crane pitched for the Giants. If Crane lost again, Keefe would be correct that he was indispensable, so he'd get his $4,500; if Crane won, Day would be correct that Keefe was just another pitcher, so Day's offer of $4,000 would be accepted. Crane secured his first victory of the 1888 season on April 26. There was no gloating by Day, though, as Keefe's capitulation in the salary negotiation was barely mentioned in the New York City newspapers.

Despite the delayed start, Keefe led the National League with a .745 winning percentage and 335 strikeouts during the 1888 season. One reason for his success was the adoption of a 140-game schedule in 1888, which added an extra two weeks of games to the previous 126-game schedule. The lengthened schedule forced manager Mutrie to use a three-man pitching rotation, which provided Keefe with more rest between starts. In 1888 Keefe also began to conserve energy by strictly focusing on his pitching and expending little effort at hitting. Once a .225 hitter at bat, he had a paltry .127 batting average in 1888; thereafter he was barely a .100 hitter in the batter's box.

Keefe also furthered his own image as a master pitcher in 1888 through a section in Jake Morse's book *Sphere and Ash: A History of Baseball*, which included some content from Keefe's previous writing about pitching in the 1884 book *Batting and Pitching*.[16]

Mutrie began the 1888 season with veteran Welch and newcomers Crane and Titcomb as his three pitchers. Once Keefe joined the team for his first start on May 1, Crane was relegated to spot duty. The Giants carried three catchers, O'Rourke, Brown and Murphy. Buck Ewing was still predominantly a third baseman, with Connor, Richardson, and Ward filling out the infield, with rookie Gil Hatfield in reserve. The Giants deployed four outfielders in Gore and Tiernan as holdovers from 1887 along with newcomers Elmer Foster and Mike Slattery.

With the immense popularity of the Giants within New York City, Keefe's image appeared in several exclusive card sets issued during 1888. Photographer Joseph Hall distributed a team photo of the Giants, dressed in white uniforms with "New York" in lettering across the shirt front for the first time to respond to the new trend to have the city affiliation displayed on player uniforms. Hall also made available individual photos of the players in cabinet cards. On tobacco cards issued in 1888, Keefe was one of only ten baseball players portrayed in the Goodwin champions set, which was diversified beyond baseball into boxers, rowers, and gunslingers like Buffalo Bill. Keefe's image also appeared on cards issued by Green & Blackwell Chewing Gum, which were the first baseball cards ever issued with gum rather than tobacco, and in the set of cabinet cards issued by the *Sporting Times*, the weekly baseball publication owned by Day.[17]

The Giants began the 1888 season sluggishly. On June 15 the team was in fourth place, six games behind league-leading Chicago, as the star-studded Giants ostensibly faced yet another disappointing finish in the National League standings. The turning point for the Giants in their ascension to first place in 1888 was the return of Ewing to the catcher's position on an everyday basis in mid–June. The consistent donning of the catcher's mask by Ewing coincided with a rejuvenation of the team's former ace pitcher, Mickey Welch. It also coincided with the commencement of Keefe's celebrated 19-game winning streak, which stretched from June 23 to August 10. This winning streak remains the major-league record, which Keefe shares with Giants pitcher Rube Marquard, who tied the record in 1912.[18]

Contemporary news reports provided no particular reason for Ewing's return to full-time catching, after he had rarely appeared behind the plate during the previous two seasons, in just one-fifth of the team's games. In 1887 Ewing took the catcher's position for only eight games. The press noted Ewing's contribution to team success as catcher, but only obliquely reported why. "Ewing, to date, has caught in his twenty-fifth consecutive game," the *New York Clipper* reported in late July. "Ewing's wonderful work behind the bat no doubt has had a great deal to do with the fine showing the New Yorks have made. Not that he alone is responsible for the high standing the team has recently taken, but his daily appearance behind the bat has given the rest of the boys more confidence. They see how hard Ewing is working to win, and therefore they feel that they must do equally as well."[19]

A more tangible reason for Ewing to catch more games in 1888 was reputedly the $1,000 bonus that Day offered to pay him if the Giants won the pennant, supplemented by $25 for each game he played over 65.[20] This is the more overt reason that Ewing was so helpful to the Giants in 1888, and to Keefe and Welch in particular. Ewing was better able to endure the physical punishment as catcher because he began to wear an oversized glove to catch pitches with his left hand, rather than use both hands. Although there was no contemporary reporting in 1888 of Ewing using his enlarged catcher's mitt, the *New York Sun* revealed in 1890 that Ewing began to wear the big mitt in 1888:

> It is just two years since Buck Ewing created a sensation by wearing an immense glove on his left hand while taking Tim Keefe's hot shot behind the bat at the old polo grounds. His first appearance with the glove, which looked for all the world like a big boxing glove crushed out flat by a road roller, caused a shout of laughter from the assemblage, but when the game was over Buck declared that his hand was not swollen a particle, and that thereafter nothing could tempt him to relinquish his new guard to his big left hand. All through that season Buck wore the glove, and soon it was recognized as indispensable in the paraphernalia of the big back stop.[21]

The dearth of contemporary news reports about the new glove was likely due to local writers sparing Ewing the embarrassment of appearing unmanly by using the oversized glove in this era of tough-guy catchers. The *New York Clipper* gave a hint of this when it wrote: "Ewing is certainly doing remarkably well, yet there are plenty of correspondents out of town who are hurling innuendoes at him. They seem jealous of the fine record he is making."[22] Those undefined "innuendoes" were undoubtedly the unmanly jokes of the era. With the Giants' success in 1888, that unmanly attitude evaporated when soon every catcher wore an oversized glove and caught the ball with one hand rather than two.

As Peter Morris related in his book *The Catcher*, Ewing used the big glove to protect his hands from injury, which was a constant problem with the two-handed catching style. The glove allowed Ewing to catch more games. It also gave him an edge in throwing out baserunners, since he could make a quicker throw to second base with his bare hand than he could with the thin glove he previously wore on his right hand.[23] However, as Morris noted, Ewing had to modify his catching style, since a padded glove on the left hand didn't enable a catcher to secure a baseball, only stop it.

Ewing was not the first catcher to use a big mitt. Doc Bushong, around 1886 in the American Association, was one of the first to pad the glove on his left hand and begin to catch one-handed rather than two-handed.[24] Bushong, who in 1888 was catching for Brooklyn after being sold by the St. Louis Browns, was a friend of Keefe and co-contributor with him to the 1889 book *Scientific Ball*. With Bushong just across the East River from Manhattan where the Giants lived and worked, Ewing may have been motivated by Bushong's popularizing of the big mitt, perhaps at the behest of Keefe to enable him to return to full-time catching. In his writing about the catcher position in *Scientific Ball*, Bushong, who believed the catcher was most responsible for a team's victory, left a small clue to this possibility: "The great number of games the New York club won last year by such a close margin as one run, might easily have been turned into victories by the opposing teams but for the fact of superb catching and throwing and thus preventing more runs from being scored."[25] During the 1888 season, the Giants won two-thirds of their one-run games, 22 of 34.

The Giants also had 21 shutout victories during the 1888 season, Keefe with eight and Welch with five. Both pitchers later in life sang the praises of Ewing. Welch, in 1908, called Ewing the "king of catchers" and credited him with much of the success of the 1888 team: "Is there today any greater baseball player than Buck Ewing was? Ah, he was the greatest of 'em all, indeed the grandest that the game has ever known. Universally acknowledged by all followers of the sport as the king of catchers."[26] Keefe was nearly as effusive in his praise of Ewing during a 1906 interview: "People say who followed the game that I was a pretty good pitcher myself. Well, anybody could pitch if Ewing was catching them. He knew how to steady a pitcher, knew all the points of the batsmen in the league and used those points to great advantage. He was always constantly up to the many tricks of the game and never forgot a weakness of his opponents."[27]

Ewing was extremely helpful in elevating Keefe into the ranks of the top two or three strategic pitchers in the National League. In an article entitled "The Art of Pitching" in the May 1889 issue of *Outing* magazine, Henry Chadwick defined a strategic pitcher:

> Now, what is strategy or "head work" in pitching? Its elements may be summed up as follows: Primarily, it is to deceive the eye and judgment of the batsman as to the character of the ball sent in to the bat, such as making it appear to be a swift ball when the pace is actually lessened by a well-disguised method of delivery, and also to suddenly change the line of its direction, through the medium of the curve; to which is added a deceptive delivery as to the height of the ball sent in over the base. To these strategic points are to be added that of watching the action of the batsman, so as to catch him out of good form for effective hitting; and, lastly, to tempt him to hit a ball to a part of the field where you have prepared your outfielders for catching it.[28]

While he named Clarkson, Galvin, and several others as noted exemplars of strategic pitching, Chadwick wrote that "the most successful of these pitchers is Keefe, of the New York team of 1888."

Keefe was by now the king of the change-up, or slow ball as it was called during that era. "Tim Keefe has the best slow ball of any pitcher in the profession. It deceives the best batters in the National League," one observer wrote. "There is no difference in the delivery of that and his speedy ball. It leaves his hand apparently in the same way, but it nears the plate so slowly that I have seen the batters invite curvature of the spine in their frantic, but fruitless, endeavors to hit it."[29]

Keefe and Ewing also developed a pitch-out play to cut down baserunners attempting to steal. Keefe described the play in his section on pitching in *Scientific Ball*: "He must first receive the catcher's sign, then watch the base-runner; see that he doesn't secure too much of a start off his delivery, so that the catcher will have an opportunity to dispose of him while stealing to second base. This plan worked quite successfully last season [1888] when a very fast runner intended to steal second base. Have the catcher stand about three feet outside the plate and pitch a fast, straight ball about breast high and right into his hands. This enables him to have a clear field in which to throw to second base."[30]

During Keefe's 19-game winning streak, the Giants won 31 of 40 games. The team catapulted from fourth place on June 27, six games behind Chicago, to first place on July 28. Then a 10-game winning streak from July 31 to August 10 extended the Giants' lead to seven games over second-place Chicago.

Keefe's personal 19-game streak

This Old Judge tobacco card distributed in 1888 was a color image of Tim Keefe in the orange and black striped shirt that the New York Giants wore during the 1887 season (Library of Congress, Prints and Photographs Division, LC-DIG-bbc-0558f).

began on a rainy day in Philadelphia on June 23, with a narrow 7–6 victory over the Phillies. Keefe hit his groove on June 26 with a four-hit win over the Phillies, as the *Philadelphia Inquirer* reported that "the Phillies could not hit Keefe" in an article entitled "Keefe Pitches a Grand Game."[31] The influence of Ewing was evident in this game, though, since Keefe took second billing in the New York papers. "The work of Buck Ewing was of the best possible order," the *New York Times* reported. "He handled the curves of Keefe in a brilliant manner and accepted all of the sixteen chances presented him without making an error of any description, not even a passed ball being charged against him. Keefe's work, too, was greatly admired."[32]

After two wins over Washington at the Polo Grounds, Keefe remained undaunted on the Giants' three-week road trip, with victories in Detroit, Pittsburgh, and Indianapolis. On July 13 in Indianapolis, Keefe hurled a four-hit shutout for his eighth straight victory, when "Keefe's curves proved enigmas to the local players."[33] He picked up his ninth and tenth wins in Chicago against the League's second-place team. Shortly after the Giants left Chicago, a syndicated article appeared in the *Chicago Inter Ocean* entitled "Tim Keefe: The Country's Greatest Pitcher."[34]

Keefe had his first bad outing in a month on July 20 in Philadelphia, when he yielded 12 hits in a 7–6 thriller that went into extra innings before the Giants secured the victory. "While the Phillies hit Keefe very hard," the *Philadelphia Inquirer* reported, "the New York pitcher was effective at critical points."[35] The *New York Clipper* captured those "critical points" in more detail:

> There is no doubt but that Keefe's wonderful headwork saves him many times from pitching a losing game. He is often batted quite hard, but as he prevents the hits from being bunched they prove of little benefit to the nine making them. This was undoubtedly the case in the game at Philadelphia on July 20. In the first inning, with men on second and third bases and one out, Keefe struck out Delehanty and Fogarty. Again, in the third inning, the second and third bases were occupied, with one man out, and Keefe proved himself equal to the emergency. He struck out Farrar, and Delehanty went out on a foul tip to Ewing. In the fourth inning the chances looked very favorable for one run at least. A good hit or even a sacrifice would have done the business, but it was not forthcoming. The bases were filled, with only one out, when Andrews was retired on strikes and Farrar went out on a fly to Foster.[36]

When Keefe defeated Philadelphia on July 28 for his fourteenth consecutive victory, the Giants wore all-black uniforms for the first time.[37] The tight-fitting black uniforms, with "New York" in white letters on the shirt, "were designed by Tim Keefe" to replace the loose-fitting white pants and shirts with maroon stockings.[38] The black togs were called Nadjy uniforms, based on a popular comic opera then playing at the Casino Theatre, in which one actress wore a "black bat" dress that was all black, with splashes of white, from "the satin shoes to the headdress representing a pair of bat's wings."[39] The inspiration of the play "Nadjy" for the black uniforms was one indication that Keefe frequented the theater district in 1888, presumably accompanied by Clara Helm as his escort.

The July 28 game was the start of a rough patch for Keefe. Although New York won that game, 4–2, the Giants needed to score two runs in the ninth inning to break a 2–2 tie. On August 1, Keefe gave up a four-run lead by allowing Washington to score three runs in the eighth and ninth innings. With the tying run on third base in the ninth inning, Keefe got Wilmot to ground out to Ward to end the game. On August 6 against Indianapolis, the Giants had to come from behind to win, 3–2. "Keefe pitched one of the games for which he is famous," the *New York Times* remarked, when a first-inning lead by the visitors "did not disturb him" but rather "seemed to stimulate him and thereafter the base hits were few and far between."[40] Another close call for Keefe came on August 10, when the Giants had to rally to defeat Pittsburgh, 2–1, for his nineteenth straight victory.

The streak came to a conclusion at the Polo Grounds on August 14 when Keefe was defeated by Chicago in his quest for a twentieth consecutive win. "Keefe pitched a winning game and had he received proper support in the fifth inning, the Giants would have had an equal chance to win the game," the *New York World* reported. "It was his first defeat after winning nineteen straight."[41]

Chicago scored the first run to take a 1–0 lead, when Spalding's team "gave an exhibition of scientific batting" that defused Keefe's strategic thinking in the pitcher's box. After Cap Anson singled, with Brotherhood compatriot Fred Pfeffer coming to bat, the *Chicago Inter Ocean* reported that "Keefe motioned to his fielders to move toward right field as Chicago's second baseman generally hits in that direction." Pfeffer then smashed the ball down the left-field line to score Anson. Chicago never surrendered the lead and Keefe's winning streak ended.[42]

Many people came out to the Polo Grounds to watch history being made. "It was not the Saturday half-holiday crowd, nor the hoodlum element that gathers there sometimes on the weekdays, but it was an assemblage of 12,000 well-dressed men and women that crowded the grand stand and the bleaching boards and swarmed all over the field," the *Chicago Inter Ocean* described the scene that day. "Carriages stood in double rows all around the big field, and two big tally-ho carriages, each drawn by six horses, drove up to the grand stand with McCaull's opera company."[43]

DeWolf Hopper and the rest of McCaull's cast of the comic opera

15. Record-Setting 19 Consecutive Wins   151

"Prince Methusalem" attended the August 14 game. Later that evening, the New York and Chicago teams both attended the performance at Wallack's Theatre. "Hopper let himself loose on the subject of baseball and the men laughed heartily at the hits the comedian threw at them," the *New York World* reported. "In honor of the occasion he recited with telling effect that humorous poem 'Casey's at the Bat,' that the audience literally went wild with enthusiasm, men got upon their seats and cheered ... it was one of the wildest scenes ever seen in a theatre, and showed the popularity of Hopper and baseball."[44]

That was the first public performance of Ernest Thayer's famous poem. "When I dropped my voice to B flat, below low C, at 'the multitude was awed,' I remember seeing Buck Ewing's gallant mustache give a single nervous twitch," Hopper recalled years later. "And as the house, after a moment of startled silence, grasped the anticlimactic denouement, it shouted its glee."[45] His hundreds of future performances of "Casey at the Bat" not only defined Hopper's acting career, but also contributed to a measure of fame for Keefe after his pitching career ended, through a belief that Thayer had modeled the poem's pitcher after Keefe.

With the National League pennant virtually locked up by the end of September, Mutrie rested Keefe and Welch for the postseason. Each pitcher appeared only once after September 27, Welch on October 3 and Keefe on October 13, the final day of the season. After the Giants clinched the pennant on October 4, the team finished with a 84–47 record, nine games ahead of second-place Chicago. Keefe posted his best-ever statistical season in the National League, with his 35–12 record in the pitcher's box, 1.74 earned-run average, and 0.937 ratio of walks and hits per inning.

Besides his 19-game winning streak in the pitcher's box during a pennant-winning season, Keefe had other positives things to be exuberant about in his life during the summer of 1888. There was his budding romance with Clara Helm, the wealthy socialite whom he was courting. A frequent visitor to the Polo Grounds in 1888, she was often observed "gazing intently" at her suitor's efforts in the pitcher's box.[46] In addition, Keefe probably was delighted by the court decision in July to mandate that 111th Street be cut through the Polo Grounds to bifurcate its expanse between 110th and 112th Streets.[47] Since Day would need to find a new playing field, Keefe believed this would increase his value because Day would need him more to attract crowds to whatever out-of-the-way location he could locate for a new ballpark.

One negative in Keefe's life was his relationship with Ward. It is unclear how bad their relationship was during the 1888 baseball season. Several newspapers published accounts in the postseason that ranged from there being "coolness" to "an undercurrent of friction" to their outright not speaking to each other.⁴⁸ Although Keefe generally scoffed at these reports for public comment, his friendship with Ward was on the rocks.

The tension could have been simply a side effect of Keefe's romantic relationship with Clara, who was Ward's sister-in-law. More likely, though, the strain was the result of Ward's overconfidence that the Brotherhood had a good working relationship with the National League. Keefe likely felt that was a false front, while Ward thought everything was copasetic with Spalding and the other owners. Ward seemed to believe he had a special connection with Spalding, who had advanced from journeyman ballplayer to master craftsman in the baseball business, as owner of the country's largest sporting goods firm and the Chicago ballclub. Keefe probably felt that Ward was daft.

Ward trusted Spalding so much that he signed on to be captain of the All-America team to play against the Chicago team on Spalding's tour to Australia in the fall of 1888. Keefe had declined the opportunity to participate in the tour, forcing Spalding to offer the pitching role to Keefe's teammate Ed Crane. With several members of the Brotherhood on the All-America team, Fred Pfeffer and Ned Hanlon besides Ward, Keefe may have expressed his concerns.

During the summer of 1888, Ward appeared conciliatory to the National League on several matters. Even though the League had reneged on its commitment to resolve the issues surrounding the $2,000 salary cap, Ward told the *New York Clipper* in May that "there are no issues between us and the National League at present," and "we have obtained all the conditions and rights we want, but we intend to perfect our organization into a beneficial institution."⁴⁹ At the only Brotherhood meeting during 1888, on June 10, there was only minor business transacted and no action proposed to tackle the salary-limit rule.⁵⁰ Ward even sounded a positive note on the reserve rule. In his book *Base-Ball: How to Become a Player*, which was published in 1888, Ward wrote: "To this rule, more than any other thing, does base-ball as a business owe its present substantial standing. By preserving intact the strength of a team from year to year, it places the business of base-ball on a permanent basis and thus offers security to the investment of capital."⁵¹

These words of Ward signal that the rift between Keefe and Ward ran deeper than mere trust of Spalding to a philosophical disagreement over the primary priority of the Brotherhood regarding the reserve rule. Ward was most concerned with eliminating the selling of players (via the sale of release technique) while Keefe was mainly concerned with salaries not being constrained by the reserve rule and instead determined by the open market. This disagreement can be seen in how the two men typically positioned the order of these two issues in their public remarks during 1889. Ward: "The players claim first that the present system of selling releases without benefit to the player is an outrage.... Next they claim that every man is entitled to receive for his services just as much as he can obtain."[52] Keefe: "We want the abolition of the [salary] classification system and we want the sale of players entirely done away with."[53]

The first line of the Brotherhood preamble of 1885 seemed to be at the heart of the disagreement between Keefe and Ward: "To protect and benefit ourselves collectively and individually." Ostensibly, the group came before each man. Ward advocated the group, while Keefe favored the individual. Ward's willingness to accept the $2,000 official salary cap with its ad hoc side deals to handle excess salary was the intellectual wedge that divided him from Keefe, who was willing to tolerate the selling of players in exchange for open-market salaries.

A more overt sign of the split between Ward and Keefe in 1888 was Ward's establishment of an executive committee to run the Brotherhood while he was away on Spalding's world tour, rather than name his deputy Keefe as the singular temporary head.[54] This group seemed to be designed to temper Keefe's ability to swerve from Ward's message during his absence.

Postseason baseball matters centered once again on the balance between pitching and hitting. As Keefe had prophesized after the ballclub owners reduced the requirement for a strikeout from four to three strikes, that balance had once again tipped back in favor of the pitcher during the 1888 season. To increase the amount of hitting, discussions turned to the idea of moving the pitcher's box farther from home plate to increase the distance between batter and pitcher.

Keefe was so riled at the constant tinkering by the ballclub owners with the pitching rules that he wrote an article for the *Boston Globe* in October 1888 to express his views on the subject. "These would-be reformers have grown to be like a whimpering baby eager for a new toy," Keefe wrote. "No sooner do they obtain the change they ask for then they bob up serenely the following year for another, which may possibly wipe out every vestige of change which their pleadings obtained the year previous. It is experiment, always experiment."[55] Keefe added:

> The same men who wished, and did at one time reduce pitching to a science, now are striving to put a premium on brute strength by placing the pitcher farther away from the batter. Some argue that five feet will make no material difference, but I do not think so. A person with plenty of strength and speed will be the most effective pitcher, and the men who depend on change of pace will be virtually "back numbers." The curve and slow ball will be lost arts in the base ball world for a certainty.... If the pitcher is removed to 55 feet [as opposed to the current 50 feet from home plate to the front line of the pitcher's box], the

team containing the best batsmen will gain a lead so early in the season that the interest in the pennant race will be gone before June.... I propose to allow the batsman to call for any particular ball he might wish, i.e., either a high or low ball, and that would produce enough batting to satisfy the most exacting [spectator]. I don't expect that the league will adopt my ideas, nor do I care, but I do think them worthy of consideration.[56]

Keefe was now thinking in the mindset of a master craftsman at his trade, not as a journeyman pitcher, believing that masters should establish the work process for the journeymen. In his mind, a non-working capitalist who provided solely funding and no labor had no business establishing work rules.

In November Ewing reportedly said about the pitching rules, "You can depend on it that a return will be made to the high and low ball and the effect will be felt by the pitchers. The greatest pitchers in the country under that rule will be Keefe, Welch and Galvin." The *Sporting Life* editorialized: "Make Keefe and Welch the greatest pitchers in the country, eh? No wonder Sir Timothy wastes the midnight oil in preparing column articles, advocating the restoration of the old high and low ball rule."[57]

As the National League champion, the New York Giants arranged a postseason series with the St. Louis Browns, the American Association pennant winner, to determine the world's championship, as the World Series was then called. It wasn't the first time that many of the Giants had played against St. Louis, since they had met in New Orleans during the 1885 postseason and again after the 1887 season in San Francisco.

It was the fourth consecutive appearance for St. Louis in the World Series. After the disputed tied series with Chicago in 1885, the Browns defeated Chicago in 1886 and lost to Detroit in 1887. The 1887 series was a lengthy best-of-15-games extravaganza played in ten different cities, which drew meager crowds for the last four games after Detroit had clinched the series in the eleventh game. The 1888 World Series was a less travel-weary affair than the 1887 road show. John Day and St. Louis owner Chris Von der Ahe agreed to play a best-of-10-games match with four games each in New York and St. Louis and the other two games in Brooklyn and Philadelphia. If an eleventh game were to be necessary, it would be played in Cincinnati. In a novel arrangement, the owners agreed to use two umpires for each game, John Gaffney of the League and John Kelly of the Association, rather than a single umpire that was customary in that era.

Keefe won four of the first eight games for the Giants, as New York clinched the series by winning six of the first eight games, rendering moot the final two games of the 10-game series.

In the first game of the series on October 16, Keefe pitched the Giants to a 2–1 victory with a three-hitter at the Polo Grounds. Of the three hits, only two were clean hits to the outfield, as the other was a scratch infield single. Just two other balls left the infield, two fly balls to Tiernan in right field. Keefe also had nine strikeouts. After the Browns won the second game to tie the series, Keefe pitched a six-hitter in the third game for a 4–2 victory. Keefe escaped bases-loaded situations in the fifth and seventh innings to secure the victory. After the Giants won the fourth game, Keefe increased the team's series lead in the fifth game with a 6–4 victory. He spotted the Browns a 4–1 lead, but the Giants scored five runs in the eighth inning to rally for victory. This was the last game the Giants ever played at the Polo Grounds in its original location at the intersection of Fifth Avenue and 110th Street.

The Giants took a commanding five-games-to-one lead in the series with a win in the sixth game in Philadelphia. As the series moved to St. Louis, the Browns won the seventh game by scoring four runs in the gathering dusk to rally to victory. Keefe shut out the Browns in the eighth game on October 25. The Giants were awarded the Dauvray Cup at the St. Louis Grand Opera House during the evening of October 27, but Helen was not there to do the honors, as she, Ward, and Crane had left St. Louis after the clinching game on October 25 to go west to Denver to meet up with the All-America team that was part of Spalding's baseball tour to Australia.

Keefe cemented a national reputation as baseball's best pitcher in 1888 with his World Series performance. He gave up just 18 hits and two earned runs in 35 innings pitched, while registering 30 strikeouts, to earn four victories. Keefe was motivated to pitch well in this postseason series to help establish a national reputation, since newspapers nationwide carried wire-service accounts of the World Series games. The national reputation would be quite helpful from a business perspective, as Keefe was on the verge on opening up his own sporting goods firm, Keefe & Becannon.

Ward sailed from San Francisco on November 18 with the rest of the Spalding tour, with the first stop slated for Hawaii before heading across the Pacific Ocean to Australia. Ward's wife was not on that ship, however, since after a disagreement in San Francisco Helen left the tour to return to New York to meet her sister Clara to travel to Europe.[58] Everyone on the tour was unable to receive communications from the United States until they reached Sydney, Australia, since there was not yet a telegraph cable under the Pacific Ocean.[59] Since Spalding, just before leaving San Francisco, had extended the tour so that it would now go all the way around the world, with stops in India, Egypt, Italy, and England before returning to the United States, Ward was unable to communicate with the United States for months, not just weeks.

An editorial in *Sporting Life*, based on an authoritative source (presumably Ward), summarized the Brotherhood situation on the eve of the National League meeting in November:

> The absence of John M. Ward, president of the Ball Players' Brotherhood, for the entire winter will not hamper the Brotherhood in the least. The government is in the hands of an executive committee, and authority has never been vested in any one official, although Mr. Ward, while on the field, had considerable power and exercised a general supervision as president and chairman of the committee. All reports to the contrary notwithstanding, there will be no meeting of the Brotherhood council until the regular spring meeting, and at the annual League meeting next Wednesday the Brotherhood will neither be represented nor request a hearing upon any topic whatever. There will be some individual grievances, perhaps, presented to the League by Brotherhood members, either in writing or in person, but the Brotherhood itself, nor any committee representing it, will not be on hand. The Brotherhood got all it wanted last winter in the way of recognition and a new contract, and is quite satisfied with its present relations to the League and with the very smooth and pleasant progress of events since.[60]

Since Ward had no concern about the salary cap, he saw no reason for the Brotherhood to be at the League meeting. With Ward fending off seasickness 1,000 miles offshore in the Pacific Ocean, the National League ballclub owners held three days of meetings beginning on November 20 in New York City.

Keefe and the rest of the New York Giants had been on top of the baseball world for four weeks after winning the World Series, until the third day of the League meeting when the owners dropped a bombshell on the ballplayers.

The agenda for the first two days of the League meeting concerned routine matters. The rules committee, seeking to increase batting in 1889, debated a return to the high-low strike zone choice by the batter, moving the pitcher farther from home plate, and changing the number of allowable balls and strikes. While most observers associated with the playing field (including Keefe) favored the return to differing strikes zones by batter as the best way to increase hitting, the committee only reduced the number of balls required for a base on balls from five to four.[61]

There was another pitching rule change for 1889 season that received little attention: the pitcher was allowed to place either foot on the rear line of the pitcher's box and the other foot did not need to be placed to the left of the center line of the box. "We abolished the imaginary line regulating the position of the feet, and now a man can put either foot on the rear line," Philadelphia owner John Rogers explained. "The rule last year was never strictly enforced. Tim Keefe, for instance, crossed one foot over the other."[62]

On the third day of the League meeting, the owners dropped their bombshell when they adopted the Brush Plan to constrain player salaries. The Brush Plan, also known as the classification plan, provided for five fixed-salary classifications that players could be assigned to: A for $2,500; B for

$2,250; C for $2,000; D for $1,750; and E for $1,500. Not only would baseball skill be a determinant for which classification a ballplayer would be assigned, but off-the-field habits would also be taken into account.[63]

The classification plan is considered to be the catalyst for the formation for the Players' League one year after that plan was adopted by the National League. But the typical Ward-outfoxed-by-Spalding explanations are oversimplified, such as Ward being "uncharacteristically oblivious to the fact that Spalding might have ulterior motives for bringing him on the trip" or "see[ing] the timing of the plan's passage as a blatant act of treachery on Spalding's part."[64] The catalyst was not Ward being naïve or Spalding exercising treachery, but rather the ballclub owners backsliding in their basic comprehension of the role of the ballplayer. The classification plan treated the player not as a craftsman with individual talents, but rather as a component that could easily be compartmentalized, like an industrialized factory worker. If Ward and Spalding had both been at that League meeting and not on their way to Australia, the Players' League would still have been formed.

Soon the League owners backed off the classification plan a bit, saying that players under reserve for 1889 would not be impacted by it. But the damage had been done in view of the Brotherhood members still in the country, led by Keefe, who saw the classification plan as distinct evidence that there was a cavernous philosophical divide between owners and ballplayers. The executive committee established by Ward quickly deviated from his wishes by making Keefe the chief spokesman and temporary head of the Brotherhood. Keefe immediately gave a long interview to Harris of the *New York Press* about his thoughts on the classification plan:

"I arrived from Albany last Tuesday morning [November 20] and have been more amused than interested to read the reports of the League meeting in New York. Though I cannot say definitely what shape the action of the Brotherhood will take, depend upon it we are not going to sit idly by and allow the League to deal as unfairly by us and in as bad faith as has been the case. They broke faith with us last year when they promised to abolish the $2,000 limit clause and did not.... It certainly is time to act. There will be plenty of fun ahead for the League. Why, it is the old $2,000 limit business over again. Do you think Ewing is going to play for any $2,500 next season, or that this rule is going to hasten his signing? Do you suppose that the New York Club is going to be without his services on account of this rule? Not a bit, depend upon it.... I shall not lose any sleep about the matter. I shan't rush to sign and I don't think any of my comrades and friends will. We won't assemble until next spring, but when our Houses of Parliament do assemble, let them tremble."[65]

Eliminating restrictions on salaries was Keefe's top priority as a Brotherhood officer, so he immediately became a firebrand on the subject and aggressively talked it up with baseball writers. He demonstrated a newfound proclivity to publicly vocalize his thoughts, rather than remain in the background and let Ward use more tempered words to describe the Brotherhood position. "This grading of players is all nonsense, because it is so impracticable. No one can undertake to do such a thing as that," Keefe criticized the classification plan. "The idea of watching the players, and rewarding the good ones! Did you ever hear of anyone being detailed to watch the actors or men in any other profession, for that matter?"[66] Keefe was virtually a proselytizer when it came to the evils of the classification plan.

Harris publicly called out Keefe on the excessive verbiage: "The Boston space writers have struck a veritable mine for specials and are working the worthy Timothy Keefe to perfection," Harris wrote. "This is all very fine for Keefe and the reporters, but it won't do the Brotherhood any good and that organization is in momentary danger of being placed in a false position. Hadn't the rest of the Brotherhood's governing council better call a halt on the loquacious secretary-treasurer?"[67]

Sullivan of the *Boston Globe* wrote that fall that "Tim Keefe, as a world's champion, is the same retiring and gentlemanly fellow he was as pitcher of the old Troy Club," adding that "Tim wears the same sized hat he did when he blossomed out as a twirler."[68] However, Keefe soon began to change in many ways, as he was sucked into the vortex of the Brotherhood's radical plan to change the nature of professional baseball. But first he grappled with the challenge "to embark in the sporting goods business" by opening a new firm, Keefe & Becannon, in January 1889.[69]

Keefe's decision to compete with Spalding in the sporting goods industry, however, turned out to have unexpectedly grave personal consequences to Keefe, which would drastically change the future direction of his life.

16

Sporting Goods Proprietor

In January 1889, when Tim Keefe established the sporting goods store Keefe & Becannon in New York City, he stepped up from his journeyman status as a ballplayer to function at the master level to follow in the footsteps of Albert Spalding (Spalding & Bros.) and George Wright (Wright & Ditson) who had earlier made the same transition from the playing field to sporting goods merchant.

Keefe's business partner was William H. Becannon, the older brother of former Metropolitans pitcher Jim Becannon, who was "a leading spirit among the amateur clubs of this vicinity for many years and will, no doubt, command their trade."[1] A correspondent for the *New York Clipper* stopped by the temporary headquarters of the new enterprise and filed this pitching-analogy-laden report of the activity at Keefe's sporting goods emporium:

> Handsome Tim Keefe and his genial partner, W.H. Becannon, sat in their cozy office, Room F, 149 Broadway, when a *Clipper* reporter called on them Jan. 21. Tim was in the box (chair) with his mail matter before him, and, after carefully sizing up the contents he would, by a graceful movement of the body, either send in a straight one to his receiver, "Buck," who stood ready to nail a customer, or he would let go one of his provokingly slow "drops," just as an inducement to some wary tradesman, and thus it went all through the game of correspondence. "They will not steal many bases on Buck," observed the reporter. "Not while I am watching them," replied Tim, with a smile.[2]

Becannon had taken a similar route in baseball as Keefe, first playing for amateur teams for several years in the 1870s before moving up to be a professional for minor-league teams. However, he never made the jump to the major leagues as a ballplayer, settling for a three-week stint as an umpire in the American Association in 1883. Becannon began working for Spalding & Bros. in 1885 when the firm opened its New York City store at 241 Broadway, before leaving its employ in January 1889 to team up with Keefe. "What Becannon lacks in fame as a player he makes up in business capacity and executive ability," *Sporting Life* reported. "The success which has attended the new firm is in great measure due to his untiring efforts and a practical knowledge of the business acquired by his long connection with the Spaldings."[3]

159

It was a bold move by Keefe to open a sporting goods company in 1889. There were many competitors in the sporting goods business in the late 1880s, including Wright & Ditson in Boston, A.J. Reach in Philadelphia, H.H. Kiffe in Brooklyn, and Peck & Snyder's in New York City. The industry was dominated by the Spalding & Bros. firm, often called "the first leisure conglomerate," which was involved in manufacturing, distribution, and publishing a large variety of sports-related items.[4] Spalding & Bros. was established in 1876 in Chicago as a partnership between Albert and his brother Walter.[5] Much like the initial structure of Spalding & Bros. where Albert continued to pitch while his brother Walter ran the business, Keefe & Becannon had a similar arrangement, where Keefe still played baseball to advertise the firm while Becannon managed the business.

Spalding was a major force in baseball, where his firm supplied the official ball of the National League. Spalding "aspired to be the John D. Rockefeller of baseball," wrote historian LeRoy Ashby in his book *With Amusement for All: A History of American Popular Culture*. "Just as Rockefeller integrated the oil business, controlling it from drilling to sales, Spalding established a highly lucrative sporting-goods business in which his plants manufactured baseball gloves, balls, and bats and moved the products through more than twenty thousand retail accounts."[6] Spalding sought to monopolize the sporting goods industry, by consolidating the other competing firms. At the time Keefe & Becannon opened for business, Spalding & Bros. already had a partial ownership of Reach, and the firm would go on to either absorb all the other major competitors, such as Wright & Ditson, or put them out of business.

Keefe & Becannon, the sporting goods firm established by Tim Keefe, was most famous for producing the Keefe Ball, as seen in this rare *Sporting Life* advertisement. The firm was also known for two specialty items, the catcher's glove popularized by Buck Ewing in 1888 and the kangaroo shoes that Keefe wore when he won 19 consecutive games in 1888.

16. Sporting Goods Proprietor

Out of the country with his world tour at the time Keefe & Becannon opened its doors, Spalding was probably livid upon his return when he discovered the new competition for sporting goods in New York City, especially since Keefe had enticed one of Spalding's top salesmen to jump ship from his New York store to team up with him. Keefe believed he was just another artisan hanging out his shingle as a master craftsman. But to Spalding and his brother Walter, Keefe's ties to the Brotherhood made his new enterprise a personal affront, not simply another business competitor.

After Keefe & Becannon occupied its permanent offices at 157 Broadway, the firm began its campaign to acquire a healthy share of the New York City market for sporting goods.[7] Like Spalding & Bros. and the other firms it was competing with, Keefe & Becannon sold more than just baseball goods: "Its general line embraces the implements and accessories of every branch of sport, including base ball, athletics, bicycling, cricket, boxing, tennis, foot ball, lacrosse, croquet, [roller] polo, skating, fishing, fencing, and gymnastics. There is nothing in any of these lines that Keefe & Becannon can not supply."[8] Baseball, though, was the specialty of the firm, which offered products that its competitors couldn't match. The *New York Press* reported that the "Ewing glove" was a cornerstone product of the fledging company, in addition to its "kangaroo Keefe shoes."[9] Keefe also did a bustling business selling black Nadjy uniforms, which the Giants had worn during the 1888 season.[10] Keefe included a little book entitled "Hints on Pitching" with every order, to encourage sales and further his image as the game's greatest pitcher.[11] However, after operating for only two years, Keefe & Becannon went out of business in 1891, a victim of the firm's over-reliance on baseball-related business from the ballclubs in the Players' League.

Keefe had been considering the establishment of a business to leverage his fame in New York City for about two years. He became serious about it in early 1888 when he transferred the ownership of his Cambridge real estate into the name of his sister Annie in order to protect himself from the claims of business creditors.[12] He had alluded to the business in the spring of 1888 when he was negotiating his salary with the New York Giants, telling Sullivan of the *Boston Globe*: "I have business here in Boston to settle up that may take me a week, and it may take a month.... I am not trying to play any bluff. When I get my business affairs fixed up ... if they want me, and I will jump in."[13] Ten months later in February 1889, Sullivan again interviewed Keefe, after he had taken a break from the business to coach the Amherst College baseball team. Keefe told Sullivan:

"All business now. I got away from Amherst for a few weeks to drum up some trade. Just got in with my samples. Yes, we're doing pretty well. Takes a long time to get acquainted, but we are picking up a trade; got the suits of both Amherst teams, varsity and freshman.... Why I took off my coat up at Amherst the other day to show how I thought a ball ought to be curved. I pitched just two balls and my arm ached for hours. That is the only time I have touched a ball since last October."[14]

Unlike previous years, Keefe didn't use the college coaching time in 1889 to prepare his right arm for the upcoming major-league season.

A few weeks after talking with Sullivan of the *Boston Globe*, in a good faith gesture to the management of the Giants, Keefe agreed to pitch a Saturday afternoon preseason game for the Giants against Brooklyn of the American Association. Harris of the *New York Press* found Keefe at his place of business on that Saturday morning. "At an early hour yesterday forenoon Mr. Timothy John Keefe, a Broadway merchant, stood behind his counter doing up a pair of kangaroo shoes for a ball crank," Harris wrote, adding that the customer "watched him eagerly as he tied up a very hard looking package, for Mr. Keefe has not been a merchant very long." When the customer asked Keefe who would be pitching for the Giants that day, "the merchant smiled sweetly, as he replied: 'I haven't signed yet, but I am going to try to help the boys out.'"[15] Brooklyn hammered Keefe, 6–0, as the star pitcher of the Giants appeared very rusty in the pitcher's box.

His poor showing in the Brooklyn game demonstrated that Keefe was preoccupied with getting his new business off the ground rather than perfecting his pitching delivery for the upcoming season. He was also immersed in an intellectual battle with the ownership of the Giants to negotiate a higher salary to continue to pitch for the Giants. Keefe's strong belief in the future success of Keefe & Becannon led him into a nasty salary squabble with the Giants, which resulted in a two-week holdout at the beginning of the 1889 playing season.

17
Successful Salary Holdout

In the aftermath of the despised salary classification plan announced by the National League ballclub owners in November 1888, Tim Keefe moved forward with his plan to stage a holdout for a higher salary to play for the New York Giants during the 1889 season. Keefe executed this second consecutive holdout by using Harris of the *New York Press* as an unwitting co-conspirator through his newspaper reports. Keefe trusted Harris because they shared twin loves, baseball and the theatre, as Harris was the dramatic editor for the *New York Press* in addition to his role as sports editor.[1]

Keefe began laying the groundwork for his holdout in December 1888 when Harris wrote in the *New York Press* that "Tim Keefe wants an increase of salary for 1889," despite Day's contention that Keefe had been the highest paid pitcher in the National League the previous year.[2] A few weeks later Harris wrote, "Keefe has not signed yet, and is not likely to for some time to come. I do not think he will do so until the eleventh hour," after he chatted with Keefe at his sporting goods store as he worked to mail advertising circulars. "Last year Keefe's salary was about $4,000, which was several hundreds less than he demanded. This season Tim will naturally want an increase, and in view of his work last season is entitled to it. Just how the New York club will be able to give it to him without interfering with the classification and grading plan is best known to Mr. Day."[3]

In the absence of any official action by the Brotherhood in regard to the salary classification plan, Keefe's holdout at least was a minimal attempt to put some pressure on the ballclub owners. "What may be done of course I cannot say. There will not be another meeting of the Brotherhood until President Ward returns to America," Keefe told Harris. "As this will not be until April, there can be no meeting until the first Eastern trip of the Western clubs."[4]

Ward had planned to be a holdout in the spring of 1889 once he returned from the Spalding world tour, to test the player-sale extension of the reserve rule. Ward had repeatedly said that 1888 would be his last season with the Giants, since he expected Giants owner John Day to sell his release for a price higher than the $10,000 price tag paid by Boston for the release of Kelly and Clarkson. By November 1888 newspaper reports indicated that Washington was willing to pay $12,000 for Ward's release.[5]

While Ward was away on the Spalding world tour, Keefe pursued a holdout to test the salary limits implicitly created by the reserve rule (and explicitly by the classification plan). Keefe focused his Brotherhood-related actions on his top priority, which was likely that of the membership as well, not Ward's top priority (the selling of ballplayers), which the council of delegates favored. Whether he intentionally hijacked the holdout stage or not, Keefe was asking for trouble once Ward reappeared on American soil.

In addition to his holdout for a higher salary, Keefe also began posturing that he had viable alternatives to pitching for the Giants and was able to sit out the 1889 season. Newspapers noted that he was busy getting the Keefe & Becannon sporting goods business off the ground. He also leaked information to the *New York World* about the value of the land he owned in Cambridge. "Another cause for this independence, it is said, is the sudden increase in value of some property owned by Tim at Cambridge, Mass.," the *New York World* reported. "Recently the town officials decided to erect a public library and selected as a site for it the ground owned by Tim ... [who] when offered a fair price for the property refused the offer. He has refused several others since, the last being $30,000. Tim, it is said, holds off for $50,000 and is confident of obtaining that sum."[6]

Of course, the *New York World* report was an exaggeration. By 1889 the public library in Cambridge was already under construction across the street from Keefe's property.[7] The city did not need to acquire any additional land for the library. There was possibly a grain of truth to the story, as Harvard College was reportedly interested in Keefe's land.[8] That interest, if sincere, was likely tepid since the Keefe property was not contiguous with the college's other land, and there were existing houses between it and Harvard Yard. However, John Day did not know that, so it could serve Keefe as an effective ploy in his bargaining with Day.

Ward didn't find out about the League's salary classification plan until the Spalding tour reached Egypt in February, where he read about it in an old American newspaper in Cairo. Simon Goodfriend wrote about the discovery in his dispatch to the *New York Sun*, which is likely how Keefe and the other Brotherhood members knew that Ward knew.[9] Ward didn't rush back home from Egypt immediately, though, but rather remained with the tour, expecting to reunite with his wife in Europe. However, Helen and her sister Clara had already left to return to the United States.[10] Once Ward knew his wife had jilted him, he left the tour in England and returned to New York City in late

March. Another reason that Ward did not immediately return to the United States was that while on the tour he worked on a plan to launch what would be known as the Players' League. He didn't want to tip his hand to the National League owners by returning too early.

The exact details of the formation of the Players' League, including the date when the concept clearly moved forward, have been lost to history, since there was no incentive for anyone involved with those activities to write them down for posterity after the collapse of the league following its lone 1890 season. Winners write history, the old adage goes, not the losers. The most comprehensive history is Ward's piece in the *Players' League Guide* (reproduced in *Sporting Life* in April 1890); Harris also penned a history in December 1889 that was published in the book *Athletic Sports in America, England and Australia*.[11] Given the relationship between Harris and Keefe, this latter history may include some of Keefe's thoughts on the matter. Keefe said little for publication about the Players' League after its 1890 season. Keefe's ledger of Brotherhood meeting minutes might have included some salient information, but no passages from 1888 or 1889 have ever been made public.[12]

The evolution of the league's formation in this chapter, as well as its eventual demise discussed in later chapters, is the author's interpretation of events, using these two sources and other snippets located in credible contemporary newspaper reports. Conventional wisdom has always been that Ward and his inner circle of team delegates evaluated different approaches, including a general strike. A more nuanced look at the limited evidence indicates that Ward and the Brotherhood likely were intent on establishing a new league from the day Ward stepped back on U.S. soil in March 1889.

In October 1889 Albert Johnson, the major financier of the Players' League, wrote that Brotherhood member Ned Hanlon told him that "he, Ward, Pfeffer, and Fogarty, on the trip around the world had thought of getting capital in each city to build the grounds for them, for which they would allow a fair percentage for the risk, the players to receive a portion of the profits."[13] This indicates that the Players' League concept moved forward sometime in late February or early March while Ward was in Europe, when "an idle fantasy was suddenly transformed into a real alternative."[14] While it is very unclear exactly what transpired in Europe, if Johnson's text is taken at face value, it indicates that some discussion had occurred back in the United States prior to the Spalding tour's departure from San Francisco, since the profit sharing element is included, which Keefe surely had a hand in crafting to mimic the ownership principle that he so dearly advocated.

Once Ward was back on American soil in March 1889, Keefe's relationship with Ward became more strained. There were at least two primary reasons for the increased tension between the two Brotherhood officers.

Keefe had rekindled his romance with Clara Helm, who had returned in January with her sister Helen, Ward's wife, from their trip to Europe. This was problematical because Clara, with Keefe's tacit approval, offered to finance Helen's return to the theater, which Ward was fundamentally opposed to.[15] Clara and Helen soon returned to Europe in late May for a two-month stay following a quarrel between Ward and his wife about her return to acting.[16]

In addition, Ward was surely annoyed at Keefe for pushing his own agenda, not Ward's, in the aftermath of the salary classification plan and in displacing Ward as the prominent salary holdout that spring. However, Keefe's holdout quickly turned into an effective distraction as the Brotherhood lightning rod in the public forum, so that Ward could work unencumbered behind the scenes on the plans for the Players' League. With Keefe's holdout tied to the classification plan, Ward easily camouflaged his efforts to start a new league through a disinformation campaign with the baseball writers. Ward publicly focused all the Brotherhood's activities during the summer of 1889 on the classification plan, which was a red herring. Any newspaper discussions about a new league printed before September 1889, notably by Harris in the *New York Press*, were dismissed as ridiculous by most observers, particularly by the ballclub owners.

With more pressing matters requiring his attention, Ward encouraged Keefe to go to the mat with the Giants in his holdout. Two weeks before Opening Day, Harris wrote about the stalemate between Keefe and Day in the *New York Press*: "Tim is having quite a quadrille with Mr. Day. Tim very naturally thinks his good work of last season entitles him to a raise in salary, and Mr. Day thinks that Tim's salary last year was too much."[17] Keefe was a very effective front man for the Brotherhood in the spring of 1889, as his holdout captured the attention of newspapermen.

On the eve of April 18, with New York City expected to close down the Polo Grounds in order to run 111th Street through the property, Keefe used this leverage to take his salary negotiation to the wire services for nationwide distribution. Newspapers across the country ran a one-sentence summation of the situation: "Keefe refuses to pitch for the New Yorks for less than $5,000 a year, and Mr. Day declines to pay over $4,000, [so] it is probable that Tim will not be with the club this season."[18] Keefe was more detailed with the baseball writers in New York City. "Yes, it is true that I have asked for an increase," Keefe told the local writers. "I have played good ball for the New York Club, the organization has made money, and I do not think that my demands are unjust.... If my terms are not agreed to I will attend to my sporting goods business and give up the diamond until matters are arranged to my satisfaction."[19]

Harris of the *New York Press*, with his personal connection to Keefe, published more intimate thoughts of Keefe during the course of the holdout, especially in the Sunday edition of the *Press* when reader circulation figures were the highest. Three days after the news broke nationally, Harris wrote this account in the April 21 Sunday edition:

> I do not believe that both parties will stand by their guns for many weeks. One or the other will, I think, give in, and there will be a compromise of some kind before June 1. I talked with Mr. Day Friday, and he was very positive in his statements. "I have offered Keefe $4,000," said he, "and I consider it enough. I shall not pay him another cent. Keefe is a great and successful pitcher, and I want his services, but those services, in my opinion, are not worth the amount he asks for them—$5,000. If he continues to refuse $4,000 we will have to do the best we can without him." I called on Keefe at his place of business and found him quite as decided as John B. Day. "I'm in a position where I can afford to wait," said Sir Tim. "I've got a good business and a little money. I don't know any better time for me to retire than now. I know $4,000 is a good deal of money, but I've made up my mind that I'm entitled to more, and I can be as obstinate as Mr. Day. I won't sign for $4,000; that's flat. If I do not get more I won't pitch a ball. If I am classified I'll retire altogether." And there you have both sides of it.[20]

With Keefe incorporating Ward's now-aborted holdout strategy to test the reserve rule by threatening to sit out the 1889 baseball season, Keefe was an extremely effective diversion to forestall the New York baseball writers from prying too deeply into what the Brotherhood was actually planning.

Opening Day of the 1889 season found the New York Giants playing in Jersey City, New Jersey, because the Polo Grounds had been shut down to make way for 111th Street. This enhanced Keefe's negotiation position, since only 3,000 fans bothered to make the trek from Manhattan to Jersey City. Previous Opening Days at the Polo Grounds typically drew 10,000 or more spectators. The Giants soon worked out a deal to use the St. George's Cricket Grounds on Staten Island. But this was even more remote from Manhattan than Jersey City. Still, John Day wouldn't budge on his offer to Keefe.

While Keefe was verbally jousting with Day about his salary for the 1889 season, Ward had signed with the Giants and was moving forward with his plan for the new league. When two games of the opening series with Boston were rained out, Ward took the opportunity to meet with several of the Boston players. Ward, now entrenched in the disinformation campaign, leaked the meeting to Will Rankin at the *New York Clipper*. Rankin wrote that "demands will be made upon the magnates during the championship season, when, if necessary, a strike could be made effective," adding that "it is pretty certain the players will make a fight against the classification plan."²¹ Ward almost assuredly used the meeting with the Boston players to vet his plan for the new league. The strike threat was clearly a red herring, since a strike would have been subscribing to the American Federation of Labor approach to labor relations, which Ward despised.

On Sunday, April 28, Harris wrote about his latest conversation with Day. "I expressed my belief that the Giants could hardly hold the pennant without Keefe's services. Mr. Day would not admit that. 'I know,' said he, 'that Keefe is a great pitcher, but he is not worth $5,000. No pitcher is. What's more, I won't give him that sum if we lose every game. If he won't sign we'll do the best we can. It will give the young fellows a show, and we'll depend on Welch and Crane to lead the van.'"²² The following Sunday, May 5, Harris tossed Day a bone, likely at the behest of Keefe: "I look for a speedy settlement with Keefe. He is ready to compromise, and it appears to me that Mr. Day is too shrewd not to meet him in the same spirit."²³

Keefe offered a compromise to Day on May 6. "Tim Keefe and Mr. Day met 'by accident' yesterday at the *Sporting Times* office," Harris wrote. "Mr. Keefe said he would sign for $4,500, $500 less than his demand when negotiations began. Mr. Day said he would not give Keefe a penny over $4,000. The magnate and the player parted as far apart as ever. Keefe says he will not play ball this season for less than $4,500. He told a *Press* reporter that he was about satisfied now that he would not do any playing this season." Harris quoted Keefe as saying, "Mr. Day has reached his limit and I have reached mine. I shall make no further effort to compromise the matter."²⁴

After Keefe met Day again on May 7, Harris wrote: "Neither side showed any disposition to weaken. Keefe called at the *Sporting Times* office in reference to an article on pitching. While there Tim ran across Mr. Day. There was some joking about joining the team, but nothing serious. Sir Tim drank a glass of water and said, 'See what you've driven me to,' and Mr. Day remarked that a man who could get $4,000 for playing ball wasn't obliged to drink water."²⁵

On May 9, the Giants played in Boston. With both Welch and Crane injured and Titcomb pitching ineffectively, Buck Ewing pitched the game for the Giants. Although New York won the game, Keefe's services were clearly needed since the pitching staff was badly depleted. Day capitulated. "After much disagreement and long haggling, President Day and Tim Keefe, the king of pitchers, have at last come to a definite understanding," the evening edition of the *New York World* reported. "Yes, I have signed," Keefe told the *World* reporter with a smile, "and that's all there is to it," declining to specify the terms. "Keefe is a trifle fat for ball-playing," the writer added, "the effect of a winter's good keeping, but he will work steadily now that he is fixed for the season."[26] The *New York Press* reported the next day that Keefe and Day had agreed to the proposed $4,500 compromise.[27] Keefe pitched his first game of the 1889 season on May 10 in Boston.

Keefe is sometimes called "the first holdout," due to his successful effort to be "the first National League player who refused to put on a uniform until his terms had been accepted after the beginning of the championship season."[28]

There was some urgency for Keefe to sign with the Giants by mid–May. First, he needed to be engaged by a ballclub in the National League to retain his status in the Brotherhood, whose first meeting was scheduled for Sunday, May 19. Second, the short-term success of the Keefe & Becannon sporting goods firms was dependent upon Keefe functioning as a professional pitcher. His latest treatise on pitching was published that spring in the book *Scientific Ball*, designed to increase his reputation as a master craftsman in the art of pitching.[29] Keefe's opening paragraph stated:

> The chief requisites for a first-class pitcher are good, quick curves, plenty of speed, and a cool head at critical moments. To be successful he must possess all of the above qualities. Speed is really the essential point in a pitcher, but he must have good command of it or his work will be more damaging to his catcher's hands than to the opposing batsmen. The same holds good with his curves. If he has not good command of them, he is certainly laboring under great disadvantage. The only way to acquire command of the ball is by continual practice. Always make it a point when pitching to have an object to pitch at. It cannot be acquired in a day or a week, but requires years of practice.[30]

A longer excerpt of Keefe's pitching section in *Scientific Ball* is contained in Appendix C.

Upon their return to New York City from Boston, the Giants played a four-game series with Cleveland, which was now in the National League, having transferred from the American Association to replace the Detroit club. This was fortuitous for the Brotherhood, as it made it much more feasible to work with Albert Johnson, the Cleveland trolley magnate who was interested in financing the new league. Arrangements for these discussions started around mid–May, with Frank Brunell, the sports editor of the *Cleveland Plain Dealer*, likely acting as an intermediary. Brunell is credited with orchestrating the Cleveland-Detroit transaction to get Cleveland back into the National League.[31] Brunell became the secretary of the Players' League, a position that seemingly was reward for some instrumental aspect of the league's formation.

The first of two formal meetings of the Brotherhood council of delegates in 1889 occurred on May 19 in New York City. Ward later characterized the meeting atmosphere as "indignation was extreme," with many of the team delegates "ready even to quit entirely rather than longer submit to such unfair treatment."[32] Harris, in his history of the Brotherhood, wrote that "Ward advised a strike, or, at any rate, the leaders were inclined to order one ... on the Fourth of July."[33] The strike vote, according to Harris, didn't pass. If a strike vote were conducted, it would have been purely for disinformation purposes. After the meeting Ward announced that he would meet with Spalding personally to discuss the classification plan when the Giants played in Chicago in late June. The *New York Clipper* published a long piece about Ward being "outspoken in his denunciation of the classification rule."[34] While publicly Ward continued to espouse this red herring to keep the owners fixated on classification, the Brotherhood secretly sped forward on its plan to establish a new league.

However, the May 19 meeting was reported to be an all-day session that lasted into the evening and "was held behind closed doors and the greatest secrecy was maintained as to what was done."[35] Little information was released beyond the re-election of Ward and Keefe as officers and the establishment of the position of vice president (to be held by Dan Brouthers).[36] This new officer position seemed to be punishment for Keefe to diminish his power within the Brotherhood, since it was later reported that Keefe, a true believer in the movement, "had to be urged to accept the nomination for secretary-treasurer of the Brotherhood."[37] With so much time spent in the meeting and so few publicized results, the meeting surely involved an extensive discussion of Ward's plan for a new league and Johnson's involvement in financing it. The distinct possibility of a new league is exactly what Harris reported in the *New York Press*:

> The two things which they desire to have arranged more equitably are reforms that justice would seem to dictate. The players claim first that the present system of selling releases without benefit to the player is an outrage and if it is continued each man must be paid one-half of whatever sum is given for his release. Next they claim that every man is entitled to receive for his services just as much as he can obtain, and so no man or corporation of men have a right to say "your services are worth so much and you shall not receive any more." This is what the classification rule means, and Mr. Ward and his associates will demand its abolishment. The alternative will be the desertion of the league by every member of the Brotherhood, and the formation of a new league by the Brotherhood and certain capitalists who, they claim, are ready to stand by them.[38]

Although he had revealed the Brotherhood's big secret, no one took Harris seriously.

In early June, Johnson began meeting with Brotherhood members, first with Hanlon when his Pittsburgh team was playing in Cleveland. The National League schedule very conveniently required Cleveland to play a four-week homestand from June 6 to July 6 against six of the other seven league teams (all except Indianapolis). This lengthy homestand enabled most of the Brotherhood members to talk with Johnson to understand how the new league would operate.

Attendance was so bad at the Giants' games played at remote Staten Island that the morning game of the Decoration Day twin bill attracted a mere 500 spectators; the crowd was not much better at the afternoon game, when only 5,000 or so ventured across New York Harbor to watch the Giants. On June 14, the Giants left for a three-week road trip, which included a stop in Cleveland, where Keefe and his teammates met with Johnson to discuss plans for the new league. When the Giants returned on July 8, their new playing facility in Manhattan was ready.

Day reached agreement in mid–June to lease half the available land in Coogan's Hollow in the far northern section of Manhattan, at the intersection of Eighth Avenue and 155th Street.[39] Day called the new ballpark the New Polo Grounds, since baseball fans had become accustomed to that name for the place where the Giants played their ballgames. Interestingly, the work to build the new ballpark was interrupted on June 24 when some unauthorized men began to fence in part of Day's leased grounds, claiming they were "acting under instructions from A.L. Johnson of Cleveland."[40] This seems to indicate that plans were well under way to lease the adjoining land in Coogan's Hollow for the New York team in the forthcoming Players' League.

After winning his first three games after ending his holdout, Keefe went into a tailspin by losing four of his next five games, culminating in a 10–7 loss on June 6 at the South End Grounds in Boston. "The New York directors feel very sore about Keefe's poor work and no one can blame them," Harris wrote in the *New York Press*. "I think it safe to predict that Sir Tim will soon strike his gait and regain the confidence of the public, which is decidedly waning."[41]

What was bothering Keefe wasn't his arm, but rather that his youngest sister, Annie, was dying. In what could only have been a heart-wrenching moment, Keefe visited his dying sister on June 7 at the family home in Somerville, outside Boston, to not only console her but also to have her sign paperwork to transfer back to him the official ownership of his land in Cambridge.[42] Annie Keefe died on June 23, 1889, at the Keefe home in Somerville, the third member of the family to die of consumption within two years.[43] Keefe received the news of his sister's death when the Giants arrived in Chicago that evening. In an article entitled "Keefe's Sister Is Dead," the *New*

York World reported that a telegram awaited him in Chicago and that he planned to take the earliest possible train to return home.[44]

As evidenced by the trust he had in her with his real estate holdings, Annie was Keefe's favorite sister. The importance of Annie was also evident by an article published the day after her death in the *Boston Globe*. Although clearly written for the sports section, the article appeared in the news section, probably at the behest of Sullivan, who as the city editor was also in charge of sports. "It was evident that the sad news received by Keefe affected every man in the club, as many of the men knew Miss Keefe personally, and all were aware how much Tim thought of her," the *Globe* wrote.[45] Sullivan also positioned the story of Annie's funeral, held at St. Joseph's Catholic Church in Somerville, on the front page of the *Globe*'s evening edition.[46] Annie was buried in the Keefe family plot at St. Paul's Cemetery, next to her father and her sister Margaret.[47]

The loss of Annie as his confidant pushed Keefe closer to Clara Helm, who was in Europe with her sister Helen at the time of Annie's death. In fact, Clara had spent a good deal of the previous eight months in Europe, not in New York City, and wouldn't return until late July. The long absence accelerated Keefe's desire to marry her.

While still mourning the death of his sister, Keefe stopped by the offices of the *Boston Globe* before leaving Boston to rejoin the Giants in Indianapolis. "You have a great batting team and that inexplicable dogma of the fatalists, luck, seems to be with you," Keefe told baseball writer Tim Murnane. "Besides, the Boston club thus far have met with no serious accidents. Luck was with the New Yorks last season; we all felt it, and played accordingly, but this year we seem to be handicapped at every point."[48] Keefe then rattled off the list of injured Giants, including Ward, Crane, Welch, and Slattery.

Ward had mysteriously hurt his arm while the Giants were playing in Cleveland, so he was out of the lineup from June 20 to July 8. This gave Ward more time to work on the Brotherhood plan and meet with members of the other teams on the lengthy road trip. When the Giants reached Chicago, Spalding brushed off Ward regarding the proposed meeting, saying the salary classification issue could wait until the National League meeting in November. Ward publicly feigned indignation at the rebuff. "They were afraid to meet us and discuss the points which were to have been raised," Ward said. "That's the size of it."[49] Privately, though, Ward couldn't have been more pleased, since he wanted no action to occur. This cleared the way for the new league and inspired overconfidence in the owners that the Brotherhood situation was well in hand.

The disinformation campaign by the Brotherhood was in high gear between the aborted meeting with Spalding in Chicago and the next Brotherhood meeting on July 14 in New York City. "Ward says while the Brotherhood threatens nothing yet, it would be an extremely unwise move for the National League to try the effect of delays, postponements or begging the question," the *New York Clipper* reported.[50] Keefe, using some clever language that hinted at the planning for a new league, said: "Spalding and a few of the moneyed people may regret their step. I won't say what the Brotherhood will do but we will move ... there is one thing certain, they won't classify as many men this fall as they think."[51]

As Ward later noted in his brief history of the Players' League, "There then remained nothing else for the players to do but to begin organizing on a new basis, and this course was decided upon at a meeting of the representatives of the various Brotherhood chapters held at the Fifth Avenue Hotel, New York, on July 14, 1889."[52] At that meeting, the Brotherhood conducted a status update on the financial backers in each city for the new league and then voted to execute the plan to create the new league for the 1890 season. Of course, that's not what Ward told the baseball writers, who blandly reported that the "secret session" was held for "the purpose of obtaining the ideas of the men about the future actions to be taken."[53] However, the new league soon became one of the worst-kept secrets of the summer of 1889.

With the plan to create the Players' League for the next season now firmly in place, the New York Giants played exceptionally well during the second half of the 1889 season. The close race between New York and Boston to determine the National League champion inspired greater public interest in baseball, especially regarding the individual ballplayers, which could only help successfully launch the Players' League.

After languishing in the middle of the standings during the first half of the season, the Giants put together a seven-game winning streak at the beginning of July to vault into second place on July 13. This put the Giants two games behind first-place Boston, setting the stage for the two teams to go at it hammer and tong (the "tooth and nail" expression of that era) for first place over the next three months. While Keefe, Welch, and Crane in the pitcher's box were sufficient to propel the Giants into second place, the team needed a solid fourth pitcher to successfully weather the second half of the 140-game season. Many doubleheaders lurked on the horizon to make up rained-out games from earlier in the season, the result of a new league rule that required the playing of rainouts rather than to simply ignore those games, as has been the previous practice.

The key to the Giants' pennant drive in 1889 was the acquisition of pitcher Hank O'Day in late July from the last-place Washington team.

Although he had a 2–10 record with Washington that season and had posted a league-high 29 losses in 1888, O'Day more than capably augmented Keefe, Welch, and Crane by winning nine of the ten games he started for the Giants in 1889.

In August the popularity of the Giants increased a notch in New York City when the *New York World* erected a "Baseball Bulletin Board" in front of its offices on Park Row.[54] Baseball fans could now watch the progress of Giants' road games to vicariously participate as a spectator. The first game posted on the Bulletin Board was the August 6 game in Chicago. Keefe lost a 7–1 lead in top of the ninth inning, when he allowed seven runs to score. The Giants tied the game in the bottom of the ninth before scoring two runs in the tenth inning to win the game. The crowd in front of the *New York World* building cheered their hero, Keefe.

On August 18 the Giants, just a game and a half out of first place, arrived in Boston for a three-game series with the league leaders at the South End Grounds. On Monday, August 19, the two teams tied, 4–4, with Crane in the pitcher's box for the Giants. Keefe was absent from the game. That afternoon Keefe married Clara Helm in a private ceremony in Worcester, Massachusetts, 40 miles west of Boston, at the home of Alonzo Sanderson, a Methodist minister.[55] The marriage was not revealed to the public until a few days later. Keefe did pitch the next day, August 20, but he lasted only three innings, being relieved by Welch in the fourth inning of the Giants' 12–2 defeat. "It was decided that Keefe had been pounded enough, so he was consigned to the seclusion of the bench," the *Boston Globe* reported about the apparently distracted, newly married pitcher.[56] The Giants left Boston on August 21 after losing again, to fall three and a half games behind Boston.

On the way back to New York City, Keefe's secret marriage was disclosed to a writer, who was presumably tipped off by one of the Keefe's teammates. "It was a fitting sequel to the long and checkered love affair," the *New York World* commented. "The affair was kept absolutely quiet until last evening when it began to be whispered about on the steamboat Providence, on which the Giants were traveling homeward."[57] Baseball fans first found out about the marriage on August 22 when an afternoon newspaper printed the announcement of the marriage and sent newsboys to sell papers at the Polo Grounds, where Keefe was pitching for the Giants against Philadelphia. In the fourth inning the newsboys arrived and started hawking, "All about Tim Keefe getting married." Since the Giants were batting at the time, the players were seated on the bench. "Ward looked over at Keefe and laughed," the *New York World* reported. "Tim promptly blushed and hung his head. Connor gave Keefe a facetious poke in the ribs."[58]

Harris of the *New York Press* was not surprised at the announcement, since he knew that Keefe and Helm had been engaged for over a year, despite all the "tall prevaricating" that Keefe did about that subject. "Tim has been kept very busy receiving congratulations, and he deserves to be congratulated, because he has married a very charming woman of some means," Harris wrote. "Mrs. Keefe has secured a husband of ability intellectually, a handsome man and a man well fixed in the world's goods. Both are lucky in their choice and deserve happiness."[59] Upon the return of the newlyweds to New York City, the *New York World* reported that "Mr. and Mrs. Keefe have taken a handsome suite of apartments at the Marlborough," where they could live a grand lifestyle and attend the theater often.[60]

Why did they select Monday, August 19, as their wedding date? After Clara returned from Europe in late July, the Giants were traveling on the road and didn't return east until the series in Boston in mid–August. Since it was the Giants' last trip to Boston for the 1889 season and there would be little time between the end of the season and the expected formal announcement of the Players' League, August 19 was the first (and last) realistic opportunity for a marriage ceremony where relatives of both sides could possibly attend. However, Clara's sister Helen was reportedly the only family member present at the wedding, as no one attended from the Keefe family.[61]

It is unclear why they got married in Worcester, 40 miles west of Boston, although it likely was related to St. Joseph's Catholic Church in Somerville. They couldn't get married there, as Keefe may have wanted to, since Clara was not of the Catholic faith; in that era the Catholic Church frowned on mixed marriages between people of different faiths. A larger issue likely was

During the National League pennant race between New York and Boston in 1889, the *New York World* regularly published cartoons to augment its coverage of the Giants' games. When the Giants clinched the pennant on October 5, 1889, this cartoon appeared on the front page of the evening edition of the *World*, showing Giants manager Jim Mutrie disposing of the Boston ballclub into a proverbial bean pot.

that his mother and sisters may not have approved of his marriage outside the Catholic faith, so there was no need to be married near Boston. Having a Methodist minister perform the ceremony at the minister's home in Worcester ensured the couple's privacy, at least for a few days.

As the Giants began the stretch run in September for the National League pennant, the first specific rumors were reported about a "great scheme" being organized by Al Johnson of Cleveland in conjunction with the Brotherhood to monopolize the baseball market. "The gentleman who gave me these facts, if they are facts, was in a position to know, and although I laughed at him and tried to show him how absurd such a move would be, he said he got his information from a source that could not be questioned," Indianapolis baseball writer A.G. Ovens wrote. "He maintained that, whether the scheme was ever carried through or not, it was now under consideration and would be attempted."[62] Most observers scoffed at the idea. "I look upon the scheme as utopian and I am surprised that people can entertain any serious notions in favor of it," a Pittsburgh ballclub official told the *Pittsburgh Dispatch*.[63]

A 12-game winning streak in September put the Giants in a tie with Boston for first place, which the two teams essentially shared over the final three weeks of the season. With both teams on the road to finish the 1889 season, Mutrie overused Keefe and Welch down the stretch in the battle for the pennant, while Boston used Clarkson in the pitcher's box for nearly every game (all but three). As the two titans wrestled for the pennant on the playing field, the rumors of a new league took on a life of their own in the newspapers.

In an article on September 21 entitled "War on the League: The Brotherhood Anxious to Shine in the Base-Ball World," Harris of the *New York Press* reported that several men were ready to sign a lease on the land next to the New Polo Grounds to be used by a New York ballclub in a new league. Giants president John Day laughed at the idea. "The whole thing sounds pretty fishy. In the first place no names are given. Secondly, the rent talked of is excessive, and thirdly, nobody would be fool enough to lease grounds for a ballclub without players and a League to play in," Day told Harris. As for the Brotherhood players leaving the League and starting their own club, Day said, "It is all nonsense. There will be no secession, and there will not be an opposition league. The differences between the players and the League, if there are any, will be amicably adjusted in good time."[64] An unidentified person, who was "close to the leadership of the Brotherhood," possibly Keefe, gave the *Press* details of the plan for the new league.

With so many rumors swirling in the newspapers, and basically the cat out of the bag in New York City, the Brotherhood decided to get out in front of the story and have Frank Brunell, now the sports editor at the *Chicago Tribune*, furnish the real facts of the plan and acknowledge that a new league would operate for the 1890 season. Brunell's article appeared on September 22 with this opening paragraph: "The story of the formation of a gigantic baseball trust, which has been hinted at for the last ten days by various papers in the cities where baseball interests the people, can be told by The Tribune in detail."[65] The *Chicago Tribune* article was reprinted the following day in newspapers across the nation. Since it was now official that a baseball rebellion was under way, the pennant race gained increased attention as baseball fans wondered where their favorite players would play the next season.

New York and Boston went into the last game of the season on October 5 tied for first place. New York defeated Cleveland, 5–3, while Boston lost to Pittsburgh (when Galvin defeated an exhausted Clarkson, 6–1), to give the Giants their second consecutive National League title. Keefe won the last game of the season for the Giants. "When Keefe said yesterday that he would pitch the game of his life he told the truth," the *New York Times* reported. "From the outset he shot the ball across the plate with rare speed and accuracy and had the Cleveland batters completely at his mercy. Beads of perspiration dropped from his brow, but he continued his telling work until the last man was retired in the ninth inning."[66] Showing his interest in the theater, Keefe promised the game ball, if victorious, to actor A.S. Lipman in "The Burglar," then playing in Chicago after its run in New York City.[67]

Back in New York City, a huge crowd cheered the victory outside the *New York World* building, when its Baseball Bulletin Board pronounced the Giants' victory, when telegraph reports reached the building minutes after the game ended.[68] When the Giants reached Jersey City after their celebratory train ride back to New York City, "Tim Keefe led the champions as they came from the train, and as soon as the crowd recognized him there was a shout of delight that echoed and re-echoed through the big building," Will Rankin later wrote in a retrospective of the scene. "It was some time before the players could make their way to the waiting ferryboats," to cross the Hudson River to Manhattan, where more crowds met the players with cheers outside the ferry house.[69]

In some ways it was amazing that the New York Giants won the 1889 pennant to repeat as National League champion with all the distractions that the ballplayers were immersed in. However, in other ways the distractions were helpful, since many players, including Keefe, were excited to look forward to the start of a new league and an end to the battle with the League ballclub owners. Because of his late start and the many matters on his mind other than baseball, Keefe did not pitch especially well during the 1889 season. He produced only 28 wins, as he missed a seventh consecutive 30-win season.

Keefe's mind was clearly on the Brotherhood and not baseball as the Giants prepared to meet Brooklyn in the 1889 World Series. "We want the abolition of the classification of the players and we want the sale of players entirely done away with," Keefe told Harris at the *New York Press*, in a continuation of the disinformation campaign to the very end that left open the hope of a peaceful resolution with the League owners. While not acknowledging the Brotherhood's plan for a new league, Keefe did respond to a question about its potential for success. "I do not see why not. The public will go to see base ball, no matter who is at the head of the movement. If Clarkson is to pitch for the Brotherhood, in [Boston] the public will go to see him play, no matter if there is another club charging but twenty-five cents admission. The same is true in New York, and, in fact, in all of the cities."[70]

The strong geographic rivalry between Brooklyn and Manhattan should have made for a formidable atmosphere when the Giants met the American Association champion in the World Series that fall. Keefe was in the pitcher's box on October 18 for the first game of the World Series at the New Polo Grounds, but a tired Keefe was ineffective as the Brooklyn batters pummeled him for five runs in the first inning. Although down, 5–0, the Giants rallied to go ahead, 10–8, at the end of the seventh inning. Keefe did not pitch well, but he should have won the game, since the umpire refused to stop the game for darkness even in the emerging dusk. Brooklyn touched Keefe for four runs in the eighth inning to win, 12–10.

After Crane won the second game, Welch didn't pitch much better in the third game than Keefe had in the opener, being pulled after five innings in an 8–7 loss. Obviously, both pitching workhorses were tired and looking forward to the Brotherhood announcement after the World Series concluded. When Brooklyn won three of the first four games, Mutrie sat both Keefe and Welch for all of the remaining games (except for using Keefe for three innings of relief in the seventh game). New York then won the next five games to win the series behind Crane (three wins) and O'Day (two wins). O'Day was the pitching hero, winning the sixth game, 2–1, and the deciding ninth game, 3–2, on October 29.

The Giants held a breakup meeting on October 30 in their clubhouse at the Polo Grounds. By now, everyone, including Day and Mutrie, knew this was the end of the New York Giants as they had known the team for the past several years, so the atmosphere was a bit gloomy. As for the future, Day was still optimistic. "I guess the boys really mean to go it alone and I'm sorry for it. One thing is for certain, that the National League can and will live. It has capital, prestige, the faith of the public," Day told the *New York World*. "The intended desertion will hurt us, of course, but even though the new organization proves ever so successful it cannot kill the League."[71] Day was now more sanguine about the existence of the Brotherhood league, since a few days earlier he had been offered the presidency of the new league. The offer arose from the respect that Keefe, Ward, and the other Giants players had for Day as a baseball executive. However, Day turned down the position "to stand by his old comrades."[72]

On November 4, 1889, the Brotherhood announced the formation of the Players' League to compete with the National League. The rebellion of some of the country's last remaining artisans commenced, in which the ballplayers intended to demonstrate the continued existence of the free labor ideal. Or so they thought.

18
Establishing the Players' League

On November 4, 1889, the worst-kept secret in America became public knowledge when the Brotherhood announced the formation of a new baseball league in which its members, basically the vast majority of ballplayers currently in the National League, would play during the 1890 season. The new league was formally called the Players' National League of Professional Base Ball Club, but was known more commonly as the Players' League. The apostrophe after "Players" in the name of the league was important, because it denoted the possessive form rather than a mere adjective. The apostrophe signified that the league was controlled by the players; without the apostrophe, the connotation would have been simply a league comprised of players.

Brotherhood president John Ward drafted a long announcement about the rationale for the formation of the Players' League, often called the "Brotherhood manifesto," which focused on Ward's largest gripe about the National League. "Players have been bought, sold, and exchanged as though they were sheep instead of American citizens," Ward wrote. "We believe it is possible to conduct our national game upon lines which will not infringe upon individual or natural rights."[1] Naturally, there was no reserve rule in the Players' League and no selling or releasing of ballplayers during the season.

There was nary a word about Keefe's top priority, the elimination of income limitations, and not one mention of "salary," "compensation," or even "classification plan." In the furor over the announcement, the *New York Times* reported that Keefe "acted as secretary" of the meeting, where "he threw ink with as much skill and proficiency as he curves an out-shoot," while recording player grievances as he "took them down in shorthand."[2] Chicago infielder Fred Pfeffer was portrayed as a larger figure in the Brotherhood movement than Keefe.

There were eight ballclubs in the Players' League. Six clubs represented cities already in the National League (Boston, Chicago, Cleveland, New York, Philadelphia, and Pittsburgh), one club was in an existing American Association city that was soon to transfer to the National League (Brooklyn), and one club was in Buffalo. Each ballclub was governed by an eight-man board of directors, comprised of four ballplayers and four capitalists. At the November 7 meeting between players and capitalists, the financial structure of how ballclubs would operate was solidified to provide for profit sharing with the ballplayers and some cross-subsidization of other ballclubs:

> Each club stands on its own basis. After all expenses and a contribution of $2,500 has been made to the prize fund, the first $10,000 of profit goes to the stockholders. The next $10,000 or any part thereof is to be put into a pool to be divided pro rata among all the players of the League at the end of the season. A second pool will be made of all profits or any portion thereof exceeding $20,000. This second pool will be divided, half to the eight clubs and half to the players. It will thus be seen that no club will contribute to the support of another club unless its profits exceed the sum of $20,000.[3]

This financial structure differed substantially from the plan first devised by the Brotherhood, as initially unveiled in Brunell's article in the *Chicago Tribune* in September 1889 as well as initial reports after the Brotherhood announcement. As originally contemplated, the new league was to be run as a monopoly trust, like Standard Oil, with "all expenses and receipts [being] pooled for the general benefit." The first $10,000 of combined profits was to go to the prize-money pool for the ballplayers, the next $80,000 to the capitalists, the next $80,000 to the ballplayers, and the excess profits to be divided evenly between the ballplayers and the capitalists. This approach came across distinctly in the original proposed name of the new league, the United Baseball Association. The *Chicago Tribune* headline had been quite telling: "A Great Ball Trust."[4]

Most analysis about the Players' League has focused on its final structure as agreed upon in November 1889, not on its original design that was unveiled in September 1889. Its actual structure was fatally flawed, since it basically mirrored the structure of the National League with two huge deficiencies: (1) the expected return to the capitalists was lower, since some profits were shared with the ballplayers, not retained in their entirety, and (2) there was less assurance that ballplayers would remain with the ballclub, with player contracts of a three-year duration, not in perpetuity as with the reserve rule. Once the negotiations between capitalists and ballplayers were concluded on November 7, 1889, the Players' League was virtually doomed to failure.

Of greater historical interest is the original structure envisioned in September 1889, which was effectively to be a holding company where the capitalist stockholders (and ballplayers through a profit-sharing component) would share the pooled financial results of all eight ballclubs. This was an adaptation of the prevailing successful business model of the 1880s to organize an industry monopoly, such as Standard Oil in the oil refining business.

While Standard Oil had used a corporate trust to effectuate this kind of business structure, as did the consolidations of the sugar and whiskey industries, by 1888 holding company legislation had been passed in New Jersey to allow a company to own stock of other companies.[5]

Keefe, as a student of business, and Ward, as a lawyer, would have been cognizant of these developments as they studied ways to organize the Players' League. The amount of capital needed to run the new league as a monopoly negated the possibility of it being wholly owned by the ballplayers, so a partnership between the capitalists and ballplayers (through the newfangled concept of profit sharing) was devised to divide the pooled profits of all the ballclubs.

In the fall of 1889, operating a monopoly was perfectly legal, since it was not until 1890 that Congress passed the Sherman Antitrust Act. For the Players' League, the holding company approach would have been a monopoly initially concerning talented ballplayers; once the other two major leagues were forced out of business, it could then control the supply of the product (ballgames). However, one big problem for the Players' League was that industry monopolies invariably evolved as a combination of existing businesses, with a strong leader at the top, such as John D. Rockefeller at Standard Oil. The Players' League would have been an attempt to organize a monopoly among eight new companies without a strong existing leader. This explains why a baseball man like John Day was recruited in October 1889 to be the president of the new league. Had Day accepted the challenge, major-league baseball likely would have evolved very differently than it did.

If the holding company structure with a strong leader had been actually implemented, the Players' League arguably would have succeeded in toppling the National League. However, the capitalists in New York and Boston did not want to subsidize the losses likely to occur in the other six ballclubs, so they twisted arms at the November 7 meeting to have each ballclub stand on its own so that the initial returns to its stockholders would be based solely on that club's financial results. Other than by Harris at the *New York Press*, there was little reporting of this drastic change in the operation of the Players' League. If the Players' League had remained a holding company with pooled financial results, the New York capitalists would have had much less incentive to bail out, as they did, soon after the 1890 season ended.

Keefe left no indication of his opinion about this drastic change in profit distribution. From his public comments during the next 12 months, he didn't seem to be overly concerned about it, probably since the profit-sharing element addressed his top priority. That turned out to be a huge error by Keefe.

The New York ballclub in the Players' League was primarily financed by capitalists Edward Talcott, a stock broker, Cornelius Van Cott, a politician and postmaster of New York City, Edwin McAlpin, a tobacconist who had connections among the elite in New York City, and Frank Robinson, a brother-in-law of McAlpin.[6] Keefe was also a stockholder in the New York Players' League ballclub, having invested $1,000 in ten shares of stock.[7] It wasn't just business with these four capitalists; it was also personal. Talcott, Van Cott, McAlpin, and Robinson were all Republicans, the opposite political persuasion of John Day, who had ties to the Democratic machine at Tammany Hall.[8] McAlpin seemed motivated by his ego and increased social stature. Van Cott clearly was motivated by political gain. Robinson was there to watch over his brother-in-law's investment. Talcott was a cold-hearted businessman.

At the beginning of the 1890 season, the *New York World* wrote that the motivation of Talcott was that "he loved the game and wished to see it played freed from the sales system and other wrongs done the players and the game by the dictators whose alleged safeguard was and still is the reserve rule." This seems straight from a press release by Ward, as it mirrored his motivation. However, the *World* also described Talcott as having "earned the reputation of being one of the brightest traders on the floor of the Stock Exchange," since he made every cent of his $300,000 fortune "by his own brains and pluck."[9] Talcott most certainly was in it for the money. "E.B. Talcott said he believed the Brotherhood was a good investment for any capitalist," the *New York Herald* wrote. "He expects to make money out of his stock."[10] Little did Ward or Keefe or any of the other ballplayers on the Giants suspect that Talcott viewed this transaction as just another stock deal, buy low and sell high.

Van Cott, ever the politician, said the right things about the new venture when the new league was announced: "My interest in the Brotherhood is simply and purely a matter of principle," Van Cott told the *New York World*. "I don't believe in the buying and selling of men, and that is why I am with the players. I am a Republican because I don't believe in slavery, and this is a damn sight worse than slavery. I am in favor of smashing anything that denies a man his rights and tries to buy and sell him like a bale of cotton, whether it's in ball playing or anything else. I am willing to do anything I can to help the boys, although I haven't seen a game of ball in two years."[11] Van Cott's lack of baseball affection was a troubling omen.

Harris, in his typical prescient mode, immediately wrote about the apparent duplicity of the Players' League financiers after his interview with an unidentified New York capitalist (who was likely Talcott):

> I asked a capitalist today how long he thought it would take the League to fill the places of the men who are preparing to desert their employers. He thought, perhaps, two years, certainly three at most. When pressed, he admitted that

when the moment arrived there wouldn't be a great deal of money for either Players' League or National League. What is to become of the players when the capitalists got enough and draw out? "Oh," was the reply. "There'll be money made for a couple of years anyhow, and then, well, that's too far off to speculate about now." There you have it. The men who are going into this venture are not philanthropists. Very few of them have any sympathy with the poor, abused base ball "slave." They are in it for the money and when it ceases to be profitable the players may shift for themselves. I wish the boys success with all my heart, but somehow I cannot bring myself to believe that they will get there.[12]

The Brotherhood announced its grand plan on November 4 before all the details had been worked out, since the concept needed to be in place prior to the scheduled National League meeting in mid-November. That turned out to be a significant tactical error, since it gave the capitalists leverage over the ballplayers in crafting the final financial underpinnings of the league. The *New York Times* mentioned this on November 7 when it wrote that the ballplayers' original proposition "does not appear to exactly meet the views of some of the financial backers," who considered the organization "in a crude state" where the players "will have to make many concessions before the men will put up their money."[13] The next day the pooling scheme was abolished. The resulting financial arrangement further exposed the motivation of the capitalists to be profit over philosophy.

The entire starting lineup and pitching corps of the New York Giants pledged to play for the New York club in the Players' League, leaving Day and Mutrie will no talent to put on the field. One big challenge for Keefe and his compatriots was the overlapping schedules of the two teams, which created a direct competition for spectators, especially when the Players' League club established its ballpark right next to the existing New Polo Grounds, where the National League team conducted its games.

In many ways, it was miraculous that Keefe and Ward as Brotherhood officers held together as many of the 120 or so members as they did to join the fledgling Players' League, as there was a very small attrition rate of defection back to the National League. While the players were guaranteed their 1889 salaries for the 1890 season, the risk was enormous for the average ballplayer, especially those with families to support. If the new league failed, they faced the very real possibility of being blacklisted by the National League and left with no way to earn a baseball income. Ward has been given most of the credit for keeping the Brotherhood membership together, but Keefe no doubt had a much larger role in maintaining the solidarity.

One telling indication of Keefe's increased role was a *Chicago Inter Ocean* headline on November 1: "J. Montgomery Ward to Be Deposed and Tim Keefe Elevated."[14] The newspaper reported that Keefe was to replace Ward as

Brotherhood president. Keefe even pre-announced details of the new league on November 1, including team rosters.[15] However, just a few days later, Ward was re-elected president. "There may be personal differences between Ward and Keefe, but they are one in the Brotherhood," the *Philadelphia Inquirer* wrote. "They recognize the fact that unity of action is absolutely necessary for the common good."[16] Although Keefe was more aligned with the goals of the ballplayer membership than was Ward, Keefe capitulated in the quest for the presidency and control of the agenda, for reasons that became evident publicly just a few weeks later. Ward's transfer to the Brooklyn ballclub was one immediate outcome of this disagreement, so that the two men no longer needed to cross paths on a daily basis.

Keefe seemed to be the point person for communication with the ballplayers and took a much more active role in public relations with the baseball writers. "We expect to have obstacles thrown in our way, but we are bound to win in the end," Keefe said in late November. "The League will no doubt flood us with injunctions, and there may be plenty of civil suits for damages instituted, but we will be fully prepared for all this." As to the number of ballplayers he expected to sign with Players' League clubs, Keefe responded heartily, "I may say all of them. There will be but very few defections."[17]

One of the first player defections was Jack Glasscock, who re-signed with Indianapolis. "Yea, it's true. Glasscock has gone back on us," Keefe said sadly. "But what can you expect of a man who wears a No. 12 shoe and a No. 6 hat? He is a traitor of the worst type, and will always be branded as such. He attended meetings regularly, and led us to believe that he was with us, in order to get information for the League magnates. He is a man destitute of honor or decency."[18]

Another early defection was star pitcher John Clarkson, who returned to the Boston ballclub in the League in early December. Soon thereafter, the first members of the New York Giants abandoned the Players' League club to go back to the National League. In a late-December article entitled "Tiernan Turns Traitor," the *New York World* reported that outfielder Mike Tiernan was the "first Brotherhood baseball player in the New York Club to desert his companions for the National League," when he signed with Day for a $1,000 raise in salary.[19]

Keefe, a dyed-in-the-wool Brotherhood believer, certainly agreed with the *World*'s "traitor" and "desertion" characterizations. "My, what a pity it is that the Brotherhood did not contain one third less of the League players and have men of stronger character. We would have been much better off," Keefe commented on Clarkson and Tiernan. "When I hear of these continual desertions, how the actions of these same persons last summer come vividly to my mind. 'Why don't you come at them now,' was the common remark. 'We've got them where we want them, and you can count on us every time. Stick? Why, we'll stick or perish.' Yea, they'll stick, but they didn't say which side they would stick to."[20] However, most Brotherhood members stuck with the Players' League. By year-end 1889, 77 of the 118 players who had finished the 1889 season in the National League had signed contracts to play in the Players' League for 1890; 21 players from the American Association had also joined up.[21]

John Day used the Tiernan signing to entice other players to return to the Giants, by visiting them at their offseason homes. "There isn't money enough in New York city to buy me to jump my contract with the Brotherhood," Roger Connor told Day when he visited his home in Waterbury, Connecticut, in late December. "The New Yorks' first baseman was as immovable as a mountain," the *New York Sun* reported. "Connor told Mr. Day that he cared not what Tiernan or any other player did. That he had signed with the Brotherhood, and he was going to stay by that organization until the last."[22]

While most of the Giants stood by the Brotherhood, pitcher Mickey Welch soon joined Tiernan as a renegade from the Brotherhood, when he signed a personal contract with Day for a $4,000 salary guaranteed for three years. Welch, with a large family to support, sought security, which the Players' League could not offer him. When Welch visited the Keefe & Becannon store to deliver the news, though, Keefe did not denigrate him about his decision. "Tim is not the man to let a business transaction interfere with his personal feelings," the *New York Sun* reported about the meeting. "He shook hands with Welch, with the remark that every man knew his own business."[23] Keefe understood what it meant to take care of family. Indeed, Keefe and Welch remained life-long friends, unlike his relationship with many of the other ballplayers on the championship New York Giants team of 1888 and 1889.

At the first meeting of the New York Players' League ballclub in December 1889, Keefe and Ewing were selected as player representatives on the ballclub's board of directors. Van Cott was elected president, Talcott as vice president, and Robinson as secretary-treasurer.[24] In effect, though, Talcott was the managing director. A week later, McAlpin was elected president of the Players' League in the first league meeting of the new organization. Unfortunately, McAlpin was more of a titular head of the league. Brunell, the baseball writer, was elected league secretary.[25]

Keefe was tapped to serve on the grounds committee, along with Talcott and Van Cott, where he was very involved in the effort to construct a new ballpark.[26] Keefe had announced the new grounds two months earlier, which were located at 115th Street and Eighth Avenue, "just above the present diamond of the Giants."[27] The new playing facility was called Brotherhood Park.

While the recently married Ewing was still back at home in Cincinnati, Keefe was the acting manager of the New York Players' League ballclub until Ewing returned to the city in March. Keefe did much of Ewing's duties during his absence, such as scheduling spring exhibition games, handling player contracts, and negotiating construction contracts for the new ballpark.

At the first owners' meeting of the Players' League in mid-December, the Rules Committee approved two major rule changes from those used in the National League. First, two umpires would be used for each game, rather than one. Second, the pitcher's box was lengthened by six inches to be six feet long and four feet wide, with its front line moved a foot farther from home plate, so the pitcher would deliver the ball with his back foot 51 feet, six inches from the plate.[28] The thinking of the Rules Committee, comprised of three ballplayers (Ward, Ewing, and Pfeffer) and two capitalists (Hart of Boston and Hilt of Philadelphia), was that these changes would increase the volume of hitting to encourage spectators to attend ballgames.

The Rules Committee also awarded the contract to provide baseballs for the Players' League games to Keefe & Becannon. With its bid to provide the balls for free, Keefe's firm beat out three other competitors for the contract. Lovell Arms Company wanted $4 per dozen baseballs; Shibe & Company offered to supply the balls for free as well as publish the league guide and pay the league a percentage of its retail sales; H.H. Kiffe offered to supply the balls for free and pay the league a $3,500 bonus.[29] Spalding & Bros., the country's leading sporting goods firm, obviously did not bid due to its conflict of interest in support of the National League.

There were some howls of favoritism in the awarding of the baseball contract to Keefe's firm. While the bid wasn't as overtly financially favorable to the league, Keefe's firm was most likely to spend money on marketing the Players' League's name, giving the league a lot of publicity in its competition for customers with the established National League. The *New York Sun* provided a more detailed explanation:

> Mr. Hart says that the stories about the granting of the League ball to Keefe & Becannon are very misleading. He was on the committee which had that matter in charge, and the contract was granted to the highest bidder. Tom Lovell's bid was lower than Herman Kiffe's, which again was lower than Keefe & Becannon's. Kiffe put in a bid for the ball and League guide, and Keefe's firm put in a bid for the ball alone. Another firm wanted the guide, and was willing to pay for it, so that the combined bid of Keefe and the guide men was $750 better for the Players' League than Kiffe's bid and a good deal better than Lovell's. The Players' League finally decided to issue its own guide, and gave the ball to Keefe & Becannon.[30]

A possible conspiracy theory would have Keefe stepping aside in the election for Brotherhood president in exchange for the baseball contract to further his ambition to be a sporting goods magnate. The *New York Press* implied this soon after the Brotherhood election in early November, when it reported there was "not much doubt that Keefe & Becannon will furnish the base ball supplies for the new league."[31]

One intangible factor in the contract award likely was that Keefe was more amenable to providing a "lively" ball to encourage more scoring to entice spectators to Players' League games, compared to the low-scoring National League games with its dead ball. While the use of a "rabbit ball" ostensibly would be anathema to a strategic pitcher such as Keefe, by 1889 he was leaning more toward being a businessman than a pitcher, probably because the 33-year-old could sense that he had only one or two more viable years left as a pitcher. There were sporadic reports that Keefe used liniments and mustard plasters to keep his right arm limber. In any event, Keefe signed a three-year contract to supply the official baseball to the Players' League.[32]

Exactly how or when the decision to use a lively ball was made is unclear. There doesn't appear to have been specifications provided to the bidders to produce a lively ball. It may have been a verbal quid pro quo between the Rules Committee and Keefe, made in conjunction with the decision to move the pitcher farther from home plate. Or Keefe may have made the decision himself. Because the Keefe Ball was very lively, it could have been the manufacturer that made the ball a bit too lively. Early in the 1890 season, Harris wrote, "Tim, who is always honest, admits that it is too lively."[33]

Keefe was not being charitable in providing the Keefe Ball to the league for free; it was a business decision designed to earn a profit in a tangential manner. He could sell the Keefe Ball to retail customers to earn some money on the contract. He also had an inside track to supply uniforms and equipment to the ballclubs in the Players' League. Keefe made a huge bet that the Players' League would succeed, advertising Keefe & Becannon as the "Outfitters to the Players' National (Brotherhood) League and Manufacturer of The Keefe Official Ball."[34]

While Keefe was intellectually committed to the Players' League movement, he did take precautions to protect his financial commitment. On the same day that the Rules Committee awarded the baseball contract to Keefe & Becannon, Keefe transferred ownership of his real-estate property in Cambridge from himself to his mother, Mary Keefe. This ensured that creditors could not reach this asset for legal judgments against him, because Keefe & Becannon was organized as a partnership, not a corporation, so he was personally liable for financial losses.[35]

In late December 1889, the New York Giants served legal papers on Ward as the ballclub pursued an injunction to stop Ward (and by implication Keefe and the other Brotherhood members) from jumping to the Players' League and thus enforce the reserve rule inherent in his National League contract. A hearing in *Metropolitan Exhibition Company v. Ward* was scheduled for January 1890.

"Now that the 'bomb' has been fired and we know what it is, I don't feel alarmed in the least," Keefe said. "Now that we have seen their hand, I can say I think it is very weak, so weak, in fact, that I was greatly surprised. Unless they have something stored away that we haven't heard of I haven't the least fear for the Brotherhood's safety."[36] As the hearing date neared, Keefe commented: "Why, they have no show on earth to beat the players. Their argument that the players signed amounts to nothing, as we had to sign that kind of a contract or be blacklisted by the clubs under the National Agreement. It was a case of 'get into line or get off the earth,' and we preferred to get into line and do a little planning for the benefit of the players."[37]

In mid–January Judge Morgan O'Brien denied the injunction and ruled in favor of Ward, saying that the contract was indefinite and lacked mutuality. "The court noted there were no fixed terms or conditions in place for Ward's 1890 contract," Patrick Thornton wrote in *Legal Decisions That Shaped Modern Baseball*. "Judge O'Brien said that all Ward had actually contracted to do was to give the club the right to reserve him, with the terms to be agreed upon at a later date. He did not agree to enter into a contract for 1890 on the same terms and conditions he did for the 1889 season."[38] Essentially, O'Brien ruled that the reserve rule was unenforceable in court. Upon hearing the verdict, Keefe was jubilant: "If this isn't a Fourth of July for the Brotherhood I don't know anything about it. Tuesday night I was so certain that we would win that I would have bet anybody $10 to $1."[39]

After the National League lost that court battle, the League owners tried bribery by offering substantial contracts to stars like Mike Kelly of Boston and Buck Ewing of New York. Both turned down the money for the sake of the Brotherhood.[40] Keefe said that Mutrie offered him a deal to return to the League team, but he obviously turned it down.[41] The Giants eventually also sued Keefe, having papers served to him in early March just as he was leaving for New Jersey to coach the baseball team at Princeton College for a few weeks.[42] None of these actions put a crimp in the resolve of the Players' League to cripple the National League.

Keefe had an advantage over other Players' League pitchers since he had easy access to the official ball to be used for the 1890 season and could practice with it during the preseason drills he conducted with the Princeton College baseball team. Combined with the foot-and-a-half longer pitching distance, Keefe could experiment with adjustments to his delivery to remain as effective in the pitcher's box as he had been the previous two seasons. "Tim Keefe has been putting in some valuable time at Princeton College under the watchful eye of Professor Robinson," the *New York Press* reported in late March. "He has the great New York pitcher in perfect form, so he told me the other day. As an illustration of how good he was, Keefe put twenty-seven balls straight across the plate in succession one day last week. Tim goes over daily to put the collegians through a course of his own."[43]

In one of the first instances of modern spring training conducted in the southern part of the United States, the New York Players' League team sailed to Savannah, Georgia, in mid–March for several days of limbering up and preseason drills in a warm climate. Keefe, however, did not participate due to his "business engagements" back in New York City.[44] In another bad omen, Keefe & Becannon was not the popular hangout for ballplayers awaiting the beginning of the 1890 season. Most players, whether in the National League or Players' League, preferred Nick Engel's saloon or the Spalding & Bros. store, since one writer noted that at Keefe & Becannon "Timothy only talks business there."[45]

With Keefe more focused on business than baseball, the Players' League was poised to start its fateful 1890 baseball season.

19
Capitalists Desert the Ballplayers

The battle for baseball fans in New York City commenced on April 19, 1890, when the National League and Players' League teams both staged their season-opening game at home in their neighboring ballparks in northern Manhattan. The Players' League team outdrew the National League team that day by nearly a 3-to-1 margin, as 12,013 fans packed the newly built Brotherhood Park while only 4,644 attended the game at the Polo Grounds.[1]

For New York baseball fans, the choice was simple. The Players' League team was completely recognizable, because it was essentially the lineup of the previous year's National League team but with Hatfield replacing Ward at shortstop, Slattery substituting for Tiernan in right field, and John Ewing (Buck's brother) taking the spot of Mickey Welch on the pitching staff. On the other hand, the players on the National League team were all strangers, except for Tiernan and Welch, with the majority being men that Giants president John Day had acquired (on credit, not with cash) from the defunct Indianapolis team, including Jack Glasscock and Jerry Denny who had reneged on their commitment to the Brotherhood.

Tim Keefe was in the pitcher's box for the Players' League team in the season opener, after leading the team onto the field at Brotherhood Park before a wildly cheering crowd. New Yorkers were passionate about their baseball heroes, but the adrenalin quickly dissipated once they saw an inferior product displayed on the diamond. Philadelphia defeated New York that afternoon, 12–11, when nearly a dozen errors were committed by each side and both pitchers were "touched up beyond the expectation of almost everyone present" for numerous base hits in what would soon be known as the quintessential high-scoring Players' League game.[2] The culprit was the foot-and-a-half longer pitching distance and the lively Keefe Ball used by the Players' League.

The quality of play was not much better at the National League game at the Polo Grounds, where the Giants were shut out by the Philadelphia

Phillies, 4–0, as the undermanned team managed to produce only three hits. Hard-throwing Amos Rusie was in the pitcher's box for the Giants, collecting the first of his league-leading 34 losses that season. Rusie, one of the many former Indianapolis players on the field for the Giants, had potential, though, as he would lead the National League in strikeouts in 1890, but he was quite wild, as he also led the League in bases on balls and wild pitches.

After Keefe lost not only the season opener but also his next two outings, he went on a six-week winning streak, showing that he had mastered how to best throw the lively ball and effectively use the longer pitching distance. On May 14 Keefe "was in fine fettle and made the ball talk as it went waltzing by the big sluggers" in New York's 11–4 victory over Boston at the new Congress Street Grounds.[3] On May 24 he hurled one of the few shutouts in the high-scoring Players' League in a 6–0 win over Cleveland. Keefe secured his 300th career win in early June, although to no newspaper fanfare at the time. His victory on June 7 put the Giants into second place in the Players' League standings, which, unfortunately, was the closest the team would get to first place all season.

Business was booming at the Keefe & Becannon sporting goods store, so Keefe enlarged the premises to handle the customer demand. An article entitled "Keefe & Becannon: The New and Prosperous Sporting Goods Firm" in a May issue of the weekly *Sporting Life* newspaper helped spread the word.[4] The early euphoria for the Players' League seemed to position Keefe for huge success in the sporting goods business.

By late May, the Players' League team had clearly won the attendance battle between the two New York City baseball teams, even if just on a relative eye-balling basis, since both teams grossly inflated the turnstile counts provided to newspapers. For baseball fans, there was more interest in the familiar players of the former National League team now in the uniforms of the Players' League team, rather than the "ersatz Giants" that the fans considered to be imposters in National League uniforms.[5]

However, the Players' League team soon lost the publicity war. John Day strong-armed most of the city's daily newspapers to focus coverage on the National League and downplay the Players' League. As a result, the largest circulation newspapers, the *New York World* and *New York Sun*, had only superficial coverage of the Players' League games. Publishers also supported Day by reassigning baseball writers whom they suspected to be sympathetic to the Brotherhood; most notably, June Rankin no longer covered baseball at the *New York Herald*.[6] William Harris, a confidant of Keefe in his past salary negotiations with the Giants, left the *New York Press*; his writing for *Sporting Life* and wire services in 1890 continued to be insightful, but it was much less influential.[7] Any objectivity for the Players' League at the weekly *Sporting Times* evaporated in July, when Day ceded ownership of the newspaper to the Spalding brothers as part of the National League's financial bailout of the New York Giants.[8]

Tobacco cards were no longer distributed in 1890, further reducing the publicity opportunity for the New York Players' League team. The five major cigarette manufacturers, which controlled 90 percent of the market, had consolidated that spring to form a tobacco trust called American Tobacco Company.[9] As Dave Jamieson wrote in his history of baseball cards, "The tobacco trust had virtually no competition [for cigarettes], and without competition there was no need for costly advertising—certainly not for elaborate insert cards, as much as the public adored them."[10] With the tobacco trust in place, there was no need for what many called the "picture-giving business," so Goodwin and Allen & Ginter, two of the five companies in the trust, discontinued the inclusion of baseball cards into their cigarette packaging. Also largely disappearing were photographer-produced cabinet cards, which had drafted off the popularity of tobacco cards. In 1890 there were virtually no cards distributed of the ballplayers on the New York Players' League team.

The baseball competition in New York City financially crippled Day as he tried in vain to compete with the Players' League ballclub. By July he had lost tens of thousands of dollars and was nearly bankrupt, having raided the profits of his tobacco business to shore up the Giants. Talcott and the other capitalists backing Keefe's ballclub in the Players' League probably thought they had Day right where they wanted him, which would force him to sell out to them, figuring who in New York City would bail him out at that juncture. Talcott and the capitalists didn't anticipate a rescue party comprised of non–New Yorkers who had a vested interest in keeping Day's ballclub viable.

Several owners of other National League ballclubs game to Day's rescue, since they understood that the National League needed a strong presence in New York City or else their franchises would be worthless. In mid-July Chicago owner Albert Spalding orchestrated the bailout. Spalding (through his brother Walter), Soden of Boston, Reach of Philadelphia, and Abel of Brooklyn provided more than $60,000 of cash in exchange for stock in the ballclub; Brush canceled the $25,000 debt owed him for ballplayers purchased from his Indianapolis team, in exchange for stock. Day lost control of the ballclub's destiny, but he still was its president, albeit as a minority owner, with merely $20,000 left in stock holdings.[11]

Talcott tolerated Keefe during the first half of the 1890 season, as his excellent pitching kept the team in the hunt for the Players' League pennant. While he appreciated Keefe's business perspective, Talcott was probably put

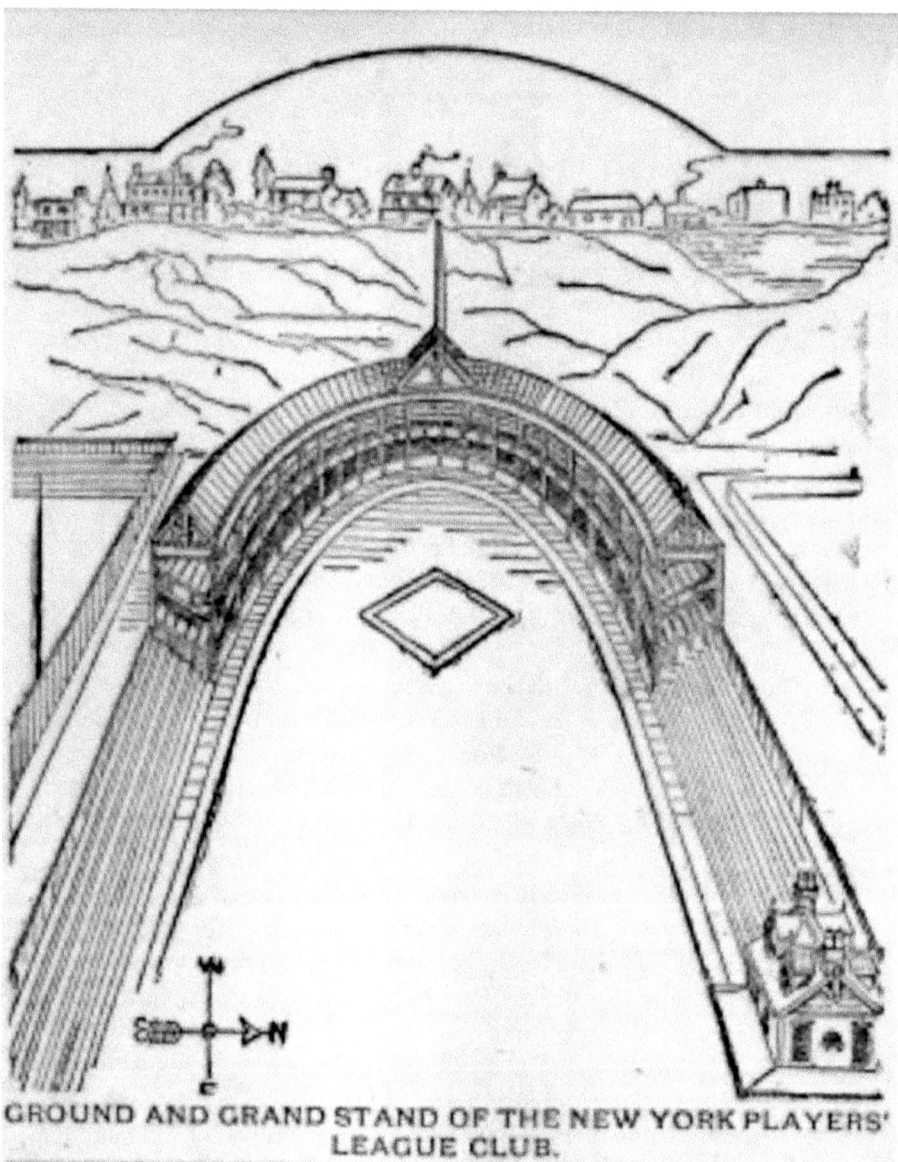

GROUND AND GRAND STAND OF THE NEW YORK PLAYERS' LEAGUE CLUB.

The one lasting aspect of the 1890 New York ballclub in the Players' League was its playing grounds, Brotherhood Park, shown here in a line drawing that appeared in *Sporting Life* in April 1890. In 1891, this facility became the third vintage of ball grounds that were known as the Polo Grounds, when the Players' League club was absorbed by the New York Giants club of the National League.

off by Keefe's rabid, uncompromising belief in the Brotherhood and ballplayer "rights" to the game's earnings. In contrast, Buck Ewing had a more even keel with regard to both baseball and business, which Talcott would have considered to be a more rational perspective. Keefe was too headstrong for Talcott's taste, since Keefe prioritized the Brotherhood and his sporting goods business ahead of the baseball team. Soon, Ewing was tight with Talcott, while Keefe was outside the inner circle.

Keefe's extreme dedication to the Brotherhood was exemplified by two episodes during the spring. In mid–May he spent a Sunday off day by taking the train to Philadelphia to visit Jim Fogarty and convince him to remain with the Players' League, since he was rumored to return to the National League.[12] In early June, when the two New York City teams traveled to their next games in Philadelphia on the same train (in the same car), Keefe and his teammates traveled in silence; reportedly, Keefe sat next to Glasscock, whom he considered a deserter, and never spoke one word to him.[13]

With the National League ballclub owners prepared to weather the 1890 season financially following the bailout of the New York Giants, the Players' League quickly lost its attendance edge during the second half of the season. The high-scoring ballgames due to the lively Keefe Ball turned away spectators rather than drawing them to the ballpark. *Sporting Life* later wrote that one of the biggest problems with the Players' League was "its unwise, radical changes in the playing rules, which more than any other cause handicapped the new League, inasmuch as the increased pitching distance and lively ball necessarily made a favorable comparison of Players' League contests played on new grounds with the small-score, dead-ball game of the National League impossible."[14]

While the Players' League had a monopoly on the game's best ballplayers, the conditions under which their talents were displayed didn't work in favor of the new league. Talcott was probably miffed at Keefe in this regard as well, since his business produced the lively Keefe Ball that was, at least in part, responsible for the unpopular high-scoring games in the Players' League. For example, the August 16 game when Boston defeated New York, 16–15, was "one of the most unsatisfying games of the season, and the large crowd was not slow in showing its true feelings," the *New York Times* reported. "It was not a ball game, but a travesty on it. It reminded one more of the circus ring than the base ball field."[15] The tying run scored for Boston in the ninth inning on a passed ball by Ewing and the winning run scored on a wild pitch by Hatfield, who was the third New York pitcher used that day.

With only modest newspaper publicity and waning spectator interest in the high-scoring ballgames, matters came to a head for the New York Players'

League team in mid-August when the loyalty of manager Ewing was called into question. Ewing admitted that he had talked with Giants president Day in Boston on the recent road trip. "No man has worked harder or more faithfully for the welfare of the Players' League than I have, and I defy any one to point out a case where I have been derelict in my duty," Ewing told the *New York Sun*. "I saw no harm in it, and I would do it again, the same as any gentleman should. There was nothing said between Mr. Day and myself that the entire public should not know."[16]

The subject of the conversation with Day was more than mere banter between two old acquaintances. Day proposed that Ewing lobby his teammates to consolidate the two New York teams. Ewing reportedly did communicate Day's offer to Keefe, Richardson, and Connor. All declined to consider it, to one degree or another. Keefe reportedly refused to even listen to Ewing, by walking away from him as soon as he began to talk about returning to the National League.[17]

Historians have typically cast Ewing as the villain in the Players' League demise. Whether Ewing or Day was the instigator of the August discussion, and their future interactions, remains unclear, as are Ewing's motivations for participating in them. Ewing's biographer justified his actions by writing that "Ewing, the consummate poker player, played the hand he had dealt himself," since he had recently married and had a child on the way.[18] Interestingly, Talcott, who had stood next to Ewing during the *Sun* interview, listened to Ewing's words "with feelings of keen regret," the *New York Sun* noted, before Talcott remarked, "When Ewing gives up, we will stop; that's as sure as you live."[19] This appears to be the turning point, when Talcott began seriously contemplating a consolidation of the two ballclubs and how he could come out on top in the transaction.

When Ewing told Harris, now writing for *Sporting Life*, that the ballclub's directors knew all about his conversations with Day, Harris postulated an interesting scenario. "Buck's admission in this latter regard has aroused a good deal of curiosity here. What was the purpose of these mysterious conferences with Mr. Day?" Harris inquired. "Was Buck an unofficial representative of the Players' League, sounding Mr. Day as to a compromise? Or was it an amalgamation? Can it be that the New York end of the Players' League, through Ewing, are trying to capture Mr. Day instead of Mr. Day trying to capture Ewing?"[20]

As with many of Harris's conjectures during the past three seasons, he had an uncanny ability to unearth significant grains of truth where others took things at face value. Talcott was likely hunting Day, not the other way around. The motivations of Talcott were soon exposed in a *New York Sun* editorial. "Mr. Talcott and his associates may have been great capitalists, but their professions of being sincere well wishers of base ball were manifestly as false as their [attendance] figures," the *Sun* took Talcott to task at ruining the game of baseball. "They have brought shame on it, to no man's profit and to all ball players' detriment. The country can only hope for better things next year."[21]

The New York team remained in the hunt for the Players' League pennant until Keefe broke his finger on August 19 while he was shagging fly balls before the game. Because Keefe didn't wear a glove, he caught flies with his bare hands. In catching one of Mike Slattery's fly balls, he injured his right hand "when a ball more difficult than the average came down and split the index finger of Tim's right hand in a bad manner."[22] After having surgery to repair his broken finger, Keefe tried to pitch again on September 8, but lasted only one inning because the injured finger impacted his delivery. "Keefe was not himself," the *Boston Globe* reported. "The game was virtually lost to Boston, however, in this short time, as four bases on balls, a hit by a pitched ball, followed with hits by Nash and Irwin, gave the home team five runs."[23] Keefe also had two wild pitches in his short stint, as Boston romped to victory, 18–6, in yet another classic high-scoring Players' League contest due to the lively Keefe Ball.

With Keefe unable to contribute on the baseball diamond, Talcott dispatched him to St. Louis in September, ostensibly to recruit ballplayers from the Browns team in the American Association to play in New York for the 1891 season.[24] The move seems disingenuous, since Talcott was by now likely in active pursuit of consolidation with Day's Giants. The scouting assignment did isolate Keefe from Ewing, to remove any impediment, since to say that Keefe was "outspoken against amalgamation" was an understatement.[25] By mid–September, Talcott was clearly on the road to amalgamation (i.e., consolidation), when the *New York Sun* wrote about Talcott's disappointment with his team:

> I think that away down in his heart Mr. Talcott does not take so much stock in ball players as in the earlier stage of the season. It has been his ambition to have the New Yorks win the championship. And why shouldn't they have won it? There is not one valid reason. Some of the players have treated Mr. Talcott shabbily. He went into this scheme with them, and has worked faithfully to further their interests. All this kindness on his part has gone for naught.... I think he has come to a realization of the fact that the ball players are "out for the stuff," and that they care just as little for him, excepting for the almighty dollar, as they did of Mr. Day.[26]

Talcott may have been thinking about Keefe as one of the money-grubbing ballplayers when he spoke to the *New York Sun* writer. Talcott reportedly stopped paying most of the ballplayers in September, including Keefe, Richardson, and O'Rourke.[27]

As the team stumbled to a third-place finish, eight games behind first-place Boston, Keefe compiled a 17–11 record during the 1890 season. While Keefe's absence down the stretch hurt the team, Talcott, though, blamed Crane for the team not winning the pennant. "The principal reason, and I do not hesitate to say it, lies with Crane," Talcott reasoned. "We thought with the foot and a half added to the distance between the pitcher's box and the plate that he would be much speedier and more effective than other pitchers, as he had the physical strength to hold out. But he did not keep himself in condition and today we are in third position. That is the long and short of it."[28]

Since Keefe had returned to New York City from St. Louis by late September, he likely attended the opening of "The Whirlwind," starring his sister-in-law Helen Dauvray Ward, at the Standard Theatre.[29] The Wards were separated by that time, and soon would be on their way to divorce court. Clara Keefe's financing of her sister's theatrical dreams did not help the situation.[30] "The Whirlwind" was both a critical fiasco as well as a financial debacle; the production closed within a month.[31] Keefe likely didn't feel too badly at the time about several thousands of dollars going down the drain, since he was optimistic about the future of the Players' League. That attitude, though, quickly changed.

Almost every ballclub in both leagues lost money in 1890 and the two leagues were on the path to mutual assured destruction. The New York Players' League club was no exception, as it reportedly lost $8,000 (nearly one-half of its paid-in capital of $20,000), not counting the investment in Brotherhood Park, which made the loss for its capitalists even greater.[32]

Once the 1890 season ended in early October, the heads of the two New York ballclubs were primed for a compromise solution to end the baseball war. President Day of the National League club said: "I am in favor of a settlement if one can be consistently arranged. I think the idea of a conference between the leagues a good one."[33] Talcott of the Players' League club told the *New York Herald*: "I am in favor of a compromise if possible. I want to see the League and Brotherhood come together and talk over the situation in a business-like manner. Mr. Day is a business man, and I feel sure that he is willing to have a consultation with us. The two leagues can come together easily, and by making concessions on both sides, I think the trouble of the past season can be fixed up."[34]

While both gentlemen appeared ready to sit down at the negotiating table, Keefe was absolutely adamant against it. Keefe told the *New York Press*: "I believe that there ought to be some kind of a talk to try and come to terms, but I don't see what kind of an arrangement can be made. Some one is pretty sure to get the worst of the bargain, and I know that that one won't be the Players' League. Still, if anybody will suggest some equitable arrangement I believe there'll be a show for the settlement of the dispute."³⁵ Ward, the Brotherhood president, on the other hand, signaled compromise. "It is evident to everybody that war is a losing game ... thousands of dollars have been thrown away and it is about time we cried halt ... of course it is a bitter pill, but for the sake of peace and harmony we will swallow it."³⁶

A peace conference among the three major leagues convened on October 9 in New York City. Talcott was one of the three representatives for the Players' League and Day one of the three men for the National League to participate in discussions with the American Association to try to decide the best way to run professional baseball. Spalding, just back from Europe, also represented the National League. The Brotherhood was not invited to the discussions.

While formal discussions were conducted among the nine men from the three major leagues, Talcott also met with Day on the side to discuss the specific New York City situation. Spalding also conducted secret meetings with several of the New York Players' League ballplayers. "President A.G. Spalding of the Chicago club had several pleasant carriage rides (after dark) with Buck Ewing," Will Rankin wrote in a retrospective about the consolidation of the two New York ballclubs. "Then Buck induced one or two other players to accompany him. It soon became known that it was a 'diamond cut diamond' deal on all sides. Moves were soon made for meetings of the moneyed men and consolidation plans were mapped out."³⁷ With Ewing on board, Talcott made good on his August comment about giving up the ship when Ewing did. Keefe, most certainly, was not one of the ballplayers seen in Spalding's carriage.

It took only one week for the capitalists of the New York Players' League ballclub to officially desert the Brotherhood ballplayers and consummate a deal to consolidate the two New York City ballclubs. On October 14, Talcott and Day, both with big smiles, emerged from a meeting at Van Cott's office. Talcott let Day have center stage to convey the deal. "There will be but one club in New York city next season. That is now practically settled," Day told the *New York Sun*. Asked about the input of the Players' League ballplayers, Day responded: "The players are not in this matter. The whole settlement lies just where it ought to. The players have not been considered. The matter has been talked over from a business standpoint to see how the present condition of affairs could be bettered."³⁸

Talcott confirmed the deal the following day, but provided very few details.³⁹ There were few details because this was just the first shoe to fall.

What league would the consolidated ballclub be in? Who would be in charge? What ballplayers would be retained? These details would fall into place during the next two months. Papers were signed in mid–December to finalize the deal.[40]

Ewing's role as key participant in the consolidation talks was cemented on October 14, when he was spotted that morning at the Stock Exchange to talk with stockbroker Talcott. "To Ewing probably more than any one is due the credit for paving the way to their meeting [on October 14]. Ewing's good sense told him that the war was a fatal one, and that a compromise must be had or the game must die out and the players get no more princely salaries," the *New York Sun* reported. "He has been working harder than if he was behind the bat every day. No one has worked harder to bring about a compromise than he. In the middle of the season he tried to bring Messrs. Day and Talcott together."[41]

The *Boston Globe* dispatched writer Tim Murnane to New York City to cover the big story. "Talcott seems to be merely putty in Buck Ewing's hands. These two men are always seen together when there is any base ball business, and their aim now seems to be in getting the pick of their present players into line, and then dictating to the Players' League what they would like to see done for the good of the game," Murnane wrote about his lunch with Talcott and Ewing at Nick Engle's saloon. "There is very little doubt but Eddie Talcott and John B. Day have come to a full understanding, and the only hitch now will be with Talcott delivering the goods." Murnane didn't specify what he meant by "the goods," but that became clear later in his article when he wrote: "Mr. Talcott seemed to be at sea and much worried over the turn things had taken during the last few days. His hope of being able to dictate to the majority of the Players' League clubs was fast dying out."[42]

From Murnane's report, it seems clear that the deal between Talcott and Day was contingent on Talcott bringing about the elimination of the Players' League, so that the consolidated New York City ballclub would play in the National League without any local competition. Talcott may also have been asked to destroy the Brotherhood organization as well, to eliminate obstacles to running the consolidated ballclub as efficiently as possible, from an expense standpoint.

Keefe was a three-time loser in this deal between Talcott and Day, which not only killed off the New York Players' League club, but also resulted in the demise of the Players' League itself as well as the Brotherhood organization.

In one of his last columns in *Sporting Life* before he died, Harris once again was able to make sense out of confusion. "The players are naturally very much put out because the capitalists are preparing to compromise and consolidate with the National League without giving them an opportunity to assist in arranging the details," Harris wrote after the deal with Talcott and Day went public. While the ballplayers complained about having to reunite with the former Brotherhood men who had deserted the Players' League in 1890 to return to the National League, Harris zeroed in on their anger. "The real reason seems to be to those who look under the surface that the completion of the deal now in progress will practically eliminate the Ball Players' Brotherhood, either as dictators or factors, in the prosecution of the base ball business. Should the deal go through, the Brotherhood, while it would still have some importance, would not have any further control of the business, and, beyond its utility as a beneficial organization, would cease to be a power."[43]

To Keefe and many other Brotherhood members, the establishment of the Players' League was supposed to have been about devising a fundamentally better way to conduct the business of baseball, to better divide the rewards between ballplayers and capitalists. Now, it was abundantly clear that the capitalists had never, for one second, subscribed to that philosophy. The ballplayers had been duped. And now they had absolutely nothing to show for all the sacrifices they had made and the risks they had taken.

The Brotherhood held its last meeting on October 20, 1890. Members voiced their concerns, but there was little the organization could do. "The men are agitated to no small degree over the fact that the financial backers of the League and Brotherhood have formed a little mutual admiration society," one newspaper summarized the meeting.[44] Ward tried to barge his way into the three-league peace talks then under way, but he was denied entrance at the door.

In his last remarks as a Brotherhood officer, Keefe was livid that the Players' League capitalists had even talked to the National League magnates. "I am surprised that our capitalists are having anything to do with the other people. The more they go near the League people the worse it is apt to be for the Players' League," Keefe told the *New York Sun*. "The fact is the more the buzz saw is fooled with the more liable it is that somebody will get hurt. Three weeks ago the Players' League had the National League beaten; things don't look quite that way at present."[45] As to what would happen to the Brotherhood should the capitalists conclude negotiations with the National League, Keefe was a true believer to the end: "Why, that's impossible. In the first place the players would stick together to a man, and it is quite possible that in case our backers got tired we might find some new ones, but then there's no use of discussing that point."[46]

By mid–November, though, Keefe had resigned himself to the reality of the end of the Brotherhood and a consolidated New York ballclub for the 1891 season. "I don't see as I shall have anything to say about it," Keefe told the *New York Sun*. "It will be a case of must [join] or not play at all. In fact, I may not even be asked to play."[47]

After the October 1890 deal for the capitalists in the New York Players' League ballclub to combine with the stockholders of the New York National League ballclub, the demise of the Players' League was certain. It just took three months of intrigue and backstabbing to work out the funeral arrangements. The "chief undertaker" was Albert Spalding, who, according to his biographer, acted "like any good capitalist, Spalding kept his mouth shut, took command of the situation, and began the process that led eventually to the collapse of the Players' League."[48] As Spalding later wrote, "unconditional surrender was the only possible solution," whose terms, to his surprise, "were greedily accepted" by the Players' League capitalists.[49]

The Players' League officially ceased to exist by mid–January 1891. Besides the consolidation of the two ballclubs in New York City, mergers were also negotiated with the competing clubs in Chicago, Brooklyn, and Pittsburgh. The Players' League clubs in Boston and Philadelphia were transferred to the American Association. The National League bought out the Cleveland club, although litigation about that liquidation lingered on for several years. The Buffalo ballclub simply dissolved.

Keefe had misguided trust in Talcott, perhaps because he was so immersed in his own Keefe & Becannon sporting goods business during the 1890 season (especially concerning the Keefe Ball). Keefe was also distracted by his relationship with Clara during the first year of his marriage, as they relocated from the city to the suburbs to live in a "beautiful residence in Yonkers."[50] Keefe's insistence on independence, while Ewing and Ward turned out to be more malleable on working arrangements within a capitalist business structure, also was a consideration. In the end Keefe's stance as an implacable zealot of Brotherhood dogma, and the labor theory of value in general, seriously impaired his future in baseball.

Talcott engineered a deal that turned out very well for him, when, in 1893, he became the majority stockholder in the New York Giants ballclub in the National League.[51] However, the deal was not nearly as beneficial for minority stockholder Tim Keefe.

20
Aftermath of the Players' League

The collapse of the Players' League in January 1891 completely changed the direction of Tim Keefe's life, since he had expected the Keefe & Becannon sporting goods firm to be his post-baseball future. Instead, the league's demise resulted in the bankruptcy of Keefe & Becannon in May 1891.

Keefe worked furiously during the winter of 1891 to save Keefe & Becannon from insolvency. Unfortunately, Keefe had to inject his own funds in the company, since payments due from the Players' League ballclubs piled up as uncollectible. Money owed to Keefe & Becannon included $557 by the Pittsburgh club, $450 by Buffalo, and $328 by Brooklyn.[1] He also spent money to file a law suit against the Players' League, hoping to recover his losses from the first year of his three-year contract to furnish baseballs to the league for free, in exchange for the right to sell the ball on a retail basis in his store. One writer estimated that Keefe had fronted $1,125 for 225 dozen baseballs used by the league during the 1890 season.[2] The lawsuit had little merit, though, since Keefe could still sell the Players' League baseball, albeit with little buyer demand.

Two weeks after the start of the 1891 baseball season, Keefe's lawyer, Abram Dittenhoefer, appeared in court to dissolve the Keefe & Becannon partnership and apply for a receiver. The court filing noted that the two partners "cannot conduct the business amicably" and that Keefe had contributed more capital to the firm than did Becannon. "Keefe says that by their agreement each put $2,500 into the business, but since that time he has advanced a good deal of money to the firm, while Becannon has not," the *New York Press* reported on the situation.[3] On May 8 the court appointed a receiver to handle the firm's creditors.

An offer by Walter Spalding to have Spalding & Bros. acquire Keefe & Becannon at a rock-bottom price was a likely cause of the rift between Keefe and his business partner. Keefe, ever independent, would have refused the offer, while Becannon, sensing the end in sight, would have wanted to sell. Following the dismantling of the Keefe & Becannon firm over the summer, Becannon did go back to work at Spalding & Bros.[4]

The dissolution of Keefe & Becannon wiped out Keefe financially. Most of his limited funds went to satisfy creditors of the firm, although the receiver only paid off the debts at cents on the dollar. "He was one of the most zealous workers in behalf of the baseball rebels, and if that organization had proved a success Keefe would probably have been benefited more largely than any other one man in the country," the *New York Tribune* wrote later in 1891. "If the Players' League had proved a success, Keefe would probably have become wealthy, but it did not, and Sir Timothy's coffers were materially drained."[5] Fortuitously, Keefe had transferred ownership of his Cambridge real estate into his mother's name in late 1889, so he still had that asset in reserve.

Although John Day was nominally still the president of the New York Giants, he was by no means in charge of the 1891 Giants team. The other seven members of the board of directors clearly were calling the shots in the management of the ballclub, to be carried out by Edward Talcott as vice president, Frank Robinson as secretary, and Walter Spalding as treasurer.[6] Keefe was a partial owner of the Giants, since his stock in the Players' League ballclub had been converted into stock of the recapitalized National League ballclub, but his $1,000 of stock represented less than one percent of ownership.[7]

Even though the Brotherhood had lost the war to the National League, Keefe did not abandon his Brotherhood ideals. He still firmly believed that a ballplayer should be paid his market worth when held captive by a ballclub under the reserve rule. In February 1891 Keefe told Talcott that he "would only play for the same money he got last year, $4500; which is $500 less, he claims, than he can get from another league club ... [otherwise] he wants his release."[8] Although just a year and a half ago they had been partners to build the now-defunct New York Players' League ballclub, Keefe got no sympathy from Talcott, who summarily rejected Keefe's salary demand.

Keefe left New York City in early March to once again coach the baseball team at Princeton College.[9] He returned to college coaching with a renewed vigor. In the long run, he thought this avenue would now have a more prominent role in his post-baseball future than it had in the past, given the imminent collapse of Keefe & Becannon. In the short run, he tutored a promising pitching pupil, Lawrence Young, to make a good showing in Princeton's exhibition game in early April against the Giants. "The Princeton College team will be stronger, in my opinion, than ever before," Keefe told a writer from the *New York Sun*. "The New York team will not have a picnic, either, when they meet them, and if they are not careful it is just as likely as not that they may have to succumb to the orange and black."[10]

Keefe had to sign with the Giants early in 1891 and could not afford to stage a holdout at the beginning of the season, as he had been able to do in

1888 and 1889. In order to keep Keefe & Becannon afloat, he needed the cachet of being a current member of the Giants. He also needed to be one of the Giants for the April 4 exhibition game with Princeton, to maximize that publicity for business development purposes. Unlike 1888 and 1889, Keefe had no negotiation leverage, since he was no longer the team's top pitcher; Amos Rusie now had that honor.

In 1891 baseball writer William Harris, who was ill and would die that July, was no longer writing for the *New York Press*. Therefore, inside information that Harris had written about in Keefe's 1888 and 1889 salary negotiations was lacking in newspaper reports of his 1891 negotiation.

Keefe seemed to feel entitled to a fair wage as partial restitution for his failing sporting goods business, which arguably had been eviscerated by the merger of the two New York ballclubs, which then precipitated the merger between the two leagues. "He lost a pile of money in the Players' League fight by furnishing the various clubs with sporting goods," *Sporting Life* reported in March. "He feels that he cannot afford to come down in his salary like some of the other players who lost nothing."[11] Added stress for Keefe was the pressure on him to support his mother and two unmarried sisters, since he needed to replace the income that had been provided by his sister Annie, who had died in June 1889, and his sister Ellen, who was engaged to be married in December 1891.[12]

Keefe's best negotiation leverage was that he would bring New York City fans back to the National League games. "One thing can be said, if Keefe is not a member of the team there will be a great howl of indignation from the public," one writer believed. "Outside of Ewing he is the most popular player who will be on the New York team."[13] It was debatable, though, whether or not Keefe was still a gate attraction. Buck Ewing thought so. "The management can't afford to dispense with the greatest pitcher in the profession. Keefe is not obstinate, and will compromise," Ewing told the *New York Press* in mid–March. "I know what I am talking about when I say that Keefe's appearance in the box swells the receipts from $600 to $1,000 whenever a strong team plays against the Giants."[14]

The management of the Giants thought Keefe's value had diminished from the glory days of 1888 and 1889, and thus sought to reduce his salary by $1,000, from $4,500 to $3,500. Day told writers his typical hard line that "he will get $3500 or nothing."[15] Manager Jim Mutrie communicated the same $3,500 offer a few days later, which Keefe, of course, refused, telling him, "I want the same money I got last year, $4500." When a writer asked Keefe about Mutrie's reaction, Keefe replied that he "nearly fainted."[16] Day and Mutrie were only figureheads by this time, with no decision-making authority. Talcott represented the views of management, which was heavily influenced by the stockholders who had bailed out the ballclub in July 1890. Walter Spalding, the club's treasurer, was the most visible member of the bailout faction.

By the end of March, Keefe had to cave in to management's $3,500 salary offer. When he met with Talcott on March 30, Keefe dropped his salary demand to $4,000 and agreed to return $500 if the ballclub did not make money during the 1891 season.[17] On March 31 both parties agreed to a deal, at undisclosed details. "Director Talcott called on him at his Broadway store and, after a brief consultation, they went to J. Walter Spalding's office," the *New York World* reported. "There a League contract was produced and Tim signed his name to it. He declined to state what his salary is to be, but said he was satisfied with it."[18]

To Talcott and Spalding, Keefe was a transition cost, along with both Day and Mutrie whose days with the New York Giants were also numbered. Amos Rusie was the ace pitcher for the Giants now, not Keefe nor even Welch. Talcott likely accepted some small compromise in exchange for Keefe tutoring the young Rusie. There is some evidence that Keefe did help tutor Rusie. The *New York Sun* reported a few years later that Keefe suggested that Rusie develop a slow ball to save his arm from throwing too many fastballs.[19] However, as soon became evident, any respect that Talcott had for Keefe as a master craftsman in the pitcher's box quickly evaporated.

On April 4 in the exhibition game between Princeton College and the Giants, Keefe's prize pupil, Princeton pitcher Lawrence Young, displayed excellent results. "Tim Keefe has been coaching the pitchers of the Princeton team all winter, and he certainly has developed two remarkably fine twirlers," the *New York Press* reported. "Twelve times the New Yorks faced Young, and he struck out five, putting the Giants out in one, two, three order in each inning. Young has remarkably good control of the ball and a quick jump curve which is very deceptive to the batter."[20]

At the 1891 season opener on April 22, spectators returned to the National League ballgame in New York City with a "combination of League yells and Brotherhood howls" that was reminiscent of the team's glory years. "When the last spectator turned over his half dollar to the weary ticket seller," the *New York Times* reported, "a glance at the turnstiles showed that 17,835 persons had passed through the gates."[21] Rusie lost to Clarkson in the opener, 4–3.

It must have been incredibly awkward for Keefe to sit on the Giants' bench and watch two Brotherhood disbelievers pitch the season opener, as well as be associated with the Giants' lineup that was less than one-half former Brotherhood members and largely comprised of Brotherhood deserters and

League stalwarts such as Glasscock, Denny, Tiernan, and Rusie (with Welch also on the bench). Not only had the two New York teams consolidated for 1891, but their operations had too. The Giants played their games in 1891 at the old Brotherhood Park, now rechristened to be the third vintage of the Polo Grounds. The former New Polo Grounds of 1889 and 1890, adjacent to Brotherhood Park, was abandoned and became known as Manhattan Field.

To publicly demonstrate that Keefe wasn't the same pitcher in 1891 that he was during the 1888 and 1889 championship seasons, Mutrie was forced (by an unidentified person in ownership) to start Keefe in the second game of the season on April 23. Keefe, never a fan of pitching in the cold weather, was unimpressive against the Boston batters, as he gave up seven runs in the fifth inning of an 11–6 loss. The *New York World* headlined its article on the game: "Keefe Vigorously Hammered and the Giants Defeated."[22] "The Boston batsmen appeared to learn the secret of Keefe's pitching, and they sent the ball in all directions," the *New York Times* reported. "He tried his stock of curves, shoots, drops, slow and speedy balls, but he couldn't stop the fusillade."[23]

That April 23 appearance was the first of several blatant attempts by the ownership of the New York Giants to embarrass Keefe. Talcott, a devout capitalist and Keefe's former ally in the Players' League ballclub, who clearly had been disingenuous in his avowed support for the Brotherhood movement, made no attempt to rescue Keefe from the forthcoming charade. The next embarrassment for Keefe was to sit on the bench for six weeks before pitching in another game.

After the staged failure of Keefe in the pitcher's box, reports soon surfaced in Philadelphia and New York newspapers about discussions to move Keefe to the Philadelphia Phillies. "I will sign either Keefe or Sharrott if I can get them," manager Harry Wright told the Philadelphia writers.[24] Mutrie was more circumspect with the New York City writers, saying there was no deal, while Keefe was very noncommittal, saying he liked Philadelphia, but that he'd shop his services to the highest bidder if he were to be released.[25]

Keefe sat on the bench for the entire month of May. During this period, Ewing injured his arm and couldn't play, so he, as captain, essentially became the bench manager, as Mutrie was cast aside. It was Ewing who largely executed management's whim regarding Keefe for the remainder of his days with the Giants. Keefe did not get his next chance to pitch until June 4 against Cincinnati at the Polo Grounds. Allowing only three hits in the 4–2 victory, Keefe "astonished the critics who have been asserting that Sir Timothy had outlived his usefulness as a ballplayer."[26] He was also victorious the next time he stepped into the pitcher's box on June 15, defeating Chicago. These would be his only victories with the Giants in 1891, though, as he finished his tenure with the Giants in 1891 with a 2–5 record.

After he lost the game on June 19, ownership set him up again. On June 24 Keefe pitched only one inning, giving up three runs, before being removed from the game. "Keefe, to express his position charitably, has taken a back seat. It required just one inning for Keefe to lose the game yesterday," the *New York Times* reported. "As he walked to the bench, the majority of the cranks spoke in undertones, some shook their heads knowingly, and others who were want to cheer the favorite pitcher on every possible occasion in past years gave unmistakable evidence of disgust at the poor work."[27] When Welch entered the pitcher's box in the second inning, some writers smelled a rat, though. "When Keefe was put in to pitch Wednesday it was the intention to take him out of the box at the very first opportunity," *Sporting Life* reported. "As evidence of this it is only necessary to record a brief dialogue that took place before the game between Manager Mutrie and a reporter: 'Who is going to pitch for you to-day, Jim?' asked the reporter. 'Well, Keefe will go in for the first,' replied Mutrie, in a hesitating manner. The deduction, in view of subsequent events, is perfectly plain."[28]

Keefe had to face his baseball demons on his own during the summer of 1891, as "reduction sale" advertisements for Keefe & Becannon appeared in the *New York World* and *New York Press*. In what was to become an annual summer excursion, Clara Keefe boarded a ship bound for London, England, on July 11 to visit sculptors in Europe and talk with representatives of the World's Fair planned for 1892 in Washington, D.C., to honor the 400th anniversary of the arrival of Christopher Columbus in the New World. "Mrs. Keefe intends while abroad to secure ideas for the design of a statue to be exhibited at the World's Fair," the *New York Herald* reported. "This statue will be exhibited together with a bust of Mr. Chauncey M. Depew who has promised her sittings as soon as he returns from Europe."[29]

The verdict on Keefe as pitcher seemed solid by mid–July. "Keefe's work has been very poor. He has neither speed nor control, and without these elements a pitcher is of no earthly use," the *New York Press* reported. "John B. Day and Manager Mutrie may have a little sentiment for the old players but the new element in the Board of Directors certainly has not, and why should they? Business is business in base ball as in everything else."[30] In the July 16 game in Cleveland, "Keefe was hit unmercifully throughout the game," the *New York Press* reported. "The once great Sir Timothy was a presumably sadder and wiser man."[31] When the Giants returned to New York City following that game, Keefe demanded his release rather than remain with the Giants.

The Giants gave Keefe his 10-day notice of release on July 21, to be effective July 31. "His work has not suited the management this season, and as he has been drawing a big salary, it was deemed advisable to let him go," the *New York Times* reported. "This news will be received with regret by the lovers of baseball in this city. Keefe has been a big favorite here."[32] There was a tinge of bitterness in Keefe's words when he spoke to sportswriters after his release was announced:

> I hate to leave New York, am very fond of it, and would do all in my power for New York, but what am I to do? I have been systematically done [in] by the management of the New York Baseball club. I was told at the commencement of the season that I had been hired simply as a bench player; now I know it. They would not let me play, and when I did get a chance, I worked under a disadvantage. I feel that I am just as good a player as I ever was.[33]

A few days later Keefe elaborated on his situation: "I have been expecting this action of the management for some time. It is in line with their policy toward me ever since the beginning of the season. The whole thing has been brought about by one man. I will not mention his name, but all my friends know whom I mean."[34] The *New York Press* reported that Keefe "had an idea that the Chicago element of the Board of Directors was against him and that there was a systematic scheme to down him."[35] By "Chicago element," Keefe meant Walter Spalding, the treasurer of the Giants and co-owner of the Spalding & Bros. sporting goods firm.

During the 10-day period before his release was final, the Giants' ownership took one more opportunity to embarrass Keefe by taking him on the team's trip to Boston, ostensibly for a farewell pitching appearance against his hometown team. Scorecards were printed in Boston with Keefe in the lineup for the game on Saturday, July 25, but Ewing put Welch in the pitcher's box. Ewing told reporters that Keefe would pitch on Monday, July 27, but again Welch pitched the game. "Who is keeping Keefe out of the box?" the *New York Press* inquired.[36]

At the game on Tuesday, July 28, the defrocked Mutrie showed up at the South End Grounds with a newly signed pitcher for the Giants named Andy Dunning, late of the Manchester, New Hampshire, team in the New England League. Ewing put Dunning in the box rather than Keefe. With so much evidence that management was unnecessarily hazing Keefe, the Giants players intentionally failed to support Dunning and essentially threw the game to Boston. Dunning was shelled for five runs in just two innings of work, with four of the runs being unearned due to errors by the Giants.

To avoid a lopsided defeat, Ewing was forced to put Keefe in the game for his final performance in a New York Giants uniform. "Poor Dunning looked for assistance from Keefe, who was sitting on the bench prepared to play. The genial Keefe hated to watch the slaughter of the innocents, and he consented to relieve Mutrie's new find," the *New York Times* described the situation.[37] The Boston crowd cheered when Keefe took the field in the third inning, the *Boston Globe* reported, also noting that "the old Cambridge boy was given a hearty reception when he walked to the plate in the third inning."[38]

In its article entitled "Keefe Given Half a Chance," the *New York Herald* exposed the indignity that management had imposed on Keefe, writing that there were "very flimsy excuses" provided by management for not using Keefe. Management claimed "the club was afraid to lose games" due to his poor pitching, but yet "it sees fit to take chances on an untried minor leaguer ... while Keefe occupies a seat on the bench."[39] This article surely drew a wry smile from Keefe.

A week before his final day with the Giants on July 31, the *Boston Globe* wrote this about Keefe: "Everybody knows him, and everybody likes him. That is, everybody but one man. This one man is connected with the management of the club, and to his influence Keefe's release is said to be due.... The real animus of Tim's release has not yet been ascertained, and probably never will be."[40] That unidentified member of management was Walter Spalding.

Spalding naturally denied he had any influence in the Keefe situation, going so far as to release a lengthy statement in October that was in the vein of he "doth protest too much":

> During the entire season I have had nothing to do with the active management of this club. I have simply performed my duties as its treasurer. I have not at any time advised the engagement or release of any player, nor did I know of Mr. Keefe's release until after it had been given out. To substantiate what I have said I wish to read you this letter which I received to-day from Mr. John B. Day. I did not ask for it, but Mr. Day sent it to me of his own volition:
>> To the Public: Whereas, Some newspapers have for some time since been insinuating that Mr. J.W. Spalding has interfered with the management of the New York Ball Club, and that he has interfered with my prerogatives in connection with the club, I wish to say in justice to Mr. Spalding, that since the team took the field in the spring he has had nothing to do with the management of the club whatever, nor has he in any way interfered with me in reference to the club or its affairs. Very respectfully, John B. Day.
>
> This was given to me by Mr. Day of his own volition, and merely to put at rest these stories that I am dictating the policy of the New York Club.[41]

Of course, Spalding, as treasurer of the ballclub, had substantial input into all financial decisions and no doubt pressured Day into releasing Keefe to save money, especially when all of ownership was seeking to recoup the losses from the 1890 season.

Whether Spalding pushed for Keefe's release because the Keefe & Becannon firm had been a competitor to his own sporting goods firm is impossible

20. Aftermath of the Players' League

to tell. Keefe, though, did believe Spalding was against him "on account of business rivalry."[42] Interestingly, Spalding & Bros. bought some assets of Keefe & Becannon in the liquidation of the partnership, including the trademark for the "Buck Ewing Mitt," which had been a cornerstone product of the firm when it opened for business in 1889.[43] Keefe may have taken that purchase as evidence that the treasurer of the Giants was against him.

Keefe was the first departure in the dismantling of the championship team of 1888 and 1889. Mutrie was fired as manager after the end of the 1891 season, replaced by Pat Powers for 1892. Welch pitched his last game for the Giants in May 1892. Ewing and O'Rourke were traded after the 1892 season. The last member of the champion Giants to play for New York was Mike Tiernan, who continued to patrol the outfield at the Polo Grounds until the 1899 season.

John Day remained in his diminished role as president of the Giants through the 1892 season, when he was replaced by Van Cott.[44] Day became destitute in the 1890s because he could not continue to earn a sufficient income in his wholesale tobacco business, which supplied cigar makers with high-quality tobacco leaves grown in Connecticut to use as cigar wrappers.[45] The setback for Day was the change in the cigar business beginning in 1891, where imported tobacco leaves from Sumatra replaced Connecticut-grown leaves as the cigar wrapper preferred by consumers.[46] The Sumatra-grown tobacco dominated the U.S. cigar business by 1893 and thus devastated Day's business. It wasn't until 1900 that growers in Connecticut discovered that they could replicate the quality of the Sumatra leaf by growing tobacco plants in shaded fields, but by then it was far too late to save Day's business.

Keefe's days as a pitcher were not yet over in 1891, though, as he played two more seasons with the Philadelphia Phillies before ending his major-league career in 1893.

21
Ending His Pitching Career in Philadelphia

Following his last day with the New York Giants on July 31, 1891, Tim Keefe waited a few days to strike a deal with Harry Wright to play for the Philadelphia Phillies until he knew where he would stand in Wright's pitching plans for the rest of the season. Wright was already using four pitchers and the team had no room on its roster for a fifth twirler.

Clarity regarding Keefe's role with the Phillies arrived on August 10 when Wright released pitcher Ed Cassian. Wright now could use an experienced pitcher with Keefe's credentials. On August 11, Keefe agreed to pitch for the Phillies, after negotiating a deal at unpublicized salary rates. "His contract with us is at a certain figure for the remainder of the season," Wright told reporters. "Should we wish to reserve him, however, we have his price [for 1892]."[1]

Keefe pitched his first game in a Phillies uniform on August 19, an 8–7 loss to Brooklyn in Philadelphia. "Tim Keefe made his first appearance as a Quaker and he quaked to the extent of twelve hits and seven bases on balls," the *Philadelphia Inquirer* reported on his inconsistent pitching performance, which included allowing four runs in the ninth inning to blow a 7–4 lead.[2] He secured his first victory for Philadelphia on August 22 when he defeated his former New York Giants teammates, 9–5, on the grounds in Philadelphia. While he was certainly motivated to defeat his former team, Keefe refused to pitch at the Polo Grounds. Wright indulged Keefe by agreeing to his request not to pitch in the five-game series in September with the Giants at the Polo Grounds. Keefe's motive was revenge, "as he thinks his attractive powers will be the means of putting too much money in the New York treasury."[3]

However, Keefe was rusty in the pitcher's box, since he hadn't pitched on a regular schedule since he broke his finger in August 1890 and had been seldom used by the Giants earlier in 1891. After defeating Pittsburgh on August 31, Keefe lost his next five games, as his new catcher, Jack Clements, had difficulty getting used to the variety of pitches Keefe threw. Not having the hugely partisan crowd that he was used to at the Polo Grounds also took

Keefe some time to acclimate. The losing streak was snapped on the last day of the season when Keefe defeated Boston on October 3. Keefe finished with an uninspired 3–6 record during his two months with Philadelphia, as the team chugged its way to a fourth-place finish in the National League standings, 18 games behind pennant-winning Boston.

In December 1891 the landscape of the National League changed dramatically as the result of the League's three-day conclave with the rival American Association to determine how the two organizations should be merged in order to improve profitability of the remaining ballclubs. In the end, the National League created a 12-team league for 1892 by absorbing four Association clubs (Baltimore, Louisville, St. Louis, and Washington) and buying out the other clubs. To help pay for the buyout and recover losses incurred during the Players' League war, the National League owners agreed to expand the playing schedule, allow Sunday games, reduce player salaries, and shrink roster size. None of these ramifications were good news for Keefe.

For the 1892 playing season, the National League owners agreed to conduct a 154-game schedule in a split-season format, with the first half to be played from April 12 to July 13 and the second half to run from July 14 to October 15. The first-place finishers of the two halves would meet in a playoff series to determine the pennant winner. The owners copied this idea from the minor-league Eastern Association, which had used the format to salvage its 1891 season.

Keefe had no shortage of motivation to resurrect his reputation as one of the game's best pitchers. However, Keefe needed to be in better physical condition than he had been for a few years, in order to endure the longer playing season in 1892. He expected manager Wright to have him on a short lease, given the lack of top form that Keefe had exhibited in the pitcher's box the previous year. Keefe needed to perform well in 1892 or his pitching career was likely over.

The possibility of his pitching career ending in 1892 would have been terrible timing for Keefe. In March 1892, in a non-public sign of his impending financial difficulties, Keefe mortgaged his Cambridge property with the City Five Cent Savings Bank to generate $2,500 that he needed to cover some of his debts and to supplement the reduced salary he was being paid for the 1892 season.[4] The mortgage was for a three-year period, which was typical for the era. Banks then only granted short-term loans on property, for one-half or less of its value, with interest to be paid semi-annually (in this case, six percent) and the principal amount due in full in a balloon payment at the end of the term. Keefe presumed he could overcome his money problems within three years; however, his judgment didn't come to fruition.

In early January 1892 Keefe wrote a letter to Wright, posted from Somerville, to update him on his physical fitness for the 1892 season:

I am in splendid shape. I take four hours of exercise every day and I am now down to 180 pounds. This is the first winter I have practiced in a gymnasium for some years, and I confidently expect to report in the spring in better condition than I have been for three years. I will be ready to report by March 1, and will go South with the club for practice if you conclude to send the club there.[5]

However, in mid-January, Keefe was authorized by the Harvard Athletic Committee to coach the Harvard College baseball team that winter to prepare the team's pitchers for the 1892 season.[6] Since his contract with Harvard called for his services to be provided through April 1, Keefe did not go to spring training with the Phillies, who trained that year in Gainesville, Florida. Harvard posted a 34–5 record during the 1892 season, so Keefe's efforts at tutoring the pitchers paid dividends. He rationalized his departure from the spring workouts of the Phillies by using the time at Harvard to develop a set of signals he could surreptitiously give Clements so that the catcher would be better prepared to receive his wide assortment of pitches.

On April 12, the signal system seemed to work well, since Keefe looked impressive on Opening Day against the Giants at Philadelphia, even though he lost, 5–4. It was the earliest date that Keefe had ever pitched a game in the major leagues, since the longer season required that games be played ten days earlier than the April 22 start of the 1891 season, and extend an extra two weeks into October.

However, ten days later, the Brooklyn batters seemed to know what pitch Keefe would throw, since they trampled the Phillies, 12–0. "Keefe hadn't pitched ten balls over the plate when it was apparent that it wasn't his day," the *Philadelphia Inquirer* reported. "It made no difference where he hurled the leather the Brooklyn bats came up against it with a crush that made the earth tremble."[7] Brooklyn catcher Tom Kinslow related a few years later how he had deciphered Keefe's signal system:

> "I knew that Keefe, not Clements, was the signal bureau, though Clem stood under the bat and made a deaf-and-dumb alphabet with his hands, just for a stall to throw us off. I studied Keefe closely for three innings without catching him in the act of tipping off signals to Clements, but I finally smelt the mouse. I noticed that Tim stood with his left foot on an angle as he was in the act of delivering the ball. Just as he was about to deliver a speedy, curveless ball, he scraped his foot in the ground, bringing it toward him till the toe pointed directly at the batsman. On a curved ball the foot was motionless. I called Ward's attention to the signal, and he tipped off our players. We hammered Tim out of the box that day."[8]

Not only was the season longer in 1892, but there were also far fewer off days to use to reschedule postponed games due to rainouts. Given the split-season format, teams couldn't wait until the fall to make up games, so teams had to immediately reschedule those postponements into second games of a doubleheader. The April 23 doubleheader was the first of ten for Philadelphia during the first half of the 1892 season, not counting the scheduled twin bills on the Decoration Day and Independence Day holidays. That put additional stress on the team's four-man pitching staff.

Philadelphia muddled through the first few weeks of the 1892 season, standing in tenth place on May 27 with a 13–19 record, 10 games out of first place. However, the Phillies then rattled off a streak of 25 wins in 28 games from May 28 through June 28, including 16 straight, to capture second place, five games behind first-place Boston. Keefe, who was 6–1 during this stretch, must have modified his signal system with Clements to avoid another sign-stealing episode as happened with Brooklyn.

On June 28 Keefe pitched the Phillies to their sixteenth consecutive victory, when he threw a three-hitter to defeat Boston, and John Clarkson, 8–1. Keefe not only pitched well but also contributed to the offense. As reported by the *Boston Globe*, "In the seventh Tim Keefe hit the ball high over the right field fence for a home run, to the surprise of himself and the disgust of his Cambridge friend, Clarkson."[9] The embarrassment of Clarkson surrendering a home run to the weak-hitting Keefe was too much for the Boston ballclub. The next day, in one of the league's first economy moves of the 1892 season, Boston released the high-salaried Clarkson after his mediocre pitching performance during the first half of the season.

Harry Wright, as manager of the Philadelphia Phillies, extended Keefe's pitching career into 1893 when he signed Keefe following his release from the New York Giants in 1891. Wright, as the National League's chief of umpires, also helped convince Keefe to become an umpire in 1894 (Library of Congress, Prints and Photographs Division, LC-DIG-ppmsca-09631).

Despite Keefe's outstanding pitching, Philadelphia never seriously threatened Boston's lead in the standings, as the Phillies lost eight of their next 16 games to finish the first half in third place. Unfortunately for Keefe, the Philadelphia ballclub also started to pare back its roster for the second half to reduce its salary expense. Keefe received his 10-day notice of release on July 11.

Since Wright really didn't want to part with Keefe, just reduce his salary, the 10-day period was in essence a tryout for Keefe. After losing a tight, 1–0, game on July 13, Keefe then tossed two excellent games, a four-hit victory on July 18 and a three-hit shutout on July 21. Although he had demonstrated how effectively he could still pitch, the best Keefe could wrangle from Wright to stay on the team was a lower salary reduction, $125 a month from Wright's proposed $150 cut.[10] These business tactics would never have been tolerated during the Brotherhood years, but there was little Keefe could do now, especially since he needed the income following the bankruptcy of his sporting goods business.

On his own with his wife in Europe—"Mrs. Tim Keefe sailed for England on Wednesday to visit her sister, Mrs. John Ward, who has made a hit on the London stage"—Keefe continued to pitch well during the second half of the season.[11] His pitching performance invited warm newspaper commentary, such as "Tim Keefe demonstrated that he has lost none of his cunning as a pitcher," he was "the Keefe of old," and "Tim Keefe was in old-time form."[12] Still, the Phillies were never in contention during the second half and finished in fifth place, as Keefe compiled a 19–16 record over the full season.

In October 1892, in the first public sign of Keefe's financial problems, he pitched in two postseason exhibition games for the Phillies. On October 18, he yielded just two hits in eight innings in a game with a team from Camden, New Jersey; three days later he pitched in a game against the team from the University of Pennsylvania.[13] Since Keefe hadn't pitched in a local postseason exhibition game since 1886, he obviously needed the money in 1892.

To supplement his baseball income, during the winter of 1893 Keefe worked as a roller polo referee in the New England Polo League, which had professional teams located in the Massachusetts cities of Brockton, Waltham, and Worcester along with the Rhode Island cities of Pawtucket and Providence. Roller polo, what today is called street hockey, was a popular sport in that era for working-class spectators since it was one of the few sports played indoor at night under artificial light. "Tim Keefe is now the model referee, being the [John] Gaffney of polo," the *Boston Globe* noted.[14] He was not just impartial when it came to enforcement of the rules, but he was also concerned about player safety in the rough-and-tumble game of roller polo. In reporting on the game between Waltham and Worcester, the *Globe* wrote, "Tonight's game was also marked by considerable rough play, and many times during the evening Referee Keefe was called upon to warn the players to be more careful."[15] Little did Keefe realize that his stint as a referee was a warm-up for his next baseball job.

More ominously, from a financial perspective, Keefe was one of the first Philadelphia ballplayers to sign a contract for the 1893 season, which came at another salary reduction in the ballclub's continued austerity move. Keefe seemed desperate for money, as the renowned contract negotiator was willing to accept whatever salary the ballclub would pay him to continue to pitch in the major leagues. According to newspaper reports, it was an income level the former star pitcher "gracefully accepted," although no doubt with gritted teeth.[16]

The National League owners abandoned the unpopular split-season schedule used in 1892 and reverted to the conventional full-season format for 1893, although cutting back the number of games from 154 to 132. To attract more spectators to the ballpark to bolster the profitability of their ballclubs, the owners instituted a pitching change to introduce more hitting into the game:

> The pitcher's boundary shall be marked by a white rubber plate twelve inches long and four inches wide, so fixed in the ground as to be even with the surface, at the distance of sixty feet six inches from the outer corner of the home plate so that a line drawn from the centre of the home base and the centre of the second base shall give six inches on either side. The front line of the box in 1892 was distant fifty feet from the home base, [with] the pitcher's pivot foot standing on the back line of the box five feet six inches back of its front line. Under the new rule the pitcher's box has been reduced to twelve inches by four inches, the front line of which is sixty feet six inches distant from the home base."[17]

This new pitching distance introduced in 1893 has remained unchanged to modern times.

Keefe believed the existing pitching distance was just fine. "Any change would tend toward more bases on balls," Keefe said, "thus compelling a pitcher to put the ball over the plate with as little delay as possible."[18] Keefe also claimed the longer distance wouldn't affect him, so that he "will be more effective than ever."[19] However, the new pitching changes did negatively impact Keefe. As he coached the Harvard College pitchers during the winter of 1893, it must have been frustrating for the 36-year-old Keefe to try to find a way to successfully adapt to this significant change in the pitching rules that basically destroyed his livelihood.

One month into the 1893 season, the *Sporting Life* provided its readers with an informative analysis of the pitching changes, concluding that it wasn't the increased distance that was the problem but rather the elimination of the expansive pitcher's box in favor of the tiny rubber:

> The increased distance doesn't count so much. The ball comes a trifle slower, but that does not matter; it is that little rubber slab that has fixed the pitchers. Formerly a twirler could change his position from side to side of the box, and obtain extra leverage on every curve; but tied down to a limited chunk of rubber, his speed is impaired, his curves are simply annihilated, and the ball instead of coming now from one point and then another, comes again and again over the same limited course. It's like pitching down a two foot alley. The ball is there; it isn't going to wriggle away as it used to do, and all you have to do is to step out and paralyze it. So far as the increased distance goes it is all right. But the rubber slab isn't.[20]

Many pitchers continued to try to sustain their customary pitching style in 1893 at the longer distance, but failed to successfully adapt to the new pitching rules. Bill Hutchinson was the most visible casualty. He had averaged 40 wins a season for the previous three seasons, but he dropped down to just 16 wins in 1893. Only three pitchers successfully adapted to consistently dominate batters: Cy Young, Amos Rusie, and Kid Nichols. All three averaged 30 wins a season both before and immediately after the rule changes. The conventional wisdom is that fastball pitchers, such as these three, made the switch easier than curveballers, which as the *Sporting Life* article notes were more dramatically impacted. Cy Young biographer Reed Browning also conjectured other reasons. "About the same time, the site from which the pitcher made his deliveries became elevated," Browning wrote, adding that Young may also have learned how to best use the rubber to push off from to get extra power in his motion.[21]

Without the ability to move around the pitcher's box to deliver pitches from different angles, Keefe had a hard time adjusting to the "two foot alley" where he had to throw the ball. At age 36, he was more impacted by the longer pitching distance than younger pitchers due to the natural aging process that increased the strain on his right arm. Basically, he tired more quickly now.

Keefe repeatedly couldn't close the deal in 1893, as too often he failed to hold a lead in the late innings. The first signal of trouble was the April 29 game when Keefe gave up five runs in the ninth inning to allow Brooklyn to tie the game. Brooklyn then went on to defeat Philadelphia, 11–10, in ten innings by scoring off Taylor, whom Wright had inserted to replace Keefe. Despite winning more often than he lost, Keefe often exhibited "wildness" or was "pounded hard" by opposing batters, according to *Philadelphia Inquirer* reports during the 1893 season. Keefe obviously struggled to find a way to fool hitters with his slowball that was that much easier to hit when thrown from five feet farther away.

21. Ending His Pitching Career in Philadelphia

Wright's patience with Keefe ended in August after two more high-profile blown ballgames. On August 11, at the Polo Grounds, the New York Giants scored three runs off Keefe in the ninth inning to tie the game, and then went on to win in the tenth inning. The last straw came on August 15 when Keefe "pitched in good form" for the first six innings, but then "showed a woeful lack of judgment in distributing his bases on balls" to allow Boston to score six runs in the last three innings to defeat Philadelphia.[22] This was the last game that Keefe ever pitched in the major leagues.

Wright gave Keefe his release the next day. While most newspaper reports indicated that Keefe was released in a salary reduction move, the Philadelphia correspondent to *Sporting Life* put the separation more bluntly: "Keefe's salary was no bigger than that of any other Philadelphia player. Not a player on the team gets over $1800. Keefe was released because, after being carried nearly two seasons, he could not be relied upon to be in condition when called upon."[23]

Although unmentioned in the press at the time he pitched his last major-league ballgame, Keefe retired as the career pitching leader in strikeouts with 2,564 (a record broken by Cy Young in 1908) and had the second-most career victories with 342, just behind Pud Galvin.

There were certainly no hard feelings between Wright and Keefe over the release, since Wright tapped Keefe to umpire the game with Boston on August 17 when regular umpire Jack McQuaid was sick. "After dilly-dallying around for a few minutes, Sir Timothy Keefe was called upon to look after the interests of both clubs in the game," the *Philadelphia Inquirer* reported. "Some of the cranks were afraid Tim would have it in for the Phillies on account of having been given his walking papers by Harry Wright, but the veteran twirler umpired in a manner calculated to make Gaffney or Lynch green with envy."[24] There were no complaints from Wright after Boston defeated the Phillies. Impressed with the comportment of Keefe as an umpire, Wright probably marveled at how Keefe was able to contain his emotions to be as impartial as he was that day.

Keefe returned to New York City to consider his options. He was spotted at the Polo Grounds on August 30 watching the Giants' game, where he told a *New York Sun* writer that he had "decided to rest for the balance of the season," adding that he didn't care "to accept offers from minor league clubs."[25] A few weeks later another New York sportswriter ran into Keefe, who said his arm "has many a good game left in it," indicating that he hoped to return as a major-league pitcher for the 1894 season.[26]

As it turned out, Wright was a key factor in Keefe's next position in baseball, after Wright was fired as the manager of the Phillies that November.

22

Harvard Baseball Coach

In January 1894, Tim Keefe had to confront his future beyond professional baseball, after being a major-league pitcher for 14 years. Wintering at his mother's home in Somerville, Keefe's only official connection to baseball was as the preseason coach for the Harvard College baseball team, which practiced one mile away on the Harvard campus in Cambridge. In his third consecutive year as Harvard coach, Keefe adopted a more public persona as head tutor for the Harvard pitchers in 1894, as he actively courted newspaper coverage of his work.

As he monitored the workout of players in the indoor cage in the Cary Building on the Harvard campus in early January, Keefe told Tim Murnane of the *Boston Globe*: "Of course I cannot say that Harvard has anything like the chances she had last year, but the material is up to the average and several of the men show considerable promise. A number of men under my charge have shown a decided improvement in the short time we have been at work."[1] The outlook for the 1894 team was "not very favorable," with only Joe Wiggin and Andy Highland topping the list of possible pitchers, Keefe confessed to the student writer for the *Harvard Crimson*, who then added in his published article that "a few months' training under T.J. Keefe ought to make both of them much more effective than last spring."[2]

Reprints and paraphrases of this Boston-generated commentary about Keefe made its way into newspapers published in New York, Chicago, and Philadelphia as well as the baseball weeklies. Soon after Keefe was rehired in January, the *Chicago Inter Ocean* headlined its article on the Harvard nine: "Harvard Battery Work: Keefe Exercises the Various Candidates for the Points."[3] The *New York Press* wrote that Keefe "does not speak very encouragingly of a bright outlook," adding that he "says there is plenty of good material, but it needs a great deal of training to get into good form."[4] In April, the *Philadelphia Inquirer* reported: "Captain Wiggin and Coach Keefe are working hard to develop strong team play in order to counterbalance the lack of individual merit, but as yet their labors have met with very little return, and the inexperience of the candidates makes this an exceedingly difficult task."[5]

These newspaper reports helped to publicize Keefe's teaching ability and his vast repository of baseball knowledge, which Keefe hoped would lead to a full-time position somewhere on the baseball landscape. The Harvard job paid a few hundred dollars, which was good for three months of part-time work but hardly would pay the bills for the entire year. With his future no longer in sporting goods or his original plan to leverage his shorthand skills, Keefe needed a steady income, since he continued to suffer financial difficulties following the Players' League debacle, which was compounded by the nation's severe economic depression that began in 1893. Despite the publicity of his baseball teaching skills, he still had no job prospects by March 1894.

To raise money to live on that summer and to pay off the $2,500 principal on the mortgage he had obtained in 1892 on his Cambridge property, Keefe sold one-quarter of his still-undeveloped land on Cambridge Street in mid–March.[6] The *Cambridge Chronicle* reported that the Brock brothers would build a double house facing Cambridge Street, overlooking the grounds of the Cambridge Public Library, and a single house on the Irving Street side of the land.[7]

As Keefe watched the erection of the double house at 1673 Cambridge Street on his former property, not very far from Harvard College, Keefe likely started to contemplate the possibility of building such a rental structure on the remainder of his Cambridge Street land at the corner of Trowbridge Street. In this thinly developed area of the city of Cambridge, there were only a few houses on Irving Street and just one house on Trowbridge Street, as the house at 1673 Cambridge Street was the first dwelling on Cambridge Street between Irving and Trowbridge. Looking east from Keefe's remaining parcel, there was empty land for one block, then the sheds of the West End Street Railway on the next block.

This painting by sports artist Dick Perez depicts Tim Keefe in his early 30s, when his baseball career was winding down and he began to devote more time to coaching college baseball teams during the offseason (dickperez.com).

Sportswriter friends reported how Keefe's right arm was in great shape from the Harvard workouts, as he subtly angled for another shot at pitching on the major-league diamond. Rumors that various teams were considering Keefe also made their way into print, no doubt planted by friends of Keefe. Cincinnati was a popular mention, where old friend Frank Bancroft was the business manager. No team seriously considered the 37-year-old Keefe, though. He might have had a chance at returning to the major leagues if he proved himself capable in the minor leagues, but he refused to swallow his pride by pitching in the minors.

Keefe attended several major-league games during the spring of 1894 to network among his former associates, both in baseball and in the press. The *New York Sun* reported that he was at the Polo Grounds in early May, as he made his way north from New Jersey where Harvard had played Princeton the day before.[8] The *Boston Globe* noted Keefe's attendance at a game in June at the Congress Street Grounds, the former ballpark of the Players' League team in Boston, which the National League team was using temporarily while the burned-down South End Grounds were being rebuilt.[9] In late June Keefe did secure a workout with the Boston team, "but it was not a favorable trial," thus ending any hope that Keefe would once again pitch in the major leagues.[10]

Although Keefe coached three more years at Harvard College, he was never able to leverage that role into a baseball job elsewhere. Keefe might have anticipated working there as a full-time coach, since the Harvard Athletic Committee did vote in December 1895 to search for one, but a full-time baseball coach was not actually hired until 1900.[11] Despite the *Harvard Crimson* headline in January 1896 "Keefe Will Coach the Pitchers," he would always be just a temporary figure on the Harvard campus.[12]

During the winter of 1896, Keefe teamed up with Tommy Bond, in a reunion of their coaching 15 years earlier, to work with the Harvard pitchers. Harvard retained Bond into the spring to continue his work during the playing season as an "instructor of base ball" who would be "at the services of any student of the University who desires to learn the national game."[13] In his final winter coaching at Harvard in 1897, Keefe mentored sophomore pitcher Percy Haughton, who went on to a highly successful football coaching career at Harvard.[14]

With no prospects for full-time employment in the summer of 1894, Keefe needed another vocation to leverage his master status as a baseball pitcher. The one person who was interested in hiring Keefe for a baseball-related job was National League president Nick Young.

23

Umpire in the National League

During the summer of 1894, National League president Nick Young was having a devil of a time maintaining a full crew of umpires. Of the seven men Young had hired as umpires at the beginning of the 1894 season, only four remained on the job by the Fourth of July holiday: Tom Lynch, Tim Hurst, Bob Emslie, and Jack McQuaid. One of the three who had quit was Jim O'Rourke, Keefe's former teammate with the New York Giants, who was replaced by John Gaffney. Young wanted to hire Tim Keefe to be an umpire.

In the gentlemanly era of early baseball, it had been an honor to be designated as an umpire, as one who knew the rules and could interpret them fairly. This carried over to the amateur era of the 1870s, when Keefe was first schooled as a ballplayer. In the professional game, though, ballclub owners were reluctant to pay for competent umpires. The National League didn't regularly use paid umpires until 1878 and didn't have its own full-time staff of umpires until 1883. Even then, the owners didn't support the umpires in disputes with ballplayers, which fueled continual disrespect for the umpire, who "became the sacrificial lamb, the villainous blamesake upon which fans could toss their collective frustrations."[1] As Larry Gerlach wrote in his history of the umpire, "The transformation of the umpire from esteemed arbitrator to despised villain was largely deliberate. As club owners and league officials recognized that umpire baiting boosted gate receipts, they refused ... to curb rowdiness, and even joined sportswriters in depicting umpires as scoundrels and scapegoats ... in an era when 'Kill the umpire!' was not mere rhetoric."[2]

If it were just Young's interest in him, Keefe would have likely declined the offer to become an umpire. While he had both the aptitude (knowledge of the rules and a good eye for the strike zone) and occupational experience (a dozen games umpired while an active ballplayer), Keefe had little interest in dealing with the increased rowdiness among the ballplayers. But Keefe was influenced by Harry Wright, who was now the league's Chief of Umpires, a job created to keep Wright in the game following his dismissal as manager in Philadelphia. Wright, whose duties were largely confined to communicating with umpires and evaluating their performance, persuaded Keefe that the league needed competent men like him who could heighten the integrity of the game. In August 1894, Keefe accepted the job as a National League umpire. It didn't pay nearly as well as being a ballplayer, but it did provide a regular income.

His first umpiring assignment was the August 3 game at the revamped South End Grounds in Boston. "Tim Keefe made his first appearance as a league umpire, and got through without a kick," the *Boston Globe* commented on his umpiring debut, adding that he "seemed just a little nervous."[3]

The National League generally assigned only one umpire to a game; for a few important games, the league would assign two umpires. "Working alone, an umpire, no matter how resourceful and experienced, could never have a good view of all or even most of the plays he had to call," historian Charles Alexander wrote about the umpire's plight. "Besides resorting to a variety of tricks on their opponents when the umpire wasn't looking (some dirtier than others), players stormed and raged, shoved and shouldered the umpire himself when close calls went against them."[4]

As much as he could, Keefe emulated John Gaffney, the venerable umpire who controlled the game through tact and diplomacy. Gaffney would also stand behind the catcher until the batter reached base, then go behind the pitcher for a better view of the action on the bases, a method of positioning he instituted in 1888.[5]

Young gave rookie umpire Keefe a light schedule for the remainder of the 1894 season. Keefe wasn't assigned to any games at the Polo Grounds, where he preferred not to umpire, given his strong ties to spectators in New York City as well as his dislike for the ownership of the New York Giants (who would sell out after the 1894 season). When first-place Baltimore met second-place New York in Baltimore, Young assigned two umpires to the series, with Lynch taking the home-plate duty while Keefe called the bases. Keefe spent the final three weeks of the season in Louisville to call the games of the league's last-place team in front of tiny crowds that during the week might be fewer than 100 people.

A novelty for Keefe was working on Sunday again, since Louisville played Sunday baseball, which continued to be prohibited by law in most states on the East Coast. It was the first time since 1884 that Keefe had participated in a Sunday game at the major-league level, when he pitched for the Metropolitans of New York in the old American Association, which played Sunday games on the road. Neither the New York Giants nor the Philadelphia Phillies played Sunday games on the road, since both ballclubs adhered to a strict Sabbatarian philosophy.

One hallmark of Keefe's umpiring philosophy became evident in

Louisville at the tail end of the 1894 season, where half of the games were stopped before the completion of nine innings. Keefe liked to use his authority to curtail games due to darkness long before dusk was apparent, in order to ensure the safety of the ballplayers.

He umpired 47 games during the 1894 season and generally received good reviews in the press. But he had a much more difficult year in 1895, when his judgment was repeatedly questioned by ballplayers, many of whom had played with him or against him just two years earlier.

Although Keefe returned to coach the Harvard College baseball team over the winter of 1895, he was not as vigilant about staying in shape by participating in the Harvard workouts, since he had no hope of returning to the major leagues as a pitcher. As he began his first full season of umpiring, his lack of physical conditioning quickly showed. In the Decoration Day twin bill in the heat of Washington, D.C., Keefe left the afternoon game in the fifth inning "since he was so affected by the intense heat."[6] Unfortunately, Keefe soon gained a reputation among the ballplayers as an umpire who wasn't man enough to deal with the heat. Umpires needed to be in as good shape as, if not better than, the ballplayers themselves.

As Peter Morris described in his article on umpires subtitled "The 19th Century Umpire as Sprinter," by the 1890s "an increasing number of them began to race about the diamond in order to render their decisions. Naturally, umpires who did so were expected to get to the appropriate bases as quickly as the players themselves. The umpire—who was already required to have eagle eyes, expert knowledge of ever-changing rulebooks, implacable dignity in the face of abuse, a booming voice, and a host of other skills—was now also being called upon to show great foot speed."[7]

Just three weeks into the 1895 season, Keefe was already melancholy about his fate as an umpire, as indicated by an interview he gave in Pittsburgh: "I didn't think that I would ever even be umpiring and I believe now that if some of the boys would stop and think they may have to be umpires themselves someday they would not do so much kicking." He didn't harbor any desire to ever don a baseball uniform again, saying: "I had my day as a pitcher, that was all there was to it. My arm seems to be just like it used to be, but I couldn't get up any speed." The Pittsburgh writer concluded: "He says he will have to be driven out of the business."[8]

Players on the Baltimore and Cleveland teams did drive Keefe from the game. They were the two rowdiest teams in the National League, stocked with brash Irish-American ballplayers seeking every advantage to win ballgames, including umpire intimidation. John McGraw, third baseman of the Baltimore Orioles, was hated by many umpires, since they would often be surrounded by ringleader McGraw and several of his teammates to vehemently complain about a call made by the umpire. "John McGraw would flower and flourish as an umpire's nemesis without equal," his biographer wrote of the "belligerent, quarrelsome, unprincipled on-field personality."[9] Patsy Tebeau of the Cleveland team also came to be despised by umpires.

Like many a man before him, Keefe took to drinking to ease his stress. There were times when he was accused of imbibing too much. In mid-May a Louisville fan accused Keefe of being intoxicated while umpiring.[10] Then McGraw accused Keefe of drinking following the July 23 game he had umpired in Pittsburgh. "Look here, old man, you sent out for a bottle yesterday," McGraw taunted Keefe outside the ballpark. "I was sick," Keefe replied. McGraw then responded, "Sick! Drunk, you mean. You were drunk all last week in Chicago, too."[11]

Part of the stress felt by Keefe was the impending dissolution of his marriage. He and Clara had drifted apart. She began traveling with him at the beginning of the 1895 seasons, but by Pittsburgh she went her separate way to prepare for her annual overseas excursion. A brief item in *Sporting Life* in May 1895—"Mrs. Keefe is making the Western trip with her husband"—was one of the last public indications that they were still together.[12]

For the first half of the 1895 season, Keefe was generally tolerated by the players and fans. "He is not as accurate on balls and strikes as he might be, but he does not make any of those egregious blunders that some of his fellow umpires do," one commentator described his umpiring. "Keefe has the air of a man who is well versed in his business, without being domineering or seeming infallible."[13] But after a run-in with McGraw and several other Baltimore players in the Baltimore-Pittsburgh series in July, ballplayers and fans began to routinely lose respect for Keefe as an umpire.

It all started in a doubleheader on July 22 when Keefe "took sick" in the third inning of the second game, once again due to the effects of the heat. Although he returned to umpire the game on July 23, the *Baltimore Sun* reported that he was "in no condition to work" and "all through the game he gave dreadful decisions on balls and strikes." Keefe set off the Orioles that day when he ejected Hughie Jennings from the game for complaining that Keefe had blown the call on a curveball thrown by the Baltimore pitcher.[14] "When he put one out of the game, there was war to the death," the Pittsburgh correspondent to *Sporting Life* reported. "There was no need of the display by McGraw and the others," which included the aforementioned drinking comment.[15]

Then in September Keefe was assigned to umpire his first games at the Polo Grounds, the one location where he had expressly told Nick Young that he didn't want to work. Tired after working several doubleheaders there, Keefe had an especially tough single game on September 11, when he was "erratic in decisions" in the Boston–New York game. "Tim Keefe had a trying time of it, as he had decisions to make all through the game, and, as it is a difficult matter to please everybody, he had to stand an unusual amount of abuse from the players as well as the spectators," the *New York Times* described his challenge.[16] The *New York Evening Telegram* was more pointed in its examination of Keefe: "Unless Keefe can stiffen his spinal column he will never succeed as an umpire. He should drop all thought of being a 'good fellow.'"[17]

Even though the Giants won that game, partly as a result of Mike Tiernan scoring from second base as the Boston players forgot about him as they argued with Keefe about his safe call on the play at first base, the fans at the ballpark weren't any more sympathetic to Keefe than the ballplayers. "In a grilling battle between the Giants and the Bostons, however, Keefe, absolutely honest, made several close decisions against the New Yorks," umpire Tim Hurst later told the *New York Sun*. "Before the game ended Keefe was the target for a volley of abuse. He was hooted and hissed and finally a mob tried to handle him roughly as he made his way to the dressing room. Believe me, boys, Keefe actually broke down and wept. The admirers of former days had turned against him in less than two hours."[18]

His return to the Polo Grounds in late September for the season-ending series between the Giants and pennant-winning Baltimore was no more ego-boosting to Keefe than the Boston series had been two weeks earlier. In a doubleheader on September 27, after McGraw and the Orioles complained so much about Keefe's umpiring in the first game, Keefe refused to umpire the second game. After the game he openly complained about Nick Young, saying that he shouldn't have assigned him to these games without a second umpire to officiate the bases. Still irritated the next day, with both the Baltimore players and the league president, "Keefe ordered McGraw, who was on the coaching lines, off the field, and when he refused to go Keefe called a policeman to put him off."[19] Keefe was very bitter about the ignoring of his desire not to umpire at the Polo Grounds: "Nick Young is not treating me justly. He knows very well that I do not care to umpire in this city, where I played ball so long, as I have many friends here, and, by umpiring honestly, I cannot please everybody."[20]

Young selected Keefe to umpire the postseason Temple Cup series, played by the first-place and second-place teams in the league to provide a bonus for the players, not to determine a league champion, which was undisputedly the first-place team during the season, Baltimore. Whether or not Keefe was being rewarded for being an honest umpire or penalized for his September outbursts was debatable, since the Temple Cup combatants that fall were the league's two rowdiest teams, Baltimore and Cleveland. At least there was some solace for Keefe in that Young deployed a two-man umpiring system for the entire Temple Cup series, in an attempt to dampen the mischief. Jim McDonald teamed with Keefe to umpire the initial games in Cleveland.

A more boisterous crowd than the usual regular-season gathering in Cleveland greeted umpires Keefe and McDonald for the first game on October 2. "There were kicks against the decisions of both umpires—kicks by the Baltimores, kicks by the Clevelands, and kicks from the thousands of lusty throats [among the spectators]," the *Chicago Inter Ocean* reported.[21] "A more unruly crowd of spectators never attended a National League game," the *Baltimore Sun* reported. "The conduct of many was almost beyond comprehension ... the rougher element not only annoyed the Baltimore players by hurling epithets, but threw missiles at them and even rushed out upon the field to prevent them from making plays."[22]

In the bottom of the ninth inning, Cleveland scored two runs to defeat Baltimore, 5–4. The winning run scored on Zimmer's grounder to Jennings at shortstop, after second baseman Kid Gleason couldn't turn the double play to nab the slow-footed Zimmer at first base. Keefe made the crucial call at first base, inciting the Baltimore critics to accuse Keefe of home-crowd favoritism.

When Baltimore lost the second game the next day, the catcalls for Keefe got even louder, as the umpires could do nothing to stop the Cleveland fans from throwing beer bottles, cushions, and tinhorns at the Baltimore players. "One thing is certain, and that is the Baltimore players want Keefe and McDonald to umpire the cup games in Baltimore, but here [in Cleveland] the Orioles would like to have Emslie and Hurst, who are not influenced by home crowds," the *Baltimore Sun* commented. "In fact, they demand Keefe and McDonald in Baltimore, and if the others are sent there, Hanlon's men will probably register a strong kick with President Young."[23]

During the second game, word arrived in Cleveland that Harry Wright had died that day. Keefe did not umpire the third game on October 5, as Tim Hurst took his place. Keefe likely attended Wright's funeral in Philadelphia on October 6, where "thousands of old friends took a last look at 'dear Old Harry.'"[24] Without Wright in his corner to champion the integrity of league umpires, Keefe was less interested in doing the job.

Keefe was in Baltimore for the resumption of the Temple Cup series on October 7, after Cleveland had won the first three games of the best-of-seven-games competition. Keefe teamed with Hurst, and needed to avoid the riot outside Union Park after Baltimore won the fourth game, where fans retaliated for the treatment shown the Baltimore players in Cleveland by throwing rocks, sticks, and rotten eggs at the Cleveland players as they left the ballpark. When Cleveland won the fifth game to clinch the exhibition series, Keefe no longer had to risk his life to umpire a Temple Cup game.

In the fall of 1895, Keefe decided to build a two-family house on his remaining Cambridge real estate. In October 1895 Keefe received a building permit for a wooden dwelling to be built by John McIssac at the corner of Trowbridge Street and Cambridge Street.[25] Keefe, inspired by his father's life work as an independent carpenter, chose a local builder for his house who was a master craftsman. McIssac, who lived in Cambridgeport and was the same age as Keefe, "came to Cambridge in 1882 and learned the trade of a carpenter, which he followed as a journeyman for a few years," the *Cambridge Chronicle* wrote about McIssac's progression as an artisan through the apprentice–journeyman–master system. "He studied architecture in Boston, and in 1887 engaged in the business of contractor and builder on his own account in this city."[26]

In December 1895, Keefe mortgaged the property to raise $4,500 to

Tim Keefe was fond of this painting of a baseball game by Henry Sandham after he retired from umpiring in 1897. Note the umpire at the bottom left that resembles the mustachioed Keefe (Boston Public Library, Print Department).

build the house, with a loan from East Cambridge Savings Bank.[27] Reflecting the deteriorating nature his credit rating, the bank would only grant Keefe a one-year term for the loan, with full repayment of the principal amount due in December 1896. Once the house at 1653 Cambridge Street was completed, his mother and two sisters moved out of the Springfield Street house in Somerville to live with Keefe in one of the units while he rented the other unit to help provide an income. Despite his reputation as a Cambridge native, this was the first time since Keefe was a young boy in the early 1860s that he had actually resided within the city limits of Cambridge.

By the start of the 1896 season, Keefe despised being an umpire. "Some of my enemies must have got me that position," Keefe said ten years later. "I did not like umpiring. Did you ever see a man who did?"[28] Not all love was lost between Keefe and umpiring, though, since he had a Henry Sandham painting of a baseball game, with an umpire in the foreground (who resembled Keefe) on the wall in his house for many years after retiring from umpiring.[29] He tried a few more times to do the right thing as an umpire, but he not only couldn't change the perspective of the fans and the ballplayers during the 1896 season, they disrespected him even more.

In the May 10 game between Brooklyn and Louisville, Keefe needed a police escort to leave the ballpark in Louisville after Brooklyn won, 3–1, with a three-run rally in the seventh inning. "The principal feature of the game was the poor work of Umpire Keefe," the *Brooklyn Eagle* reported. "He came out [of the ballpark] guarded by half a dozen policemen, who had all they could do to prevent the people from administering a severe rebuke."[30]

Three days later in Chicago, the spectators and ballplayers were livid after Keefe didn't call interference on Boston first baseman Tom Tucker after he had allegedly tackled a Chicago baserunner. "A menacing howl arose from the stands, men shook their fists at Keefe, while [Cap] Anson was attempting to convince Keefe that Tucker's interference was intentional and that the runner should be given second base. Keefe was obdurate," the *Boston Globe* reported. On the next play when Keefe gave the Chicago batter only a double, not a home run, after his long fly ball bounced off the outfield stands, the ballpark went wild once again. "From the stand there came a thundering roar. One fat man waddled down the main aisle of the grand stand and pleaded with those about him to go on the field and do violence to Keefe. The latter stood near the plate while the Chicagos danced about him like a swarm of dervishes. Their threats were to no avail. From this time until the close the spectators taunted Keefe at every opportunity."[31]

The final straw for Keefe was Cleveland first baseman Patsy Tebeau during the series in Boston over the Decoration Day holiday. In the May 29 pre-holiday game, after Tebeau caught the third out at first base, he threw the soiled ball over the fence so that Keefe would have to put a new ball in play, thus giving Cleveland an advantage as they batted next. However, "one of the most disgraceful scenes ever seen at the South End Grounds," then occurred, according to *Boston Globe* writer Tim Murnane. When Keefe ordered Tebeau to the bench, he called Keefe a "vile name ... one which would cost him dearly if brought to court." When Keefe ejected Tebeau from the game and asked a policeman to escort Tebeau from the field, five Cleveland players swarmed around Keefe and swore at him. Tebeau, with his head poking over the fence gate, was "still calling on his crowd to give it to Keefe ... a shrewd move, for after this Keefe could only see every play favorable to the Cleveland bulldozers." But Murnane didn't back up Keefe, though. "If Keefe had the backbone of a Lynch at least five of the foul-mouthed Cleveland crowd would have been put out of the grounds, but unfortunately Mr. Keefe lacks the ability to handle men of the Cleveland stamp."[32]

Keefe abdicated the next day in the holiday twin bill. In an article headlined "Keefe Blind: Boston Discouraged by His Decisions," Murnane castigated Keefe once again for his poor work. "Umpire Tim Keefe had a case of the blinds. He was dead to the world most of the time, and held a guessing bee with himself as the boss guesser. The home team got the small end of everything until the crowd jeered him continually, and Patsy Tebeau smiled with satisfaction. He had hypnotized Keefe and was so sure of the game that he enjoyed the distress of the Boston men."[33]

Following the debacle of Keefe being a single umpire for the Cleveland games in Boston, National League president Nick Young tried to appease Keefe by pairing him with Stump Wiedman as a two-man umpiring crew. Keefe tolerated that system for just two weeks, until disgust overwhelmed him and he tendered his resignation following the June 17 game that he umpired in Washington.[34] However, Young did not accept Keefe's resignation because he was so desperate to retain quality umpires. Young instead suggested that Keefe take some time off to reconsider his decision. A week and a half later, Young convinced Keefe to return as the single umpire for the Cleveland-Chicago series that began on June 29. However, Keefe, usually a paragon of integrity, seemed intent on forcing Young to fire him.

In an article entitled "Keefe's Poor Work," Chicago sportswriter Bill Phelon reported his observations that Keefe had intentionally blown calls: "I never, in all the years I have watched base ball, saw such umpiring as Tim Keefe's. Tim was afraid of Tebeau—simply frightened to death of the Cleveland leader—and he threw the harpoon into our pitchers in the calling of balls and strikes in a way that was simply outrageous. Ball after ball that cut the plate square in two he called wrongly ... the press box here is on the ground floor and right behind the catcher, and we distinctly saw not one or two, but twenty good straight ones cut the plate, only to be called balls by Keefe."[35] If his actions in that game were not enough to discredit his impeccability as an honest umpire, Keefe also befouled his reputation for integrity by failing to show up for the morning game of the Fourth of July holiday twin bill in Chicago (he did umpire the afternoon game). Neither action caused the hoped-for result of being removed from his job as umpire.

Since the league president wasn't going to fire him for being grossly incompetent as an umpire, Keefe had to resort to quitting on the job. His last day as a National League umpire was the July 6 game in St. Louis, where he walked off the field in the fifth inning and forced the two teams to use ballplayers as substitute umpires for the remainder of the game.[36] The next day Keefe telegraphed his resignation to the National League office:

> My sole reason for leaving the field yesterday and for then and there determining to sever my connection with the national game forever is that base ball has reached a stage where it is absolutely disgraceful. It is the fashion now for every player engaged in a game to froth at the mouth and emit shrieks of anguish whenever a decision is given which is adverse to the interests of the club to which he belongs. This may not be wearying to the general public, but it is certainly disgusting to the umpire who gives decisions disinterestedly and as he sees the plays. The continual senseless and puerile kicking at every decision has been infinitely trying to me and I have been considering for some time whether I had not better resign. I can apparently please nobody.[37]

The intolerable situation reached a breaking point for Keefe when it became deeply personal, not simply baseball. The *Brooklyn Eagle* reported a conversation that Keefe had with an unidentified Chicago ballplayer over the Fourth of July holiday: "I can't stay in a business which makes my friends abuse me and mistrust me. I can't have people whom I have had for associates for years pass me up when they meet me."[38]

To most people, Keefe was just another piece of umpire roadkill on the baseball turnpike. Few defended him, with the notable exception of Jake Morse of the *Boston Herald*, who wrote: "When we know of players hurling the quintessence of profanity, at umpires, driving one out of the business, a gentleman and a fine fellow—Tim Keefe—and then throwing balls over fences and spiking new balls, it is time to throw all personal feelings to one side and rally for the defense of the game."[39]

With his mother and two sisters now Cambridge residents, after settling into their newly built, but heavily mortgaged, house at 1653 Cambridge Street, Keefe still needed an income to support himself and the other members of the household. With his brother now married, with two children, and operating his own plumbing business, the onus fell on Keefe to look after his mother and two unmarried sisters.

Through his sporting connections in New York City, Keefe knew bicycle-race promoter Pat Powers, who, as one of his many roles, was also president of the Eastern League minor-league baseball organization. Powers was most famous for sponsoring an annual six-day bicycle race in Madison Square Garden. "This grueling race began at one minute past midnight on Monday morning and went straight through to 10 p.m. Saturday," Peter Nye wrote in his history of American bicycle racing. "It was an excruciating test of stamina made worthwhile by a purse of $10,000 in gold double-eagle coins weighting sixteen pounds. The six-day race around the steeply banked board track, ten laps to the mile, went for 142 hours of continuous competition." The winner of this excruciating endurance test received $1,300, a huge amount for six days of work.[40]

In early August, Powers coaxed Keefe into becoming an umpire in the Eastern League. Powers pounced on the availability of a high-quality umpire such as Keefe and sold him on the lower stress level of making game decisions in the minor leagues compared to that at the major-league level, as well as lower physical fatigue traveling the compact eight-city league comprised of Providence, Rochester, Buffalo, Syracuse, Toronto, Springfield, Scranton, and Wilkes-Barre. But first Powers had to create an opening for Keefe on the league's umpiring staff. After attending games throughout the circuit, Powers finally fired Herman Doescher on August 20 under the guise of "bad judgment in declaring a forfeit in the Providence game" two days earlier. Keefe umpired his first Eastern League game on August 21 in Scranton, Pennsylvania.[41]

Keefe did find less stress as an umpire in the Eastern League, where the players were more intent on advancing to the National League than showing up an umpire. "Tim says that the Eastern League players pay more attention to ball playing and as a rule let the umpire alone," the *Wilkes-Barre Times* reported after the 1896 season. "Players in the big league are apt to blame the umpire for almost every play that goes wrong."[42] The fans at the minor-league ballpark were also more forgiving. One of Keefe's worst experiences was having a cushion thrown at him by a fan in Syracuse after he had called out a runner at second base. Considering the abuse heaped on him in Baltimore and Cleveland, the Syracuse situation was tame. The police even went into the stands to chase down the cushion-throwing fan, a rare occurrence in a major-league ballpark.[43]

Tough financial times continued for Keefe. Unable to repay or refinance the impending balloon mortgage payment due in December 1896, Keefe had to sell more of his Cambridge land in order to avoid foreclosure on his new house. In November 1896 he sold 12,000 square feet of his remaining property to Michael Harty for enough money to allow the East Cambridge Saving Bank to discharge the mortgage.[44] Keefe's once-vacant neighborhood was starting to fill in. Harty, who operated several grocery stores in Cambridge, squeezed three two-family homes (at 1657, 1663, and 1667 Cambridge Street) onto land that originally had been two house lots. Ernest Flentje, a German immigrant who was a sausage importer, built a huge stone house at 1643 Cambridge Street across from Keefe's house on the corner of Trowbridge Street.

After returning to umpire in the Eastern League in the spring of 1897, Keefe's umpiring career came to an abrupt end during the summer of 1897 when he suffered a broken collarbone in a July 17 game at Springfield, Massachusetts. He was injured in "an accident which knocked out Tim Keefe in the ninth inning" when a foul tip off the bat of Springfield first baseman Dan Brouthers "struck him squarely in the left shoulder while close up behind the bat ... and broke Keefe's collar bone." After remaining in the game for several minutes, "Keefe tottered and fell to the ground" and was forced to leave the game. The bone was set at his hotel room.[45] After recuperating for a few weeks, Keefe returned on August 7 to umpire a game in Providence. However, he lasted only a few games because the pain was just too intolerable to continue, and soon resigned his position.[46]

Keefe did attempt to return to the National League umpiring staff for the 1898 season, when the ballclub owners voted to employ a two-man system for all games during the expanded 154-game season. However, his injury, and negative reputation from the events during the 1896 season, precluded his return.

24

Retirement from Baseball in Cambridge

After he umpired his final ballgame in 1897, Tim Keefe severed his relationship with baseball and lived a quiet life for another three decades in Cambridge, Massachusetts.

Keefe didn't return to coach the baseball team at Harvard College during the winter of 1898. Instead, Harvard enlisted Ted Lewis, a pitcher with the Boston team in the National League and graduate of Williams College, to coach the team. "It was a radical change on the part of the Harvard Athletic Committee to appoint a young pitcher like Ted Lewis in place of Tim Keefe, who has been coach at Harvard for so many seasons," *Boston Herald* writer Jake Morse commiserated with the apparent snubbing of Keefe, who had no formal education beyond grade school, for the college-educated Lewis.[1]

However, Keefe likely gave up the coaching post voluntarily, sensing impending changes in the baseball program at Harvard. A new philosophy of coaching was on the horizon, which changed the emphasis from training players in the winter to winning ballgames in the spring. While the college was on the verge of employing its full-time baseball coach in 1900, the baseball team began taking an annual trip to the South in 1898 to train outdoors in the warmer climate, which soon took precedence over the indoor training that Keefe had mostly provided. Also in 1898, the Harvard baseball team began playing its home games at the Soldier's Field athletic complex, located across the Charles River in Boston, where Harvard Stadium was soon to be built for the football program. By relocating all athletic contests away from the Harvard campus, there was a heightened importance to winning in all sports, not just baseball.

One of Keefe's last public appearances was in June 1898, when he participated in a reunion game with other members of the 1884 championship Metropolitan team. "Tim Keefe pitched well for a couple of innings," the *New York Herald* reported of the game on June 26 in Weehawken, New Jersey, against the West New York Field Club. Not surprisingly, the "Old Mets of

1884" lost, 12–4.[2] After that ballgame, Keefe steadfastly remained out of the public eye. As one writer noted during the summer of 1899, "One rarely hears the name of Tim Keefe mentioned now. The former great pitcher seems to have dropped entirely out of sight and sound."[3] Indeed, during the last three decades of his life, Keefe was a virtual recluse, with only rare public commentary or appearance.

While Keefe remained out of public view, his name carried on in corrupted versions of the poem "Casey at the Bat" that began appearing about 1900 in a number of anthologies of humorous verse. These versions of Thayer's poem substituted the line "He signaled the pitcher" with "He signaled to Sir Timothy," and more specifically indicated Keefe through the change of the term "the writhing pitcher" to "the New York pitcher."[4]

Needing to replace his baseball-related income, the 41-year-old Keefe had a four-unit apartment building constructed in 1898 on the remaining undeveloped portion of his land in Cambridge. The apartment building, whose address was 87–89 Trowbridge Street, was squeezed onto the small section of land next to the house at 1653 Cambridge Street, where his widowed mother (who technically still owned the property) lived with his two spinster sisters, Katherine and Mary. In December 1897 the city of Cambridge issued a building permit for a "brick and frame house to contain four tenements" at the Trowbridge Street location, to be built by John McIssac, the same carpenter who built Keefe's adjacent house on Cambridge Street.[5] A month later, in an article entitled "Double House on Trowbridge Street," the *Cambridge Chronicle* described the house:

> The front entrance is to be reached across a piazza on Trowbridge Street. This is 7 feet in width and 22 feet long. Above on the second story, a neatly designed balustrade will extend about it. Two bay windows on the front of the house will serve the parlors both on the lower floor and on the second story. The roof is pitched, and in the Trowbridge Street gable there will be three dormer windows, the two smaller ones being treated to colored glass. The two suites on the first floor consist of a parlor, two chambers, dining room, kitchen, pantry and china closet, bath room, and a chamber each on the floor above. Similarly, the two suites on the second floor have each the same number of rooms, with the addition of two chambers for each suite.[6]

This article, no doubt planted by Keefe, helped him to secure responsible tenants to live in the four units. Keefe needed to attract tenants to his building since Trowbridge Street was relatively vacant at the time, since most of the other lots, owned by the heirs of now-deceased Mary Brown (from whom Keefe had originally purchased the land), had yet to be developed.[7] Some of the first tenants at 87 Trowbridge Street were George Raymond, a dentist, and Daniel Smith, a lawyer.[8]

However, eventually, Keefe had to advertise for tenants: "Two new and handsome suites of 8 and 7 rooms, all improvements, at 87 Trowbridge Street; open plumbing, set trays and range, good location, opposite school and public library; five minutes' walk from Harvard Square; plenty of land. Apply at 1653 Cambridge Street."[9] Keeping the building occupied was a major priority, since the building was highly leveraged. To provide funds to build the house, estimated in the building permit to cost $8,500, Keefe secured a $5,000 mortgage from the East Cambridge Savings Bank.[10] Since the length of the mortgage loan was short, just one year, the bank considered the building to be a risky loan. In order to refinance that amount every year, the bank needed assurance that the building had full occupancy with tenants who made timely rent payments.

All units in Keefe's two buildings were occupied at the time of the 1900 federal census. In the Trowbridge Street building, there were four tenants: two stay-at-home widows, one stenographer, and one traveling salesman. In the Cambridge Street house, Keefe's mother, his two sisters, and three lodgers (all Harvard law school students) lived in one unit, while a widow and her son lived in the second unit.[11]

Curiously, Keefe was not recorded in the 1900 federal census as a resident in either of his two buildings in Cambridge. Nor can he be located in any Massachusetts location or in any of the other 44 states in the nation at the time. He also was not listed in the *Cambridge Directory* at the time (and would not be until 1907). Clearly, given this lack of public record, Keefe seemed to be more than just a recluse. He was in hiding.

A 1902 article in the *Boston Post* entitled "What Five Noted Veterans of the Baseball Diamond Are Doing Today" reported on five former major-league ballplayers with local roots: Keefe, Gid Gardner, Mike Slattery, Mert Hackett, and Jack Manning. However, the section about Keefe was by far the shortest, with just two paragraphs that skimped on details. The article only gave a vague hint about what Keefe was doing, noting "Mr. Keefe is in business in New York and has long since given up active baseball."[12]

One reason to hide was to avoid creditors. In December 1902, Keefe declared bankruptcy. "Timothy J. Keefe, 1653 Cambridge Street, has filed a bankruptcy petition," the *Cambridge Chronicle* reported about a 1902 court filing. "He owes $3,758.55, with no assets."[13] Keefe was broke, contrary to newspaper reports indicating that he was doing well financially, such as this 1901 report in the *New York Morning Telegraph*: "Keefe is now in Cambridgeport, Mass., where he has money invested in real estate, from which he derives an income sufficient to enable him to live comfortably."[14]

The bankruptcy petition may have been related to a second reason for hiding, since Keefe was involved in a divorce proceeding. While court filings are elusive to verify the timing of the divorce, Keefe reported his marital status as "divorced" in the 1910 federal census (a status he reaffirmed in the next two decennial censuses).[15] Compounding the mystery of the dissolution of his marriage, his wife, Clara Keefe, disappeared from public documents and newspaper reportage in 1896. Interestingly, this was the same year that her sister, Helen Dauvray, married Albert Winterhalter, three years after the finalization of her divorce from John Ward, Keefe's former teammate on the New York Giants and fellow officer in the Brotherhood. Rather than take an annual voyage to Europe, Clara may have permanently relocated to London or Paris, two places she often visited when Helen had lived in Europe during the early 1890s.

Another, more intangible, reason for hiding was to avoid public scrutiny as a failure. Keefe had failed in the effort to create the Players' League, failed at being a businessman in the sporting goods firm Keefe & Becannon, and failed at being a major-league umpire. Now he was failing at money and marriage. In that era, failure was considered to be a character flaw. Both John Day and Jim Mutrie were shunned due to the 1890 failure of the New York Giants, not withstanding that both men had no control over the circumstances. To Keefe, it was better to be forgotten than to be viewed as a failure.

Keefe seemed to have little fondness for the twentieth-century version of the New York Giants, who were managed by John McGraw, his nemesis when he had worked as an umpire. The Giants won the National League pennant in 1904, the team's first championship since 1889 when Keefe had pitched the team to the title. In early October, McGraw's 1904 team played the 1889 Giants in a benefit game at the Polo Grounds. Keefe did not participate in this game, which was won by the current-day Giants, 10–8. As one newspaper wag noted, though, the score could easily have been 100–8 had McGraw's men played the game to the best of their ability. Mickey Welch returned to the Polo Grounds to pitch for the 1889 team. However, as the *New York World* reported, "Welch still can pitch a bit, but he failed to fool the youngsters, who landed on his curves whenever they got ready."[16]

Welch was the only former member of the Giants that Keefe maintained a friendship with following his retirement from baseball. Welch lived in Holyoke, Massachusetts, about 100 miles west of Cambridge. In a 1906 interview, Keefe said, "I haven't seen anything of my old chums for some time. Once in a while I go up to Springfield and when I do I always go over to Holyoke to spend the night with Welch."[17] There was a similar feeling from Welch, who told baseball writers in both 1907 and 1908 that he intended to visit Keefe in Cambridge and "renew the good old days."[18]

24. Retirement from Baseball in Cambridge

Although he was a National League pitcher in the nineteenth century, Keefe became an American League baseball fan in the twentieth century. In the 1906 interview noted above (granted to talk about Buck Ewing, who was critically ill at the time), Keefe remarked, "Well, I try to keep up with baseball fairly well. I run in to Boston occasionally to see a game on the American League grounds. Collins, who is a fine fellow, has a fast team. It is well balanced and I like to see them play."[19]

Keefe may have been an American League fan for the simple reason that it was much easier for him to get to the Huntington Avenue Grounds, where the Boston Americans played their games, compared to the more complicated excursion to the South End Grounds, which were also now in a dilapidated neighborhood. But the telling clue to the change in his partisanship between leagues was his reference to Boston's player-manager Jimmy Collins. The American League grew out of the Players Protective Association, the next subsequent collective body of major-league ballplayers to form after the Brotherhood collapsed. The American League fostered ownership potential for ballplayers, which the Brotherhood had tried to espouse in the formation of the Players' League. Players in the American League could realistically aspire to ascend to ownership, as Collins had with the Boston ballclub (he was acting president in 1906). Former ballplayers Charlie Comiskey and Connie Mack were already in ownership.[20]

One of Keefe's rare public appearances occurred in February 1909 when he attended the funeral in Cambridge of fellow nineteenth-century pitching great John Clarkson. "It is not often that one sees Tim Keefe," Jake Morse, now editor and founder of *Baseball Magazine*, commented. "The veteran pitcher of the old Mets and the New Yorks looked very well indeed. He has some real estate property in Cambridge and occupies most of his time looking after it."[21]

Four months later Keefe attended the funeral of his mother, Mary Keefe, who died in June 1909.[22] She was laid to rest in St. Paul's Cemetery next to her husband and daughters Margaret and Annie. Beyond the sadness of Mary's death, there was the legal matter of the change in property ownership for the houses at 1653 Cambridge Street and 87–89 Trowbridge Street. To keep the properties beyond the reach of his creditors, Keefe had arranged for his mother's will to transfer ownership of the two properties in equal shares to his sisters Katherine and Mary.[23] While he continued to maintain the properties, he successfully kept his name off their deeds.

In July 1912 New York Giants pitcher Rube Marquard tied Keefe's record of 19 consecutive victories. However, as Marquard approached the 19-win threshold, there was little mention of Keefe's name. Most baseball observers were baffled by the exact mark that Marquard was chasing, since the state of recordkeeping at the time was not nearly as exact as it is today. "He has smashed the wonderful showings of both Jack Chesbro and Ed Reulbach, both of whom had run 14 victories in succession," *The Sporting News* reported after Marquard's 16th straight victory. "He needs two more triumphs to match Radbourne's figure of 18 straight and that is the mark he is shooting at." As for the 20 straight by Jack Luby or the 19 consecutive by Keefe, "there is nothing positive to prove it."[24] Soon, though, Luby's streak was determined to be just 17 in a row, and Keefe's streak of 19 was verified to be accurate. Only then was Keefe's name thrust into the spotlight as the rightful record holder.[25]

Marquard tied Keefe's record on July 3 in a 2–1 victory over Brooklyn. "Rube Marquard, the wonderful left handed pitcher of the New York Giants, has equaled the generally accepted major league record of nineteen consecutive victories made by Tim Keefe in 1888," the *New York Tribune* noted about the accomplishment.[26] However, Marquard failed in his bid to break the record when he lost his next start on July 8 against Chicago. After the game, Marquard remarked: "Of course, I am sorry I did not win my twentieth game. I would be a fool to deny it.... I am not worrying over my first defeat a little bit. In fact, I feel easier in my mind now that the strain is off. I did worry nights before every game, and now I can go into every game I pitch hereafter and not be bothered with any old records or new ones."[27]

In 1912 pitcher Rube Marquard tied Keefe's record of 19 consecutive victories. Keefe had established the record in 1888, when he led the New York Giants to their first National League pennant (Library of Congress, Prints and Photographs Division, LC-DIG-bbc-1406f).

There was no mention of Keefe's name by Marquard, probably because most baseball observers felt that Marquard had established the "modern" record, because Keefe's streak occurred in a different era at a shorter pitching

24. Retirement from Baseball in Cambridge 241

distance. As one newspaper noted: "As a matter of fact, there is no comparison between these records of the two last named, as in the days of Keefe far less depended upon the pitcher, and the work was less strenuous and exacting, while baseball had not been developed to such an exact science."[28]

The reaction of Keefe, if any, to Marquard's record-tying performance went unrecorded at the time, as no Boston or New York City newspaper, nor *Sporting Life* and *The Sporting News*, published remarks from an interview with Keefe. Nor were there any published remarks concerning Keefe's thoughts about Walter Johnson and Smoky Joe Wood challenging the record with their 16-game win streaks later in 1912, which established the American League record for consecutive pitching victories.

Keefe not doubt would have graciously congratulated Marquard on equaling his record, but he likely would have been annoyed at the downplaying of his 1888 streak that Marquard had tied. Back in 1906, Keefe had offered this opinion on the nature of baseball since he played the game: "There have been changes and changes, but I can't see really, for the life of me, that the players of today excel those of the period just before the Brotherhood broke up. It seems to me that was the most prosperous time that the game has ever known. Certainly there are no better batters today than there were then."[29] Although he didn't say it directly, Keefe probably felt that the pitchers of 1906 were no better than those in his day.

In September 1914 Keefe viewed the modern-day players when the Boston Braves invited Keefe and Welch to watch the team on its way to the National League pennant. In a photograph published in the *Boston Globe*, Keefe still looked like the Sir Timothy of old, sporting a mustache and wearing a suit and bowler hat.[30]

As more buildings were erected on Trowbridge Street after 1900 to fill in the neighborhood, Keefe, whose occupation was listed in the 1915 *Cambridge Directory* as "real estate," was busy with the upkeep on his four-unit apartment building there. The city of Cambridge issued building permits for alterations on this building in 1913 and 1915.[31] It appears that Keefe swung a hammer once again as a carpenter, as he was named as the builder on the 1913 building permit (the company founded by McIssac, the house's original builder, was named on the 1915 permit).

In 1915, a niece, Helen Brodbine, lived with Keefe and his two sisters in their 1653 Cambridge Street residence.[32] Helen, the oldest daughter of Keefe's sister Ellen, was then taking classes at nearby Radcliffe College, the female extension of all-male Harvard University, to complete her bachelor's degree.[33] In 1915 Helen received her degree from Trinity College in Washington, D.C., the women's school at all-male Catholic University.[34]

Carrying forward her father's belief in education, Ellen Brodbine was insistent that her children, both sons and daughters, obtain a good education. At the time of Helen's college graduation, Ellen Brodbine was a widow raising nine children by herself, after her husband had died in 1911.[35] All nine children graduated from college, including her four daughters, which was very rare for that era.[36] Two daughters went on to establish careers, rather than settle for being a wife and mother, which again was rare for the period. Ann Brodbine, a graduate of Trinity College, established her own travel agency in Boston in 1921, and operated it for 65 years until she sold it in 1986.[37] Mary Paula Brodbine, a graduate of Emmanuel College, became a high school teacher.[38] Ann and Mary Paula were frequent visitors to 1653 Cambridge Street, especially in the later years of their Uncle Tim, Aunt Katherine, and Aunt Mary.

In 1928 Keefe granted a lengthy interview to *Boston Globe* sportswriter Ford Sawyer. Talking to Keefe at a Red Sox game at Fenway Park, Sawyer noted "the 70-year-old real estate owner is unknown to the vast majority of the thousands who are urging on their Boston favorites." Keefe, who now regularly attended ballgames once a week, told Sawyer that baseball was "fundamentally the same old game" as back in the 1880s, and that he particularly liked to watch Ty Cobb.[39]

Keefe lived a placid life in Cambridge in his later years. His niece Mary Paula Brodbine, who provided help to him when needed, recalled that he was "a tall dignified man with a fair complexion, a magnificent mustache, and a quiet but genial disposition" who was "an omnivorous reader, interested in mathematics, and had a warm sense of humor."[40]

Tim Keefe died on April 23, 1933, in Cambridge.[41] Following a requiem mass at St. Paul's Church, he was buried in Cambridge City Cemetery.[42] Newspapers in Boston, New York, and cities across the country printed obituaries to honor Keefe, recounting his feats with the New York Giants of nearly a half century earlier.

Two New York sportswriters wrote special columns to eulogize Keefe. John Kieran of the *New York Times* wrote of the remembrances of an elderly man who saw Keefe pitch in the 1880s: "So Tim Keefe is dead. Well, I suppose it doesn't mean much to the young fellows who go out and root for Lefty Grove. They think they have a great pitcher on the Giants now, this Carl Hubbell. Maybe he is a great pitcher. But the Giants had other great pitchers, greater than Hubbell. They had Matty, and Amos Rusie—and Tim Keefe. Tim with his mustache, and Buck Ewing catching him; there was a battery!"[43] Joe Vila of the *New York Sun* chased down Mickey Welch and wrote about his remembrances of Keefe: "I never saw a pitcher better than Keefe. I well remember how he and I used to alternate in the box in the '80s and how Buck

Ewing, the best catcher of all time, worked with us. Keefe was a master strategist, a powerfully built athlete. He knew the weak points of every hitter in the National League.... He knew more about pitching than many of the young men of today."[44]

Following Keefe's death, his sisters Katherine and Mary continued to live in the house at 1653 Cambridge Street, which they co-owned with each holding a one-half interest.[45] In February 1941, both women made arrangements for the house on Cambridge Street, and the adjoining property on Trowbridge Street, to remain in the hands of the Brodbine family following their deaths, by converting the legal ownership in the properties into a joint tenancy with right of survivorship.[46]

Four months after the property conversion into joint tenancies, a baseball museum in upstate New York in the little village of Cooperstown celebrated its two-year anniversary in June 1941. Two decades later the museum would rescue Keefe from being just a footnote to baseball history, when he was selected for inclusion in its adjoining Hall of Fame exhibit hall.

25
Hall of Fame Selection

Tim Keefe was not a popular choice of the Baseball Writers' Association of America in the 1936 balloting to select the inaugural class to be inducted into the soon-to-be-built Hall of Fame in Cooperstown, New York. Keefe received just one vote from the 78 baseball writers who participated in the special election for the nineteenth-century-stars component of the initial Hall of Fame class.

No nineteenth-century stars were selected for the Hall of Fame's inaugural inductees, since no old-timer received the required 75 percent of the balloting. Cap Anson and Buck Ewing topped that vote with just over 50 percent. Among pure nineteenth-century pitchers, Hoss Radbourn did the best, collecting 16 votes (21 percent) to finish in seventh place, with John Clarkson the next best with five votes. Keefe tied for 35th spot in the old-timer election with his one solitary vote.[1]

With such minimal support in the first year of voting, Keefe's name quickly evaporated from Hall of Fame consideration, since by the 1930s Keefe was a footnote to baseball history. His pitching exploits for the New York Giants in the 1880s were now long forgotten. Keefe's name was now more famous as the mythical pitcher in "Casey at the Bat," since Dan Casey did promotions to further his titular fame from the poem's title. At a "Casey Night" in May 1938, the 76-year-old Casey took swings at a minor-league game in Baltimore. He swung at and missed the first two serves from Rogers Hornsby, the former major leaguer who was Casey's foil as the pitcher, but on the third pitch he stroked a hit to left field, rather than strike out as his namesake had done in Thayer's poem. As for his success that evening, Casey said, "Hornsby didn't have as much on the ball as Tim Keefe did" back in that inspirational August 1887 game.[2]

Casey went to his grave in 1943 believing Keefe to be the model for the pitcher in Thayer's famous poem. "Doesn't Thayer designate New York as the visiting team—doesn't he refer to their pitcher as Sir Timothy and doesn't he say he ground the ball to his hip before releasing the pitch?" one obituary writer recalled of a frequent exhortation by Dan Casey to anyone who would listen. "That was the way Tim Keefe worked and he was known all over the league as Sir Timothy."³ Unfortunately, Casey remembered the corrupted versions of Thayer's poem, which were commonly published in a variety of newspapers and books in the early years of the twentieth century, not the original poem.

In 1939, after the baseball writers failed to elect any old-timers in the previous two annual elections, an impromptu Old-Timers Committee was established to rectify the lack of nineteenth-century stars being named to the Hall of Fame. The three-man committee, comprised of Commissioner Kenesaw Mountain Landis, National League president Ford Frick, and American League president Will Harridge, named four old-time players to the Hall of Fame: Anson and Ewing, the top vote-getters in the 1936 election; Radbourn, the top pitcher in that election; and Candy Cummings, the alleged inventor of the curveball. The committee also named executives Albert Spalding and Charles Comiskey, who had also been ballplayers in their day.

Radbourn was generally acknowledged in 1939 as the greatest pre–1893 pitcher, recognized largely for his prodigious 60-win season in 1884 (since adjusted to 59 wins). In his biography of Radbourn, writer Charles Achorn attributes the 1939 selection to the strength of a 1909 article in *Baseball Magazine*, penned by Boston sportswriter Jake Morse, entitled "The Greatest Pitcher That Ever Lived."⁴ When the top baseball writers of the 1920s, such as Grantland Rice and Hugh Fullerton, were canonizing Christy Mathewson and Walter Johnson as the best pitchers ever, they also opined that Radbourn was the best of his era, even though they never saw Radbourn pitch.⁵ Few, if any, writers postulated that anyone other than Radbourn was the premier pitcher of the pre–1893 era, so the Old-Timers Committee had an unimpeachable selection in Radbourn.

As for the other pitcher selection in 1939, it's difficult to comprehend how the committee chose Cummings over Keefe and Clarkson, especially when Cummings polled zero votes in the 1936 special balloting for nineteenth-century stars. *The Sporting News* openly questioned the committee's decision in an editorial: "Many are at a loss to account for the selection of Cummings over others whose records in the game are more impressive ... the distinction of being the first to perfect the curveball seems to be shared equally by Fred E. Goldsmith and Cummings and no conclusive evidence has yet been produced to show that one preceded the other."⁶ So Cummings was inducted into the Hall of Fame along with Radbourn, while the other 300-game winners from the pre–1893 era—Keefe, Clarkson, Galvin, and Welch—all needed to wait another generation for their posthumous invitation to the Hall of Fame.

Among knowledgeable fans of baseball history, though, Keefe was a worthy candidate for the Hall of Fame. In a 1942 fan poll conducted by *The Sporting News* in connection with a Hall of Fame crossword puzzle contest, Keefe received the sixth-most votes (1,640) to finish behind Lefty Grove, Ed Delahanty, Hugh Duffy, Dan Brouthers, and Jesse Burkett as men who should be inducted into the Hall of Fame.[7] Since Grove was then still an active player and thus ineligible, Keefe was deemed by the fan poll to be the pitcher most deserving of Hall of Fame selection.

Such sentiment didn't carry over to the expanded Old-Timers Committee that was created in 1944 following the death of Commissioner Landis. In 1945 and 1946, the Old-Timers Committee minted 21 new Hall of Famers, which included the other top four vote-getters in the 1942 fan poll, pre–1900 players Mike Kelly and Jim O'Rourke, and five post–1900 pitchers (Joe McGinnity, Eddie Plank, Jack Chesbro, Rube Waddell, and Ed Walsh). Even though the Old-Timers Committee packed the Hall of Fame with nearly two dozen new members, pre–1893 pitchers such as Keefe and Clarkson were not considered worthy, victims of continued prejudice against pitchers from the era prior to the establishment of the 60-foot pitching distance in 1893.

In 1953 the Old-Timers Committee was replaced with a reconstituted Veterans Committee. In 1960, after a fourth consecutive year without any Hall of Fame inductees selected by the baseball writers, the Veterans Committee took matters into its own hands to create more Hall of Famers. Veterans Committee member Paul Kerr, named president of the Hall of Fame in 1961, enlisted the help of Lee Allen, the historian at the Hall of Fame, in the effort to increase the number of Hall of Famers.

"Allen was interested in biographies, in ballplayers as people," baseball analyst Bill James described Allen in his book *The Politics of Glory: How Baseball's Hall of Fame Really Works*. "He wanted to know everything about everybody who ever played baseball."[8] Allen actively tracked down biographical information that was lacking in the Hall of Fame files, often traveling to places off the beaten path to chase down details about former ballplayers.

Fortunately for many forgotten nineteenth-century ballplayers, Kerr "allowed Allen, even encouraged Allen, to advise and support the Veterans Committee."[9] Allen did the research on candidates and wrote up their accomplishments for the Veterans Committee to select from. Without the efforts of Allen, Keefe may never have been enshrined in the Hall of Fame. He was one of the fortunate players to be among the "Lee Allen's Picks," as Bill James termed them, which included Billy Hamilton and John Clarkson in addition to Keefe.

Noted baseball writer Fred Lieb had started the public lobbying for worthy nineteenth-century players with a July 1960 article in *The Sporting News*. Lieb named twelve players unjustly left out of the Hall of Fame, with Keefe prominently mentioned near the top of that list.[10]

The momentum for the nineteenth-century pitchers picked up steam in 1961 after Milwaukee Braves pitcher Warren Spahn won his 300th game in August 1961. Newspapers across the country reported that Spahn was the 13th such pitcher to achieve that milestone, the last being Lefty Grove in 1941, and printed the list of the other 12 pitchers who had 300 career victories. Eight of those dozen pitchers were already in the Hall of Fame, all except Keefe, Clarkson, Welch, and Galvin. Spahn's accomplishment initiated discussion of the informal criteria for a pitcher with 300 wins to be an automatic Hall of Famer.

In 1963 Clarkson was elevated to Hall of Fame status. How the Veterans Committee determined that Clarkson should be recognized ahead of Keefe is undocumented. It was apparently based on the fact that Clarkson was involved in one of the first player sales in baseball history, thus supposedly making him more valuable than Keefe. Following the announcement of the 1963 inductees, articles in *The Sporting News* by Veterans Committee member Dan Daniel and historian Lee Allen both noted that Clarkson was "the second player to be sold for a big purchase price," the same $10,000 amount paid to acquire Mike Kelly in the inaugural blockbuster player sale.[11] As regards Keefe, the New York Giants, of course, had refused to sell him to another team, despite the substantial price tag that a transfer of Keefe would have fetched.

The injustice of leaving Keefe out of the Hall of Fame was righted in February 1964, when the Veterans Committee finally selected Keefe for induction, along with five others: Burleigh Grimes, Miller Huggins, Red Faber, Heinie Manush, and John Ward. The Associated Press dispatch, though, indicated that Keefe and Ward were secondary picks among the six selections, calling them "two men from pre–1900 days."[12] There was no fanfare in the New York City newspapers over Keefe's elevation to one of the greats in baseball, as they were fixated on the selection of Huggins, the former Yankees manager in the Babe Ruth era.

Responses were just as tepid in his earlier stomping grounds. A columnist for the *Troy Times Record* remarked, "But how many people remember that Tim Keefe, the old-time pitcher who was elected to the shrine last week, played in Troy as a member of the Haymakers for three seasons when the Collar City team was a member of the National League?"[13] The answer, of course, was that very few remembered him. Ditto in the Boston newspapers, which all carried wire service accounts without mentioning the local angle that Keefe was born and raised within five miles of downtown Boston.

Getting the Veterans Committee to select Keefe was the easy part for Allen. Unfortunately, when he went to deliver the news to Keefe's relatives, he came up empty-handed. Only three survivors had been listed in Keefe's obituary in 1933, "three sisters, the Misses Katherine and Mary Keefe of Cambridge, and Mrs. Ellen Brodbine of Revere."[14] None of the three sisters were in the Cambridge telephone book 30 years later, since all of them had died, Katherine in 1943, Mary in 1952, and Ellen in 1948. "I was unable to find any trace of his descendants in Cambridge," Allen later wrote in his "Cooperstown Corner" column in *The Sporting News* about the detective work thrust upon him once again.[15] Allen couldn't locate a Keefe descendant in Cambridge because his most direct descendants didn't possess the Keefe surname. Tim had no children and the three children of his brother Daniel, who had died in 1925, were daughters who had all married. As Allen recalled the saga of tracking down a Keefe descendant, "Thinking that if anyone in Boston could be of help, it would be Harold Kaese of the Globe. I phoned him and was happy to hear him say: 'You're in luck. About a half-hour ago, I got a call from a Miss Brodbine, who is Tim Keefe's niece.'"[16] There were several Brodbine nephews and nieces still alive, the children of Tim's sister Ellen.

Ann Brodbine had called Kaese at the *Boston Globe*. She and two sisters, Mary Paula Brodbine and Katherine Brodbine Shea, met with the sportswriter a few days later. "I'm so glad he made it," Ann told Kaese. "He should have made it sooner." The nieces showed Kaese a scrapbook with yellowed newspaper clippings that touted Keefe's accomplishments in baseball. "If you will look at these scrapbooks, you'll see that T.J. was certainly one of the best," Mary Paula proudly told Kaese.[17]

Mary Paula Brodbine represented her uncle at the Hall of Fame induction ceremony on July 27, 1964, in Cooperstown.[18] The text on Keefe's plaque at the Hall of Fame reads: "Righthander who won 346 games for Troy, Mets, Giants and Phils in only 14 seasons. His record streak of 19 straight triumphs paced Giants to flag in 1888. One of first pitchers to use a change of pace delivery." Mary Paula Brodbine made many trips back to Cooperstown, "where she befriended Mrs. Babe Ruth and had a lasting friendship with 1971 inductee Rube Marquard and his wife."[19] Marquard, another pitcher for the New York Giants, shared the record with Keefe for 19 consecutive pitching victories.

Curiously, another choice of the Veterans Committee in 1964 was John Ward, a teammate of Keefe with the New York Giants. Ward was also a compatriot of Keefe as one of the officers of the Brotherhood of Professional Base Ball Players. The pairing of Ward and Keefe as Hall of Fame selections in the same year could be an indication that Lee Allen was trying to rectify an injustice by previous Veterans Committee members who seemingly had blackballed the two renowned renegade players, since the Brotherhood-inspired Players' League had nearly put the National League out of business in 1890 and seriously impacted ballclub profits for years thereafter. If Allen had not died in a car accident in 1969, this curiosity about the committee's past neglect of both Keefe and Ward might have come to light.

The elevation of Keefe and Clarkson to Hall of Fame status initiated the 300-win benchmark as a de facto automatic qualifying standard for Hall of Fame selection. While pre–1893 pitchers Pud Galvin and Keefe-teammate Mickey Welch were voted in by the Veterans Committee in 1965 and 1971, respectively, the real acid-test for the 300-win threshold came with Early Wynn.

Wynn won exactly 300 games, with his last, immortality-inducing, victory coming at age 43 in 1963. Since he had struggled to get to the 300-win plateau, would the BBWAA vote Wynn into the Hall of Fame via the front door, or would he have to wait until he was eligible for selection by the Veterans Committee? In his first year of eligibility for the Hall of Fame in 1969, Wynn polled just 28 percent of the vote. However, he gained momentum during the next two years, garnering 47 percent in 1970 and 67 percent in 1971. In his fourth year of eligibility in 1972, Wynn finally made it over the required 75 percent threshold when he was named on 76 percent of the ballots.

Newspaper columnist Leonard Koppett initially did not side with Wynn, but changed his mind by 1972: "The whole Wynn case is based on an impressive statistic. He won 300 games. No one ever has claimed he was the greatest pitcher of his time, even for a couple of years. But the argument (to which I have now yielded) is that such a statistic, taking 23 years to accomplish, is worth recognition in itself, on the grounds of rarity."[20]

In 1973, with the 300-win benchmark now firmly established for automatic Hall of Fame status, Warren Spahn, a 363-game winner, breezed into the Hall of Fame in his first year of eligibility. At the same time, Keefe's legacy to the baseball world was just beginning to take shape, after lying dormant for more than three-quarters of a century.

26

Unsung Pioneer of Ballplayer Rights

For several years after Keefe's induction into the Hall of Fame in 1964, his nieces, who now owned his former home at 1653 Cambridge Street in Cambridge, Massachusetts, had a sign placed on the property to signify the house's historical significance. In 1976 the *Cambridge Chronicle* cheekily referred to the somewhat unsightly sign as "a shrine of sorts commemorating Tim Keefe."[1]

This sign gained a small amount of literary prominence as part of the setting in the 1971 short story entitled "The Plumber," written by John L'Heureux. Everyday, a retired plumber, a widower who lived in a small apartment on Trowbridge Street, sat in a park on Cambridge Street, where in the summer he could view "Tim Keefe's house with the garden in front." After his lunch, he would devote "an hour to gaze on the wonder of the Tim Keefe garden," which was "a garish affair, three feet wide and nine feet long, into which were crowded four display tables ... which overflowed with petunias" planted in enamel basins and clay pots placed on cement blocks and the steps of a small ladder. "Standing at the garden, he could shift his gaze to the left and admire the sign above the door. It was an enormous sign in red and white, proclaiming that this was the home of Tim Keefe, Hall of Fame pitcher for the New York Giants. Above the sign, propped on a table, a carousel horse galloped into the air, a monkey astride his back holding a little banner that once again proclaimed Tim Keefe."[2]

A more dignified sign denoting "Timothy J. Keefe Square" was eventually erected by the city of Cambridge in front of the house at 1653 Cambridge Street to signify where Keefe had lived for the last three decades of his life. More than a century after its construction in 1896, this house was still standing in 2014. Keefe's four-unit rental house on Trowbridge Street, which was erected in 1898, had a shorter lifespan, though, being replaced in the 1950s by a nondescript, 7-story, 25-unit brick apartment building. The house at 1653 Cambridge Street was Keefe's most publicly visible legacy, one that provided a substantial financial return to his descendants. Keefe had paid just a few thousand dollars for the land and the material and labor to build that house; in 1991 Keefe's niece Mary Paula Brodbine sold the house for $225,000.[3]

Keefe also left to his descendants a less public, privately treasured legacy: the ledger in which he, as secretary, recorded the meetings of the minutes of the Brotherhood of Professional Base Ball Players. That Keefe held onto this ledger for decades following the demise of the Brotherhood and the Players' League in 1890 indicates how strong his belief was regarding ballplayer rights. After Mary Paula Brodbine died in 2002, her heirs sold the ledger at auction in 2004 for a reported price tag of $99,000.[4] "At first glace it shows up as an old, threadbare ledger book, something insignificant you might find among the vestiges of an old general store," Rosemary McKittrick wrote in an online article about the auction of the Keefe ledger. "At second glace, it's much more. In fact, this ledger could be one of the most historically important pieces of baseball memorabilia to cross the auction block."[5]

McKittrick wasn't just engaging in hyperbole with her description of the ledger. "Keefe's ledger is important for two reasons," McKittrick wrote. "Baseball players were documented taking their first stand against what they viewed as tyrannical owners. Also, the autographs of the players who signed the ledger are extremely rare."[6] While Keefe would have wanted the former explanation to be the reason why his ledger had fetched so much money at auction, it was the latter reason—the autographs—that escalated the price to just under six figures. Keefe's signature was particularly valuable due to its scarcity. "Keefe's signature is one of the great mysteries in the field of Hall of Fame autographs," Ron Keurajian wrote in his book *Baseball Hall of Fame Autographs: A Reference Guide*. "I know of no genuine signatures in existence. I am told a couple of signatures were released by the Keefe estate, but I have never seen them. All the Keefe signatures I have examined were the product of forgery."[7]

Retention of that ledger by Keefe and his niece for all those years indicates that he would have wanted his legacy to be his role in the Brotherhood. However, that legacy didn't begin to have any widespread public recognition until the 1970s, when major-league ballplayers finally gained contractual rights to free agency.

Well into the 1920s, the Brotherhood movement was still part of the conscientiousness of both Keefe and Ward, the president of the Brotherhood, since both men were true believers to their death. Speaking at the National League Jubilee in 1925, which celebrated the beginning of the league's 50th year of existence, Ward disregarded sentiment and gave "a spirited defense of both the Brotherhood and the Players' League, which included a brief but pointed explanation of why, fully thirty-five years earlier, the players had been right and the owners—some of them still alive, some of them in that very room—wrong."[8] However, the ballclub owners were unfazed by Ward's comments, as they were then quite secure in their labor practices. Three years earlier, in 1922, the U.S. Supreme Court in *Federal Baseball v. National League* had unanimously decided that major-league baseball did not constitute interstate commerce and thus was not subject to federal antitrust laws.[9]

The Brotherhood, already an historical footnote by 1925, then became an obscure piece of trivia for the next half century, as few people wrote about the cause that was so vibrant to Keefe and Ward. Graduate students Harold Seymour in the 1950s and David Voigt in the 1960s wrote PhD dissertations about baseball history that, in part, touched upon the Brotherhood movement. However, even the publication of these two dissertations in book form in 1960 and 1966, respectively, ignited little popular interest in the Brotherhood. As a novelty piece, *Sports Illustrated* published an article by Leonard Shecter in 1968 about the Brotherhood. Shecter described the nascent union as "the invention of a Philadelphia sportswriter, William H. Voltz ... [who] tried to introduce it in 1885 and was met with vast mistrust and almost as much disinterest ... [before] nine New York Giant players got together to form a branch of the Brotherhood, and the idea started to catch on."[10]

The *Sports Illustrated* article in 1968 came a few months following the first collective bargaining agreement ever negotiated with the major-league ballclub owners. While the Players Association had been in existence for more than a decade, it took the hiring of a professional labor negotiator, Marvin Miller, for the Players Association to begin to make progress to the change the restrictions in the reserve clause. Previously, the members of the Players Association had been more interested in a pension plan to take care of their needs *after* their baseball careers were over rather than fixing issues impacting them *during* their careers.

Interest in the Brotherhood started to percolate in 1970 when St. Louis Cardinals outfielder Curt Flood, with the assistance of the Players Association, sued major-league baseball to obtain his free agency after he was traded to the Philadelphia Phillies. As part of his early coverage of *Flood v. Kuhn*, Leonard Koppett provided readers of the *New York Times* with not only a short history of the Brotherhood, on the 80th anniversary of the so-called Brotherhood War, but also why it was important: "A review of the Brotherhood War sheds some light on the intensity of emotion in today's struggle, which centers on Curt Flood's antitrust suit."[11] Flood's case went all the way to the U.S. Supreme Count, where the justices ruled against Flood and upheld the legal precedent that baseball was not subject to federal antitrust laws.

The Brotherhood gained more public attention in 1974 when Oakland Athletics pitcher Jim "Catfish" Hunter was declared a free agent after arbitrator Peter Seitz ruled that Oakland owner Charlie Finley had defaulted on a contractual salary payment due Hunter. Venerable baseball writer Red Smith wrote about Ward's efforts with the Brotherhood in an article entitled "The Catfish Hunter of His Time."[12] While the Hunter case was a contract anomaly, the Messersmith case in 1975 was a direct challenge to the reserve clause. Los Angeles Dodgers pitcher Andy Messersmith intentionally did not sign a contract for the 1975 season as a test case that the option in the reserve clause was simply a one-year option, not an option in perpetuity as the owners had always believed it to be. Arbitrator Seitz sided with Messersmith and declared him to be a free agent. Hunter and Messersmith both signed lucrative contracts to play for different teams as a result of their free agency. In the 1976 collective bargaining agreement, the Players Association and the ballclub owners agreed to a six-year period where clubs could reserve a ballplayer before he became a free agent (with salary arbitration rights in the interim).

In April 1976 *The Sporting News* published a lengthy article about the history of the Brotherhood and its connection to free agency, entitled "89 Years Ago: Players' Revolt."[13] The first extensive coverage of the Brotherhood came in 1980 with the publication of the book *The Imperfect Diamond: The Story of Baseball's Reserve System and the Men Who Fought to Change It*. Authors Lee Lowenfish and Tony Lupien devoted the entire Part I to the Brotherhood.[14]

As salaries substantially rose for ballplayers due to their newfound mobility rights, many law and economics professors wrote about the impact of baseball free agency over the next three decades. A few scholars focused on the impact of the Brotherhood movement, most notably Ethan Lewis in his 1995 master's thesis "'A Structure to Last Forever': The Players' League and the Brotherhood War of 1890" and Robert Ross in his 2007 PhD dissertation "'We are the People!': Geographies of the Industrial Production of Culture and the Rise and Fall of the 1890 Players' National League of Professional Base-Ball Clubs."[15]

Ward was the centerpiece to the pre-history of the challenge to the reserve clause, since he had been the president and chief spokesman for the Brotherhood. Keefe was usually mentioned only in passing, perhaps as Ward's brother-in-law or as the provider of the official baseball for the Players' League. Often Keefe was simply a footnote, which was both figuratively and literally the case in the book *Legal Decisions That Shaped Modern Baseball* as footnote number 97 to the second chapter.[16] However, this does not mean that Keefe had an unimportant role in the Brotherhood, just an unrecognized one.

Tim Keefe was truly an unsung pioneer of ballplayer rights, as this book has sought to portray. Slowly, Keefe is beginning to receive more posthumous public recognition for his role in the Brotherhood. A book produced in 2014 by the Hall of Fame to commemorate its 75th anniversary provided this paragraph in its description of Keefe: "Keefe and Ward formed the Brotherhood of Professional Base Ball Players, the game's first players' union. Five years later, the group would form the Players' League, a one-year experiment in player control of the game."[17]

Part of Keefe's Brotherhood-related legacy is the easy availability of a multi-million-dollar salary for a pitcher in the twenty-first century. In this regard, it was inevitable that Keefe's ultimate legacy would not be as a strategic pitcher, but rather as a statistical pitcher: 342 career wins as a pitcher (still among the all-time top ten) and 19 consecutive wins in 1888 (still the major-league record). Whenever any modern-day pitcher approaches these milestones, Keefe's name is evoked.

When two American League pitchers, Roger Clemens in 2001 and Roy Halladay in 2003, neared Keefe's record for consecutive victories in a season, newspapers once again trumpeted Keefe's name. Clemens was stopped at 16 games, while Halladay was stymied at 15 games.[18] When Clemens faced off against Greg Maddux on April 29, 2005, sportswriters reported that it was the first time that two 300-game winners had faced each other in a National League game since 1892, when Keefe met Galvin in their waning days as pitchers.[19] Clemens and Maddux both went on to surpass Keefe on the all-time win list.

The day in 2007 when Maddux tied Keefe for eighth place on the all-time win list with his 342nd victory, writer Alan Drooz of the *San Diego Union-Tribune* did some research into the nineteenth-century pitcher whose record Maddux had approached, commenting that both pitchers, roughly the same size at 5-foot-10 and 180 pounds, were "a master of the change-up."[20] Since Keefe had been neglected by the baseball community for most of the previous one hundred years, the title of that article fittingly was "So, Who the Heck Was Tim Keefe?"

Tim Keefe was a great strategic pitcher in the nineteenth century and an unsung pioneer of ballplayer rights as the secretary of the Brotherhood of Professional Base Ball Players.

Appendices

A: Tim Keefe on Pitching*

There is also no department in the game that plays so important a part in the result of a contest as that of pitching. It is not enough that the pitcher should have speed, a remarkable curve of a certain kind, or great endurance and pluck. The first essentials, next to the ability to deliver the ball, are coolness and judgment; and in most all cases these qualities are concomitant, the player who possesses judgment will be cool and collected, able to abide the fortunes of war like a true soldier if need be, and stand punishment if the other team happens to master his delivery temporarily.

Strategy, too, plays a most important part in the pitcher's work. The number of pitchers who understand their men thoroughly have been very few, and this can only be gained by careful observation and study and long experience. Bobby Mathews probably understands the player who faces him as well as any one who occupies the points to-day. Bond was also very successful in this art, and contrived to place his field with remarkable success.

The ability to combine the various curves with a change of pace is what is most bothersome to the batsman. Nothing exasperates a batsman so much, and weakens him to so great an extent, as to be prepared for an in-shoot and then strike at a ball several inches on the other side of the plate, or to expect a swift ball, only to strike at a ball that drops short.

BEFORE THE DELIVERY

Stand with the ball resting in the hands, upon the hip, out of the sight of the batter.... The idea of this is to allow the arrangement of the ball in the fingers, for the different curves, unobserved by the batter. A ball delivered from this position will generally prove very puzzling.

---

*Source: T.J. Keefe, "Curve Pitching," in *Batting and Pitching, with Fine Illustrations of Attitudes: A Thorough and Practical Treatise*, by John Morrill and T.J. Keefe (Boston: Wright & Ditson, 1884), 23–30.

Straight Ball

Hold the ball between the two fore fingers and the thumb, and throw the ball straight from the shoulder, with as much speed as possible, care being taken to retain command of the sphere. If the batsman stands forward, well up to the plate, and moves up in the act of striking, the proper ball to deliver would be the in-ball, i.e., a straight ball over the inside corner of the plate; if he stands well away from the plate, and has a habit of stepping back, the proper point to strive for will be the outside portion of the plate.

Out-Curve—Slow Ball

Hold the ball well pressed in the palm of the hand with the last three fingers. Deliver it with the same motion as is used with the straight ball over the outside corner of the plate, except that the wrist should be twisted so as to turn the hand upwards in delivering the ball.

Swift Drop Ball

Hold the hand directly under the ball, and in delivering let it slide off the ends of the fingers. The arm must be brought nearly straight up and down with the body in this delivery, the ball kept at the height of the knee, the lower the better, as more of a drop can be acquired to deceive the batter.

Swift Out-Curve

The ball should be held as in the delivery of a straight ball. Hold it tightly between the fore fingers and thumb, and the motion of letting it leave the hand should be done with such a quick snap of the wrist as to allow the hand to turn under as much as possible.

The In-Shoot

Throw the ball out from the shoulder, letting it pass off the ends of the first two fingers. It is a ball that should be worked on the inside corner of the plate, and that should have more speed to it than the out-curve. It should shoot in very quick just before reaching the plate. If the batter has a habit of stepping back from the plate, the ball should be worked from the outside corner.

Rising Ball

Hold the ball in the same manner as in the out-curve. When delivering, stoop over, throwing the hand well under and out from the body. Never pitch a ball to a right-handed batter above the waist, if possible; and for a left-handed batter, keep it high and over his shoulder. It is a ball that should have plenty of speed.

Hints to Pitchers

Do as little catching or throwing before or during a game as possible, as the hand, or rather fingers, ought to have their natural feeling, that with little throwing as possible goes a great way to give a pitcher command in delivering the ball.

B: Tim Keefe on Shorthand*

To the Editor of *Browne's Phonographic Monthly*:

There is probably no art more trying to one's patience than that of phonography. I am not possessed with an over-amount of that most agreeable quality, and during my early experience with the mysteries of phonography have often worked myself into a state bordering on madness, especially after studying hard for three months with poor results …

My profession for the past ten years has been base ball a profession well established in New York at the present time. I became a member of the New York Club in 1883, and while connected with that organization acted in the capacity of pitcher. Having plenty of leisure time during the base ball season, at home also and while traveling, thought that I would undertake to master the intricacies of the art of shorthand writing. After trying to unlearn what I had learned of the Park Row system I accomplished that difficult undertaking, and can assure you that the unlearning was the harder task.

Benn Pitman's system was the one taken up, and really the one I follow today; have looked over Graham and use parts of that system occasionally. Never had an instructor, and what knowledge I have acquired has been through books relating to the art. I have witnessed some of the leading stenographers at work at Washington, both in the Senate and House, also at some of the New York courts. The official stenographers at Washington have decidedly the easier time. I consider a person who can take testimony correctly in court a wonderful person. The strain on one's nervous system is apparently more than the ordinary person can endure. Two hours work in a court room on a warm day must be far more trying to the nerves than to pitch in an exciting game under a burning sun. The latter is no easy task, but I prefer it to the former.

Being secretary of the National Brotherhood of Base Ball Players, the minutes of the meetings are taken down in shorthand. It not only offers an opportunity for good practice, but it saves considerable valuable time.

*Source: T.J. Keefe, "A Pitcher's Opinion of Phonography," *Browne's Phonographic Monthly*, January 1889.

Mr. W. Wallace, the great base ball player correspondent of San Francisco, keeps the record of different clubs and players in shorthand and has done so for years. I do not expect to ever gain a livelihood by stenography—at least, not at present, and certainly not while pitching is so remunerative. From the present to the first of January, my address will be very uncertain. After that date, I intend to locate in New York, and you can count me a willing subscriber to your valuable Monthly.

Very respectfully yours,
T.J. Keefe
Somerville, Mass.
December 3, 1888

C: Tim Keefe on Strategic Pitching*

If the pitcher's delivery be ineffective, the strongest support avails him but little. The chief requisites for a first-class pitcher are good, quick curves, plenty of speed, and a cool head at critical moments. To be successful he must possess all of the above qualities. Speed is really the essential point in a pitcher, but he must have good command of it or his work will be more damaging to his catcher's hands than to the opposing batsmen. The same holds good with his curves. If he has not good command of them, he is certainly laboring under great disadvantage. The only way to acquire command of the ball is by continual practice. Always make it a point when pitching to have an object to pitch at. It cannot be acquired in a day or a week, but requires years of practice. Some of the leading League pitchers of the present day are men who have acquired the art from books that treat on the subject, *i.e.*, gained the idea, and worked at it until they became proficient and could pitch the ball at a given target.

The pitcher should be careful in beginning, for a bad habit or a poor position once acquired requires almost unremitting effort to overcome, and the result is almost a new beginning. The pitcher will experience as much trouble in the change as he would if he were just learning the art. During my experience as a coacher I have had pitchers under my instructions, who have made a poor commencement because their style of holding the ball was defective. Instead of holding every ball they pitch the same, they will grasp the out-curve ball wholly between the fingers and pitch it in that manner, while the same pitchers will hold and pitch their speedy or in-ball with two fore-

---

*Source: T.J. Keefe, "Pitching," in *Scientific Ball*, by Fred Pfeffer (Chicago: N.F. Pfeffer, 1889), 43–49.

fingers and thumb The result is that the batsman can tell by looking at their hands what particular ball they intend to deliver ...

Every beginner should make it a practice to hold every ball, no matter whether out-curve and drop, an in or slow ball, the same. No doubt by pitching the out-curve wholly with the fingers it will be larger, but the larger or deeper the curve the sooner it is perceptible to the batter, for a deep curve ball will apparently curve sooner after leaving the pitcher's hand than a fast, quick one; but the advantage gained by holding it between the thumb and fore-finger is that it baffles the batter in regard to what particular ball the man in the box intends to send in.

Secondly, he will have a far better out-curve, for it will be quicker and considerably faster, and a short, quick curve will prove more effective than a very deep or large one. Of course all young pitchers like to see a good curve on the ball when delivered, and as the curve delivered by the use of the fingers entirely is deeper than any delivered in a different manner, it is not surprising that so many young pitchers acquire a bad habit in the beginning ...

The pitcher in taking his position should stand erect, facing the batter, holding the ball on a level with his shoulder and between the two fore-fingers and thumb, with his left hand covering the ball. When in the act of delivering, he should bend his body as far back as possible, thereby relieving his arm of considerable strain, bringing his arm first down and then above his head, so that the swing of it will describe a circle while in the act of delivering the ball ...

As I said before, the pitcher has no time to use so many varying deliveries. In the first place, after one or two bad or unfair balls have been delivered by the pitcher, he is then compelled to pitch the ball properly over the plate. In such cases he will generally rely on the ball that he has the best command of, which is, in eight cases out of ten, the fast, straight ball. A good, quick out-curve and drop, a fast in-ball and a slow ball, are about all that is necessary for a pitcher to have command of to be effective. Indeed, very few of the most noted pitchers use anything but this delivery, and, with good command, it will enable any pitcher to go through a season's campaign successfully.

The pitcher often finds himself placed in very trying positions. Nothing but a cool head and perfect control of his temper will bring him through creditably. He is sometimes placed in such straits through the incompetency of the umpire, or through some error of his support, or perhaps through his own blunder. At a critical point in the game, when the score is exceedingly close, the umpire, through poor judgment, gives the batter his base on called balls; the next man makes a safe hit. The pitcher, who, at this point, is working like a "beaver" to deceive the following batsman, has four unfair balls and two strikes on the latter. He then has one ball to pitch in which either to dispose of the batsman or give him his base. He delivers it just where the batter called for it, but the umpire doesn't agree with him, and gives the batter his base on called balls.

This is enough to demoralize the most undemonstrative pitcher in the profession. If he loses his temper at this stage of the fight, his chances for saving the game are very poor indeed. There is only one course to pursue: settle down and work all the harder. Continue pitching as if you were sure of winning under all circumstances. Never mind what the umpire's decisions are; it will do no good to fume and fret over them, for he will not change them. All that can be done is to make the best of the situation and work with a greater determination ...

The successful pitcher is the one who will pitch as well at critical points as when his club has a sure lead and the result of the game is a certainty. Anybody can pitch when there is nothing at stake or when victory is certain. Practice until you can pitch as well at critical points as when you have a winning lead. Never lose your temper or get discouraged, no matter how poor your support may be. Always remember that you are paid to pitch and not to find fault with anybody on the field. Do your best every minute. Go into the game with all the confidence that you can muster. When you step into the box at the beginning of the game, consider yourself the best pitcher in the country and the only one. With such confidence and good command of your delivery there is nothing to fear.

D: Pitching Changes Keefe Adapted to, 1880 to 1893

Delivery and Arm Motion

Year	League	Change
1880	NL	Ball release not above waist
1883	AA	Ball release not above shoulder
1885	NL	Overhand ball release (one foot fixed on back line of pitcher's box, rescinded in June)
1887	NL	One foot fixed on back line of pitcher's box
1893	NL	One foot fixed on pitching rubber

Pitcher's Box Dimensions

Year	League	Change
1880	NL	6 feet long by 4 feet wide
1886	NL	7 feet long by 4 feet wide
1887	NL	5.5 feet long by 4 feet wide
1890	PL	6 feet long by 4 feet wide
1891	NL	5.5 feet long by 4 feet wide
1893	NL	eliminated, replaced by 1-foot-wide pitching rubber

Pitching Distance

Year	League	Change
1880	NL	45 feet from front line of pitcher's box

1881 NL 50 feet from front line of pitcher's box
1887 NL 55.5 feet from back line of pitcher's box
1890 PL 57 feet from back line of pitcher's box
1891 NL 55.5 feet from back line of pitcher's box
1893 NL 60.5 feet from pitching rubber

Strike Zone

1880 NL Batter can choose high or low zone
1887 NL One zone for all batters

Base on Balls

1880 NL 8 balls
1881 NL 7 balls
1885 NL 6 balls
1887 NL 5 balls
1889 NL 4 balls

Strikeout

1880 NL 4 strikes
1881 NL 3 strikes
1887 NL 4 strikes
1888 NL 3 strikes

Hit Batsman

1880 NL Called ball
1884 AA Batter takes first base
1885 NL Called ball
1887 NL Batter takes first base

Length of Regular Season

1880 NL 84 games
1883 AA 98 games
1884 AA 112 games
1886 NL 126 games
1888 NL 140 games
1892 NL 154 games
1893 NL 132 games

Chapter Notes

Chapter 1

1. *New York Press*, May 31, 1888.
2. William Harris, "Sketches of Baseball Writers," in *Athletic Sports in America, England and Australia*, edited by Henry Clay Palmer (Philadelphia: Hubbard Brothers, 1889), 610. In this early history of baseball writers, Harris provided historians with a perspective on the craft in an age when bylines were mostly pseudonyms and actual names were just beginning to be published.
3. Ibid., 602–603. Articles written by Sullivan in the *Boston Globe* were attributed to "Featherweight" and those in *Sporting Life* were bylined "Mugwump."
4. Obituary of William Harris, *Boston Globe*, July 8, 1891.
5. Jerry Nason, "The W.D. Sullivan Years, 1884–1910," *Boston Globe*, February 13, 1972.
6. Richard Barber, *The Knight & Chivalry* (New York: Charles Scribner's Sons, 1970), 36.
7. Harold Perkins, *The Origins of Modern English Society* (London: Routledge & Kegan Paul, 1969), 273–274.
8. Will Rankin, "Was an Artist: Tim Keefe the Best Pitcher of His Day," *The Sporting News*, January 30, 1897.
9. Henry Harrison, *Surnames of the United Kingdom* (Baltimore: Genealogical Publishing, 1969), 242.
10. Jay Dolan, *The Irish Americans: A History* (New York: Bloomsbury, 2008), 62.
11. Ibid., 103.
12. Steven Riess, *Touching Base* (Westport, CT: Greenwood, 1980), 154–155.
13. Robert Burk, *Never Just a Game: Players, Owners, and American Baseball to 1920* (Chapel Hill: University of North Carolina Press, 1994), 67, 244.
14. Rex Burns, *Success in America: The Yeoman Dream and the Industrial Revolution* (Amherst: University of Massachusetts Press, 1976), 1.
15. Judy Hilkey, *Character Is Capital: Success Manuals and Manhood in Gilded Age America* (Chapel Hill: University of North Carolina Press, 1997), 126.
16. Bruce Laurie, *Artisans Into Workers: Labor in Nineteenth Century America* (New York: Noonday, 1989), 35.
17. "Tim Keefe: The Country's Greatest Pitcher," *Richmond Dispatch*, July 29, 1888.
18. Ronald Mendel, "Labor Republicanism," in *Encyclopedia of U.S. Labor and Working-Class History*, edited by Eric Arneson (New York: Routledge, 2007), 762.
19. Eric Foner, *Free Soil, Free Labor, Free Men: The Ideology of the Republican Party Before the Civil War* (New York: Oxford University Press, 1970), 18.

Chapter 2

1. Naturalization record of Patrick Keefe, National Archives, Boston U.S. Circuit Court, Volume 9, Page 70.
2. *Cambridge Directory*, 1853.
3. Bob Reckman, "Carpentry: The Craft and Trade," in *Case Studies on the Labor Process*, edited by Andrew Zimbalist (New York: Monthly Review, 1979), 75.
4. *Cork Examiner*, August 11, 1845.
5. Dolan, *The Irish Americans*, 69–70.
6. Kerby Miller, *Emigrants and Exiles: Ireland and the Irish Exodus to North America* (New York: Oxford University Press, 1985), 294.
7. Dolan, *The Irish Americans*, 77.
8. Naturalization record of Patrick Keefe.
9. Charles Elliot, *Somerville's History* (Somerville, MA: Privately published, 1896), 39.
10. Miller, *Emigrants and Exiles*, 317–319.
11. Naturalization record of Patrick Keefe.
12. *Cambridge Directory*, 1852.
13. Samuel Eliot, *A History of Cambridge, Massachusetts, 1630–1913* (Cambridge, MA: Cambridge Tribune, 1913), 117.
14. *Cambridge Directory*, 1853; State census of 1855, Massachusetts Archives, dwelling #1283, family #1556 in Ward 2 of Cambridge.
15. Marriage records for 1855, Massachusetts Archives, Volume 88, Page 52.
16. Naturalization record of Patrick Keefe.

263

17. Ibid.
18. Elliot, *Somerville's History*, 39.
19. Mark Erlich, *With Our Hands: The Story of Carpenters in Massachusetts* (Philadelphia: Temple University Press, 1986), 22.
20. Robert Christie, *Empire in Wood: A History of the Carpenters' Union* (Ithaca: Cornell University Press, 1956), 25.
21. Reckman, "Carpentry: The Craft and Trade," 80–81.

Chapter 3

1. Birth records for 1857, Massachusetts Archives, Volume 106, Page 204.
2. Baptismal records for St. John's Church in East Cambridge, Catholic Archdiocese of Boston Archives.
3. *Cambridge Directory*, 1860.
4. Federal census of 1860, U.S. Census Bureau, Series M653, Roll 508, Page 324.
5. National Park Service, *The Civil War Defenses of Washington, Part 1* (Washington: U.S. Government Printing Office, 2006), 20–21.
6. Harold Kaese, "Keefe Fanned Mighty Casey," *Boston Globe*, February 9, 1964. Patrick Keefe was definitely not a soldier in the war, according to the extensive records published in *Massachusetts Soldiers, Sailors, and Marines in the Civil War* (Boston: Adjutant General, 1937).
7. Lee Allen, "Keefe's Dad Made Bullets in Rebel Prison," *The Sporting News*, April 4, 1964.
8. Charles Sanders, *While in the Hands of the Enemy: Military Prisons of the Civil War* (Baton Rouge: Louisiana State University Press, 2005), 79; Ellis Coulter, *The Confederate States of America, 1861–1865* (Baton Rouge: Louisiana State University Press, 1950), 470–473, 478.
9. Civil War draft registrations, National Archives, Sixth Congressional District of Massachusetts.
10. Birth records for 1864, Massachusetts Archives, Volume 169, Page 105.
11. Keefe burial site, Cambridge City Cemetery, Elogium Path, Lot 6206.
12. Death records for 1863, Massachusetts Archives, Volume 166, Page 62.
13. State census of 1865, Massachusetts Archives, dwelling #579, family #645 in Somerville; *Somerville Directory*, 1869–1887.
14. State census of 1865. Although no street addresses are denoted in that census, neighbors of Patrick Keefe were William Crumley and Samuel Wright, who both resided on Oak Street in the 1869 *Somerville Directory*.
15. Elliot, *Somerville's History*, 59.
16. Davis Dyer and Daniel Gross, *The Generations of Corning: The Life and Times of a Global Corporation* (New York: Oxford University Press, 2001), 22–25, 28.
17. Allen, "Keefe's Dad."
18. *Cambridge Chronicle*, June 12, 1869, and July 6, 1872.
19. John Thorn and John Holway, *The Pitcher* (New York: Prentice Hall, 1987), 4, 6.
20. *Cambridge Chronicle*, June 9, 1866.
21. *Cambridge Directory*, 1870–1871.
22. Birth records for 1866, Massachusetts Archives, Volume 187, Page 222; birth records for 1868, Massachusetts Archive, Volume 206, Page 127; birth records for 1870, Massachusetts Archive, Volume 224, Page 243.
23. *Somerville Directory*, 1870.
24. Clay McShane and Joel Tarr, *The Horse in the City: Living Machines in the Nineteenth Century* (Baltimore: Johns Hopkins University Press, 2007), 30.
25. Federal census of 1870, U.S. Census Bureau, Series M593, Roll 631, Page 396.
26. *City of Somerville Annual Report*, 1873–1880.
27. "Daniel Keefe," in *Regiments and Armories of Massachusetts: An Historical Narration of the Massachusetts Volunteer Militia, with Portraits and Biographies of Officers Past and Present*, edited by Charles Winslow Hall (Boston: W.W. Potter, 1901), 52–53.
28. W.J. Rorabaugh, *The Craft Apprentice: From Franklin to the Machine Age in America* (New York: Oxford University Press, 1986), 8.
29. Ibid., 132.
30. Elliott, *Somerville's History*, 59–60.
31. Christie, *Empire in Wood*, 27.
32. Reckman, "Carpentry: The Craft and Trade," 80–81.
33. Erlich, *With Our Hands*, 25.
34. Death records of 1872, Massachusetts Archives, Volume 248, Page 251.
35. *Cambridge Directory*, 1875–1876.

Chapter 4

1. Warren Goldstein, *Playing for Keeps: A History of Early Baseball* (Ithaca: Cornell University Press, 1989), 99.
2. "T.J. Keefe," *New York Clipper*, May 22, 1880.
3. *Boston Daily Advertiser*, March 20, April 22, and July 21, 1874. The Boston newspapers sometimes referred to the Tremont club as Fremont, when the typographer apparently misinterpreted the cursive-written capital "T" as an "F."
4. *Boston Daily Advertiser*, August 17, 1874.
5. Thorn and Holway, *The Pitcher*, 5–6.
6. T.J. Keefe, "Curve Pitching," in *Batting*

and Pitching, with Fine Illustrations of Attitudes: A Thorough and Practical Treatise, by John Morrill and T.J. Keefe (Boston: Wright & Ditson, 1884), 14.
7. Albert Spalding, *America's National Game* (New York: American Sports Publishing, 1911), 484–485.
8. *Boston Daily Advertiser*, April 23, 1875.
9. *New York Clipper*, May 8, 1875.
10. Peter Morris, *The Catcher: How the Man Behind the Plate Became an American Folk Hero* (Chicago: Ivan R. Dee, 2009), 44.
11. *Sporting Life*, June 1, 1895.
12. *New York Clipper*, May 29, 1875.
13. *New York Clipper*, June 19, 1875.
14. *Boston Daily Advertiser*, August 7, 1875.
15. Will Rankin, "Marvelous Growth of Baseball in New York City from its Humble Origins," *New York Press*, July 30, 1905.
16. *Taunton Gazette*, October 21, 1875.
17. *Lowell Courier*, October 23, 1875.
18. *Boston Globe*, November 19, 1875.
19. *Boston Daily Advertiser*, July 24, 1876.
20. *New York Clipper*, April 22, 1876.
21. Goldstein, *Playing for Keeps*, 98.
22. Ibid., 129.
23. "T.J. Keefe," *New York Clipper*.
24. *Lewiston Evening Journal*, July 5, 1876.
25. "Tim Keefe, the Base Ballist," *Somerville Journal*, July 6, 1889.
26. *Somerville Directory*, 1877.
27. *Cambridge Chronicle*, November 27, 1875, and January 1, 1876.
28. *Boston Daily Advertiser*, August 7, 1877.
29. *Boston Daily Advertiser*, August 16, 1877.
30. *Boston Daily Advertiser*, October 19, 1877.
31. Morris, *The Catcher*, 121–122.
32. Land record dated November 30, 1877, Middlesex South Registry of Deeds, Book 1458, Page 103.
33. Land record dated January 4, 1878, Middlesex South Registry of Deeds, Book 1461, Page 511.
34. Walter Galenson, *The United Brotherhood of Carpenters: The First Hundred Years* (Cambridge: Harvard University Press, 1983), 11, 14.
35. *New York Clipper*, November 17, 1877.

Chapter 5

1. *Boston Daily Advertiser*, March 4, 1878.
2. *New York Clipper*, March 23, 1878.
3. Frank Pope, "The Clintons of '78: Manager Fayerweather Gives Reminiscences," *Boston Globe*, March 24, 1889.
4. *New York Clipper*, June 1, 1878.

5. Pope, "Clintons of '78."
6. *Westboro Chronotype*, July 6, 1878.
7. *New York Clipper*, July 27, 1878. The other two games that Keefe appeared in as a pitcher were mop-up innings on June 27 vs. Springfield and August 2 vs. New Bedford.
8. Morris, *The Catcher*, 59, 72.
9. *Clinton Conant*, August 17, 1878.
10. Karen Nugent, "Heirloom Diamond: Clinton Ball Field Crowned as World's Oldest," *Worcester Telegram*, October 4, 2007.
11. *Clinton Conant*, September 7, 1878.
12. Pope, "Clintons of '78"; *New York Clipper*, October 19, 1878.
13. *Boston Herald*, October 27, 1878.
14. Bob Richardson, "Thomas Henry Bond," in *Nineteenth-Century Stars* (Kansas City: Society for American Baseball Research, 1989), 15.
15. Obituary of Tommy Bond, *The Sporting News*, January 30, 1941.
16. Keefe, "Curve Pitching," 14–15, 17.
17. *Somerville Directory*, 1879–1893.
18. Federal census of 1880, U.S. Census Bureau, Series T9, Roll 546, Page 339.
19. *Sixth Annual Report of the* [Massachusetts] *Bureau of Labor Statistics*, 1875, 221–236.
20. *New York Clipper*, April 19, 1879.
21. *Clinton Conant*, April 19, 1879.
22. *New York Clipper*, May 17, 1879.
23. *Boston Herald*, May 31, 1879.
24. *Clinton Conant*, June 14, 1879.
25. *Boston Herald*, June 14, 1879.
26. *Utica Morning Herald*, June 23 and 24, 1879.
27. *Utica Morning Herald*, July 5, 1879.
28. *New York Clipper*, July 19, 1879.
29. *Utica Morning Herald*, July 14, 1879.
30. *New Bedford Evening Standard*, August 5, 1879.
31. *New York Clipper*, August 23, 1879.
32. *Albany Evening Times*, October 7, 1879.
33. *New York Clipper*, November 25, 1879.
34. Ibid.
35. Morris, *The Catcher*, 84.
36. *New Orleans Times-Picayune*, January 25, 1880.
37. *New York Clipper*, February 14, 1880.
38. *New Orleans Times-Picayune*, February 9, 1880.
39. *New York Clipper*, February 21, 1880.
40. *New York Clipper*, February 28 and March 13, 1880.
41. Morris, *The Catcher*, 135, 144.
42. *New York Clipper*, March 20, 1880.
43. *New York Clipper*, April 17, 1880.
44. *New York Clipper*, April 3, 1880.
45. *Buffalo Commercial Advertiser*, October 3, 1879, as reprinted in *Early Innings: A Documentary History of Baseball, 1825–1908*, edited

by Dean Sullivan (Lincoln: University of Nebraska Press, 1995), 114.
46. Bryan Di Salvatore, A *Clever Base-Ballist: The Life and Times of John Montgomery Ward* (New York: Pantheon, 1999), 158–159.
47. "A.J. Bushong," *New York Clipper*, September 18, 1880.
48. "T.J. Keefe," *New York Clipper*.
49. Federal census of 1880, U.S. Census Bureau, Series T9, Roll 805, Page 344.
50. *Troy Daily Times*, June 11, 1880.
51. *Albany Evening Times*, June 11, 1880.
52. *Troy Daily Times*, June 2, 1880.
53. *Albany Evening Times*, July 6, 1880.
54. *Troy Daily Times*, July 7, 1880.
55. *Boston Daily Advertiser*, July 22, 1880.

Chapter 6

1. *Chicago Inter Ocean*, August 7, 1880.
2. *Troy Daily Times*, August 13, 1880.
3. *Cleveland Herald*, August 18, 1880.
4. Philip Shirley, "A Chat with Keefe," *Sporting Life*, February 24, 1906.
5. *Troy Daily Times*, September 16, 1880.
6. Minutes of National League meeting on October 5, 1880, National Baseball Hall of Fame Library.
7. Ford Sawyer, "He Pitched 19 Straight Wins," *Boston Globe*, May 27, 1928.
8. National League salary report reprinted in *Sporting Life*, April 5, 1890.
9. *New York Clipper*, December 18, 1880.
10. *Troy Daily Times*, July 16, 1881.
11. Peter Morris, *A Game of Inches: The Stories Behind the Innovations That Shaped Baseball: The Game on the Field* (Chicago: Ivan R. Dee, 2006), 224–225.
12. Morris, *The Catcher*, 92.
13. Sawyer, "He Pitched 19 Straight Wins."
14. Ibid.
15. *Chicago Inter Ocean*, September 28, 1881.
16. Don Rittner, *Troy: A Collar City History* (Charleston, SC: Arcadia, 2002), 53, 129.
17. John Foster, "The Evolution of Pitching," *The Sporting News*, December 24, 1931.
18. *Cleveland Leader*, August 18, 1880, reprinted in *Troy Daily Times*, August 19, 1880.
19. Roger Angell, *Season Ticket* (Boston: Houghton Mifflin, 1988), 196.
20. David Nemec, *The Beer and Whisky League: The Illustrated History of the American Association* (New York: Lyons & Burford, 1994), 22.
21. National League salary report reprinted in *Sporting Life*, April 5, 1890.
22. *Troy Daily Times*, August 24, 1882.
23. Roy Kerr, *Roger Connor: Home Run King of 19th Century Baseball* (Jefferson, NC: McFarland, 2011), 47–48.
24. *Cleveland Herald*, October 2, 1882.
25. Roy Kerr, *Buck Ewing: A Baseball Biography* (Jefferson, NC: McFarland, 2012), 34–35.
26. *New York Herald*, October 13, 1882.
27. *Troy Daily Times*, October 11, 1882.
28. *New York Herald*, October 13, 1882.
29. *Troy Daily Times*, October 11, 1882.
30. *National Police Gazette*, November 10, 1883.

Chapter 7

1. *Troy Daily Times*, October 21, 1882.
2. *Harvard Crimson*, April 14, 1883.
3. *New York Clipper*, January 29, 1881.
4. Obituary of Tommy Bond, *The Sporting News*, January 30, 1941; Di Salvatore, *Clever Base-Ballist*, 180.
5. Ronald Smith, *Sports and Freedom: The Rise of Big-Time College Athletics* (New York: Oxford University Press, 1988), 126.
6. *New York Clipper*, March 19, 1892.
7. *Yale News*, February 2, 1881.
8. Smith, *Sports and Freedom*, 166–167.
9. *Princetonian*, February 25, 1881.
10. *Harvard Crimson*, March 9, 1882.
11. *Yale News*, February 2, 1882.
12. Minutes of the June 15, 1882, meeting of the Harvard Athletic Committee, Harvard University Archives.
13. Minutes of the June 17 and September 27, 1882, meetings of the Harvard Athletic Committee, Harvard University Archives.
14. Minutes of the February 20, 1883, meeting of the Harvard Athletic Committee, Harvard University Archives.
15. *Harvard Crimson*, June 22, 1883.
16. *Boston Globe*, January 6, 1884.
17. Minutes of the January 21, 1884, meeting of the Harvard Athletic Committee, Harvard University Archives.
18. *Harvard Crimson*, November 16, 1883; *Princetonian*, February 18, 1887.
19. T.J. Keefe, "Pitching," in *Scientific Ball*, by Fred Pfeffer (Chicago: N.F. Pfeffer, 1889), 46.
20. *Harvard Crimson*, November 14, 1888.
21. Minutes of the November 27, 1888, meeting of the Harvard Athletic Committee, Harvard University Archives.
22. Minutes of the December 12, 1888, meeting of the Harvard Athletic Committee, Harvard University Archives.
23. Smith, *Sports and Freedom*, 171.

Chapter 8

1. *New York Times*, January 25, 1938.
2. *New York Clipper*, December 16, 1882.
3. Stew Thornley, *Land of the Giants: New York's Polo Grounds* (Philadelphia: Temple University Press, 2000), 14–18.
4. "Tim Keefe: The Country's Greatest Pitcher."
5. Rankin, "Was an Artist."
6. Sawyer, "He Pitched 19 Straight Wins."
7. "A Declining Baseball Star: Timothy J. Keefe, Once the First Pitcher Among Baseball Players," *New York Tribune*, October 4, 1891.
8. *New York Clipper*, April 21, 1883.
9. *New York Clipper*, May 5, 1883.
10. *Baltimore Sun*, May 4, 1883.
11. Edward Achorn, *The Summer of Beer and Whiskey* (New York: Public Affairs, 2013), 100.
12. *St. Louis Globe-Democrat*, June 18, 1883.
13. Craig Carter, ed., *Complete Baseball Record Book* (St. Louis: Sporting News, 2002), 87. The team record set that day by the Metropolitans for fewest hits allowed in a doubleheader lasted more than one hundred years. On April 12, 1992, the Boston Red Sox broke that record when they gave up just two hits, when Matt Young pitched a no-hitter in the first game and Roger Clemens threw a two-hitter in the nightcap.
14. *Sporting Life*, July 8, 1883.
15. *St. Louis Globe-Democrat*, June 18, 1883.
16. Achorn, *Summer of Beer and Whiskey*, 173.
17. *Brooklyn Eagle*, March 29, 1901.
18. *New York Times*, November 28, 1883.
19. National League salary report reprinted in *Sporting Life*, April 5, 1890.
20. *Sporting Life*, October 8, 1883.
21. Dolan, *The Irish Americans*, 140.
22. Terry Golway, *Machine Made: Tammany Hall and the Creation of Modern American Politics* (New York: Liveright Publishing, 2014), 108–109.
23. *Cleveland Herald*, April 5, 1884.
24. Edward Achorn, *Fifty-Nine in '84: Old Hoss Radbourn, Barehanded Baseball & the Greatest Season A Pitcher Ever Had* (New York: Smithsonian Books, 2010), 72.
25. Keefe, "Curve Pitching," 25–30.
26. Morris, *Game of Inches*, 149–150, 170.
27. Thornley, *Land of the Giants*, 20.
28. *New York Times*, May 14, 1884; *New York World*, May 14, 1884.
29. *Baltimore Sun*, May 2, 1884.
30. *Cleveland Herald*, June 1, 1884.
31. *Sporting Life*, June 18, 1884.
32. *New York Clipper*, June 28, 1884.
33. Harris, "Sketches of Baseball Writers," 597, 603.
34. Pamela Bakker, *Eyes on the Sporting Scene, 1870–1930: Will and June Rankin, New York's Sportswriting Brothers* (Jefferson, NC: McFarland, 2013), 39, 51.
35. George Juergens, *Joseph Pulitzer and the New York World* (Princeton: Princeton University Press, 1966), 119.
36. Ibid.
37. Harris, "Sketches of Baseball Writers," 593.
38. *New York World*, October 12, 1884.
39. Harris, "Sketches of Baseball Writers," 605.
40. Bakker, *Eyes on the Sporting Scene*, 79.
41. Howard Chudacoff, *The Age of the Bachelor: Creating an American Subculture* (Princeton: Princeton University Press, 1999), 187.
42. *National Police Gazette*, August 9, 1884.
43. Keefe, "Curve Pitching," 17.
44. *New York Times*, July 18, 1884.
45. *New York World*, July 18, 1884.
46. *Sporting Life*, October 1, 1884.
47. Rankin, "Was an Artist."
48. *New York Clipper*, November 1, 1884.
49. Achorn, *Old Hoss Radbourn*, 268–269.
50. Morris, *Game of Inches*, 117, 139, 162.
51. *New York Times*, October 24, 1884.
52. Frank Graham, *The New York Giants*, first edition 1952 (Carbondale, IL: Southern Illinois University Press, 2002), 7.
53. *Sporting Life*, November 19, 1884.
54. *New York Clipper*, November 29, 1884.
55. *Boston Daily Advertiser*, December 19, 1884.
56. *Boston Globe*, December 23, 1884.
57. *New York Clipper*, January 3, 1885.

Chapter 9

1. *New York Clipper*, December 29, 1883.
2. *New York Clipper*, February 7, 1885.
3. *New York Clipper*, December 6, 1884.
4. *New York Herald*, February 15, 1885.
5. *New York Clipper*, March 14, 1885.
6. *New York Times*, March 8, 1885.
7. Land record dated March 13, 1885, Middlesex South Registry of Deeds, Book 1696, Page 197.
8. *Sporting Life*, April 15, 1885; *New York Times*, March 27, April 7, and April 13, 1885.
9. *New York World*, April 13, 1885.
10. *National Police Gazette*, May 23, 1885.
11. National League salary report reprinted in *Sporting Life*, April 5, 1890.
12. Paul Dickson, *Dickson Baseball Diction-*

ary, third edition (New York: W.W. Norton, 2011), 366–367.
13. *Sporting Life*, June 17, 1885.
14. T.J. Keefe, "Curves or Liners: The Vexed Question in Base Ball Circles," *Boston Globe*, October 21, 1888.
15. *New York Times*, June 10, 1885.
16. *Boston Globe*, October 14, 1885.
17. Keefe, "Curves or Liners."
18. James Hardy, *The New York Giants Base Ball Club: The Growth of a Team and a Sport, 1870 to 1900* (Jefferson, NC: McFarland, 1996), 67.
19. Wesley Stout, *Once a Clown, Always a Clown: Reminiscences of DeWolf Hopper* (Boston: Little, Brown, 1927), 76.
20. *New York Times*, July 23, 1885.
21. Edwin Burrows and Mike Wallace, *Gotham: A History of New York City to 1898* (New York: Oxford University Press, 1999), 1149.
22. *Boston Globe*, October 14, 1885.
23. Rankin, "Was an Artist."
24. Kerr, *Buck Ewing*, 55–56.
25. *New York World*, October 18, 1885.
26. *New York Herald*, October 19, 1885.
27. *New York Times*, October 19, 1885.
28. T.J. Keefe, "The Brotherhood and Its Work," *Players' National League Base Ball Guide*, 1890, in *Early Innings: A Documentary History of Baseball, 1825–1908*, edited by Dean Sullivan (Lincoln: University of Nebraska Press, 1995), 196.
29. "Completed Auction Archive," *Hunt Auctions*. 2004. Web. Only the names were documented in Keefe's 1890 published account of the meeting. The addresses are from a photo of the meeting minutes in Keefe's ledger, when it was sold at auction in August 2004.
30. Keefe, "The Brotherhood and Its Work."

Chapter 10

1. T.J. Keefe, "A Pitcher's Opinion of Phonography," *Browne's Phonographic Monthly*, January 1889.
2. *Sporting Life*, March 26, 1884.
3. *Sporting Life*, September 1, 1886.
4. *New York Herald*, June 1, 1888.
5. Carole Srole, *Transcribing Class and Gender: Masculinity and Femininity in Nineteenth-Century Courts and Offices* (Ann Arbor: University of Michigan Press, 2009), 42.
6. *Sporting Life*, August 4, 1886.
7. *Sporting Life*, April 5, 1890.
8. *New York Times*, August 27, 1885.
9. *Sporting Life*, November 11, 1885.
10. Ibid.
11. *Sporting Life*, August 4, 1886.
12. *St. Louis Globe-Democrat*, July 5, 1885; *National Police Gazette*, June 27, 1885.
13. Harris, "Sketches of Baseball Writers," 598–599.
14. *Cleveland Herald*, January 17, 1884; Harris, "Sketches of Baseball Writers," 584.
15. *Cleveland Herald*, May 29 and June 1, 1884.
16. *Cleveland Herald*, April 2, 1884.
17. Mary Ann Clawson, *Constructing Brotherhood* (Princeton: Princeton University Press, 1989), 5.
18. Ibid., 14.
19. Ibid., 81.
20. Reckman, "Carpentry: The Craft and Trade," 75–76, 87–88.
21. Di Salvatore, *Clever Base-Ballist*, 25–31.
22. Ibid., 179.
23. Robert Ross, "We are the People!": Geographies of the Industrial Production of Culture and the Rise and Fall of the 1890 Players' National League of Professional Base-Ball Clubs," PhD dissertation, Syracuse University, 2007, 106–107.
24. Laurie, *Artisans into Workers*, 51.
25. Ibid., 66.
26. Stuart Blumin, *The Emergence of the Middle Class: Social Experience in the American City, 1760–1900* (New York: Cambridge University Press, 1989), 69.
27. Steve Leikin, *The Practical Utopians: American Workers and the Cooperative Movement in the Gilded Age* (Detroit: Wayne State University Press, 2005), 2–4, 33.
28. Gerald Grob, *Workers and Utopia: A Study of Ideological Conflict in the American Labor Movement 1865–1900* (Evanston: Northwestern University Press, 1961), 44.
29. Leikin, *Practical Utopians*, 5, 112, 164.
30. "Co-operation in America," *Boston Globe*, May 20, 1888.
31. Daniel Rodgers, *The Work Ethic in Industrial America 1850–1920* (Chicago: University of Chicago Press, 1974), 45.
32. "New Literature: Profit Sharing," *Boston Globe*, April 7, 1889.
33. Rodgers, *Work Ethic*, 48.
34. Ibid.

Chapter 11

1. *New York Times*, November 1, 1885.
2. *New Orleans Times-Picayune*, November 23, 1885.
3. A.J. Bushong, "The Catcher," in *Scientific Ball*, by Fred Pfeffer (Chicago: N.F. Pfeffer, 1889), 53.

4. *New York Clipper*, January 16, 1886.
5. *Sporting Life*, February 3, 1886.
6. Kerr, *Buck Ewing*, 81.
7. *New York Clipper*, March 13, 1886.
8. Sawyer, "He Pitched 19 Straight."
9. *New York Sun*, April 4, 1886.
10. *New York Clipper*, May 8, 1886.
11. *New York Times*, April 30, 1886.
12. Ibid.
13. Ibid.
14. *Frank Leslie's Illustrated Newspaper*, May 8, 1886.
15. Keefe, "The Brotherhood and Its Work."
16. *New York Times*, June 1, 1886.
17. Hardy, *New York Giants*, 64.
18. *Chicago Inter Ocean*, June 6, 1886.
19. *Frank Leslie's Illustrated Newspaper*, July 10, 1886.
20. Bob Lemke, ed. *2011 Standard Catalog of Baseball Cards* (Iola, WI: Krause, 2010), 253.
21. Dave Jamieson, *Mint Condition: How Baseball Cards Became an American Obsession* (New York: Atlantic Monthly Press, 2010), 21.
22. Bakker, *Eyes on the Sporting Scene*, 82–83.
23. Harris, "Sketches of Baseball Writers," 593.
24. Howard Tuckner, "Giants' First Batboy Is Not Entirely Alone," *New York Times*, September 29, 1957.
25. Elizabeth Cromley, *Alone Together: A History of New York's Early Apartments* (Ithaca: Cornell University Press, 1990), 18.
26. Chudacuff, *Age of the Bachelor*, 85–86.
27. Roy Rosenzweig and Elizabeth Blackmar, *The Park and the People: A History of Central Park* (Ithaca: Cornell University Press, 1992), 214.
28. *New York World*, evening edition, August 13, 1888.
29. "Tim Keefe: The Country's Greatest Pitcher."
30. John Tebbel and Mary Ellen Zuckerman, *The Magazine in America, 1741–1990* (New York: Oxford University Press, 1991), 66–67.
31. Michael Immerso, *Coney Island: The People's Playground* (Piscataway, NJ: Rutgers University Press, 2002), 30.
32. Charlie Bevis, *Sunday Baseball: The Major Leagues' Struggle to Play Baseball on the Lord's Day, 1876–1934* (Jefferson, NC: McFarland, 2003), 53, 283.
33. Don Jensen, "Everyone Went to Nick's," *Base Ball: A Journal of the Early Game*, Spring 2009.
34. Keefe, "The Brotherhood and Its Work."
35. *Sporting Life*, August 4, 1886.
36. *Brooklyn Eagle*, August 22, 1886.
37. *Boston Globe*, August 13, 1886.
38. Mike Roer, *Orator O'Rourke: The Life of a Baseball Radical* (Jefferson, NC: McFarland, 2005), 125, 134.
39. Roer, *Orator O'Rourke*, 134; Kerr, *Buck Ewing*, 28; Stevens, *Baseball's Radical for All Seasons*, 54.
40. *New York Clipper*, August 21, 1886.
41. *New York Times*, September 7, 1886.
42. *Sporting Life*, February 24, 1886.
43. *New York Times*, April 9, 16, and 24, 1886.
44. *New York Times*, November 15, 1886.

Chapter 12

1. Land record dated July 26, 1886, Middlesex South Registry of Deeds, Book 1759, Pages 132–135.
2. Ibid.
3. Ibid.
4. Land record dated December 23, 1886, Middlesex South Registry of Deeds, Book 1781, Page 93.
5. Biography of Mary Ridgely Brown, Maryland State Archives, SC 3520-2282.
6. Biography of Frank Brown, Maryland State Archives, SC 3520-1473.
7. Dolan, *The Irish Americans*, 87.
8. Land record dated February 21, 1888, Middlesex South Registry of Deeds, Book 1838, Pages 412–413. Also transferred to his sister was the mortgage on the Blackwell property transacted three years earlier in 1885.
9. Arthur Gilman, ed., *The Cambridge of Eighteen Hundred and Ninety-Six* (Cambridge: Riverside Press, 1896), 82–86.
10. Ibid.
11. *New York Clipper*, December 19, 1887.
12. *Cambridge Tribune*, March 24, 1888.
13. *New York World*, evening edition, April 19, 1888.
14. *New York World*, evening edition, April 20, 1888.
15. *New York World*, April 20, 1890.
16. *Cambridge Directory*, 1879.
17. *Boston Globe*, June 22, 1888.

Chapter 13

1. *New York Times*, November 15, 1886.
2. Keefe, "Curves or Liners."
3. *New York Clipper*, November 27, 1886.
4. *New York Evening Telegram*, April 2, 1887.
5. *New York Clipper*, November 27, 1886.
6. *Sporting Life*, December 15, 1886.
7. *Princetonian*, February 18, 1887; *New York Evening Telegram*, March 28, 1887.

8. *Sporting Life*, April 6, 1887.
9. *New York Tribune*, May 15, 1887.
10. *New York Clipper*, April 9, 1887.
11. John Thorn, "Baseball's Lost Chalice," *Base Ball: A Journal of the Early Game*, Fall 2011.
12. Keefe, "Curves or Liners."
13. *New York World*, July 10, 1887.
14. *Somerville Journal*, July 16, 1887; Death records for 1887, Massachusetts Archives, Volume 383, Page 213.
15. The Keefe family plot in St. Paul's Cemetery is located just to the left of the cemetery's entrance on Broadway in the town of Arlington. A six-foot-high, white marble monument marks the Keefe plot.
16. "Daniel Keefe," *Regiments and Armories*, 52–53.
17. Obituary of Ellen Brodbine, *Boston Globe*, August 1, 1948; obituary of Annie Keefe, *Somerville Journal*, June 29, 1889; listing of 1883 high school graduates, *Somerville Annual Report*, 1883.
18. Death records for 1888, Massachusetts Archives, Volume 392, Page 211. Margaret Keefe may have taken courses at the so-called Harvard Annex, the Society for the Collegiate Instruction of Women, which was later known as Radcliffe College, but alumni records are very sketchy for the early years of this institution that began offering college-level study in 1882.
19. *Cambridge City Directory*, 1887–1888.
20. *Cambridge Tribune*, January 2, 1892; Kaese, "Keefe Fanned Mighty Casey."
21. *New York World*, July 20, 1887.
22. Robert Tiemann, "Major League Attendance," in *Total Baseball*, 7th edition (Kingston, NY: Total Sports Publishing, 2001), 74.
23. Jamieson, *Mint Condition*, 27.
24. Ibid., 22.
25. Ibid.
26. Lemke, *Baseball Cards*, 260.
27. Ibid., 156.
28. *New York Evening Telegram*, August 8, 1887.
29. *New York Evening Telegram*, September 3, 1887.
30. *New York Herald*, May 22, 1887.
31. *New York Clipper*, March 12 and August 13, 1887.
32. *New York Clipper*, October 8, 1887.
33. Spalding, *America's National Game*, 514–517.
34. George Tuohey, *A History of the Boston Base Ball Club* (Boston: M.F. Quinn, 1897), 92.
35. John Ward, "Is the Base Ball Player a Chattel?" *Lippincott's Magazine*, August 1887.
36. Ibid.
37. *Sporting Life*, September 21, 1887.
38. *New York Times*, August 21, 1887.

39. Jim Moore and Natalie Vermilyea, *Ernest Thayer's "Casey at the Bat": Background and Characters of Baseball's Most Famous Poem* (Jefferson, NC: McFarland, 1994), 209.
40. Jack Miley, "I Did So Strike Out!" *Collier's*, May 21, 1938.
41. *New York Sun*, September 4, 1887.
42. *National Police Gazette*, September 17, 1887.
43. *New York Times*, September 6, 1887.
44. *New York Clipper*, September 3, 1887.
45. *New York Times*, September 19, 1887.
46. *New York Times*, December 22, 1887.
47. *San Francisco Evening Bulletin*, October 20, 1887; *Sporting Life*, January 11, 1888.
48. *San Francisco Evening Bulletin* and *New York Times*, October 26, 1887.
49. *New Orleans Times-Picayune*, October 31, 1887.
50. *New Orleans Times-Picayune*, November 1, 1887.
51. *Dallas Morning News*, November 14, 1887.
52. Mike Kelly, *"Play Ball": Stories of the Diamond Field*, 1st edition 1888 (Jefferson, NC: McFarland, 2006), 79–81.
53. Touhey, *Boston Base Ball Club*, 190–191.
54. *New York Clipper*, November 26, 1887.
55. *Boston Globe*, February 13, 1888.
56. Glenn Moore, "Ideology on the Sportspage: Newspapers, Baseball, and Ideological Conflict in the Gilded Age," *Journal of Sport History*, Fall 1996."
57. *Los Angeles Times*, November 21, 1887.
58. *San Francisco Evening Bulletin*, November 25, 1887.
59. *Los Angeles Herald*, November 27, 1887.
60. Moore and Vermilyea, *Ernest Thayer's "Casey at the Bat,"* 221.
61. *San Francisco Evening Bulletin*, December 7, 1887.
62. Randall Brown, "Baseball by the Beach," (Santa Cruz) *Good Times*, November 10, 2010.
63. *San Francisco Evening Bulletin*, December 27, 1887.
64. *Sporting Life*, February 15, 1888.
65. Death records for 1888, Massachusetts Archives, Volume 392, Page 211.

Chapter 14

1. *Boston Globe*, April 24, 1888.
2. *Boston Globe*, evening edition, April 24, 1888.
3. Thorn, "Baseball's Lost Chalice."
4. *New York Directory*, 1888.
5. Federal census of 1880, U.S. Census Bureau, Series T9, Roll 880, Page 417.

6. *New York Times*, March 9, May 19, October 12, and October 15, 1887.
7. *New York Times*, April 24, 1888.
8. "Ladies Who Love the Game: Portraits of Some Female Enthusiasts at the Polo Grounds," *New York World*, May 6, 1888.
9. *New York Daily Graphic*, November 21, 1888.
10. Ibid.
11. *New York World*, November 11, 1888.
12. Chudacoff, *Age of the Bachelor*, 65.
13. *New York World*, evening edition, November 17, 1888.
14. Di Salvatore, *Clever Base-Ballist*, 232.
15. *Sporting Life*, November 21, 1888.
16. Di Salvatore, *Clever Base-Ballist*, 328.
17. Tim Keefe folder, National Baseball Hall of Fame Library.
18. Obituaries of G. Edward Gibson, *Cornell Civil Engineer*, February 1924, and *Albany Evening Journal*, December 22, 1923; biography of Gibson in *1903 Class Book* of Cornell University.
19. *New York World*, July 10, 1891.
20. *Sporting Life*, November 21, 1888.

Chapter 15

1. *Boston Globe*, March 12, 1888.
2. *Boston Globe*, February 13, 1888.
3. Ibid.
4. *Sporting Life*, February 9, 1888.
5. *New York Times*, March 3, 1888.
6. *Chicago Inter Ocean*, April 10, 1888; *New York Press*, April 12, 1888.
7. *New York Press*, April 12, 1888.
8. *Boston Globe*, April 18, 1888.
9. *New York Times*, April 20, 1888.
10. *New York Press*, April 13, 1888.
11. *Boston Globe*, evening edition, April 20, 1888.
12. *Sporting Life*, April 25, 1888.
13. *Boston Globe*, April 24, 1888.
14. Ibid.
15. *New York Times*, April 28, 1888.
16. Jacob Morse, *Sphere and Ash: A History of Baseball*, first edition 1888 (Columbia, SC: Camden House, 1984), 39–40.
17. Lemke, *Baseball Cards*, 14, 153, 168, 337.
18. Craig Carter, ed., *Complete Baseball Record Book* (St. Louis: Sporting News, 2002), 82.
19. *New York Clipper*, July 28, 1888.
20. *Sporting Life*, November 7, 1888.
21. "The Catcher's Glove," *New York Sun*, April 27, 1890.
22. *New York Clipper*, July 28, 1888.
23. Morris, *The Catcher*, 150.
24. Ibid., 143–144.
25. Bushong, *Scientific Ball*, 51.
26. "Mickey Welch Likes Old-Timers," *Boston Globe*, February 9, 1908.
27. Shirley, "Chat With Keefe."
28. Henry Chadwick, "The Art of Pitching," *Outing*, May 1889.
29. *New York Clipper*, March 1, 1890.
30. Keefe, *Scientific Ball*, 46.
31. *Philadelphia Inquirer*, June 27, 1888.
32. *New York Times*, June 27, 1888.
33. *New York Times*, July 14, 1888.
34. *Chicago Inter Ocean*, July 22, 1888.
35. *Philadelphia Inquirer*, July 21, 1888.
36. *New York Clipper*, July 28, 1888.
37. *New York Press*, July 29, 1888.
38. *New York Press*, July 22, 1888.
39. *New York Times*, April 2, 1888.
40. *New York Times*, August 7, 1888.
41. *New York World*, August 15, 1888.
42. *Chicago Inter Ocean*, August 15, 1888.
43. Ibid.
44. *New York World*, August 15, 1888.
45. Stout, *Once a Clown*, 81.
46. *New York World*, May 6, 1888.
47. *New York Times*, July 15, 1888.
48. *Brooklyn Eagle*, November 13, 1888; *New York Press*, November 15, 1888.
49. *New York Clipper*, May 26, 1888.
50. *New York Times*, June 11, 1888.
51. John Ward, *Base-Ball: How to Become a Player, with the Origin, History, and Explanation of the Game* (Philadelphia: Athletic Publishing, 1888), 119–120.
52. *New York Press*, May 19, 1889.
53. *Sporting Life*, October 16, 1889.
54. *Sporting Life*, November 21, 1888.
55. Keefe, "Curves or Liners."
56. Ibid.
57. *Sporting Life*, November 21, 1888.
58. Di Salvatore, *Clever Base-Ballist*, 232.
59. Thomas Zeiler, *Ambassadors in Pinstripes: The Spalding World Tour and the Birth of the American Empire* (Lanham, MD: Rowman & Littlefield, 2006), 65–66.
60. *Sporting Life*, November 21, 1888.
61. *New York Times*, November 21, 1888.
62. *New York Sun*, December 8, 1888.
63. *Sporting Life*, November 21, 1888.
64. Mark Lamster, *Spalding's World Tour: The Epic Adventure That Took Baseball Around the Globe—And Made It America's Game* (New York: Public Affairs, 2006), 50; Di Salvatore, *Clever Base-Ballist*, 244–245.
65. *Sporting Life*, November 28, 1888.
66. *Sporting Life*, December 26, 1888.
67. Ibid.
68. *Sporting Life*, November 7, 1888.
69. *New York Times*, November 18, 1888.

Chapter 16

1. *New York Clipper*, January 12, 1889.
2. *New York Clipper*, January 26, 1889.
3. "Keefe & Becannon: The New and Prosperous Sporting Goods Firm," *Sporting Life*, May 31, 1890.
4. Hardy, *New York Giants*, 105.
5. Peter Levine, *A.G. Spalding and the Rise of Baseball* (New York: Oxford University Press, 1985), 72–73.
6. LeRoy Ashby, *With Amusement for All: A History of American Popular Culture* (Lexington, KY: University of Kentucky Press, 2006), 99.
7. *New York Directory*, 1889.
8. "Keefe & Becannon," *Sporting Life*.
9. *New York Press*, February 6, 1889.
10. *Sporting Life*, March 20, 1889.
11. *Sporting Life*, March 27, 1889.
12. Land record dated February 21, 1888, Middlesex South Registry of Deeds, Book 1838, Page 412.
13. *Sporting Life*, April 25, 1888.
14. *Sporting Life*, March 6, 1889.
15. *New York Press*, April 14, 1889.

Chapter 17

1. Harris, "Sketches of Baseball Writers," 610.
2. *New York Press*, December 7, 1888.
3. *New York Press*, January 27, 1889.
4. Ibid.
5. *New York Times*, November 25, 1888.
6. "Twirler Tim Is Rich," *New York World*, January 14, 1889.
7. Gilman, *Cambridge*, 83.
8. *Somerville Journal*, July 6, 1889.
9. Lamster, *Spalding's World Tour*, 168–169.
10. *New York Times*, January 30, 1889.
11. "The Rebellion: The Inception, Growth and Culmination Which Resulted in the Players' League Described by Ward," *Sporting Life*, April 5, 1890; William Harris, "The National League" and "The National Brotherhood," in *Athletic Sports in America, England and Australia*, edited by Henry Clay Palmer (Philadelphia: Hubbard Brothers, 1889), 124–128, 144–150.
12. Ross, "We are the People!" 103.
13. *Philadelphia Inquirer*, October 30, 1889.
14. Lamster, *Spalding's World Tour*, 254.
15. *New York Times*, April 10, 1889; Thorn, "Baseball's Lost Chalice," footnote 15.
16. *New York Times*, May 30, 1889.
17. *New York Press*, April 12, 1889.
18. *Chicago Inter Ocean*, April 18, 1889.
19. *New York Times*, April 18, 1889.
20. *New York Press*, April 21, 1889.
21. *New York Clipper*, May 4, 1889.
22. *New York Press*, April 28, 1889.
23. *New York Press*, May 5, 1889.
24. *New York Press*, May 7, 1889.
25. *New York Press*, May 8, 1889.
26. *New York World*, evening edition, May 9, 1889.
27. *New York Press*, May 10, 1889; National League salary report reprinted in *Sporting Life*, April 5, 1890.
28. Joe Vila, "Tim, Once Giants' Star Pitcher, First 'Holdout,'" *New York Sun*, February 5, 1931.
29. *Chicago Inter Ocean*, June 16, 1889.
30. Keefe, *Scientific Ball*, 43.
31. Harris, "Sketches of Baseball Writers," 583.
32. *Sporting Life*, April 5, 1890.
33. Harris, "The National League," 124.
34. *New York Clipper*, June 8, 1889.
35. *New York Clipper*, May 25, 1889.
36. *New York Times*, May 20, 1889.
37. *New York Clipper*, June 1, 1889.
38. *New York Press*, May 19, 1889.
39. Thornley, *Polo Grounds*, 41–42.
40. *New York Times*, June 25, 1889.
41. *New York Press*, June 9, 1889.
42. Land record dated June 8, 1889, Middlesex South Registry of Deeds, Book 1911, Page 361. Keefe neglected to transfer ownership of the mortgage on the Blackwell property, which needed to be disposed of later in 1890 by his sister Ellen, the administrator of Annie's estate. Land record dated August 7, 1890, Middlesex South Registry of Deeds, Book 1990, Page 200.
43. *Somerville Journal*, June 29, 1889; Death records for 1889, Massachusetts Archives, Volume 401, Page 225.
44. *New York World*, June 24, 1889.
45. *Boston Globe*, evening edition, June 24, 1889, page 4.
46. *Boston Globe*, evening edition, June 26, 1889, page 1.
47. Gravestone in Keefe family plot at St. Paul's Cemetery in Arlington, Massachusetts.
48. *Boston Globe*, June 28, 1889.
49. *Sporting Life*, July 17, 1889.
50. *New York Clipper*, July 6, 1889.
51. *Sporting Life*, July 10, 1889.
52. *Sporting Life*, April 5, 1890.
53. *New York Clipper*, July 27, 1889.
54. *New York World*, August 7, 1889.
55. Marriage records for 1889, Massachusetts Archives, Volume 399, Page 480.
56. *Boston Globe*, August 21, 1889.
57. *New York World*, August 23, 1889.
58. Ibid.
59. *Sporting Life*, August 28, 1889.

60. *New York World*, August 23, 1889.
61. *Boston Globe*, August 23, 1889, page 4.
62. *Sporting Life*, September 11, 1889.
63. *Pittsburgh Dispatch*, September 12, 1889.
64. *New York Press*, September 21, 1889.
65. Frank Brunell, "A Great Ball Trust: The Brotherhood Has Organized a New League." *Chicago Tribune*, September 22, 1889.
66. *New York Times*, October 6, 1889.
67. *New York World*, evening edition, October 5, 1889.
68. *New York World*, evening edition, October 7, 1889.
69. Rankin, "Crisis in Affairs of New York Club Came During War With Brotherhood," *New York Press*, August 18, 1905.
70. *New York Press*, October 12, 1889.
71. *New York World*, evening edition, October 31, 1889.
72. *New York Times*, October 29, 1889.

Chapter 18

1. *Boston Globe*, November 5, 1889.
2. *New York Times*, November 5, 1889.
3. *New York Press*, November 8, 1889.
4. Brunell, "A Great Ball Trust"; *New York Times*, November 7, 1889.
5. Jerry Markham, *A Financial History of the United States: From Christopher Columbus to the Robber Barons (1492–1900)* (Armonk, NY: M.E. Sharpe, 2002), 356.
6. *New York World*, April 20, 1890.
7. *Sporting Life*, October 17, 1891. Ewing, Richardson, Crane, Connor, and O'Rourke were five other ballplayers who were also stockholders.
8. Steven Riess, "The Baseball Magnates and Urban Politics in the Progressive Era, 1895–1920," *Journal of Sport History*, Vol. 1, No. 1 (1974).
9. *New York World*, April 20, 1890.
10. *New York Herald*, November 4, 1889.
11. *New York World*, November 4, 1889.
12. *Sporting Life*, November 6, 1889.
13. *New York Times*, November 7, 1889.
14. *Chicago Inter Ocean*, November 1, 1889.
15. *New York Times*, November 2, 1889.
16. *Philadelphia Inquirer*, November 4, 1889.
17. *Sporting Life*, November 27, 1889.
18. *Chicago Inter Ocean*, November 22, 1889.
19. *New York World*, December 22, 1889.
20. *New York Sun*, January 1, 1890.
21. *Sporting Life*, January 8, 1890.
22. *New York Sun*, January 1, 1890.
23. *New York Sun*, January 14, 1890.
24. *New York Times*, December 10, 1889.
25. Obituary of Brunell, *Chicago Tribune*, November 17, 1931. Brunell became much more famous as a writer about horse racing than baseball, as the founder of the *Daily Racing Form* in 1894.
26. *New York Sun*, January 1, 1890.
27. *New York Times*, November 2, 1889.
28. *New York Times*, December 18, 1889.
29. *Philadelphia Inquirer*, December 18, 1889.
30. *New York Sun*, January 1, 1890.
31. *New York Press*, November 8, 1889.
32. *New York Clipper*, March 22, 1890.
33. *Sporting Life*, May 3, 1890.
34. *Sporting Life*, June 28, 1890.
35. Land record dated December 17, 1889, Middlesex South Registry of Deeds, Book 1947, Page 522. His wife, Clara, also had to consent to the transfer, as she signed the deed to release "all right of on to both dower and homestead in the granted premises."
36. *New York World*, evening edition, December 24, 1889.
37. *Sporting Life*, January 8, 1890.
38. Patrick Thornton, *Legal Decisions That Shaped Modern Baseball* (Jefferson, NC: McFarland, 2012), 34.
39. *Buffalo Courier*, January 30, 1890.
40. *New York Press*, February 19, 1890.
41. *New York Clipper*, February 22, 1890.
42. *New York Press*, March 6, 1890; *Princetonian*, February 19, 1890.
43. *New York Press*, March 30, 1890.
44. *New York Clipper*, March 22, 1890.
45. *Sporting Life*, March 19, 1890.

Chapter 19

1. *New York Times*, April 20, 1890.
2. *Sporting Life*, April 26, 1890.
3. *Boston Globe*, May 15, 1890.
4. "Keefe & Becannon," *Sporting Life*, May 31, 1890.
5. Hardy, *New York Giants*, 110.
6. Bakker, *Eyes on the Sporting Scene*, 97.
7. Obituary of William Harris, *Sporting Life*, July 11, 1891.
8. *Sporting Life*, July 12, 1890.
9. Patrick Porter, "Origins of the American Tobacco Company," *Business History Review*, Spring 1969.
10. Jamieson, *Mint Condition*, 28.
11. Rankin, "Crisis in Affairs." Soden and Walter Spalding each infused $25,000 while Abel and Reach contributed $6,500 apiece.
12. *Philadelphia Inquirer*, May 19, 1890.
13. *Sporting Life*, June 14, 1890.
14. *Sporting Life*, October 11, 1890.
15. *New York Times*, August 17, 1890.
16. *New York Sun* August 12, 1890.
17. *New York Times*, August 11, 1890.
18. Kerr, *Buck Ewing*, 115.

19. *New York Sun* August 12, 1890.
20. *Sporting Life*, August 20, 1890.
21. *New York Sun*, August 28, 1890.
22. *New York Herald*, August 20, 1890.
23. *Boston Globe*, September 9, 1890.
24. *New York Herald*, September 28, 1890.
25. Ibid.
26. *New York Sun*, September 19, 1890.
27. *New York Times*, November 21, 1890.
28. *New York Clipper*, September 27, 1890.
29. *New York Times*, September 19 and 28, 1890.
30. Stevens, *A Radical for All Seasons*, 121, 143.
31. *New York Times*, October 1, 5, and 22, 1890.
32. *New York Times*, November 21, 1890.
33. *New York Press*, October 5, 1890.
34. *New York Herald*, October 7, 1890.
35. *New York Press*, October 5, 1890.
36. *New York Times*, October 10, 1890.
37. Rankin, "Crisis in Affairs."
38. *New York Sun*, October 15, 1890.
39. *New York Sun*, October 16, 1890.
40. *New York Times*, December 20, 1890.
41. *New York Sun*, October 15, 1890.
42. *Boston Globe*, October 19, 1890.
43. *Sporting Life*, October 18, 1890.
44. *New York Times*, October 21, 1890.
45. *New York Sun*, October 25, 1890.
46. *Sporting Life*, November 1, 1890.
47. *New York Sun*, November 12, 1890.
48. Levine, *Spalding*, 63–64.
49. Spalding, *America's National Game*, 288.
50. *Sporting Life*, July 12, 1890.
51. "E.B. Talcott," *New York Clipper*, July 29, 1893; obituary of Edward Talcott, *New York Times*, April 7, 1941.

Chapter 20

1. *Philadelphia Inquirer*, February 2, 1891.
2. *Sporting Life*, January 3, 1891.
3. *New York Press*, May 9, 1891.
4. Obituary of William Becannon, *New York Sun*, August 9, 1932; *Sporting Life*, October 17, 1891. Becannon did not last long at Spalding & Bros., as by 1893 he had left to start his own sporting goods firm.
5. "Timothy J. Keefe, Once the First Pitcher Among Baseball Players," *New York Tribune*, October 4, 1891.
6. *Sporting Life*, January 31, 1891.
7. *Sporting Life*, October 17, 1891. Keefe probably sold his stock in the Giants to Talcott in 1892 when Talcott was buying up stock to acquire a controlling interest in the ballclub.
8. *Boston Globe*, February 27, 1891.
9. *Princetonian*, March 4, 1891.
10. *New York Sun*, March 9, 1891.
11. *Sporting Life*, March 7, 1891.
12. *Cambridge Tribune*, January 2, 1892; *Boston Globe*, December 31, 1891; marriage records for 1891, Massachusetts Archives, Volume 416, Page 343.
13. *Sporting Life*, March 7, 1891.
14. *New York Press*, March 22, 1891.
15. *Sporting Life*, March 14, 1891.
16. *Sporting Life*, March 21, 1891.
17. *New York Press*, March 31, 1891.
18. *New York* World, April 1, 1891.
19. *New York Sun*, January 13, 1895.
20. *New York Press*, April 5, 1891.
21. *New York Times*, April 23, 1891.
22. *New York World*, April 24, 1891.
23. *New York Times*, April 24, 1891.
24. *Philadelphia Inquirer*, May 5, 1891.
25. *New York Times*, May 6, 1891; *Philadelphia Inquirer*, May 7, 1891.
26. *New York Times*, June 5, 1891.
27. *New York Times*, June 25, 1891.
28. *Sporting Life*, June 27, 1891.
29. *New York Herald*, July 10, 1891.
30. *New York Press*, July 12, 1891.
31. *New York Press*, July 17, 1891.
32. *New York Times*, July 22, 1891.
33. Ibid.
34. *The Sporting News*, July 25, 1891.
35. *New York Press*, July 26, 1891.
36. *New York Press*, July 25, 26, and 28, 1891.
37. *New York Times*, July 29, 1891.
38. *Boston Globe*, July 29, 1891.
39. *New York Herald*, July 29, 1891.
40. *Boston Globe*, July 22, 1891.
41. *Sporting Life*, October 17, 1891.
42. *Sporting Life*, October 24, 1891.
43. *Sporting Life*, April 23, 1892. The Spalding & Bros. firm may have acquired the trademark to the Keefe baseball just to ensure that it was never again produced.
44. *New York Times*, February 10, 1893.
45. Obituary of John Day, *New York Sun*, January 28, 1925; Willard Gildersleeve, *Gildersleeves of Gildersleeve, Conn.* (Meriden, CT: Journal Publishing, 1914), 41–42.
46. Meyer Jacobstein, *The Tobacco Industry in the United States* (New York: Columbia University Press, 1907), 181.

Chapter 21

1. *Philadelphia Inquirer*, August 12, 1891.
2. *Philadelphia Inquirer*, August 20, 1891.
3. *Boston Globe*, September 18, 1891.
4. Land record dated March 10, 1892, Middlesex South Registry of Deeds, Book 2101, Page 268.

5. *Philadelphia Inquirer*, January 12, 1892.
6. Minutes of the January 26, 1892, meeting of the Harvard Athletic Committee, Harvard University Archives.
7. *Philadelphia Inquirer*, April 24, 1892.
8. *Sporting Life*, December 23, 1899.
9. *Boston Globe*, June 29, 1892.
10. *Philadelphia Inquirer*, July 25, 1892.
11. *Sporting Life*, August 6, 1892.
12. *Philadelphia Inquirer*, September 10, October 1, and October 14, 1892.
13. *Philadelphia Inquirer*, October 19 and 23, 1892.
14. *Boston Globe*, December 27, 1892.
15. *Boston Globe*, December 29, 1892.
16. *Sporting Life*, March 18, 1893.
17. *Sporting Life*, April 22, 1893.
18. *Sporting Life*, December 3, 1892.
19. *Sporting Life*, March 18, 1893.
20. *Sporting Life*, June 17, 1893.
21. Reed Browning, *Cy Young: A Baseball Life* (Amherst: University of Massachusetts Press, 2003), 37, 44.
22. *Philadelphia Inquirer*, August 16, 1893.
23. *Sporting Life*, August 26, 1893.
24. *Philadelphia Inquirer*, August 18, 1893.
25. *New York Sun*, August 31, 1893.
26. *Sporting Life*, October 7, 1893.

Chapter 22

1. *Boston Globe*, January 13, 1894.
2. *Harvard Crimson*, January 27, 1894.
3. *Chicago Inter Ocean*, January 12, 1894.
4. *New York Press*, January 18, 1894.
5. *Philadelphia Inquirer*, April 8, 1894.
6. Land record dated March 15, 1894, Middlesex South Registry of Deeds, Book 2259, Page 373; land record dated March 19, 1894, Middlesex South Registry of Deeds, Book 2259, Page 228.
7. *Cambridge Chronicle*, March 31, 1894.
8. *New York Sun*, May 9, 1894.
9. *Boston Globe*, June 10, 1894.
10. *Sporting Life*, July 7, 1894.
11. Minutes of the December 21, 1895, meeting of the Harvard Athletic Committee, Harvard University Archives.
12. *Harvard Crimson*, January 21, 1896.
13. *Boston Daily Advertiser*, April 29, 1896.
14. *Boston Post*, March 8, 1897.

Chapter 23

1. David Q. Voigt, "America's Manufactured Villain—The Baseball Umpire," *Journal of Popular Culture*, Summer 1970.

2. Larry Gerlach, "Umpires," in *Total Baseball*, edited by John Thorn and Pete Palmer (New York: Warner, 1989).
3. *Boston Globe*, August 4, 1894.
4. Charles Alexander, *John McGraw* (New York: Viking, 1988), 26.
5. Peter Morris, "'A Motion as Near Flying as Any Human Being Could Attain': The 19th Century Umpire as Sprinter," *Base Ball: A Journal of the Early Game*, Fall 2008.
6. *Baltimore Sun*, May 31, 1895.
7. Morris, "Umpire as Sprinter."
8. *Sporting Life*, June 1, 1895.
9. Alexander, *John McGraw*, 26, 34.
10. *Sporting Life*, June 1, 1895.
11. Alexander, *John McGraw*, 45; *The Sporting News*, July 27, 1895.
12. *Sporting Life*, May 18, 1895.
13. *New York Press*, August 19, 1895.
14. *Baltimore Sun*, July 23 and 24, 1895.
15. *Sporting Life*, August 3, 1895.
16. *New York Times*, September 12, 1895.
17. *New York Evening Telegram*, September 12, 1895.
18. *New York Sun*, March 30, 1912.
19. *Boston Globe*, September 28 and 29, 1895.
20. *New York Evening Telegram*, September 28, 1895.
21. *Chicago Inter Ocean*, October 3, 1895.
22. *Baltimore Sun*, October 3, 1895.
23. *Baltimore Sun*, October 4, 1895.
24. *Philadelphia Inquirer*, October 7, 1895.
25. *Cambridge Tribune*, October 26, 1895.
26. Obituary of John McIssac, *Cambridge Chronicle*, April 4, 1908.
27. Land record dated December 21, 1895, Middlesex South Registry of Deeds, Book 2425, Page 552.
28. Shirley, "Chat with Keefe."
29. Kaese, "Keefe Fanned Mighty Casey."
30. *Brooklyn Eagle*, May 11, 1896.
31. *Boston Globe*, May 14, 1895.
32. *Boston Globe*, May 30, 1896.
33. *Boston Globe*, May 31, 1896.
34. *Boston Globe*, June 18, 1896.
35. *Sporting Life*, July 11, 1896.
36. *Boston Globe*, July 7, 1896.
37. *New York Herald*, July 9, 1896.
38. *Brooklyn Eagle*, July 19, 1896.
39. *Sporting Life*, July 4, 1896.
40. Peter Nye, *Hearts of Lions: The History of American Bicycle Racing* (New York: W.W. Norton, 1988), 53; *New York Times*, December 15, 1896.
41. *Buffalo Evening News*, August 2 and 21, 1896.
42. *Wilkes-Barre Times*, October 8, 1896.
43. *Philadelphia Inquirer*, June 6, 1897.
44. Land record dated November 5, 1896,

Middlesex South Registry of Deeds, Book 2510, Page 151. For mortgage discharge, see Book 2425, Page 552.
45. *Springfield Union*, July 18, 1897.
46. *Sporting Life*, September 4, 1897.

Chapter 24

1. *Sporting Life*, November 13, 1897.
2. *New York Herald*, June 27, 1898.
3. *Sporting Life*, July 8, 1899.
4. Martin Gardner, *The Annotated Casey at the Bat: A Collection of Ballads About the Mighty Casey* (New York: Clarkson Potter, 1967), 24; *Boston Globe*, September 25, 1917.
5. *Cambridge Tribune*, December 25, 1897.
6. *Cambridge Chronicle*, January 29, 1898.
7. Obituary of Mary Brown, wife of Maryland governor Frank Brown, *Baltimore Sun*, May 13, 1895.
8. *Cambridge Directory*, 1899.
9. *Cambridge Chronicle*, April 29, 1899.
10. Land record dated April 1, 1898, Middlesex South Registry of Deeds, Book 2644, Page 565.
11. Federal census of 1900, U.S. Census Bureau, Series T623, Roll 656, Page 129.
12. *Boston Post*, August 17, 1902.
13. *Cambridge Chronicle*, December 27, 1902; bankruptcy discharge dated February 17, 1903, Middlesex South Registry of Deeds, filing #7054.
14. *New York Morning Telegraph*, January 20, 1901.
15. Federal census of 1910, U.S. Census Bureau, Series T624, Roll 596, Page 142; federal census of 1920, U.S. Census Bureau, Series T625, Roll 707, Page 230; federal census of 1930, U.S. Census Bureau, Series T626, Roll 916, Enumeration District 53, Page 8.
16. *New York World*, October 7, 1904.
17. Shirley, "Chat with Keefe."
18. *Sporting Life*, March 30, 1907; *Boston Globe*, February 9, 1908.
19. Shirley, "Chat with Keefe."
20. Charlie Bevis, *Jimmy Collins: A Baseball Biography* (Jefferson, NC: McFarland, 2012), 82–83, 146.
21. *Sporting Life*, February 20, 1909.
22. Death records for 1909, Massachusetts Archives, Volume 25, Page 431.
23. Will in Docket #81913, Middlesex County Probate Court, involved in land record dated February 12, 1941, Middlesex South Registry of Deeds, Book 6471, Page 8.
24. *The Sporting News*, June 27, 1912.
25. *Sporting Life*, July 13, 1912.
26. *New York Tribune*, July 4, 1912.
27. *Sporting Life*, July 20, 1912.
28. *New York Tribune*, July 8, 1912.
29. Shirley, "Chat with Keefe."
30. *Boston Globe*, September 15, 1914.
31. *Cambridge Tribune*, April 12, 1913, and July 10, 1915. The building permits were for 87 Trowbridge in 1913 and 77 Trowbridge in 1915. In reality, the different addresses were for the same building that Keefe owned, since all the buildings on Trowbridge Street had been renumbered to reflect the greater number of dwellings standing there than had been originally anticipated when the lots were laid out 25 years earlier.
32. *Cambridge Directory*, 1915.
33. *Radcliffe College Directory*, 1922.
34. *Catholic University Bulletin*, April 1916.
35. Obituary of James Brodbine, *Boston Globe*, October 27, 1911.
36. Kaese, "Keefe Fanned Mighty Casey."
37. Obituary of Ann Brodbine, *Boston Globe*, February 21, 1988.
38. Obituary of Mary Paula Brodbine, *Boston Globe*, July 15, 2002.
39. Sawyer, "He Pitched 19 Straight Wins."
40. Kaese, "Keefe Fanned Mighty Casey"; *Cambridge Chronicle*, August 6, 1964.
41. "T.J. Keefe, Noted Pitcher, Dies at 76," *Boston Herald*, April 24, 1933.
42. Keefe burial site is on Elogium Path, Lot 6206, in the Cambridge City Cemetery. Keefe was not buried at St. Paul's Cemetery in Arlington, in the family plot where his parents are buried, as indicated by his obituaries in 1933.
43. John Kieran, "Tales of Tim Keefe," *New York Times*, April 25, 1933.
44. Joe Vila, "Tim Keefe One of Baseball's Great Pitchers," *New York Sun*, April 25, 1933.
45. Federal census of 1940, U.S. Census Bureau, Series T627, Roll 1685, Page 164.
46. Land record dated February 12, 1941, Middlesex South Registry of Deeds, Book 6471, Pages 8–11; Katherine's interest became a three-way joint tenancy among herself, her sister Ellen, and niece Mary Paula; Mary's interest became a four-way joint tenancy among herself, her nieces Ann and Mary Paula, and her nephew James Brodbine, Jr.

Chapter 25

1. *The Sporting News*, February 6, 1936.
2. *Washington Post*, May 20, 1938.
3. *The Sporting News*, February 18, 1943.
4. Achorn, *Old Hoss Radbourn*, 301.
5. Grantland Rice, "The Big 3 of the Mound," *Collier's*, April 11, 1925; Hugh Fullerton, "Baseball's Best," *North American Review*, May 1930.

6. *The Sporting News*, May 11, 1939.
7. *The Sporting News*, October 29, 1942.
8. Bill James, *Politics of Glory: How Baseball's Hall of Fame Really Works* (New York: Macmillan, 1994), 150.
9. Ibid., 155.
10. *The Sporting News*, July 6, 1960.
11. *The Sporting News*, February 9 and April 6, 1963.
12. *New York Times*, February 3, 1964.
13. *Troy Times Record*, February 7, 1964.
14. "T.J. Keefe, Noted Pitcher, Dies at 76," *Boston Herald*, April 24, 1933.
15. Allen, "Keefe's Dad."
16. Ibid.
17. Kaese, "Keefe Fanned Mighty Casey."
18. *Cambridge Chronicle*, August 6, 1964.
19. Obituary of Mary Paula Brodbine, *Boston Globe*, July 15, 2002.
20. *The Sporting News*, January 15, 1972.

Chapter 26

1. "Tim Keefe: You're the Greatest," *Cambridge Chronicle*, September 9, 1976.
2. John L'Heureux, "The Plumber," in *Family Affairs* (Garden City, NY: Doubleday, 1974), 30–34.
3. Land record dated March 5, 1991, Middlesex South Registry of Deeds, Book 21035, Page 56.
4. "Completed Auction Archive," *Hunt Auctions*, 2004, Web.
5. Rosemary McKittrick, "Simple Ledger Tells Tale of Early Union Struggle," *Live Auction Talk*, 2004, Web.
6. Ibid.
7. Ron Keurajian, *Baseball Hall of Fame Autographs: A Reference Guide* (Jefferson, NC: McFarland, 2012), 147.
8. Di Salvatore, *Clever Base-Ballist*, 396.
9. Roger Abrams, *Legal Bases: Baseball and the Law* (Philadelphia: Temple University Press, 2001), 58.
10. Leonard Shecter, "How the Class Struggle Reached Left Field," *Sports Illustrated*, November 4, 1968.
11. Leonard Koppett, "Reserve Clause Breeds Bitterness," *New York Times*, January 25, 1970.
12. Red Smith, "The Catfish Hunter of His Time," *New York Times*, April 14, 1975.
13. Wells Trombly, "89 Years Ago: Players' Revolt," *The Sporting News*, April 3, 1976.
14. Lee Lowenfish and Tony Lupien, *The Imperfect Diamond: The Story of Baseball's Reserve System and the Men Who Fought to Change It* (New York: Stein and Day, 1980), 25–53.
15. Ethan Lewis, "'A Structure to Last Forever': The Players' League and the Brotherhood War of 1890," master's thesis, Purdue University, 1995; Robert Ross, "We are the People!": Geographies of the Industrial Production of Culture and the Rise and Fall of the 1890 Players' National League of Professional Base-Ball Clubs," PhD dissertation, Syracuse University, 2007.
16. Patrick Thornton, *Legal Decisions That Shaped Modern Baseball* (Jefferson, NC: McFarland, 2012), 275.
17. National Baseball Hall of Fame and Museum, *The Hall: A Celebration of Baseball's Greats: The Official 75th Anniversary Book* (New York: Little, Brown and Company, 2014), 58.
18. *New York Times*, September 26, 2001, and August 2, 2003.
19. *New York Times*, April 30, 2005.
20. Alan Drooz, "So, Who the Heck Was Tim Keefe?" *San Diego Union-Tribune*, August 19, 2007.

Bibliography

Books and Articles

Abrams, Roger. *Legal Bases: Baseball and the Law*. Philadelphia: Temple University Press, 2001.

Achorn, Edward. *Fifty-Nine in '84: Old Hoss Radbourn, Barehanded Baseball & the Greatest Season A Pitcher Ever Had*. New York: Smithsonian Books, 2010.

———. *The Summer of Beer and Whiskey*. New York: Public Affairs, 2013.

Alexander, Charles. *John McGraw*. New York: Viking, 1988.

Allen, Lee. "Keefe's Dad Made Bullets in Rebel Prison." *The Sporting News*, April 4, 1964.

Bakker, Pamela. *Eyes on the Sporting Scene, 1870–1930: Will and June Rankin, New York's Sportswriting Brothers*. Jefferson, NC: McFarland, 2013.

Blumin, Stuart. *The Emergence of the Middle Class: Social Experience in the American City, 1760–1900*. New York: Cambridge University Press, 1989.

Bowman, Larry. *Before the World Series: Pride, Profits, and Baseball's First Championships*. DeKalb, IL: Northern Illinois University Press, 2003.

Browning, Reed. *Cy Young: A Baseball Life*. Amherst: University of Massachusetts Press, 2003.

Brunell, Frank. "A Great Ball Trust: The Brotherhood Has Organized a New League." *Chicago Tribune*, September 22, 1889.

Burk, Robert. *Never Just a Game: Players, Owners, and American Baseball to 1920*. Chapel Hill: University of North Carolina Press, 1994.

Burns, Rex. *Success in America: The Yeoman Dream and the Industrial Revolution*. Amherst: University of Massachusetts Press, 1976.

Burrows, Edwin, and Mike Wallace. *Gotham: A History of New York City to 1898*. New York: Oxford University Press, 1999.

Bushong, A.J. "The Catcher." In *Scientific Ball*, by Fred Pfeffer. Chicago: N.F. Pfeffer, 1889.

Christie, Robert. *Empire in Wood: A History of the Carpenters' Union*. Ithaca: Cornell University Press, 1956.

Chudacoff, Howard. *The Age of the Bachelor: Creating an American Subculture*. Princeton: Princeton University Press, 1999.

Clawson, Mary Ann Clawson. *Constructing Brotherhood*. Princeton: Princeton University Press, 1989.

Cromley, Elizabeth. *Alone Together: A History of New York's Early Apartments*. Ithaca: Cornell University Press, 1990.

"Daniel Keefe." In *Regiments and Armories of Massachusetts: An Historical Narration of the Massachusetts Volunteer Militia, with Portraits and Biographies of Officers Past and Present*, edited by Charles Winslow Hall. Boston: W.W. Potter, 1901.

"A Declining Baseball Star: Timothy J. Keefe, Once the First Pitcher Among Baseball Players." *New York Tribune*, October 4, 1891.

Di Salvatore, Bryan. *A Clever Base-Ballist: The Life and Times of John Montgomery Ward*. New York: Pantheon, 1999.

Dolan, Jay. *The Irish Americans: A History*. New York: Bloomsbury, 2008.

Douglas, George. *The Golden Age of the Newspaper*. Westport, CT: Greenwood Press, 1999.

Eliot, Samuel. *A History of Cambridge, Massachusetts, 1630–1913*. Cambridge, MA: Cambridge Tribune, 1913.

Elliot, Charles. *Somerville's History*. Somerville, MA: Privately published, 1896.

Erlich, Mark. *With Our Hands: The Story of Carpenters in Massachusetts*. Philadelphia: Temple University Press, 1986.

Foner, Eric. *Free Soil, Free Labor, Free Men: The Ideology of the Republican Party Before the Civil War*. New York: Oxford University Press, 1970.

Foster, John. "The Evolution of Pitching," *The Sporting News*, December 24, 1931.

Galenson, Walter. *The United Brotherhood of Carpenters: The First Hundred Years*. Cambridge: Harvard University Press, 1983.

Gelzheiser, Robert. *Labor and Capital in 19th Century Baseball*. Jefferson, NC: McFarland, 2006.

Gerlach, Larry. "Umpires." In *Total Baseball*, edited by John Thorn and Pete Palmer. New York: Warner, 1989.

Goldstein, Warren. *Playing for Keeps: A History of Early Baseball*. Ithaca: Cornell University Press, 1989.

Grob, Gerald. *Workers and Utopia: A Study of Ideological Conflict in the American Labor Movement 1865–1900*. Evanston: Northwestern University Press, 1961.

Hardy, James. *The New York Giants Base Ball Club: The Growth of a Team and a Sport, 1870 to 1900*. Jefferson, NC: McFarland, 1996.

Harris, William. "Sketches of Baseball Writers." In *Athletic Sports in America, England and Australia*, edited by Henry Clay Palmer. Philadelphia: Hubbard Brothers, 1889.

Hilkey, Judy. *Character Is Capital: Success Manuals and Manhood in Gilded Age America*. Chapel Hill: University of North Carolina Press, 1997.

Huber, Richard. *The American Idea of Success*. New York: McGraw-Hill, 1971.

Huston, James. *Securing the Fruits of Labor: The American Concept of Wealth Distribution 1765–1900*. Baton Rouge: Louisiana State University Press, 1998.

Jacobstein, Meyer. *The Tobacco Industry in the United States*. New York: Columbia University Press, 1907.

James, Bill. *The Politics of Glory: How Baseball's Hall of Fame Really Works*. New York: Macmillan, 1994.

Jamieson, Dave. *Mint Condition: How Baseball Cards Became an American Obsession*. New York: Atlantic Monthly Press, 2010.

Juergens, George. *Joseph Pulitzer and the New York World*. Princeton: Princeton University Press, 1966.

Kaese, Harold. "Keefe Fanned Mighty Casey." *Boston Globe*, February 9, 1964.

Keefe, T.J. "The Brotherhood and Its Work." *Players' National League Base Ball Guide*, 1890. In *Early Innings: A Documentary History of Baseball, 1825–1908*, edited by Dean Sullivan. Lincoln: University of Nebraska Press, 1995.

_____. "Curve Pitching." In *Batting and Pitching, with Fine Illustrations of Attitudes: A Thorough and Practical Treatise*, by John Morrill and T.J. Keefe. Boston: Wright & Ditson, 1884.

_____. "Curves or Liners: The Vexed Question in Base Ball Circles." *Boston Globe*, October 21, 1888.

_____. "A Pitcher's Opinion of Phonography." *Browne's Phonographic Monthly*, January 1889.

_____. "Pitching." In *Scientific Ball*, by Fred Pfeffer. Chicago: N.F. Pfeffer, 1889.

"Keefe & Becannon: The New and Prosperous Sporting Goods Firm." *Sporting Life*, May 31, 1890.

Kerr, Roy. *Buck Ewing: A Baseball Biography*. Jefferson, NC: McFarland, 2012.

_____. *Roger Connor: Home Run King of 19th Century Baseball*. Jefferson, NC: McFarland, 2011.

Kieran, John. "Tales of Tim Keefe." *New York Times*, April 25, 1933.

Lamster, Mark. *Spalding's World Tour: The Epic Adventure That Took Baseball Around the Globe—And Made It America's Game*. New York: Public Affairs, 2006.

Laurie, Bruce. *Artisans into Workers: Labor in Nineteenth Century America*. New York: Noonday, 1989.

Leikin, Steve. *The Practical Utopians: American Workers and the Cooperative Movement in the Gilded Age*. Detroit: Wayne State University Press, 2005.

Lemke, Bob, ed. *2011 Standard Catalog of Baseball Cards*. Iola, WI: Krause, 2010.

Levine, Peter. *A.G. Spalding and the Rise of Baseball*. New York: Oxford University Press, 1985.

Lewis, Ethan. "'A Structure to Last Forever': The Players' League and the Brotherhood War of 1890." Master's thesis, Purdue University, 1995.

Lowenfish, Lee, and Tony Lupien. *The Imperfect Diamond: The Story of Baseball's Reserve System and the Men Who Fought to Change It*. New York: Stein and Day, 1980.

Mendel, Ronald Mendel. "Labor Republicanism." In *Encyclopedia of U.S. Labor and Working-Class History*, edited by Eric Arneson. New York: Routledge, 2007.

Miller, Kerby. *Emigrants and Exiles: Ireland and the Irish Exodus to North America*. New York: Oxford University Press, 1985.

Moore, Glenn. "The Great Baseball Tour of 1888–89: A Tale of Image-Making, Intrigue, and Labour Relations in the Gilded Age." *International Journal of the History of Sport*, December 1994.

_____. "Ideology on the Sportspage: Newspapers, Baseball, and Ideological Conflict in the Gilded Age." *Journal of Sport History*, Fall 1996.

Moore, Jim, and Natalie Vermilyea. *Ernest Thayer[apost]s "Casey at the Bat": Background and Characters of Baseball's Most Famous Poem*. Jefferson, NC: McFarland, 1994.

Morris, Peter. *The Catcher: How the Man Behind the Plate Became an American Folk Hero*. Chicago: Ivan R. Dee, 2009.

_____. *A Game of Inches: The Stories Behind the Innovations That Shaped Baseball: The Game on the Field*. Chicago: Ivan R. Dee, 2006.

_____. "'A Motion as Near Flying as Any Human Being Could Attain': The 19th Century Umpire as Sprinter." *Base Ball: A Journal of the Early Game*, Fall 2008.

Nemec, David. *The Beer and Whisky League: The Illustrated History of the American Association*. New York: Lyons & Burford, 1994.

Pope, Frank. "The Clintons of '78: Manager Fayerweather Gives Reminiscences." *Boston Globe*, March 24, 1889.

Rankin, Will. "Baseball Writers Prominent in Their Day." In *The National Game*, by Alfred Spink. First edition 1911. Carbondale, IL: Southern Illinois Press, 2000.

_____. "Crisis in Affairs of New York Club Came During War With Brotherhood." *New York Press*, August 18, 1905.

_____. "Marvelous Growth of Baseball in New York City from its Humble Origins." *New York Press*, July 30, 1905.

_____. "Was an Artist: Tim Keefe the Best Pitcher of His Day." *The Sporting News*, January 30, 1897.

Reckman, Bob. "Carpentry: The Craft and Trade." In *Case Studies on the Labor Process*, edited by Andrew Zimbalist. New York: Monthly Review, 1979.

Rittner, Don. *Troy: A Collar City History*. Charleston, SC: Acardia, 2002.

Rodgers, Daniel. *The Work Ethic in Industrial America 1850–1920*. Chicago: University of Chicago Press, 1974.

Roer, Mike. *Orator O'Rourke: The Life of a Baseball Radical*. Jefferson, NC: McFarland, 2005.

Rorabaugh, W.J. *The Craft Apprentice: From Franklin to the Machine Age in America*. New York: Oxford University Press, 1986.

Ross, Robert. "We are the People!": Geographies of the Industrial Production of Culture and the Rise and Fall of the 1890 Players' National League of Professional Base-Ball Clubs." PhD dissertation, Syracuse University, 2007.

Rosenzweig, Roy, and Elizabeth Blackmar. *The Park and the People: A History of Central Park*. Ithaca: Cornell University Press, 1992.

Samuels, Edward, and Henry Kimball. *Somerville, Past and Present: An Illustrated Historical Souvenir*. Boston: Privately published, 1897.

Sawyer, Ford. "He Pitched 19 Straight Wins: Tim Keefe Tells of the Days of Ed Delahanty, King Kelly, Ed Williamson, Pop Anson; Is Enthusiastic Fan." *Boston Globe*, May 27, 1928.

Shirley, Philip. "A Chat with Keefe." *Sporting Life*, February 24, 1906.

Smith, Ronald. *Sports and Freedom: The Rise of Big-Time College Athletics*. New York: Oxford University Press, 1988.

Spalding, Albert. *America's National Game*. New York: American Sports Publishing, 1911.

Stevens, David. *Baseball's Radical for All Seasons: A Biography of John Montgomery Ward*. Lanham, MD: Scarecrow, 1998.

Stout, Wesley. *Once a Clown, Always a Clown: Reminiscences of DeWolf Hopper*. Boston: Little, Brown, 1927.

Thorn, John, and John Holway. *The Pitcher*. New York: Prentice Hall, 1987.

Thornley, Stew. *Land of the Giants: New York's Polo Grounds*. Philadelphia: Temple University Press, 2000.

Thornton, Patrick. *Legal Decisions That Shaped Modern Baseball*. Jefferson, NC: McFarland, 2012.

"T.J. Keefe." *New York Clipper*, May 22, 1880.

"T.J. Keefe, Noted Pitcher, Dies at 76." *Boston Herald*, April 24, 1933.

"Tim Keefe: The Country's Greatest Pitcher." *Richmond Dispatch*, July 29, 1888.
"Tim Keefe: You're the Greatest." *Cambridge Chronicle*, September 9, 1976.
Vila, Joe. "Tim Keefe One of Baseball's Great Pitchers." *New York Sun*, April 25, 1933.
Voigt, David Q. "America's Manufactured Villain—The Baseball Umpire," *Journal of Popular Culture*, Summer 1970.
Zeiler, Thomas. *Ambassadors in Pinstripes: The Spalding World Tour and the Birth of the American Empire*. Lanham, MD: Rowman & Littlefield, 2006.

Archival Material

Cambridge Public Library, Cambridge, MA. *Cambridge Directory*, 1850–1933.
Catholic Archdiocese of Boston Archives, Braintree, MA. Baptismal records of St. John's Church in East Cambridge, MA.
Harvard University Archives, Cambridge, MA. Minutes of Harvard Athletic Committee meetings, 1882–1908.
Massachusetts Archives, Boston, MA. Birth, marriage, and death records of the state, prior to 1910, and state census records, 1855 and 1865.
Middlesex South Registry of Deeds, Cambridge, MA. Land records, 1870–1995.
National Archives, Northeast Region, Waltham, MA. Naturalization records in Boston U.S. Circuit Court, prior to 1906, and Civil War draft registration records, 1863.
National Baseball Hall of Fame Library, Cooperstown, NY. Tim Keefe folder.
Somerville Public Library, Somerville, MA. *Somerville Directory*, 1869–1895, and *Somerville Annual Report*, 1868–1885.
U.S. Census Bureau, Washington, D.C. Federal census records, 1860–1940.
WardsMaps, Cambridge, MA. Historic maps of Cambridge and Somerville, MA.

Baseball Periodicals

National Police Gazette
New York Clipper
Sporting Life
The Sporting News

General Newspapers

Albany Evening Times
Baltimore Sun
Boston Daily Advertiser
Boston Globe
Boston Herald
Boston Post
Brooklyn Eagle
Cambridge Chronicle
Cambridge Tribune
Chicago Inter Ocean
Cleveland Herald
Clinton Conant
Harvard Crimson
Lewiston Evening Journal
New Bedford Evening Standard
New Orleans Times-Picayune
New York Daily Graphic
New York Evening Telegram
New York Herald
New York Press
New York Sun
New York Times
New York Tribune
New York World
Philadelphia Inquirer
Princetonian
St. Louis Globe-Democrat
San Francisco Evening Bulletin
Somerville Journal
Troy Daily Times
Utica Morning Herald
Westborough Chronotype

Index

Numbers in **bold italics** indicate pages with photographs

Albany, New York, ballclub 41–42, 45–48
American Association 56, 68, 85, 110, 202, 213
Amherst College 60, 140, 161
Appleton, Walter 102, 125, 134

Bancroft, Frank 43, 79, 222
Becannon, Jim 81, 159
Becannon, William 159, 203, 274n4
Bond, Tommy 25, 28, 31, 33, 37–38, 53, 61, 73, 222
Boston, Massachusetts 12, 44, 70, 99; amateur ballclubs 20, 24, 26–27, 29, 31–32; newspapers 3, 5, 76, 143; prejudice against Irish 13, 72, 90
Brodbine, Ann 242, 248, 276n46
Brodbine, Ellen *see* Keefe, Ellen
Brodbine, Helen 241
Brodbine, Katherine 248
Brodbine, Mary Paula 242, 248, 251, 276n46
Brotherhood of Professional Base Ball Players: demise 200–201; formation 90–95; Keefe as secretary-treasurer 2, 91, 92, 106, 110, 111, 113, 125–126, 152, 165–166, 173, 184–186, 188, 201, 248, 251; Keefe as temporary head 153, 157–158, 163; legacy to player rights 239, 251–254; philosophy, fundamental 96–100; planning for Players' League 126, 130, 133, 157, 165–173, 184; relations with National League 91, 125, 127, 131, 132, 141, 152, 156–157, 166, 170, 172–173, 176–178, 248; tension between Keefe and Ward 126, 151–153, 165–166, 185; Ward as president 91, 93, 110–111, 125–130, 152–153, 157, 163, 166, 170, 180, 184–185, 199, 248, 251–252
Brotherhood Park *see* Polo Grounds, third vintage
Brouthers, Dan 58, 122, 131, 170, 234
Brown, Bill 120, 145
Brown, Mary 114, 236
Brunell, Frank 95, 169, 177, 181, 186, 273n25
Burdock, Jack 111–112
Bushong, Doc 43, 44, 101–102, 133, 146

Cambridge, Massachusetts 1, 13–14, 16, 20, 30–31, 39, 115, 164, 221, 234; amateur ballclubs 20, 25, 264n3; apartment building owned by Keefe 236–237, 241, 243, 250, 276n31; land owned by Keefe 1, 2, 114–116, 161, 164, 171, 188, 213, 221, 234, 237, 239, 273n35; major-leaguers from 33, 40, 116, 140; residences of Keefe 1, 16, 229–230, 241, 243, 250–251
"Casey at the Bat" 127–128, 132–133, 151, 236, 244–245
Clarkson, John 38, 57, 64, 82, 104, 116, 117, 140, 148, 176, 185, 206, 215, 239, 244, 245, 247
Clements, Jack 212, 214
Clinton, Massachusetts, ballclub 36–37, 39–40
Connor, Roger 51, 58, 66, 85, 91, 104, 134, 145, 174, 186, 196, 273n7
Corcoran, Larry 42, 53, 54, 104
Crane, Ed 143, 152, 168, 178, 198, 273n7
Cronin, Dan 31, 32, 34
Crook, Bill 35, 36–37
Cummings, Candy 26, 245

Dauvray, Helen 121, 130, 133, 136, 155, 164, 175, 198, 216, 238
Day, John: impact of Players' League 176, 178, 182, 183, 192, 196, 198–200; owner of New York AA and NL ballclubs 52, 59–60, 66, 71, 83, 88, 204, 211, 238; tobacco business 107, 193, 211; *see also* New York NL ballclub, salary negotiations with Keefe
Deasley, Tom 85, 89, 91, 104, 121
Denny, Jerry 80, 130, 191, 207
Donohue, Peter 75–76, 85, 107
Dorgan, Mike 83, 85, 91, 121
Driscoll, John 32, 70
Dunning, Andy 209

Ernst, Harold 32, 68
Esterbrook, Tom 79, 84, 85, 91, 112
Ewing, Buck: catcher's mitt 89, 145–147, 161, 211; New York teammate of Keefe 76, 85, 89, 91, 102, 104, 112, 120, 125, 145, 168, 186, 207, 211, 244, 245, 273n7; Players' League, role in demise 195, 196, 199, 200; Troy teammate of Keefe 50, 51, 53, 57, 58, 59, 66

Fayerweather, George 35, 41
Ferguson, Bob 47, 49, 53

283

284 INDEX

Gaffney, John 40, 154, 216, 223, 224
Galvin, Pud 73, 148, 154, 177, 219, 245, 249, 254
Gardner, Gid 33, 34, 35, 36, 37, 39, 40, 47, 74, 116, 237
George, Bill 121
Gerhardt, Joe 85, 91, 106
Gillespie, Pete 59, 66, 85, 91, 104, 121
Gilligan, Barney 33, 34, 36, 39, 40, 47, 80, 116
Glasscock, Jack 185, 191, 195, 207
Goldsmith, Fred 42, 53, 54, 62, 245
Gore, George 121, 145

Hanlon, Ned 131, 152, 165, 171
Harris, William 3, 5, 142, 163, 170, 182, 192, 196, 205, 263n2
Harvard College 13, 19, 164, 241; amateur philosophy 32, 62–63, 65, 117, 235; baseball team 20, 32, 40, 214; Keefe as baseball coach 61–65, 214, 217, 220–222, 225, 235
Hatfield, Gil 145, 191
Helm, Clara: appearance 136, *137*; childhood 135–136, 139; courting by Keefe 133, 135–138, 143, 151, 166, 172; marriage (first) to Helm 136, 138; marriage (second) to Keefe 174–176, 226, 238; sculptures 137, 208; theater 133, 138, 150, 166, 198; trips to Europe 138, 139, 155, 164, 166, 208, 216, 226, 238
Holbert, Bill 49, 50, 53–54, 66, 72, 76–77, 80, 89
Hopper, DeWolf 88, 150–151

Johnson, Albert 165, 169, 170, 171, 176

Keefe, Annie 20, 115, 123, 138, 161, 171–172, 205
Keefe, Clara *see* Helm, Clara
Keefe, Daniel 17, 22, 38, 56, 123, 232, 248
Keefe, Elizabeth 20, 33
Keefe, Ellen 20, 123, 205, 241, 248, 276n46
Keefe, Katherine 17, 38, 123, 230, 236, 239, 243, 248, 276n46
Keefe, Margaret 17, 56, 123, 134, 172, 270n18
Keefe, Mary (mother) 14, 15, 16, 176, 188, 230, 236, 239
Keefe, Mary (sister) 17, 123, 230, 236, 239, 243, 248, 276n46
Keefe, Patrick 8–15, 16–19, 20, 22–23, 28, 30, 38, 56, 96, 122, 242, 264n6
Keefe, Timothy: appearance 6, *7*, 35, 42, *44*, 46, 85, *111*, *116*, *221*, 242, 254; artisan beliefs 2, 8–10, 15, 22, 23, 30, 33, 45, 51, 60, 96–97, 154, 157–158, 161, 165, 179, 201; ballplayer mobility beliefs 2, 25, 29–30, 37, 45, 58–59, 141; baseball career *see* individual ballclubs; birth 1, 15; carpenter 2, 22, 23, 25, 28, 30, 32–33, 39, 46, 96, 241; Catholic faith 7, 16, 31, 70, 109, 138, 175; character 6–8, 16, 30, 46, 55, 83, 86, 93, 109–110, 112, 116, 124, 128, 131, 137, 142, 158, 195, 202, 219, 227, 232, 238, 242; childhood 2, 18–21; death 242, 248, 276n42; education 19, 21–22, 38, 68, 110; financial position 113, 114–115, 167, 204–205, 213, 221, 230, 233, 237; Irish heritage 7, 11–12, 90, 114; marriage 138, 174–176, 202, 226, 238, 248; nickname 5, 6, 109, 208, 236; shorthand skills 92, 94, 180, 221, 257–258; signature 251; *see also* Brotherhood; Cambridge; Harvard; Helm, Clara; Keefe & Becannon; pitching style of Keefe; Somerville; umpire, Keefe as
Keefe, Timothy (grandfather) 11, 14
Keefe, Timothy (uncle) 14, 18
Keefe & Becannon sporting goods firm: bankruptcy 203, 208, 211, 274n43; inception 159–161; operation 162, 164, 169, 187–188, 190, 192, 202, 205; planning to establish 134, 143, 155, 158, 161; *see also* Players' League, Keefe Ball
Kelly, Mike 106, 125, 130–131, 189, 246

Lewiston, Maine, ballclub 27–30
Lynch, Jack 66, 77, 83

Marquard, Rube 145, 239–240, *240*, 248
Mathews, Bobby 71, 77
Mattimore, Mike 121
McAlpin, Edwin 183, 186
McGraw, John 225–226, 238
Metropolitan AA ballclub: demise 85, 88; inception 58, 66; Keefe as player 66–71, 73–77; salary negotiations with Keefe 59, 72; World Series 79–81
Mutrie, Jim: amateur player 28; Giants manager 84–85, 104, 107, 120, 144, 176, 184, 205, 207, 211, 238; Metropolitan manager 66, 67, 77, 79; minor-league manager 41, 52

National League: monopoly attitude 39, 46, 126, 213; release rule 83, 125, 140–141, 163–164, 208–209, 216; reserve rule 37, 45, 51, 58, 67, 110, 126, 141, 152, 163, 180, 183, 189, 252–253; salary limits 90, 93, 111, 131, 141, 152, 156–157
New Bedford, Massachusetts, ballclub 41
New Orleans, Louisiana 43–44, 101–102, 125, 130, 154
New York AA ballclub *see* Metropolitan AA ballclub
New York City, New York: entertainment 109–110; newspapers 3, 5, 42, 75–76, 107, 121, 124, 142, 174, 192–193; politics 72–73, 183; residences of Keefe 81, 107–108, 175, 202; theater 81, 88, 150
New York NL ballclub: inception 58, 66; Keefe as ballplayer 86–89, 104–106, *108*, 111–112, 121–128, 144–151, 171–177, 206–210; ownership 86, 83, 193, 202, 204, 211; photographs 104, 107, *108*, 124, 145; salary negotiations with Keefe 83–85, 102, 120, 141–144, 163–169, 204–206; tobacco cards 107, 123–124, 145, *148*, 193; uniforms 104,

Index

121, 145, 149–150, 161; World Series 154–155, 178
New York PL ballclub: demise 192–195, 198–200; inception 180; Keefe as ballplayer 191–197; Keefe as owner 183, 186–187, 197, 202, 204, 274*n*7; ownership 182–183, 186; salary negotiations with Keefe 184

O'Day, Hank 173, 178
O'Rourke, Jim 37, 85, 91, *105*, 106, 112, 120, 145, 211, 223, 246, 273*n*7

Pfeffer, Fred 101–102, 106, 133, 150, 152, 165, 180
Philadelphia NL ballclub: Keefe as ballplayer 212–213, 215–216, 218–219; salary negotiations with Keefe 212, 216, 217
pitching style of Keefe 9, 27, 36, 41, 42–43, 46, *52*, 55–56, 68–69, 73, *74*, 77, 87, 89, 103, *120*, 124, 147–148, 169, 207, 214, 218; arm motion permitted 19–20, 25–26, 36, 67, 73, 260; Hall of Fame selection 247–249; health of arm 38, 52–53, 62, 68, 73, 162, 188; hitting the batter 69, 72, 74, 102, 119, 261; records set 71, 145, 148–150, 192, 219, 239–241, 267*n*13; rule changes adapted to 19, 25, 26, 27, 40, 52, 67, 82, 86, 102, 118–119, 131, 156, 187, 217, 260–261; size of pitching staff 35, 53, 77, 104, 121, 144, 173, 215; writing by Keefe about 2, 9, 73, 133, 144, 161, 169, 255–260
Players' League: apostrophe, importance of 180; demise 199, 200, 202, 203; impact to baseball 179, 181–182, 197, 198, 201, 252–253; inception 173, 176–179, 180; Keefe Ball, use of 187–188, 191, 195, 197, 203, 274*n*43; structure 93, 98–100, 177, 180–182, 186
Polo Grounds: first vintage 52, 67, 88, 104, 108, *129*, 151, 155, 166, 167; second vintage 171, 184, 191, 207; third vintage 171, 176, 184, 186–187, 191, *194*, 207
Powers, Pat 211, 233
Princeton College 189–190, 204, 206

Radbourn, Hoss 73, 79–80, 86, 240, 244, 245
Rankin, June 75, 107, 192
Rankin, Will 68, 75, 76
Reipschlager, Charlie 71, 80
Richardson, Danny 85, 91, 121, 145, 196, 273*n*7
Robinson, Frank 183, 186, 204
Roseman, Jim 59, 66
Rusie, Amos 192, 205, 206, 218, 242

San Francisco, California 125, 132–134, 154
Slattery, Mike 145, 191, 197, 237
Somerville, Massachusetts 1, 13, 14, 18, 20–22, 30–31, 39; amateur ballclubs 20; Keefe family homes 2, 14, 16, 18, 21, 30, 38, 91, 116, 144, 230; real estate investment by Keefe 84, 269*n*8, 272*n*42
Spalding, Albert: ballplayer 26, 30; negotiator for National League 131, 172, 193, 199, 202; owner of Chicago ballclub 76, 125, 140, 152, 157, 245; sporting goods business 152, 158, 159, 160, 187, 190, 203
Spalding, Walter 160, 161, 193, 195–200, 204, 206
Sullivan, William 5–6, 75, 116, 135, 143, 263*n*3
Swarbush, Bill 123
Sweeney, Jerry 32, 34, 37

Talcott, Edward 183, 186, 193, 195–200, 204, 206
Tebeau, Patsy 226, 230–231
300-game winners 192, 219, 245, 247, 249
Tiernan, Mike 121, 145, 185, 191, 207, 211, 227
Titcomb, Ledell 121, 143, 168
Troy NL ballclub: demise 57–58; inception 39; Keefe as ballplayer 47, 49–54, 57–59, 247; salary negotiations with Keefe 50–51, 54, 57

umpire, Keefe as: full-time 223–234; referee in roller polo 216–217; substitute 48, 57, 69, 75, 81, 128, 219
Utica, New York, ballclub 40–41

Van Cott, Cornelius 183, 186, 199, 211
Van Haltren, George 133
Voltz, William 93–95, 252

Ward, John: childhood 96; friendship with Keefe 43, 44–45, 50, 61, 90, 138, 139, 152, 165, 185; New York teammate of Keefe 66, 83, *105*, 106, 125, 141–143, 163, 172, 185, 248; relationship with Helen Dauvray 122, 130, 138, 155, 166, 198, 238; Spalding world tour 138, 152, 155, 157, 164–165; *see also* Brotherhood
Welch, Mickey: Brotherhood member 91, 186; friendship with Keefe 186, 238, 241, 242; New York teammate of Keefe 83, 86–87, 103, 112–113, 120, 122, 123, 145, 154, 168, 174, 191, 206, 211, 245, 249; Troy teammate of Keefe 47, 49, 53, 57, 58, 66
Westboro, Massachusetts, ballclub 33–36
Williams College 64, 120
Williamson, Ned 54, 106
Wright, George 31, 37, 159
Wright, Harry: Boston manager 24, 25, 31, 48, 50–51, 76; Cincinnati manager 20; Philadelphia manager 207, 212, *215*, 219; umpire supervisor 223, 228

www.ingramcontent.com/pod-product-compliance
Ingram Content Group UK Ltd.
Pitfield, Milton Keynes, MK11 3LW, UK
UKHW041929140426
5217IPUK00014B/375